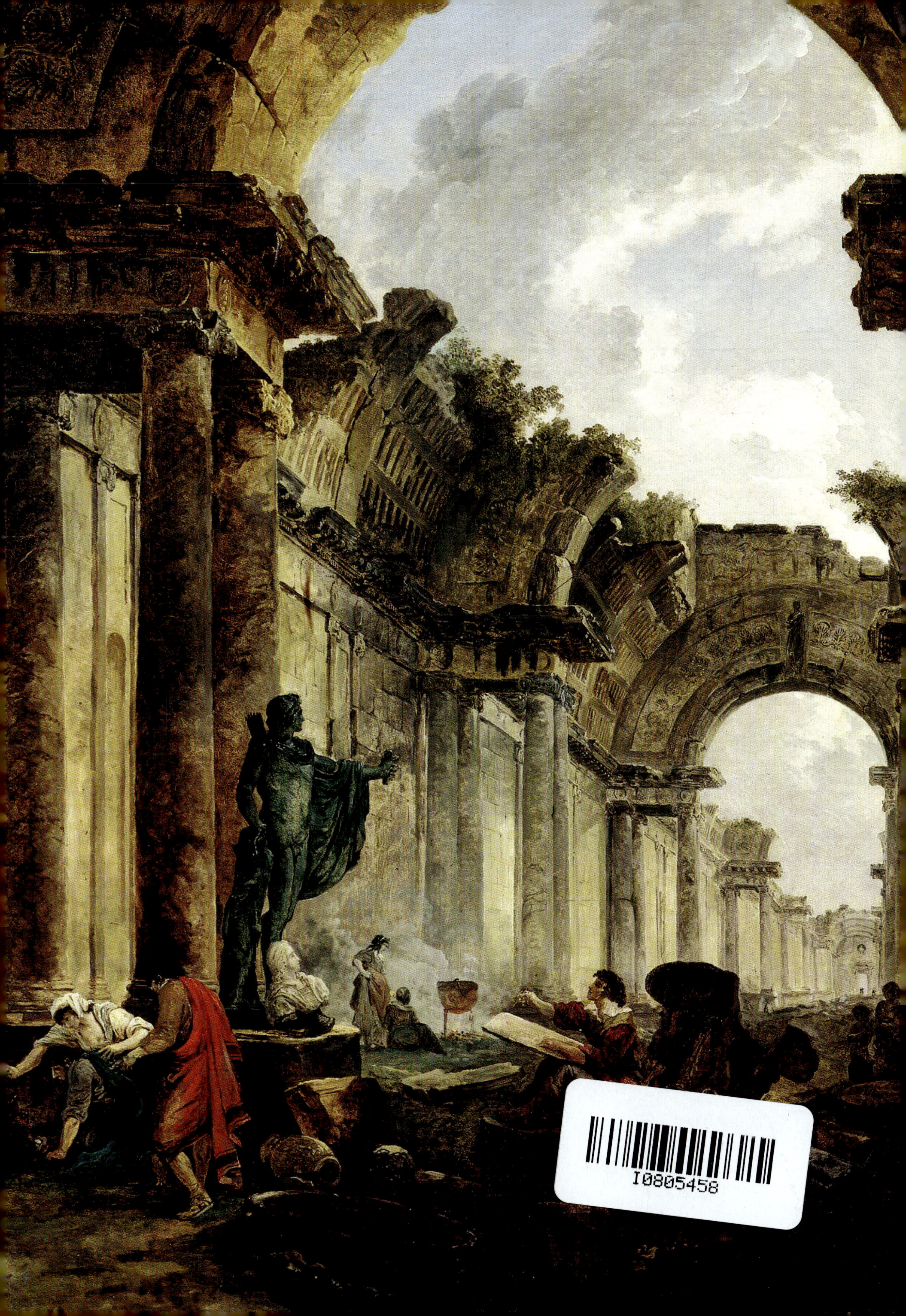

Futures&

EIGHTEENTH-CENTURY PARIS AND

Ruins

THE ART OF **HUBERT ROBERT**

NINA L. DUBIN

PUBLISHED BY THE GETTY RESEARCH INSTITUTE

The Getty Research Institute Publications Program
Thomas W. Gaehtgens, *Director, Getty Research Institute*
Gail Feigenbaum, *Associate Director*

Futures & Ruins: Eighteenth-Century Paris and the Art of Hubert Robert
Ann Bermingham, *Manuscript Consultant*
Michelle Bonnice and Diane Mark-Walker, *Manuscript Editors*

Designed by Catherine Lorenz
Coordinated by Elizabeth Kahn
Type composed by Diane Franco
Printed in China through Asia Pacific Offset, Inc.

Second edition 2012
Published by the Getty Research Institute, Los Angeles
Getty Publications
Gregory M. Britton, *Publisher*
1200 Getty Center Drive, Suite 500
Los Angeles, CA 90049-1682
www.getty.edu/publications

14 13 12 11 10   5 4 3 2
ISBN: 978-1-60606-140-4 (paper)

Front cover: Hubert Robert, *The Burning of Rome* (detail). See p. 75, fig. 31
Back cover: Jean-Laurent Legeay, *Monumental Tomb with Tree Branches.* See p. 40, fig. 19.
Frontispiece: Hubert Robert, *Imaginary View of the Grande Galerie of the Louvre in Ruins* (detail). See p. 153, fig. 65
Facing acknowledgments: Hubert Robert, *The Burning of the Opéra at the Palais-Royal* (detail). See p. 81, fig. 34
Facing introduction: Hubert Robert, *Demolition of a Church* (detail). See p. 86, fig. 36

The Library of Congress has cataloged the hardcover edition as follows:

Dubin, Nina L.
Futures & ruins : eighteenth-century Paris and the art of Hubert Robert / Nina L. Dubin.
p. cm.
Includes index.
ISBN 978-1-60606-023-0 (hardcover)
1. Robert, Hubert, 1733–1808—Criticism and interpretation. 2. Ruins in art. 3. Paris (France)—In art. 4. Art and society—France—History—18th century. I. Robert, Hubert, 1733–1808. II. Title. III. Title: Futures and ruins.
ND553.R6D83 2010
759.4—dc22

2010000637

Contents

Acknowledgments vii

Introduction 1

CHAPTER 1
The Unmade 11

CHAPTER 2
Scenes from Hell 61

CHAPTER 3
anti-edifice 109

CHAPTER 4
Posterity 151

Illustration Credits 188

Index 189

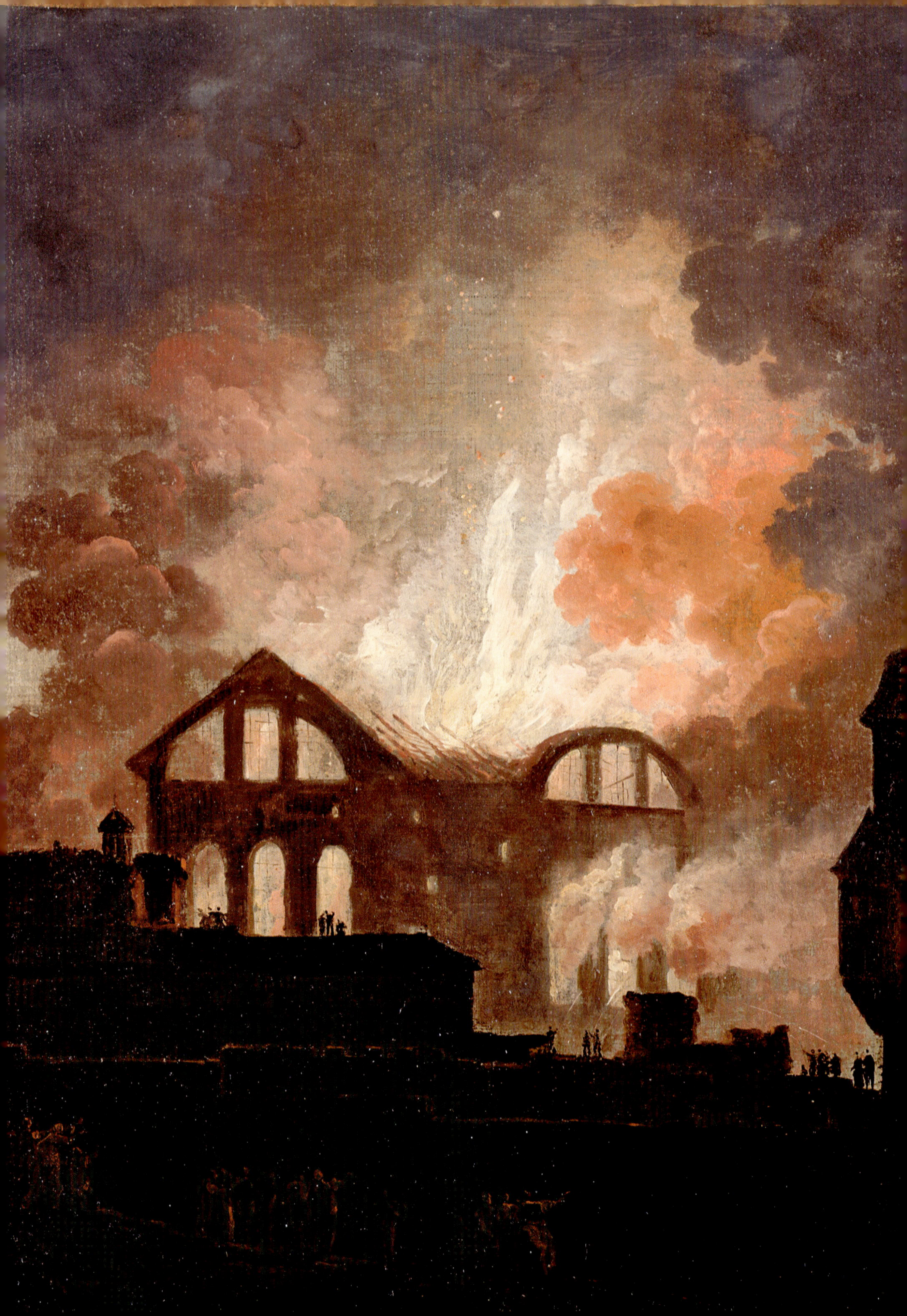

Acknowledgments

This book, about an artist navigating the passage from one epoch to another, occupied me over the course of this century's first tumultuous decade. Contemporary events formed an inescapable backdrop to its writing. In far happier ways, numerous individuals paved the way for its existence, and it is a pleasure for me to acknowledge them here. I begin with the institutions that have supported the project from the time of its first incarnation as a doctoral dissertation. A David E. Finley Fellowship from the Center for Advanced Study in the Visual Arts enabled me to spend two years in Paris, followed by a third one at the National Gallery of Art. I remain profoundly indebted to Elizabeth Cropper, Peter Lukehart, and Therese O'Malley. Further support came in the form of a Getty residential fellowship, and I can only hope that Thomas Crow, Gail Feigenbaum, and Charles Salas know just how much those nine blissful months meant to me. Revisions took place at the Institute for the Humanities at the University of Illinois at Chicago, for which Mary Beth Rose and Linda Vavra have my immense gratitude. A Dean's Research Prize and a grant from the Faculty Scholarship Support Program at UIC helped cover research costs and fund illustration acquisitions. I would be remiss if I did not acknowledge the assistance I received at museums, libraries, and archives—in particular the Bibliothèque nationale de France, the Archives nationales, the Bibliothèque d'art et d'archéologie Jacques Doucet, the Musée du Louvre, the library at the University of Chicago, and the Clark Art Institute. Another institution remains to be named, and that is the University of California, Berkeley. Between 1998 and 2006, the years of my graduate work, no more thrilling and rigorous environment for the study of French art could have existed. I have attempted over the years to convey to Darcy Grimaldo Grigsby—my dissertation adviser—and to T. J. Clark how unimaginable my work would be without them. This book continues those efforts. Others from Berkeley who have my gratitude include David Bates, Elizabeth Honig, and Anne Wagner.

A sampling of ideas in the book was published as "Robert des Ruines" in *Cabinet* 20 (January 2006). Parts of chapter 3 along with the title appeared in "Anti-Edifice: Jean Barbault's *Rome Moderne,*" in Rebecca Zorach, ed., *The Virtual Tourist in Renaissance Rome: Printing and Collecting the Speculum Romanae Magnificentiae* (Chicago: Univ. of Chicago Press, 2008).

Portions of the work were presented as public lectures and conference papers. Audiences at the University of Illinois at Chicago, the University of Chicago, and the University of California, San Diego, in particular helped strengthen the book's arguments. I thank Norman Bryson, Hollis Clayson, Marc Gotlieb, Melissa Hyde, Mark Ledbury, Jennifer Milam, Jonathan Sachs, Jon Seydl, Martha Ward, and Rebecca Zorach for facilitating such occasions. A manuscript excerpt was productively scrutinized by participants in a Chicago Consortium of Art History workshop—among them David Van Zanten and David Getsy, whose remarks inspired the title of chapter 1. Presentations at CASVA in 2004 and at the Getty during the "Duration: Persistence of Antiquity" theme year elicited discussions that decisively impacted my conception of the material.

This book also bears the imprint of conversations with friends and colleagues—many of whom influenced its writing in ways they could never have imagined. They include Jonathan Alexander, Ian Balfour, Philip Benedict, Fred Bohrer, Brigitte Bourgeois, Faya Causey, Sabina de Cavi, Kevin Chua, the late Philip Conisbee, Meg Grasselli, Talinn Grigor, Heather MacDonald, Alex Nagel, Peter Parshall, Shilpa Prasad, Susan Siegfried, Hérica Valladares, and Terri Weissman. I am indebted to the boundlessly wise and generous Benedict Leca for far more than his discovery of the watercolor that is the centerpiece of chapter 1. The late Marianne Roland Michel permitted me to consult her private archive. And Isabelle Tillerot has been a mainstay from Burgundy to Brentwood. I thankfully acknowledge the students in my graduate seminars along with my wonderful colleagues at UIC—the fellows at the Institute for the Humanities during the 2007–8 academic year as well as Esra Akcan, Ellen Baird, Catherine Becker, Robert Bruegmann, Leon Fink, Matthew Gaynor, Heather Grossman, Hannah Higgins, Victor Margolin, Virginia Miller, Robert Munman, Martha Pollak, Robin Schuldenfrei, David Sokol, and, especially, Peter Hales and Judith Kirshner. For offering assistance, wisdom, and cheer, I thank Victor Agran, Cassandra Albinson, Laure Benchimol, Philippe Bordes, Julia Bryan-Wilson, Raphael Cuir, Sarah Dreller, Darby English, Christine Giviskos, Alden Gordon, Christopher Heuer, Katie Hornstein, Jonathan Katz, Thomas Kavanagh, Louis Marchesano, Paul Maréchal, Daniel McLean, Régis Michel, Elizabeth Monroe, Deena Newman, Kathleen Nicholson, Todd Olson, Alison and Andrew Perchuk, Sanja Perovic, Alex Potts, Paula Rea Radisich, Sabine Schlosser, Tatiana Senkevitch, Rani Singh, Charles Stewart, Nancy Troy, Charles Walton, George Weinberg, Jessie Weinberg, and Sebastian Zeidler. To Ara Merjian—my home away from home—and to Elise Archias, Huey Copeland, André Dombrowski, Sarah Evans, Eve Meltzer, Bibiana Obler, John Tain, and Joseph Thometz, I owe the enriching atmosphere at Berkeley in which my project took root.

I am deeply thankful to the publications staff at the Getty Research Institute—and above all to Gail Feigenbaum—for working so tirelessly to bring this work to fruition. It did so owing to the support of Thomas Crow, Thomas Gaehtgens, and the publications committee—along with the talents of Julia Bloomfield, Michelle Bonnice, Michele Ciaccio, Rachelle Okawa, and Laura Santiago. For serving as a meticulous copy editor and reassuring conduit to every aspect of the publication process, Diane Mark-Walker has my heartfelt thanks. For her critical instincts and imaginative engagement with the text, and for acting as manuscript consultant with the perfect combination of sympathy and seriousness, Ann Bermingham has my gratitude and admiration.

Readers of individual chapters and excerpts offered valuable insights. They include Andrew McClellan, as well as the Chicago working group participants Cecily Hilsdale, Nicole Lassahn, Lucy Pick, Lisa Voigt, and Rebecca Zorach. I thank the anonymous reader who endorsed the project and—equally important—incisively detailed its weaker points. I am hugely thankful to Amy Freund, whose expert advice has become indispensable, and to two cherished interlocutors—Meredith Martin and Susan Taylor-Leduc—who shared this project with me and did so much to sustain it. For being as perceptive as critics as they are precious as friends, André Dombrowski and Bibiana Obler have my abiding affection.

Finally, this book owes everything to my family: Jesse and Shirley Jackson, Glenn and Sam Jones, Annabelle Handler, and, especially, Abbey, Rachael, Maxine, and Don Dubin. Its pages are a tribute to the limitless support and love of my sisters and parents, whose nurturing presence in my life is a constant reminder of how lucky I am.

Lest I forget, the mere typing of his name—Matthew Jackson, my solace, my light—is enough to remind me as well.

—Nina L. Dubin

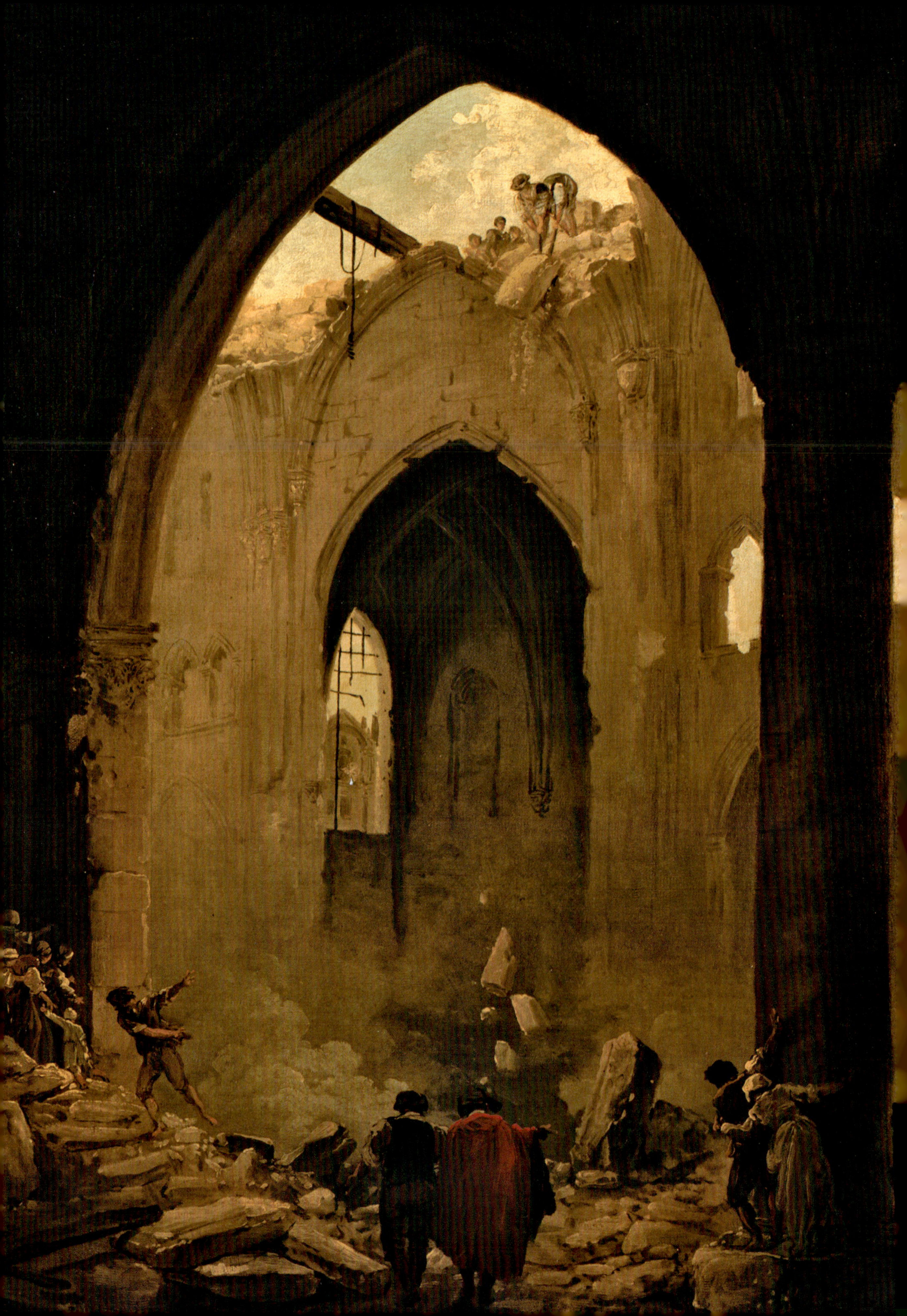

Introduction

> Who knows if on the banks of the Seine... some traveller, like myself, shall not one day sit on their silent ruins, and weep in solitude over the ashes of their inhabitants, and the memory of their former greatness.
>
> —Constantin-François, comte de Volney (1791)[1]

Few traits in modernity have proven so persistent as the compulsion to ruminate upon the prospect of a calamitous future. As the hallmark of a secular mind-set, its flowering in the history of art may be traced back to roughly 1796. In that year, the painter Hubert Robert (1733–1808) produced a fictive view of the still-unfinished Musée du Louvre in a state of ruin (see fig. 65). Featuring the skeletal structure of the Grande Galerie invaded by the elements and strewn with the remains of antique statuary, Robert's painting looks ahead in more than one sense. In the artist's drive to obliterate the museum, one might detect a preview of the sorts of aesthetic predilections that prompted late twentieth-century artists to identify art no longer with the "pictorial" but rather with "vast" and "abandoned" spaces: with that which exists beyond, and supersedes, the confines of culture.[2] Indeed, the disappearance of pictures from the walls of Robert's endless gallery secures the designation of the crumbling monument as a theater of the sublime.

What makes Robert's painting an exercise in prescience is its execution in a culture that understood itself to be modern by virtue of its capacity to envision its own destruction. Writing in the second half of the eighteenth century, Edmund Burke, Denis Diderot, and Louis-Sébastien Mercier offered vivid accounts of hypothetical catastrophes: of London destroyed by fire or earthquake, of Paris decimated by diluvial disaster. Such images of calamity were the object of meditations both morbid and pleasurable. They coincided with the belief that the most gratifying of aesthetic experiences were associated no longer with discrete objects but rather with unquantifiable events. "It is our ignorance of things that causes all our admiration, and chiefly excites our passions," stated Burke.[3] Thus when Volney envisioned the French capital silent and in ruins, he took his place in a trajectory of authors who mined the allure of the unthinkable. As manifestations of the sublime, and as sources of delight insofar as they overturned expectation—offering images of a future that bore no resemblance to the present—apocalyptic scenarios reflected the iconoclastic character of eighteenth-century aesthetic thought. In its own way, the attraction to destruction exemplified the new mental habits of a "citizen emancipated from absolutist subjection and the tutelage of the Church."[4]

This study endeavors to locate the place of Robert's art within this paradigm shift. As such, Futures & Ruins largely circumvents the usual terrain of the monograph on the early modern artist: the facts of biography and patronage, the iconography of artworks commissioned to decorate specific settings. Such questions have been ably addressed in the scholarship on Robert, though there remains a disproportion between the enormity of his oeuvre and the sparseness of the literature it has occasioned.[5] My own contribution centers on paintings that, for the most part, were not commissioned and whose early histories have gone undocumented; such works, consequently, invite consideration of their maker within a sociohistorical and conceptual framework larger than that in which Robert traditionally has been confined. My aim in undertaking such interpretive work has been twofold: to examine Robert's own sense of time in an age newly fixated on the future, and to recover the needs his art satisfied in an era of increasing estrangement from the past. Among my conclusions is that the genre of ruins with which Robert des Ruines—as he was known—was associated facilitated adjustment to a world living less and less in the shadow of its ancestors. By extension, an underlying proposition advanced in these pages is that Robert's futuristic view of the Grande Galerie in ruins, though executed in 1796, in spirit predated the Revolution, for it marked the culmination of aesthetic strategies that enabled acclimation to modernity in advance of its full-fledged arrival.

However paradoxically, ruins in the eighteenth century constituted a privileged medium for the expression of a willingness to live no longer in what J. G. A. Pocock calls a "time of continuity" but rather in a "time of contingency"; whether the former order ever in actuality existed is of less import than the sense in the period, at times the premonition, of dwelling in its aftermath.[6] As such, ruins were appreciated less as remnants of a disappearing world than as proof of a precarious one. The valorization of ruins, coinciding with the decomposition of old beliefs, the crumbling of the dictates of Classicism, modeled a capacity to tolerate uncertainty. Literally so, for they materialized the obscurity of the past. As Charles de Brosses reported from the remains of the Basilica of Constantine in Rome: "I cannot tell you what that temple was, but only that that isolated column is the most beautiful thing in architecture in the whole world, and that seeing it gives me as much and perhaps more satisfaction than the view of any complete building."[7] The comment encapsulates the imaginative pleasure afforded by ruins—one that was premised on, and helped compensate for, the irretrievability of the past.

Robert's vast oeuvre—in addition to being an astoundingly prolific painter, he also designed a number of *fabriques,* or three-dimensional ornaments, for gardens—reflects the centrality of ruins to eighteenth-century aesthetics. As Alexander Gottlieb Baumgarten proposed in 1735, sensory perception constituted a legitimate basis for knowledge and merited being the object of its own science—the science of aesthetics.[8] The fascination with ruins marked the emphasis that aesthetic theory placed on the intangibles of subjective experience. It also sublimated an unease with the disintegration of stable truths. As structures of diminished authority, ruins embodied the degraded status of ontological values, which now ceded place to an emphasis on how the mind experienced the world. In their very decay, ruins as sites of imaginative investment bore witness to the epistemological upheaval entailed by the emphasis on aesthetic experience. They thus uniquely intimated the pleasures and perils unleashed by the reign of the senses. De Brosses's preference for an unidentifiable ruin over "any complete building" exemplifies what Ernst Cassirer sees as the danger of aesthetics: "Is not sense knowledge," he asks, "the realm of the confused and indistinct, in other words, of the opposite of pure knowledge, since this realm is impenetrable to knowledge?"[9]

As I argue in what follows, the aesthetic experiences associated with ruins permitted acculturation to a "time of contingency": to a time, that is, when preoccupation with the past's failure to serve as a guide to the present permeated multiple domains—including the economic. Central to "a society which is taking leave of the past," writes Anthony Giddens, is "the notion of risk."[10] The infiltration of "an economy of anticipation" into orders of existence hitherto untouched by the marketplace, the socialization of growing numbers of people to their roles as debtors and creditors, the reliance on new financial instruments in place of intrinsically valuable currencies: such processes—and attendant perceptions of risk as an increasingly inescapable feature of urban life—form the backdrop to my study.[11] Among my claims is that the dawning of what Giddens calls "the colonisation of the future" took place in aesthetic as well as economic life; as literary historians of the eighteenth century have long recognized, the two can scarcely be separated.[12] It need not be doubted that the fixation on ruins was indistinguishable from nascent despair over the collapse of a romanticized "time of continuity." But what is equally the case is that the unfirm foundations that commentators worried would bring down the economy stirred pleasurable reverie when encountered in the form of ruins.

In considering Robert's production in light of a new temporal consciousness enforced by an economy of "incertitude," this study ventures into material that does not typically feature in accounts of eighteenth-century French painting.[13] And no doubt art historians reading this are beginning to question, with justifiable suspicion, the whereabouts of Robert in all of this. What, they are preparing to ask, does the logic of a speculative economy have to do with the art of a well-connected Frenchman famed for the facility with which he churned out views of majestic Roman monuments fallen to ruin and inhabited by the likes of shepherds and laundresses? These readers should rest assured that what follows does not seek to undermine their acquaintance with Robert. It does, however, attempt to provide a new perspective on the production of an artist whose largely obscured significance is reflected in the absence, to date, of a catalogue raisonné of his work, an artist, it could be said, whose achievements lend themselves less readily to characterization than his shortcomings: he was a notoriously flawed draftsman and what is more, he thoroughly lacked Piranesi's intensity, Watteau's melancholy, Greuze's angst, and, of course, David's gravitas.

What unifies the artists cited above is their prominence in seminal accounts of the development of modern art. Such narratives have located in the eighteenth century the origins of an investigation of medium specificity as well as of an avant-garde grounded in an oppositional mass culture.[14] Robert's absence from (or marginality in) these studies is worth taking seriously, for the difficulty of placing him within the arc of inexorable cultural evolution remains, I think, key to understanding his distinctiveness. I have in mind the peculiar stance—playful, at times ironic—that he exhibited toward his own place in painting's history. Watteau, Jean-Baptiste-Siméon Chardin, and Greuze, for instance, made modern art that hinged on the example of the Northern school; David and his generation sought to revitalize history painting. Robert's art, conversely—as evidenced by the disappearance of pictures from his view of the ruined museum—challenged this conception of painting as a site of communion between past and present. His works abound with tongue-in-cheek references to Nicolas Poussin—quotations that signal his awareness of occupying what might be described as a post-Classical universe, one with implications for the future of painting. Robert brought to the medium an attitude, molded as it was by theories of the sublime and the picturesque, that questioned not only the primacy of painting (as decreed by the Académie royale de peinture et de sculpture) but, more broadly, the authority of models. He flirted, in certain respects, with the evacuation of tradition by pursuing the possibilities of nonpainterly practices—garden design, as noted, among them. Therein lies one reason for his extraneousness to the canon. (It is also tempting grounds for considering his place in an alternative history of art. If Robert's art fails by modernist standards, many of the works I discuss here have their distant echo in a postmodern hostility to medium specificity and a concomitant embrace of the sublime.) It is a paradox to portray Robert as existing at a remove from the past: he was, after all, an artist learned in the classics, immersed in monumental antiquity, privileged with positions in the leading cultural institutions of the day, and supported by powerful patrons such as Louis XVI. This, though, is precisely what makes his perspective so revealing. It was Robert's entrenchment in tradition that makes his art a crucial index of its erosion.

This book's central concern is to situate Robert in a culture that believed itself to have already witnessed the historical breach whose future occurrence it habitually projected. Well before 1789, Paris took leave of its past. Churches were razed. Touchstones of medieval planning were expunged and long-standing communities uprooted. The sacrifice of monuments and municipal rituals alike served an effort to reconfigure the city as a locus of unimpeded circulation. For Robert, the metamorphosis of the urban landscape remained a captivating subject from the time of his return from Rome in 1765 to the final years of his life, a period during which he devoted to Paris a series of views both actual and fictive. It is these works—many of which flew in the face of academic standards—that lie at the core of my narrative. Focusing on them has, for one, prompted me to interpret Robert's capricci—his imaginary reunions of edifices—as a barometer of the modes of perception inculcated in a city bent on deracinating its monumental order. These canvases, I argue, along with his spectacular views of the fires that ravaged the Opéra and the hospital at the Hôtel-Dieu, reveal an artist whose production was shaped as much by the innovations of Giovanni Paolo Panini and Piranesi as by the impact of urban reform, the vicissitudes of real estate speculation, and the manifestos of architectural conservationists. More broadly, attending to Paris in the art of Robert has enabled me to explore the ways in which modernization—a process whose overlapping aesthetic, economic, and urban manifestations this study details—was embraced, resisted, and fantasized about more than half a century before Haussmannization. Such conflicting impulses often may be detected in the space of a single canvas, suggesting, I contend, that Robert's pictures served at once to register and to cushion the blows of what effectively amounted to the city's creative destruction.

Finally, investigating this aspect of Robert's production has led me to examine why it was that imaginings of Paris perpetually circled back, at times eagerly, but more often anxiously, to the precedent of Rome. Robert's compulsion to embed his views of Paris with specters of Rome—to cast his volatile subjects as the return of some repressed version of antiquity—evinced a distinctly modern sensibility. It did so not because the recovery of the past advanced a progressive agenda for the future, however, and in this respect my account takes part in complicating the conventional wisdom regarding Neoclassicism. As Michael Sonenscher has recently shown, it was in the eighteenth century that remembering Rome became the hallmark of a debt-ridden state obsessed with the prospect of its own decline and fall. "We are poor," wrote Charles-Louis de Secondat, baron de Montesquieu, in 1748, in a widely echoed passage, "with the riches and commerce of the whole world; and soon... we shall all be... reduced to the very same situation as the Tartars."[15] At the same time, the Eternal City represented an ideal of durability that Paris despaired of emulating. In such a climate of economic dread, to imagine a future resembling the ancient past—as Robert did, more than once—was to give expression to a peculiarly modern convergence of insecurity and confidence, fear and hope. In this sense, the inseparability in Robert's imagination of Paris and Rome, of modernity and antiquity, uniquely qualified him to produce artworks that both channeled and assuaged his age's troubled historical consciousness.

This book examines Robert's art in tandem with perceptions of modernity and with the role played by the experience of risk in driving such perceptions; for this reason, the introduction of paper money in France in 1716 sets the stage for my account. John Law's failed experiment in liberating money from its basis in metal—that is, in promoting the expansion of wealth by enhancing money's capacity to circulate—turned the country against the prospect of financial modernization, against both paper currency and the establishment of a national bank. Nonetheless, it left a profound imprint on the French psyche. It was Law who put forth the possibility that things were worth more to the extent that they dematerialized. This idea, elaborated in Georg Simmel's *Philosophie des Geldes* (1900), also functioned as a key tenet of eighteenth-century aesthetic theory. When Roger de Piles declared that "the most finished works... are not always the most agreeable," he summed up his age's conviction that the value of artworks lay in their ability to catalyze the free circulation of mental associations.[16] Along with this shift in attention from the art object to the subjective response it engendered, "finished works" were superseded in preference by incomplete ones—by inchoate objects such as the ruin, which invited imaginative completion. The cult of ruins, I suggest in chapter 1, marked the fulfillment of Law's vision of a nominalist universe that would take the place of an ontological one, of subjective value displacing "the law . . . of objects."[17] Money, states Law, "has no value in itself except in its action and movement. . . . To gain from it, you have to get rid of it."[18] In the enthrallment with ruins, one finds a similar longing for escape from the stasis of intact forms. My argument, then, is not that Law "influenced" aesthetic theory, but rather that the latter functioned as a kind of placeholder for ideas prior to their realization in financial life.

A world apprehended as undergoing the depletion of its content: this constituted Robert's quintessential subject. Its key manifestations are traced in this study. Chapter 1, surveying the expansion of *ruinisme* from mid-eighteenth-century Rome to French picturesque gardens, contextualizes the aesthetic of ruins in a culture of risk that valued the unpredictable over the constant. Chapter 2 illuminates the valence of Robert's proclivity for the "unfinished" in a speculative economy. Focusing on his paintings of urban disasters, I explore the rise of catastrophe as a sublime subject—and as a secular version of apocalypse—at a time of mistrust in the "magic of credit."[19] Chapter 3 addresses the capricci and urban landscapes executed by Robert circa 1789—including his views featuring the demolitions of the houses along the Seine's bridges and the destruction of the Bastille. Such works are studied alongside the operations of urban improvement that—geared as they were toward remaking the city in the image no longer of princely magnificence but rather of laissez-faire—foreshadowed the dismantling of the ancien régime. Produced in the midst of a financial crisis precipitated, it was believed, by the flow of worthless paper, these paintings dwell with both relish and regret on the idea of circulation. As such, they anticipate those discussed in chapter 4, namely, Robert's canvases featuring the transformation of the Palais du Louvre into a national museum—an institution predicated on the exchangeability of art in a commercial age and which, in decontextualizing artworks, emptied them of their former meanings. These four chapters, then, sequentially chronicle the loss of the past—a process made complete by the French Revolution—which is to say, they track the oscillation in Robert's production between enchantment and disenchantment. Viewed through the lens of his art, such a loss may be comprehended as the basis for modern aesthetic experience—and the ruin recognized as the condition for imagining the future.

NOTES

1 Constantin-François, comte de Volney, *The Ruins; or, Meditation on the Revolutions of Empires: And the Law of Nature* (New York: Peter Eckler, 1890), 8.

2 Samuel Wagstaff, Jr., "Talking with Tony Smith," *Artforum* 5, no. 4 (1966): 17, 19.

3 Edmund Burke, *A Philosophical Enquiry into the Origin of Our Ideas of the Sublime and Beautiful,* ed. Adam Phillips (Oxford: Oxford Univ. Press, 1990), 57.

4 Reinhart Koselleck, *Futures Past: On the Semantics of Historical Time,* trans. Keith Tribe (Cambridge: MIT Press, 1985), 22. On the emergence of catastrophe in the eighteenth century as a newly secularized subject, see Anne-Marie Mercier-Faivre and Chantal Thomas, eds., *L'invention de la catastrophe au XVIIIe siècle: Du châtiment divin au désastre naturel* (Geneva: Droz, 2008).

5 Monographs on Robert include Jean de Cayeux with Catherine Boulot, *Hubert Robert* (Paris: Fayard, 1989); Claude Gabillot, *Hubert Robert et son temps* (Paris: Librairie de l'art, 1895); and Pierre de Nolhac, *Hubert Robert, 1733–1808* (Paris: Goupil, 1910). Skilled in the arts of garden design and interior decoration as well as painting, Robert adeptly ingratiated himself with an elite class of patrons. His consequent reputation as a reactionary sympathetic to the conservative values of his powerful clientele has been called into question by recent scholarship. This includes Paula Rea Radisich's study of a series of decorative ensembles produced by the artist—works reflective, she writes, of Robert's place in a culture of Enlightenment sociability; see her *Hubert Robert: Painted Spaces of the Enlightenment* (Cambridge: Cambridge Univ. Press, 1998), as well as Jutta Held's examination of the political overtones of ruins on the eve of the Revolution in *Monument und Volk: Vorrevolutionäre Wahrnehmung in Bildern des ausgehenden Ancien Régime* (Cologne: Böhlau, 1990). Three other notable studies explore the relationship between Robert's paintings and contemporaneous ideas concerning the built environment: Hubert Burda, *Die Ruine in den Bildern Hubert Roberts* (Munich: Wilhelm Fink, 1967); André Corboz, *Peinture militante et architecture révolutionnaire: À propos du thème du tunnel chez Hubert Robert* (Basel: Birkhäuser, 1978); and Günter Herzog, *Hubert Robert und das Bild im Garten* (Worms: Wernersche Verlagsgesellschaft, 1989).

6 J. G. A. Pocock, "Modes of Political and Historical Time in Early Eighteenth-Century England," in idem, *Virtue, Commerce, and History: Essays on Political Thought and History, Chiefly in the Eighteenth Century* (1985; reprint, Cambridge: Cambridge Univ. Press, 1995), 91–92. On contingency as the essence of modernity, see T. J. Clark, "Introduction," in idem, *Farewell to an Idea: Episodes from a History of Modernism* (New Haven: Yale Univ. Press, 1999).

7 Charles de Brosses, *Lettres d'Italie du président de Brosses,* ed. Frédéric d'Agay (Paris: Mercure de France, 1986), 2:200 (letter 46); cited in Robin Middleton, "Introduction," in Julien-David Le Roy, *The Ruins of the Most Beautiful Monuments of Greece,* trans. David Britt (Los Angeles: Getty Research Institute, 2004), 24.

8 Alexander Gottlieb Baumgarten, *Reflections on Poetry: Alexander Gottlieb Baumgarten's "Meditationes Philosophicae de Nonnullis ad Poema Pertinentibus,"* trans. Karl Aschenbrenner and William B. Holther (Berkeley: Univ. of California Press, 1954), 78.

9 Ernst Cassirer, *The Philosophy of the Enlightenment* (1932), trans. Fritz C. A. Koelln and James P. Pettegrove (Princeton: Princeton Univ. Press, 1951), 340. On the aesthetics of ruins, see, for instance, Michel Baridon, "Ruins as a Mental Construct," *Journal of Garden History* 5, no. 1 (1985): 84–96; Elizabeth Wanning Harries, *The Unfinished Manner: Essays on the Fragment in the Later Eighteenth Century* (Charlottesville: Univ. Press of Virginia, 1994); John Dixon Hunt, "Picturesque Mirrors and the Ruins of the Past," *Art History* 4, no. 3 (1981): 254–70; Sophie Lacroix, *Ce que nous disent les ruines: La fonction critique des ruines* (Paris: L'Harmattan, 2007); and Paul Zucker, "Ruins—An Aesthetic Hybrid," *Journal of Aesthetics and Art Criticism* 20, no. 2 (1961): 119–30. On French Enlightenment theories of sensationalist aesthetics, see, for example, John C. O'Neil, *The Authority of Experience: Sensationist Theory in the French Enlightenment* (University Park: Pennsylvania State Univ. Press, 1996), 105–70.

10 Anthony Giddens, *Modernity and Self-Identity: Self and Society in the Late Modern Age* (Stanford, Calif.: Stanford Univ. Press, 1991), 111.

11 Jean-Yves Grenier, *L'économie d'ancien régime: Un monde de l'échange et de l'incertitude* (Paris: Albin Michel, 1996), 145. Scholarship on eighteenth-century British literature has informed my approach to this subject (see note 12). My understanding of risk and entrepreneurial enterprise in late eighteenth-century France has been shaped by three classic works authored by Jean Bouchary—*Les manieurs d'argent à Paris à la fin du XVIIIe siècle,* 3 vols. (Paris: Marcel Rivière, 1939–43); *Les compagnies financières à Paris à la fin du XVIIIe siècle,* 3 vols. (Paris: Librairie des sciences politiques et sociales,

1940–42); and *L'eau à Paris à la fin du XVIIIe siècle: La Compagnie des eaux de Paris et l'entreprise de l'Yvette* (Paris: Marcel Rivière, 1946)—as well as by Herbert Lüthy, *La banque protestante en France: De la révocation de l'Édit de Nantes à la Révolution,* vol. 2 (Paris: SEVPEN, 1961). For a concise history of risk, see Gerda Reith, *The Age of Chance: Gambling in Western Culture* (London: Routledge, 1999). On the credit market in eighteenth-century Paris, see Philip T. Hoffman, Gilles Postel-Vinay, and Jean-Laurent Rosenthal, *Priceless Markets: The Political Economy of Credit in Paris, 1660–1870* (Chicago: Univ. of Chicago Press, 2000).

12 Giddens, *Modernity and Self-Identity,* 111. See, for instance, Patrick Brantlinger, *Fictions of State: Culture and Credit in Britain, 1694–1994* (Ithaca: Cornell Univ. Press, 1996); Colin Nicholson, *Writing and the Rise of Finance: Capital Satires of the Early Eighteenth Century* (Cambridge: Cambridge Univ. Press, 1994); Sandra Sherman, *Finance and Fictionality in the Early Eighteenth Century: Accounting for Defoe* (Cambridge: Cambridge Univ. Press, 1996); and, more recently, Mary Poovey, *Genres of the Credit Economy: Mediating Value in Eighteenth- and Nineteenth-Century Britain* (Chicago: Univ. of Chicago Press, 2008). For an overview of this literature, see Martha Woodmansee and Mark Osteen, "Taking Account of the New Economic Criticism: An Historical Introduction," in idem, eds., *The New Economic Criticism: Studies at the Intersection of Literature and Economics* (London: Routledge, 1999).

13 I borrow the term *incertitude* from Grenier, *Économie d'ancien régime.* In this sense, scholarship on the subject has not yet completely shattered the illusory separation between art and the marketplace clung to by the Académie royale de peinture et de sculpture, whose members were barred from commercial enterprise. By contrast, the intersections between economics and art in eighteenth-century Britain have been productively mined, as in David H. Solkin, *Painting for Money: The Visual Arts and the Public Sphere in Eighteenth-Century England* (New Haven: Yale Univ. Press, 1993). A spur to similar such research into the visual arts in France may exist in Martial Poirson, ed., *Art et argent en France au temps des premiers modernes (XVIIe et XVIIIe siècles)* (Oxford: Voltaire Foundation, 2004); as this anthology demonstrates, despite France's failure to keep pace with the evolution of economic institutions in England, commercial culture and the growth of financial markets had no less of an impact on *mentalités* there than they did across the channel. For a comparative account of French and British political economies, see Jean-Laurent Rosenthal, "The Political Economy of Absolutism Reconsidered," in Robert H. Bates et al., *Analytic Narratives* (Princeton: Princeton Univ. Press, 1998), 64–108.

14 I have in mind, respectively, Michael Fried, *Absorption and Theatricality: Painting and Beholder in the Age of Diderot* (Berkeley: Univ. of California Press, 1980); and Thomas E. Crow, *Painters and Public Life in Eighteenth-Century Paris* (New Haven: Yale Univ. Press, 1985). For an account of Piranesi's place in the history of the avant-garde, see Manfredo Tafuri, *The Sphere and the Labyrinth: Avant-Gardes and Architecture from Piranesi to the 1970s,* trans. Pellegrino d'Acierno and Robert Connolly (Cambridge: MIT Press, 1987), chap. 1.

15 Charles-Louis de Secondat, baron de Montesquieu, *The Spirit of the Laws,* trans. Thomas Nugent (New York: Hafner, 1949), bk. 13, chap. 17, p. 217; cited in Michael Sonenscher, *Before the Deluge: Public Debt, Inequality, and the Intellectual Origins of the French Revolution* (Princeton: Princeton Univ. Press, 2007), 9.

16 Roger de Piles, "Conversations sur la peinture," in idem, *Recueil de divers ouvrages sur la peinture et le coloris* (Paris: Ch. Ant. Jombert, 1755), 62; cited in George P. Mras, "Literary Sources of Delacroix's Conception of the Sketch and the Imagination," *Art Bulletin* 44, no. 2 (1962): 105. All translations from the French are by the author unless otherwise noted.

17 Cassirer, *Philosophy of the Enlightenment,* 293.

18 John Law, "L'histoire des finances pendant la Régence" (n.d.), in John Law, *Oeuvres complètes,* ed. Paul Harsin (Paris: Librairie du Recueil Sirey, 1934), 3:366; translated in Daniel Gordon, "The Dematerialization Principle: Sociability, Money and Music in the Eighteenth Century," in Michael Kwass and Daniel Gordon, eds., "Money in the Enlightenment," special issue, *Historical Reflections/Réflexions historiques* 31 (2005): 87. Gordon's article draws attention to the revolutionary effects of Law's system on eighteenth-century thought.

19 Isaac de Pinto, *Traité de la circulation et du credit*... (Amsterdam: Chez Marc Michel Rey, 1771), 33.

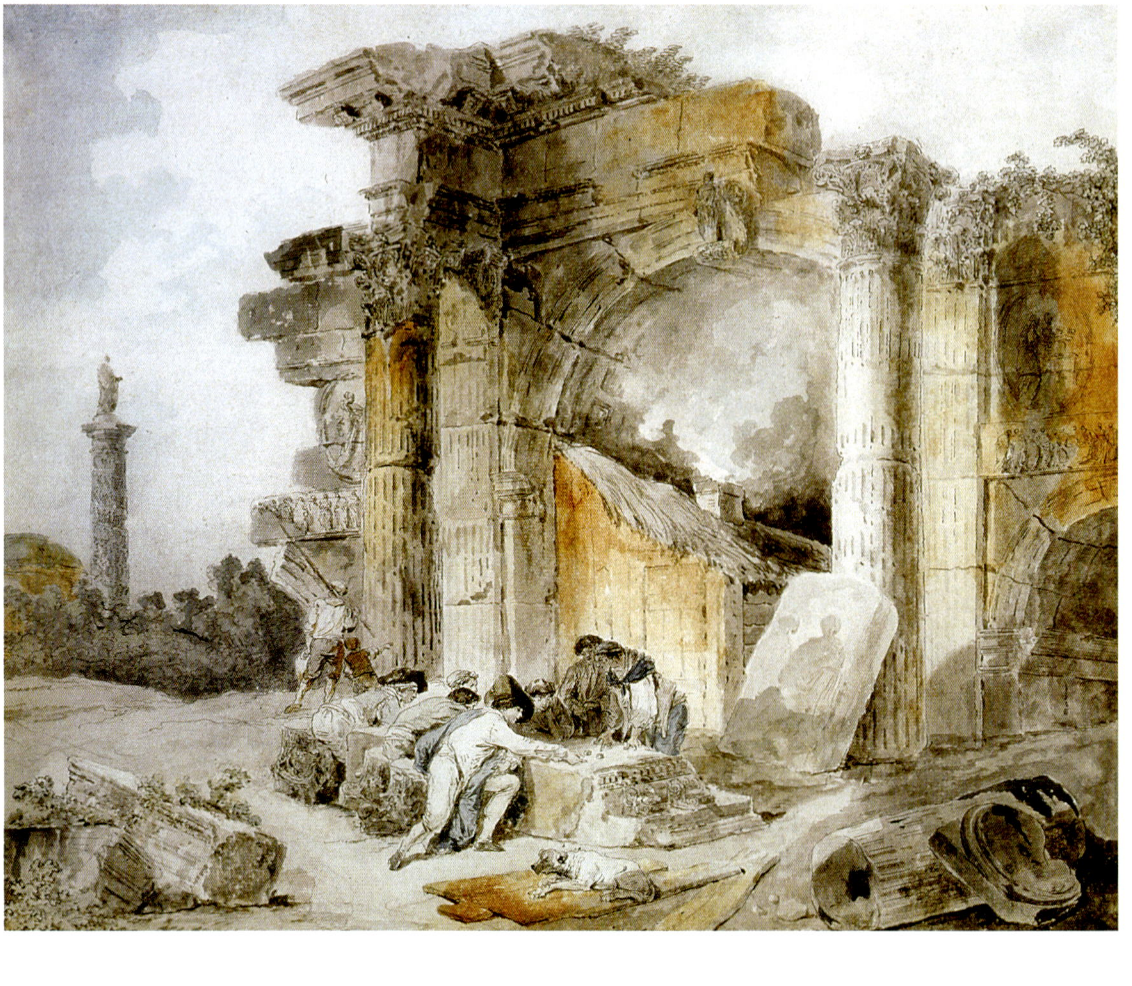

CHAPTER 1
The Unmade

> The great man is not he who most closely adheres to truth, but he who is most adept at reconciling truth and falsehood.
>
> —Denis Diderot (1767)[1]

An undated watercolor by Robert features a game of chance unfolding in a picturesque setting (fig. 1). Nestled amidst the delicate remains of an ancient landscape, a group of figures engages in a round of dice. The ruin of a once majestic edifice, now sheltering a cottage, provides the backdrop to their activity. A study in the poetics of precariousness, *A Game of Dice amidst Roman Ruins* playfully harmonizes the relationship between the ruin's residual magnificence and the modest stature of its visitors. These humble figures perch upon overturned capitals and employ a cornice fragment as their gaming table. As for the structure behind them—a caprice of disparate architectural elements supported haphazardly by fragmented columns—its own motley character makes it a monument to the vagaries of fortune. Its eroded acanthus have given way to real sprigs of foliage, just as the burning altar depicted in the medallion at right finds its counterpart in the ruin's smoky interior. Similarly, the solemn figures inscribed in the edifice's horizontal reliefs reiterate in their enactment of ritual the absorption of the dice-throwers below. Even the suspenseful pause of the game is echoed in the disruption of the ruin's narrative friezes, particularly in the abrupt sundering of the jagged structure at left.

The ruin as a site of serendipitous incident delighted such commentators as Henri Bernardin de Saint-Pierre, whose "Plaisir de la ruine"—from his twelfth *Étude de la nature* (1784)—describes nature's pleasing reconfigurations of the works of humankind. And likewise, Robert's *Game of Dice* conjures a world that lies happily hostage to chance. Overhung with greenery and colonized by the elements, the ruin—like the gamblers—surrenders its fate to irreversible fortune. Such self-abandonment to the unexpected is further thematized in the work's execution. For the quality of suspended animation that encompasses both the ludic moment captured and the abbreviated character of the ruin inheres in the condition of the watercolor. The work retains the look of the perpetually incomplete, an effect enhanced by the minimal use of color. The passages of blue and ocher that enliven the surface read as

Fig. 1. Hubert Robert (French, 1733–1808)
A Game of Dice amidst Roman Ruins, ca. 1780s (?), watercolor, pen, and ink wash, 40.5 × 49 cm (16 × 19¼ in.)
Private collection

provisional touches to a work in progress. No doubt the appearance of loose handling was carefully contrived, for "unfinished" artworks—like images of ruin—were celebrated in Robert's time as catalysts of the imagination.

It was in his review of Robert's debut exhibition in 1767 that Diderot addressed the hypnotic power of the incomplete sketch. "Why," he asks, "does a beautiful sketch accord greater pleasure than a beautiful painting? Because it has more life and fewer forms. The more forms one introduces, the more life disappears... Perhaps we find sketches so attractive only because, being somewhat indeterminate, they allow more liberty to our imagination, which sees in them whatever it likes."[2] Such valorization of the unfinished artwork abounds in eighteenth-century aesthetic thought. The comte de Caylus holds that "the curious eye and the animated imagination take pleasure... in finishing that which is often but a sketch."[3] Burke observes that visions of youth incite greater delight than those of old age, for they prompt the joys of anticipation. Similarly, in "unfinished sketches of drawing," he comments, "I have often seen something which pleased me beyond the best finishing."[4]

Indeed, the superiority of the unfinished work to the completed masterpiece, for the pleasure it afforded the beholder, constituted a key premise of aesthetic theory. Since the publication of Jean-Baptiste Dubos's *Réflexions critiques sur la poésie et sur la peinture* (1719), the artwork's effect upon the viewer had competed in interest with the artwork itself, a seismic paradigm shift that Friedrich Melchior, Freiherr von Grimm, articulates when he argues that the best of Sophocles and Euripides fall short of the art of pantomime. According to Grimm, both pantomime, which depends for its meaning upon the viewer's imagination, and music possess a "fugitive" quality that grants infinitely more satisfaction than a painting: the "most beautifully finished" productions, he maintains, remain inferior to ones that "force our imagination to finish the thought of the artist." Similarly, Diderot admires in the sketch its implication of furious vitality: "Movement, action, and even passion are indicated by a few characteristic marks, and my imagination does the rest."[5]

In short, the very insubstantiality of the incomplete work ensured its hold over the viewer—a scenario that we might analogize with the game of dice depicted by Robert. Unfinished artworks, in abdicating interpretive control to the beholder, implicitly courted chance. Replicating the thrills enjoyed at the gaming table, incomplete objects invited divestment from the established conventions of the masterpiece in favor of less certain returns. Fundamental to both the eighteenth-century passion for gambling and the discourse on aesthetic experience—with its insistence on the primacy of the viewer's subjective response—was the demotion of the faculty of reason. In both cases, the authority of past models withered before a horizon of possibilities.[6]

Robert's watercolor gestures playfully toward aesthetic consumption as a gamble, or toward gambling as an aesthetic pastime—a gambit that reflects his own canny understanding of the ruin not only as "aesthetically unintended" but also as itself a captivating instantiation of the unfinished artwork.[7] For it was precisely the incompletion of the ruin—lingering between art and nature, between irrecoverable origins and incipient destiny—that rendered it an inexhaustible repository of imaginative projection. Reviewing Robert's ruins at the Salon of 1767, Diderot describes the enjoyment uniquely afforded by the subject. "There's more poetry," he muses, "more of the accidental... in a single tree that's survived many years and seasons than in the façade of a palace. A palace must be in ruins to evoke any interest." Robert's ruins inspired Diderot's remark that "the field of the imagination is inversely proportioned to that of the eye." And as demonstrated by the critic's ekphrastic reverie, the image of the ruin—like the throw of the dice that holds its players spellbound—activates an endless chain of potentialities. For ruins "set one dreaming," both of the past—"Where are the people that erected this monument? What became of them? In what an enormous, dark mute depth my eyes wander"—and, more dramatically, of the future:

> Our glance lingers over the debris of a triumphal arch, a portico, a pyramid, a temple, a palace, and we retreat into ourselves; we contemplate the ravages of time, and in our imagination we scatter the rubble of the very buildings in which we live over the ground; in that moment solitude and silence prevail around us, we are the sole survivors of an entire nation that is no more. Such is the first tenet of the poetics of ruins.[8]

The passage reflects a novel apprehension of the ruin as an instrument no longer of remembrance but of anticipation. "Nature is always building even while she is destroying," notes Bernardin de Saint-Pierre, reflecting on the wondrous ways in which nature converted ruins into things of use.[9] It is this newly prospective, rather than retrospective, outlook that suffuses the suspended moment captured by Robert—one that marks the distance between his age's conception of ruins and that which preceded it. Before the eighteenth century, ruins functioned generally as allegories of earthly transience. "That which is firme doth flit and fall away, / And that is flitting, doth abide and stay," declares Joachim du Bellay in his *Antiquitez de Rome* of 1558, summing up his era's melancholy fixation on decay.[10] In the seventeenth century, the artists known as the Bamboccianti (meaning "clumsy dolls" or "puppets") produced views of Rome that similarly meditated upon time's victory over all things, and their precedent is one that Robert's watercolor both recalls and resists.[11] Lowly figures playing games of chance were a commonplace in the art of the Dutch painter Pieter van Laer and his followers, along with idling tramps shown lounging about, hovering over stoves, relieving themselves, and otherwise behaving ignobly (fig. 2). As an artist endlessly fascinated by the quotidian life of Rome, Robert was receptive to such motifs. The scraggly dog in the foreground of his watercolor, along with the game of dice, is a nod to the Northern tradition of genre painting that the Bamboccianti brought to bear on their Roman landscapes. Just as Watteau before him infused peasant life with mannered elegance, however, Robert substituted a lightness of touch for the brute naturalism of van Laer's circle. In the watercolor, overgrown verdure is his riposte to the excess of vulgarity showcased, for example, in the now-lost *Large Limekiln.* The efforts van Laer made to exaggerate his figures' wretchedness (as well as the scale of the limekiln) underscore the conceit that even though antiquity's monuments crumble (or, in this case, are actively destroyed), the truly immortal stuff of human frivolity endures.[12]

The gaming motif in the work of the Bamboccianti served the interests of realism as well as of morality: it recalled the presence of dice-throwers at Christ's crucifixion (those who cast lots for the clothing of Christ, as recounted in the New

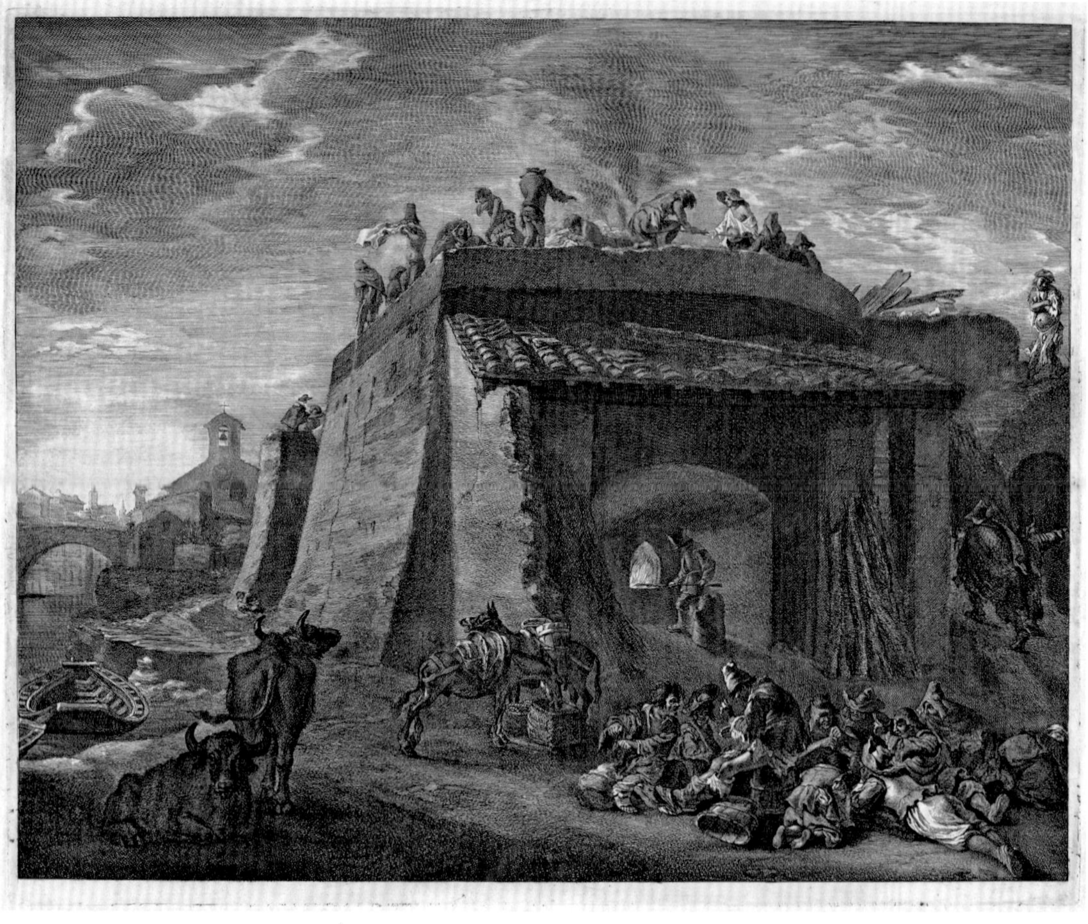

Fig. 2. Cornelis de Visscher (Dutch, ca. 1629–58), after Pieter van Laer (Dutch, 1599–ca. 1642)
The Large Limekiln, ca. 1637, etching on paper, 32.2 × 38.7 cm (12¾ × 15¼ in.) Amsterdam, Rijksmuseum

Testament) while also conveying the illusion of an unvarnished portrait of a fallen world. A view of the Campo Vaccino produced by Herman van Swanevelt makes similar use of the motif (fig. 3). Teeming with pedestrian bustle, the *veduta* presents itself as a true-to-life record of Rome's famous piazza. In the midst of laborers and merchants whose ostensibly unremarkable activities support the painting's claim to reportage, the cardplayers in the right foreground introduce the theme of *vanitas* into the landscape. The overhanging tree at right coupled with the architectural vestiges in the foreground suggest that nature and time will conquer Rome's magnificent edifices, already crowned with foliage. As in van Laer's *Large Limekiln,* only the meaningless and eternally appealing act of game playing remains impervious to decay.

Far from stirring such mournful preoccupations, Robert's ruin—bereft of its original identity—extends to the viewer the mischievous pleasures of the indecipherable. The artist employs the gaming theme to emphasize not timeless truths but their capricious disruption—an effect amplified by his choice of medium. Ill equipped, in its liquid imprecision, to support the weight of allegorical meaning, Robert's watercolor sustains irresolution, thus reveling in the coincidence between ruins, chance, and, by extension, the aesthetic of the unfinished. In the eighteenth century, revealing analogies obtained between these subjects. Writes Gerda Reith, it was in the age of mercantile capitalism and accompanying a philosophical interest in uncertainty that "chance…emerge[d] as a distinct entity *in itself,* separate from notions of fate and the

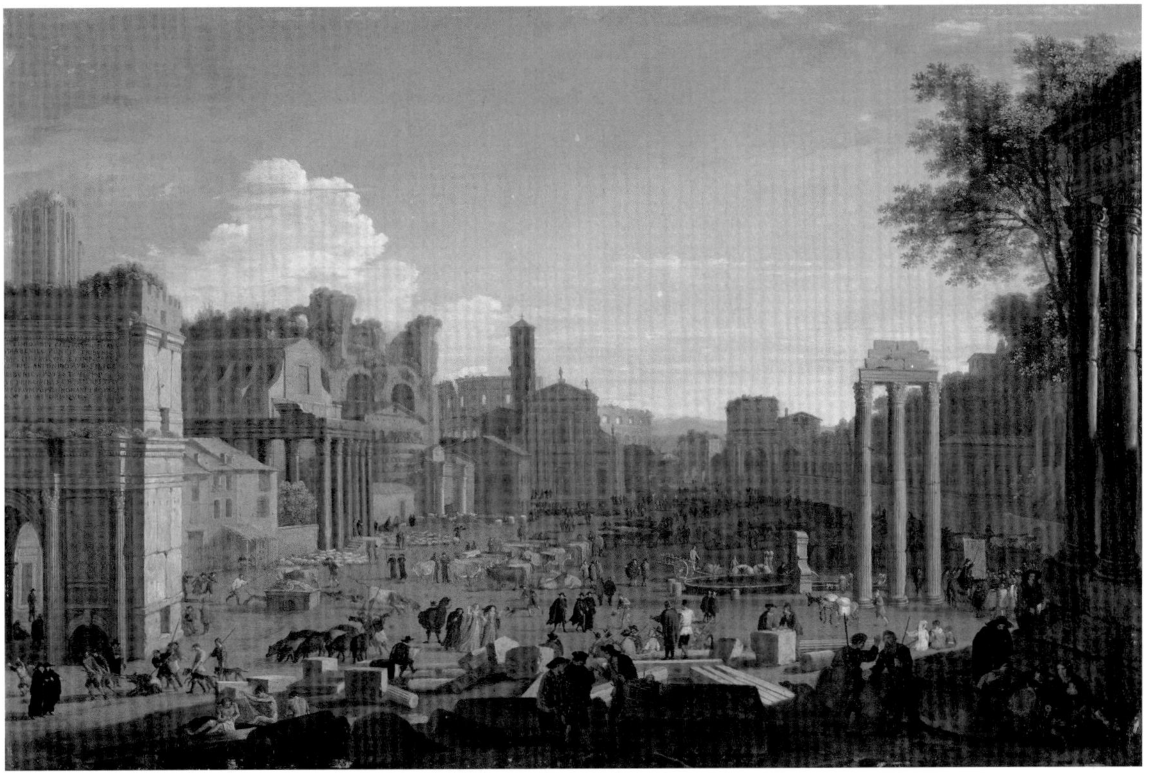

Fig. 3. Herman van Swanevelt (Dutch, ca. 1600–1665) *View of the Campo Vaccino in Rome,* ca. 1631, oil on copper, 45.4 × 67 cm (17⅞ × 26⅜ in.) Cambridge, Fitzwilliam Museum

gods."[13] Similarly, scholars have credited the eighteenth century with emancipating the ruin from its traditional meaning—dating from medieval times—as a symbol of decay and appreciating it for its "actual appearance," as "an object of pleasurable contemplation" in its own right.[14] Linking the interest in ruins with the advent of chance was the secular orientation of the period. The birth of probability theory enabled the "*secularization* of chance"—the submission of the blind goddess Fortuna, and of the divine law of providence, to a world newly unshackled from metaphysical meaning. In a parallel manner, the development of the aesthetic of the picturesque—with its delight in the formal qualities of the irregular and the variable, its affection for "rugged and broken surfaces"—diminished the ruin's symbolic overtones.[15]

This alignment of the cult of ruins with secularization, it should be said, is qualified in subsequent chapters by evidence that religious impulses did not retreat from a secularizing age so much as migrate into new aesthetic rituals; to be sure, the interest in crumbling structures proved amenable as a gauge not only of secularization but, at times, of a displaced biblical sensibility. Nonetheless, the general appeal of ruins lay in their association with the poetics of profane experience. Robert's *Game of Dice,* thematizing the courting of an unknown future, exudes this secular outlook. According to Reinhart Koselleck, eighteenth-century secularization revealed itself most critically in the emergence of a modern sense of time, an awareness of the future as distinct from the past and present. This new temporal consciousness, states Koselleck, "fundamentally ruptured the plane of Christian expectations," according to which history, endlessly constant and repeatable, was "projected in the form of a static time capable of being experienced as a tradition."[16] Following Koselleck, Niklas Luhmann asserts that preoccupation with the future, and awareness of its divergence from the past and present, is the hallmark of a modern culture of risk. "The injunction contained in modern time," he suggests, "to draw a distinction between past, present and future . . . encourages a thinking no longer amenable to any rational calculus."[17] More specifically, in an account to which this chapter will return, J. G. A. Pocock argues that the institutionalization of risk in the eighteenth century—crystallized in the foundation of the National Debt in England—fomented the conception of "a secular and historical future,"one befitting "a society now living to an increasing degree by speculation and by credit."[18]

Robert's *Game of Dice* provides a felicitous entryway into considerations of risk culture, for it emblematizes the paradox, explored in this chapter, whereby ruins functioned as sites of divestment from the past. Lending themselves to an aesthetic of play—one that compelled imaginative acquiescence to an indeterminate future—ruins assisted in the enthronement of risk. In Robert's watercolor, the architecture presents more than picturesque décor for the act of gambling. A kinship exists between the crumbling structure and the play of dice, which Robert underscores by uniting them as objects of deictic attention: the child points to the mysterious edifice, the gambler to the game. The effect is to align the cult of ruins with the age of chance—an age in which "the *perception* of . . . risks is now paramount."[19] For Robert and his contemporaries, this perception was expressed in the pervasive preoccupation with ruins.

Robert des Ruines

Robert is distinguished among his peers as an artist "smiled upon by destiny."[20] He was born in Paris in 1733 to parents who were employed by the duc de Lorraine's envoy to France, François Joseph de Choiseul, marquis de Stainville (at the time of Robert's baptism his father was recorded to have held the post of *valet de chambre*). Presumably due to his associations with the Choiseul-Stainville family, Robert attended the prestigious Collège de Navarre in Paris (it was here that he acquired his command of Latin) before commencing his career as an artist. According to Pierre-Jean Mariette, Robert received early instruction in Paris from René-Michel ("Michel-Ange") Slodtz, with whom he apprenticed from 1751 to 1753.[21] Slodtz and two of his older brothers, Sébastien-Antoine and Paul-Ambroise, were sculptor-decorators whose lucrative family workshop produced luxury goods as well as ephemeral decorations for state funerals, fireworks, and fêtes. No precise information exists concerning the nature of Robert's study with Slodtz, and one can only speculate on the influence that the sculptor's canny combinations of the ornamental and the monumental had on his pupil. Robert does appear, however, to have modeled himself after his master in some respects. Slodtz—whose commissions included designing ornaments for gardens—may have delegated tasks to his students at the time of Robert's apprenticeship.[22] Given Robert's subsequent success not only as a painter of landscapes but also as a designer of gardens and the *fabriques,* or ornamental structures, that decorated them, it is likely that a gravitation toward three-dimensional media—toward the world in excess of the tableau—was among the traits that the painter cultivated in the company of the sculptor.

Also like Slodtz, who studied at the Académie de France à Rome and enjoyed an extended tenure in the Eternal City that lasted from 1728 to 1746, Robert benefited from a prolonged stay (1754–65) in Rome, one owing at least as much to luck as to merit. In 1754, Robert accompanied Stainville's son Étienne-François (the future duc de Choiseul, prime minister to Louis XV) on his ambassadorship to Rome, and though he had not undertaken the entrance examination, Robert's admission to the Académie was arranged by Choiseul, who supported the young artist from the moment of his arrival. Robert's academic standing remained unofficial until 1759, but he nonetheless outshone the legitimate *pensionnaires* in his midst. Abel-François Poisson, marquis de Marigny, prior to granting the artist formal status, wrote to the director of the Académie, Charles-Joseph Natoire, of the positive reports that were circulating about Robert and recommended that the artist's fellow *pensionnaires* be exhorted to keep up with him.[23]

By all accounts, however, Robert remained an impossible act to follow. Despite being the most lauded pupil at the Académie, he appears to have been spared the rigors of academic training. Although the production of *académies*—life-drawings of male nude models—was a nearly daily exercise in the life of the *pensionnaires,* scant examples of such labor exist in Robert's oeuvre.[24] Nor does he seem to have furnished the king with the obligatory copies of paintings by the Italian masters. Another staple of academic routine was the production of drawings after ancient sculptures; however, while Robert was an avid draftsman of antiquities, his "copies" stray from the principles of the practice—foremost among them the rendering of volumetric form through modeling and the careful description of drapery. A sketch featuring antique statues reveals Robert's disregard for the academic premium placed on the production of highly finished drawings (fig. 4). Favoring the use of pen, wash, and watercolor, he opted for the effects of spontaneity rather than the controlled use of line. Through a combination of agitated marks and quickly applied brushstrokes, Robert's statues are less described than animated, blurred in midmotion. The page exemplifies the artist's predilection for treating the real and the imagined as interchangeable. The five statues—the Musei Capitolini's Cesi Juno and Venus; Jupiter; the Museo dei Conservatori's Hadrian from the relief Allocution of Hadrian; and a sculpture of an

Fig. 4. Hubert Robert (French, 1733–1808)
Sketch of five antique statues
From Hubert Robert, *Croquis faits à Rome par Hubert Robert en 1760,* fol. 20v
New York, Pierpont Morgan Library

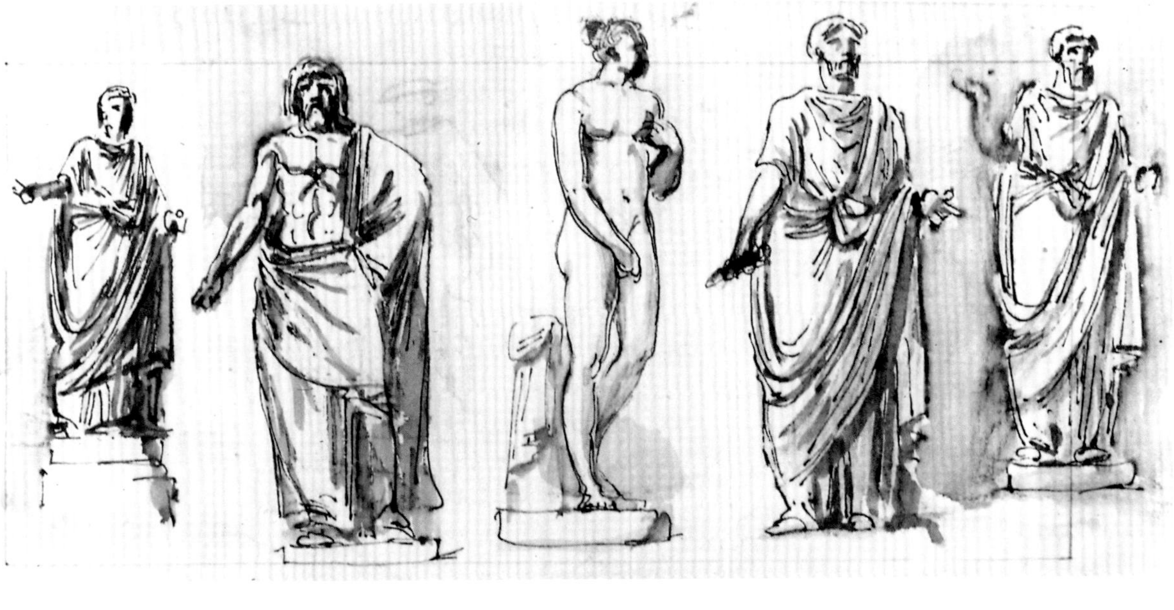

orator—appear in a sketchbook that was largely devoted to fictive views and fantastical variations on Roman monuments.

The drawing, with its attention not to internal anatomical structure but to surface incident and the broken border between the sculptures and the surrounding atmosphere, hints at the defining features of the picturesque that Robert absorbed while in Rome. Writing in 1752, Natoire lamented the decline of landscape painting and professed the hope that among his students "there would be found one who, not having the [talent] to succeed as a history painter, would take up [the art of] landscape which is so agreeable and so necessary."[25] Alert to the promise that Robert as well as Jean-Honoré Fragonard exhibited as landscape painters, Natoire led them on drawing excursions in the Roman countryside and evidently adopted a rather lax attitude toward studio practice.[26] Under the influence of his sketching companion Piranesi—who was accused by his own instructor, Giuseppe Vasi, of being "too painterly to be an etcher"—Robert cultivated a style of "painterly architecture" that emphasized sublime and picturesque effect over accurate description. The charged atmospheres of Piranesi's *vedute,* replete with cloud-strewn skies and meteorological events, left their mark on Robert, who understood better than any painter of his generation the expressive potential of negative space.[27]

Robert matriculated at the Académie at a time when the cultural climate encouraged deviation from past conventions. For the *pensionnaires* in Robert's milieu, an intense focus on the world outside the academy—manifest in the study of landscape in general and in visits to newly excavated sites in particular—reflected the growth of *anticomanie* (mania for antiquity) and its attendant temptations. The voracious market in all things antiquarian fueled the production of landscape painting. Similarly, the rediscovery of antiquity whetted the desire of artists to wander from the center of Classicism and pursue its peripheries.[28] Aided by his connections to a powerful elite, Robert was one of the first artists to visit the remote sites of recent archaeological discovery. In the company of Jean-Claude Richard de Saint-Non—a wealthy deacon, former councillor to the Parlement of Paris, and amateur artist who declared him to be "the most promising and talented young painter in the genre of architecture and ruins"—Robert toured Naples, climbing Vesuvius and studying the ruins of Paestum, Herculaneum, and Pompeii. Robert's drawings, along with Fragonard's, appeared in Saint-Non's *Voyage pittoresque; ou, Description des royaumes de Naples et de Sicile* (1781–86)—an ambitious, lavishly illustrated travel guide to the mysterious region published in Paris two decades later.[29]

Robert's travels with Saint-Non underscore the extent to which the artist's picturesque aesthetic developed in collaboration with *personnes de crédit.*[30] In 1763, Robert befriended Claude-Henri Watelet, *receveur général des finances,* and his mistress, Marguerite Le Comte, to whom Robert dedicated a series of etchings, *Soirées de Rome* (1764), featuring picturesque scenes in Rome and its countryside. By that time, Watelet had created what was reputed to be the first picturesque garden in France. Robert would later devote several drawings to Moulin Joli, as the garden was known, a "destination for Parisian society" and the basis for Watelet's seminal *Essai sur les jardins* (1774).[31] Watelet was present at the Académie royale on 26 July 1766, when Robert was given the extraordinary distinction of being admitted not only as *agréé* but also as *académicien,* a position of leadership in the institution. And it was evidently Watelet who enabled Robert to solidify his connections to Parisian high society as drawing instructor at Louis-Antoine-Auguste de Rohan-Chabot's private academy. Sessions were occasionally held in the countryside, and—alongside Watelet, a participant in the exercises—there Robert cultivated his love of the picturesque. Gardens remained central to the artist's career: in 1784, he was appointed to the post of *dessinateur des jardins du roi,* and two years later, the banker Jean-Joseph, marquis de Laborde, commissioned him to oversee the construction of his garden at Méréville.[32]

More than any other aspect of his production, Robert's activities as a garden designer reflected the lessons in the picturesque that he mastered during the course of a decade in Rome. Though little trace remains today of the sites Robert helped create, the letters he wrote to Laborde reveal an intention to create at Méréville the conditions for what might best be described as a *voyage pittoresque,* and in fact, Saint-Non's *Voyage pittoresque* offers a useful analogue to the picturesque garden. For just as the garden created the illusion of a built environment subjugated to the natural order, the *Voyage pittoresque* was written in a spirit of blithe surrender to the inexorable laws of decay. Nature's triumph over the ancient world and the irrecoverability of antiquity loom prominently in Saint-Non's work: "All these cities, so powerful, so formerly celebrated, have disappeared," notes the author. Over and over, the text posits the limits to what can be ascertained of history: of the Grotta di Pausilippo, for instance, it is known neither who built it nor when, and one can only marvel at an "enterprise [so] bold and difficult to execute" (fig. 5). So too does the *Voyage pittoresque* dwell on the role of chance presiding over both history and its revelation: the city of Herculaneum, the author reminds us, remained buried for sixteen centuries and was only discovered by "accident."[33] In the absence of archaeological fact, the text offers titillating anecdotes and picturesque views by such artists as Joseph Vernet and Louis-Jean Desprez, along with Robert and Fragonard.

Saint-Non's work illuminates the principle of the picturesque by revealing it to have been an agent of enchantment. While readers of the *Voyage pittoresque* were invited to savor the mysteries of ancient civilization and depictions of a built world overtaken by nature and ruin, visitors to Herculaneum expressed dismay over all that had been lost. As Friedrich Johann Lorenz Meyer, touring the city's decidedly unpicturesque remnants in 1783, lamented: "The most exalted imagination struggles in vain to picture a Roman city with its monuments." Works like the *Voyage pittoresque,* with their "magnificent drawings," were as misleading as the excited cries of his tour guide: "See the superb theater in Herculaneum! See the façades of the temple!" The author recalled looking in vain for "these marvels," only to find "a gate or column still more than half buried in petrified volcanic matter." Invocations of the "miserable remains of Herculaneum" resound in the travel literature.[34] Such accounts suggest that the *Voyage pittoresque,* as much as it appealed to *anticomanie,* also served as a means of substituting the superficial thrills of picturesque discovery—the "unexpected, wild, fantastic, accidental"—for the disillusionment that actual visits to the excavated sites inevitably prompted.[35] The picturesque, as presented in the *Voyage pittoresque,* was thus premised on the notion that the past was no longer meaningfully embodied and that a richness of aesthetic experience might fill the void. It was this capacity of the picturesque to deliver sensory pleasure in lieu of factual knowledge that Robert deployed in his designs for Méréville.

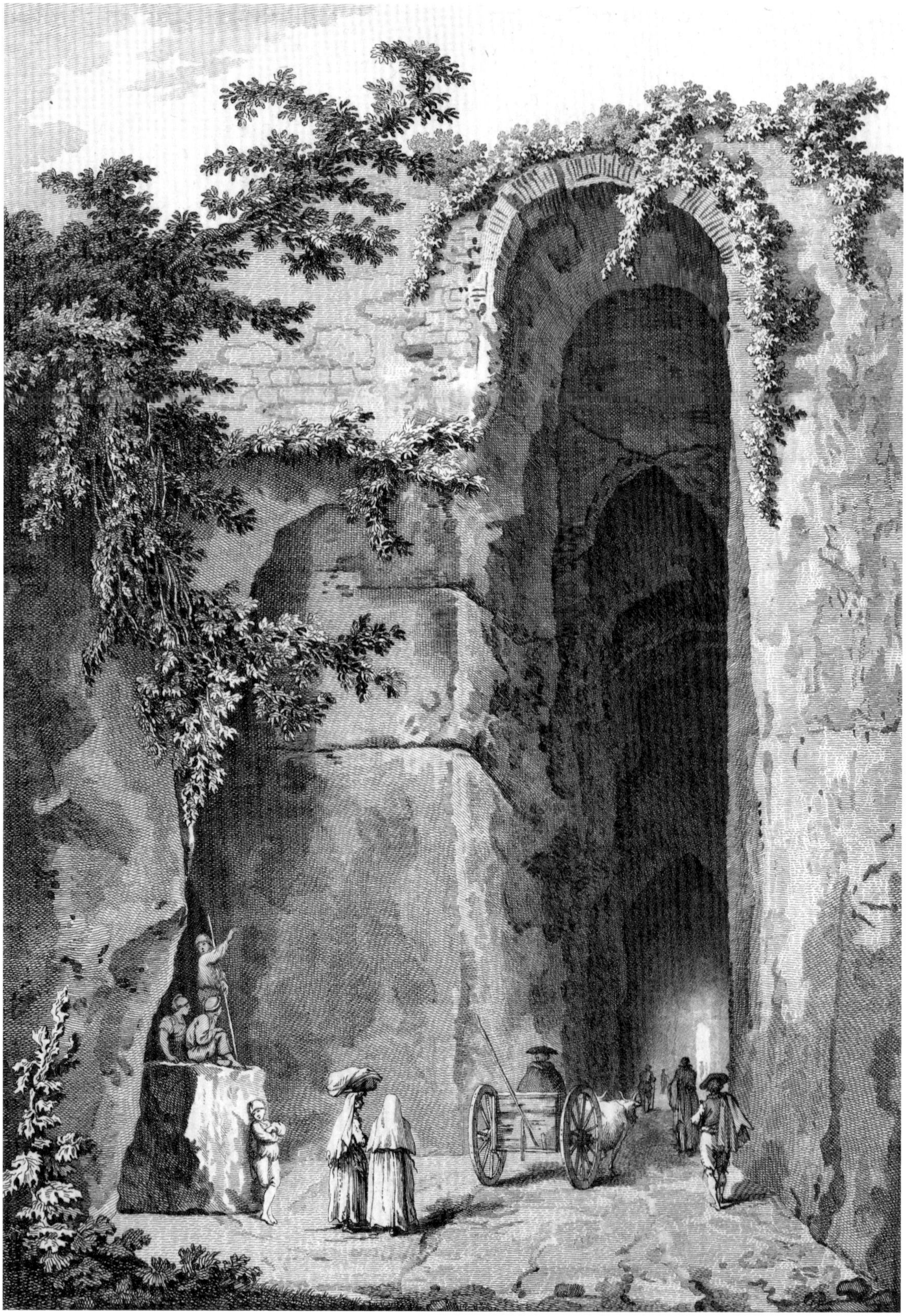

Le Jardin Pittoresque and the Pleasures of the Precarious

Robert's production at Méréville commenced in 1786, when Laborde hired him to replace the architect François-Joseph Bélanger, who was dismissed in part for his profligacy. For the next two years, the painter, working with the architect Jean-Benoît-Vincent Barré and the sculptor Augustin Pajou, among a host of other artists, oversaw the construction and installation of more than half a dozen *fabriques* for the garden.[36] The enormous commission reflected Robert's long-standing influence over the creation of *jardins pittoresques.* Noting that the artist's landscapes featuring Roman gardens were exhibited at every Salon between 1769 and 1775, Jean de Cayeux has proposed that Robert's oeuvre—with its repertoire of Roman ruins set in picturesque settings—served as an inspiration and resource for the garden proprietors and designers in his social milieu, particularly those who had never traveled to Italy. For example, such works by Robert as his drawing of Donato Bramante's Tempietto di San Pietro in Montorio—featuring the Renaissance structure recast as an ancient monument—may well have formed the basis, along with William Chambers's pagoda at Kew, of the colonnaded pagoda Louis-Denis Le Camus built at Choiseul's garden at Chanteloup (fig. 6).[37] This sort of appropriation and redeployment of a Roman ruin motif dated to the time of the Renaissance, when the dissemination of printed views of Roman landscapes promoted the adoption of antiquity's architectural forms by artists, furniture makers, and interior designers.[38] What is distinctive in the garden designers' use of Robert's ruins, however, is that whereas Renaissance *vedute* enabled the production of further objects, Robert's landscapes lent themselves to the fashioning less of things than of experiences.

Fig. 5. Hubert Robert (French, 1733–1808)
View of the entrance to the Grotta di Pausilippo outside of Naples
From Jean-Claude Richard de Saint-Non, *Voyage pittoresque; ou, Description des royaumes de Naples et de Sicile,* vol. 1 (Paris, 1781), 83

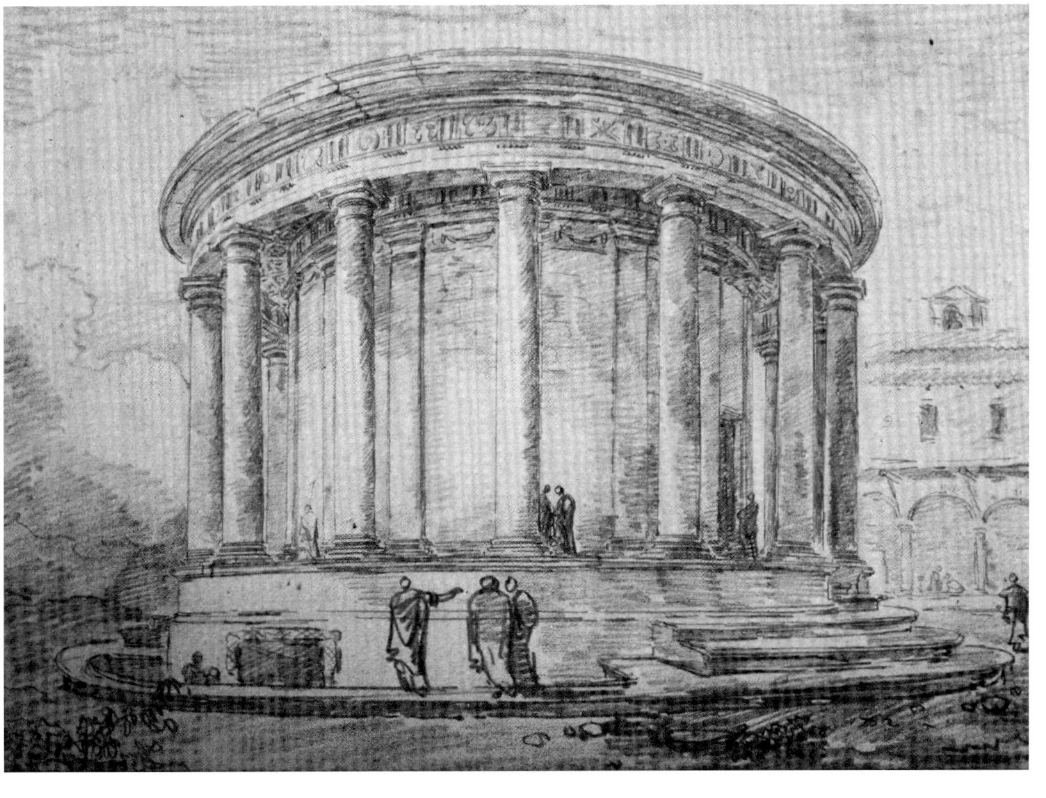

Fig. 6. Hubert Robert (French, 1733–1808)
Tempietto di San Pietro in Montorio, 1762, red chalk on paper, 33.5 × 45 cm (13¼ × 17¾ in.)
Valence, Musée de Valence

The notion, in line with contemporary theories of empirical sensationalism, that the virtue of the garden lay in its capacity to excite the senses and enliven the imagination was elaborated by Watelet. In his *Essai sur les jardins,* Watelet describes the garden's gratification of man's wish "to be constantly enthralled" and of his search for a place "where his sensibilities are intensified."[39] Though Watelet did not endorse the use of *fabriques,* preferring to minimize the role of artifice in the garden, his essay may be taken as a blueprint for what Robert aspired to create at Méréville: "if not the most grand at least the most interesting garden," as he informed Laborde.[40] In keeping with Watelet's emphasis on gardens as sites of ambulation and perpetual discovery (describing his journey along the serpentine trail of a garden, Watelet recounts, "I have discovered beautiful sights, then lost them from view, only to recover them with even greater pleasure"), the *fabriques* Robert designed promoted the park's transportive possibilities—both literal and psychological. A "gallery of caverns" measuring "168 feet in length," Robert writes to his patron of one such *fabrique,* will "fill even the most confident of souls with fright," for "who would not regard these rocks, fissures, crevices...as the marvelous work of nature?" Another dread-inducing *fabrique* was the Devil's Bridge he designed north of the château ("one advances, while trembling, over the bridge made of tree trunks and branches"), recalling the vertiginous heights of the Swiss Alps. Along with moving the souls of visitors, the *fabriques* were intended to launch the imagination to distant times and places: they included a Gothic tower; an obelisk that replicated Trajan's Column; the Temple de la Piété Filiale, inspired by the Temple of Vesta at Tivoli; a citadel; and a monument to Captain James Cook—a melancholy meditation on the New World—modeled after the fountain of the emperor Commodus in Rome, and designed, Robert writes, to inhabit the garden's "most dark and savage" corner.[41]

Such structures captivated imaginations by compelling the suspension of judgment. Describing his father's garden at Méréville in 1808—with its dramatic rock formations, its sweeping cascade, and a "grotto so spacious and so elevated it is difficult to imagine that it was made by the hand of man"—Alexandre, comte de Laborde, marvels: "There, where all was created by art, everything appeared to be the work of nature and time."[42] Thriving on disguise, the picturesque garden functioned as the ultimate "enterprise of mystification."[43] In its most theatrical manifestation—exemplified by the Parc de Monceau, created by Louis Carrogis de Carmontelle—the garden was the paradigmatic locus of the consumption of uncertainty. As Carmontelle declares in his description of Monceau, with its medley of Egyptian, Chinese, and other exotic *fabriques:* "Nature varies according to the climates.... Let us therefore vary the climates to cause us to forget where we are. Let us change the scenes of the garden like the décor of the Opera; let us create in reality that which the most able painters can only create in decoration: all times and all places."[44]

Carmontelle's statement invokes not only the reign of fantasy in the *jardin pittoresque* but also the genre's necessitation of a new kind of artist. As Michel Baridon notes, Carmontelle and his fellow pioneers in picturesque garden design considered themselves to belong to an avant-garde. Garden design had long been considered the domain of the architect, but the picturesque style rejected the uniformity and symmetry of André Le Nôtre as well as the rules of architecture.[45] As Watelet put it, the "precision" and "neatness" of architecture—with its "simple plans, symmetrical shapes, easily accessible proportions, and evenly balanced volumes"—were antithetical to the picturesque principle of unpredictability. Thus the "developer of a garden," states Watelet, will cultivate the effects of "chance" and the "fortuitous," along with the possibility of the "unexpected"; he "will favor designs full of mystery, dissimilar shapes, immediate visual impressions rather than underlying principles, and such surprises as resist uniformity." "Indecision," he writes, "is no doubt... more comfortable... than exactness, and more natural than precision."[46]

As presented by Watelet, the garden was valuable to the extent that it sustained a state of wonder. Put simply, the garden was significant less for what it meant than for what it did. This sense of the garden as a site that mobilized forms not to instantiate meaning but to sustain momentum characterizes Robert's numerous paintings featuring Méréville's bridges and waterways. The theme of the "rustic bridge" (evidently there were several in the garden) recurs in these views (fig. 7), along with the image of water cascading over rocks. As a structure whose very stability is predicated on its airy openness, the bridge, along with the rush of water, encapsulates the picturesque's hostility to the resoluteness of form—or to what Watelet called obstacle: "Is it not true," he asks, "that we enjoy seeing the convulsive action of water escaping from rocks, its violence appearing to *destroy the obstacles* that oppose its course? Yes, and our pleasure comes from the image it conveys of a recovered freedom" (my italics).[47] As an

Fig. 7. Hubert Robert (French, 1733–1808)
Temple de la Piété Filiale, Seen from a Rustic Bridge, 1785, oil on canvas, 46.5 × 55.5 cm (18¼ × 21⅞ in.)
Rouen, Musée des beaux-arts

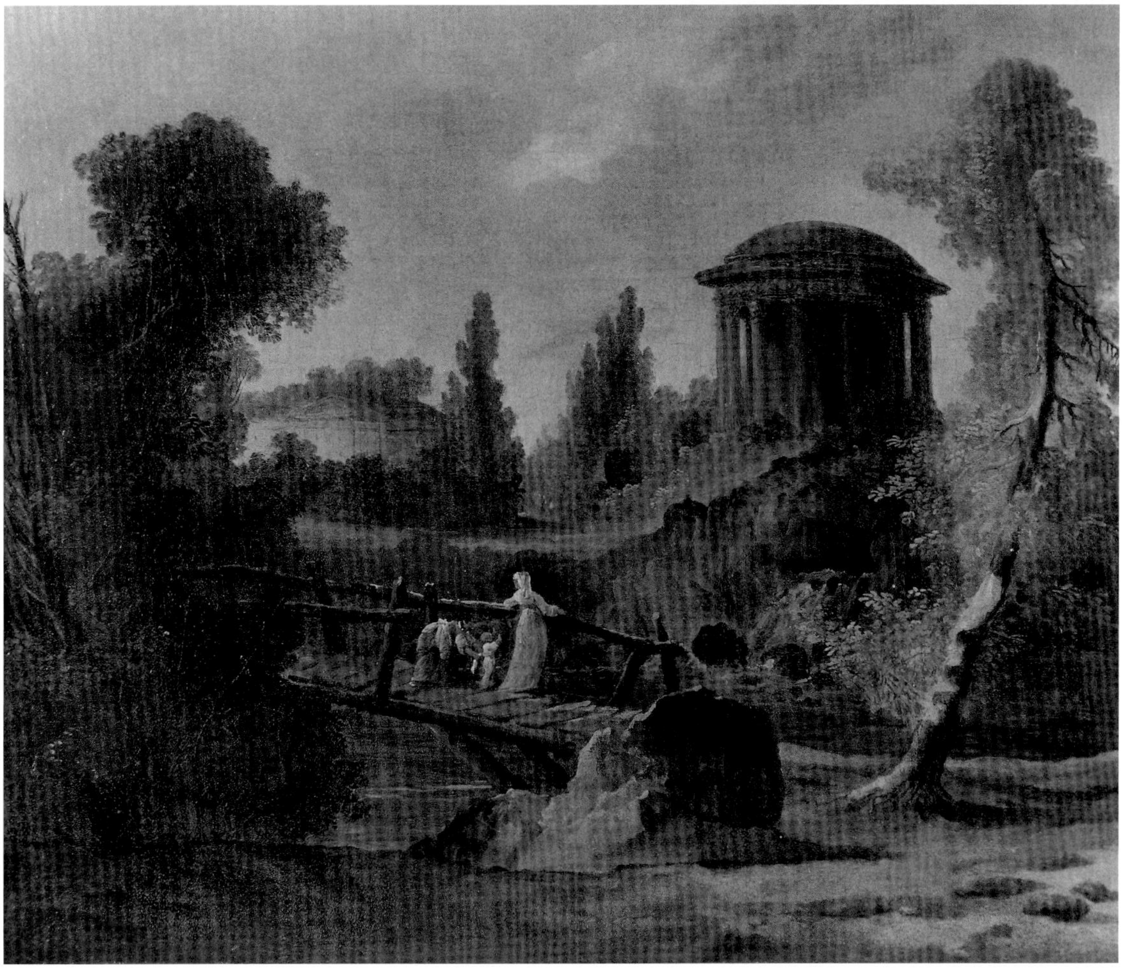

oblique testament to the delights of the unimpeded imagination, the sentiment recalls Diderot's praise of the destruction of form wrought by the unfinished sketch: "The more forms one introduces, the more life disappears." Like sketches, garden *fabriques* pleased to the extent that they evaded ontological precision. Rocks, notes Watelet, "serve as a transition from natural to artificial objects"—an observation that equally applies to wooden bridges.[48] Their identities vacillating, rocks and bridges were also subject to constant erosion. They thus reflected the appeal of *fabriques* as inherently mutable structures whose value was in inverse proportion to their constancy.

For this reason, there is perhaps no better example of a *fabrique* than the Temple de la Philosophie, modeled after the Temple of the Sibyl at Tivoli and constructed by René-Louis, marquis de Girardin, at Ermenonville (fig. 8).[49] The faux-antique *fabrique* was left intentionally unfinished, a premature ruin. Each of its six Tuscan columns was dedicated to a modern philosopher (Isaac Newton, René Descartes, William Penn, Montesquieu, Jean-Jacques Rousseau, and Voltaire), and at its base lay a broken pillar, bearing the inscription *Quis hoc perficiet* (Who will complete this?). Honoring the pursuit of knowledge, the temple also presented a token of the eighteenth-century perception of the ruin as a structure open to chance and possibility, and as aesthetically valuable insofar as it remained unfinished.

Robert participated in the creation of Ermenonville, designing the tomb of Rousseau on the Île des Peupliers (Island of poplars), situated just beneath the cliff where the Temple de la Philosophie stood. The latter structure clearly fascinated the painter, who depicted it on more than one occasion.[50] One such painting, *The Park at Ermenonville,* features the temple atop a cliff at right, and the Île des Peupliers in the background (fig. 9). Most of the canvas is devoted to sky, clouds, and water, exemplifying Robert's signature emphasis on the elemental world enveloping the ruin. The cascades in the foreground, slowly eroding the stone beneath them, reflect the painter's tendency to blur the boundaries between oppositional elements—architecture and nature, earth and sky, ground and water—the better to evoke a world in constant transition.[51] Barbara Maria Stafford writes that the eighteenth-century garden sacrificed a real engagement with nature at the altar of "untrammeled mental wandering"; the pleasures of the picturesque were "predicated on the heedless arousal of a sequence of ideas that, by definition, flee from the object."[52] And indeed, Robert's landscapes often turn on the imperceptible passage from material forms to immaterial process: note, for instance, how the luminous foliage of the tree beside the Temple de la Philosophie makes delicate contact with the similarly composed clouds above. As signaled by the peasant with outstretched hand, directing her companion's attention to a point beyond the canvas, architectonic constructions in Robert's landscapes are perpetually overwhelmed by the dynamism of their surroundings. As such, they point to the great paradox of eighteenth-century *ruinisme* exploited by the garden: namely, that it converted emblems of long-standing rootedness to the earth into fountainheads of mobility, chance, and precariousness.

Nonetheless, in Robert's *Park at Ermenonville* the Temple de la Philosophie's association with unknown prospects is unsettled by the central presence of Rousseau's tomb, its dark and enclosed structure inverting and yet completing the transparent and unfinished ruin perched above it. Of course, the temple's ruin may be interpreted itself as a rejoinder to the tomb; the point, however, is that finality and

Fig. 8. Temple de la Philosophie, Parc Jean-Jacques Rousseau
Ermenonville, France, ca. 1775

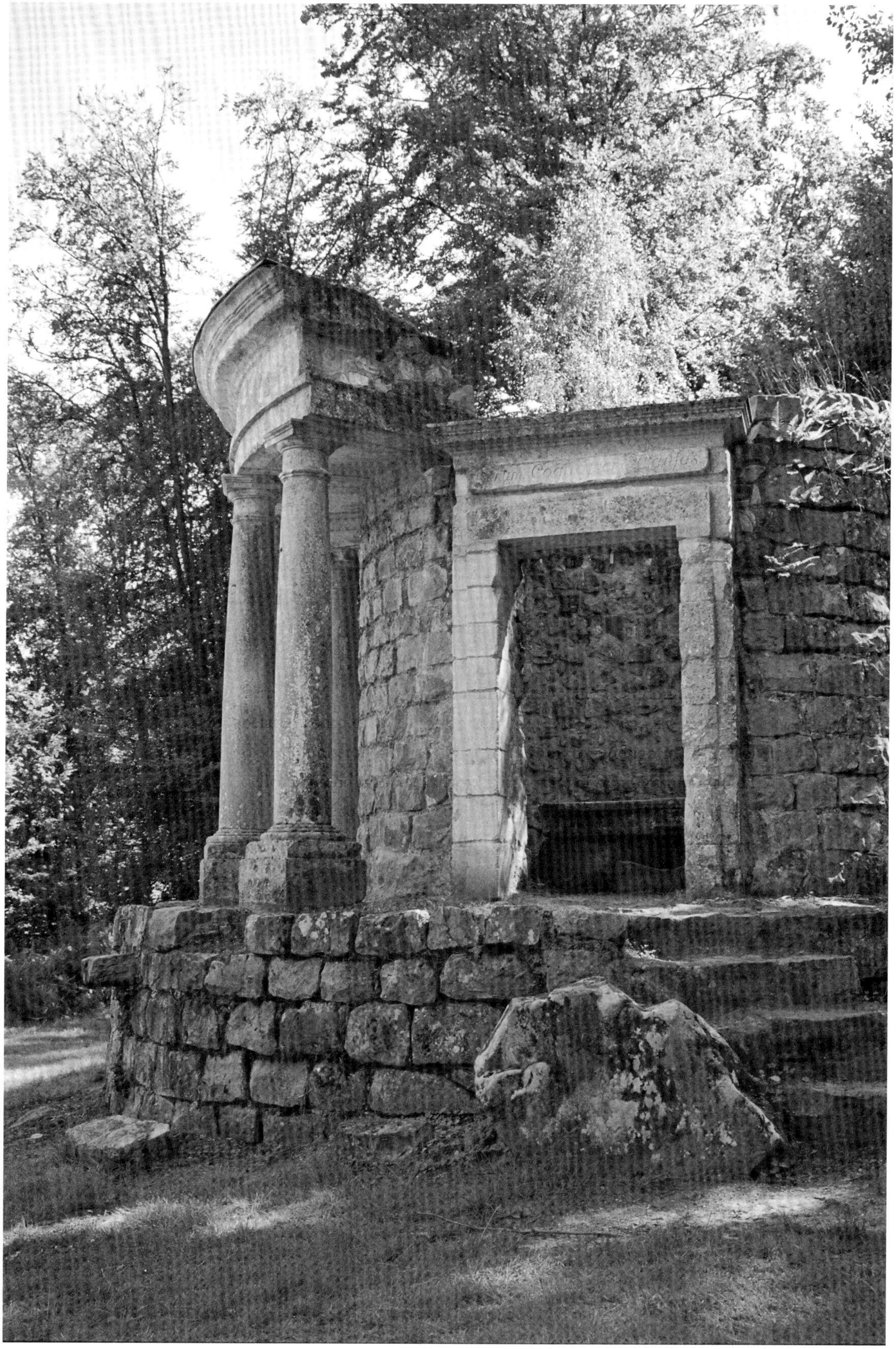

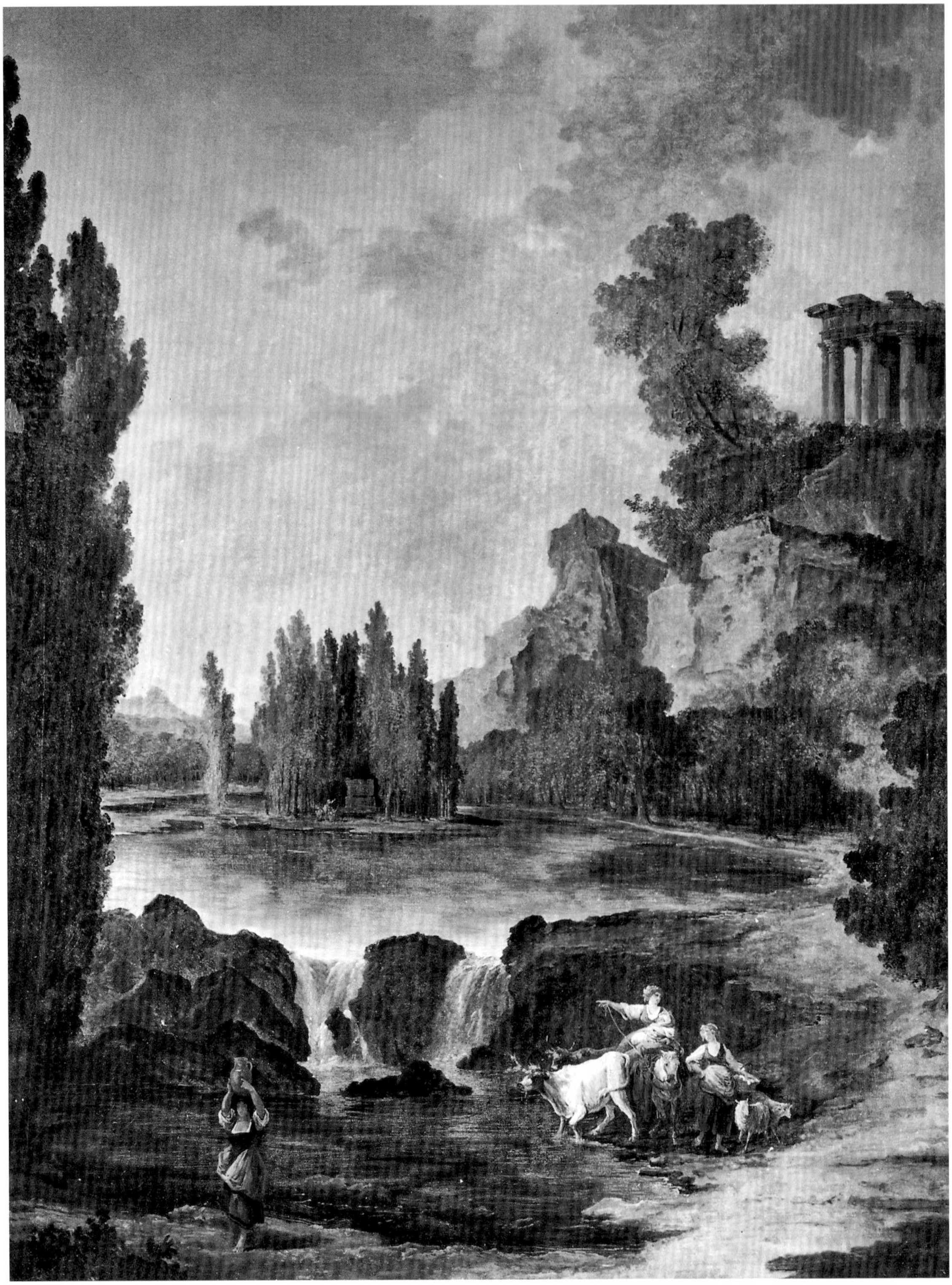

possibility become each other's shadow. The Temple de la Philosophie incarnated what Cassirer describes as the "dissolution and decline of classical theory" and the triumph of "subjectivism"—that is, the rejection of the notion that art, like reason, ought to obey "genuine, lasting and essential" principles and the growing belief that the only valid determinants of aesthetic experience lay precisely where Classical doctrine was most loath to look: in the "idiosyncrasies" and "accidental conditions of the spectator."[53] Ruins were stimulants for passionate, premonitory intuition—for imaginations no longer checked by reason, to borrow Cassirer's terminology. That decaying structures were effectively equated with incomplete sketches—which in turn were considered superior to finished artworks—marked a daring deviation from Classical thought's formerly rigid hierarchies. And given the lengths taken to invest ruins with the temporality of incompletion, a repressed uncertainty about the efficacy of this equation no doubt haunted the worship of the unfinished. As Cassirer writes, the effect of the new aesthetic, with its "ideal of *inexactness,*" is that "emotion finally becomes the only reliable criterion" of art's value—and that consequently the "work of art threatens to become a mere spectacle."[54]

Cassirer's critique has the virtue of channeling eighteenth-century apprehensions, for the period's criticism betrayed a growing unease that art—subjugated to the primacy of experience—would cease to be valued as anything other than a catalyst for successive sensations. In a review lampooning the exhibition of the king's pictures at the gallery in the Palais du Luxembourg in 1750, for instance, an anonymous critic prophetically compared the consumption of the displayed works to a kind of commodity fetishism: "[May] the holy history edify you, the profane instruct you, the poetry amuse you . . . the sky, the earth present you with images equally piquant and touching . . . all nature offer you scenes and points of views of all sorts."[55] The review satirizes the nullification of artworks under the sign of ecstatic ekphrasis, as well as an exhibition strategy that was calculated, suggests Édouard Pommier, to recreate in the gallery the spectacle of the garden.[56] Watelet's own remarks on the garden disclose an anxiety about the inability of the fleeting to compete in significance with the persistent. "Bewitching to the imagination," he writes of *fabriques,* "they enchant while we anticipate their effects; yet their charm almost always evaporates as soon as they are put into execution." Just as death lay in close proximity to Ermenonville's most famous *fabrique,* so too, Robert's painting suggests, were the touchstones of "subjectivism"—irresolution and submission to chance—synonymous with the dissolution of a prior coherence.[57]

Les Piranésiens Français and *l'Archéofiction*

What makes the *jardin pittoresque* a particularly revealing example of the destabilizing enterprise of eighteenth-century aesthetics is that the art form was itself in sync with the vicissitudes of *la mode.* Garden designers were expected to provide *fabriques* of the highest exchange value. Acknowledging the massive costs of constructing a garden or adapting one to the latest trends, Watelet warns of the potential for "ruinous effects" and "financial problems."[58] Evidence of the risks and fluctuations associated with gardens lies in the successive editions of guidebooks that appeared in the second half of the century, detailing picturesque destinations in and around Paris. "New

Fig. 9. Hubert Robert (French, 1733–1808)
The Park at Ermenonville, ca. 1786–90, oil on canvas, 194 × 142 cm (76⅜ × 56 in.) Private collection

establishments, the taste for English gardens adopted as a fashion, [and] considerable changes in several locales have once more rendered former descriptions useless and a new one more necessary," states Jacques-Antoine Dulaure, in his *Nouvelle description des environs de Paris* (1786).[59] The sequential and thus anticipatory character of garden publications—as in Georges-Louis Le Rouge's *Détail des nouveaux jardins à la mode,* which appeared in installments between 1775 and 1790—reflects the *jardin pittoresque*'s status as a barometer of evolving fads. In important ways, the prominence of ruins in *jardins à la mode* attests to their absorption into commodity culture. Facilitating this commodification was an appreciation of ruins as structures that unexpectedly deviated from stasis and predictability. Such a perception may be dated to mid-eighteenth-century Rome, following the excavations of Herculaneum and Pompeii, when *pensionnaires* at the Académie responded to antiquity's remains with a range of experimental and unconventional practices.

An account of the role played by ruins in the triumph of "subjectivism" over Classicism—so evident in the picturesque garden—properly begins in the 1740s, with the art of the first generation of French "Piranésiens." These artists—including Jérôme-Charles Bellicard, the brothers Simon and Charles Michel-Ange Challe, Nicolas-Henri Jardin, Louis-Joseph Le Lorrain, and Edmond-Alexandre Petitot—were residents of the Palais Mancini in the decade prior to Robert's arrival there. In the frequent company of Piranesi—whose workshop on the Via del Corso neighbored the Académie—they published *vedute* and archaeological illustrations, produced fantastical landscapes and architectural drawings, and designed *macchine* (elaborate wood, canvas, and stucco constructions) for popular festivals, including the annual celebration of the Chinea.[60] These artists provide a meaningful case study in the dangers of "subjectivism" insofar as their imaginations so perilously got the better of them: though they thrived as a collective while *pensionnaires* in Rome, they subsequently achieved little individual success and remained notorious for harboring chimerical fantasies. Their importance has largely been framed in terms of their influence over the formation of Neoclassicism and the "revolutionary architecture" of Claude-Nicolas Ledoux, Jean-Jacques Lequeu, and Etienne-Louis Boullée.[61] For our purposes, however, what matters about their work is its vivification of a poignant irony. A zealous recorder of antiquity's remains, their production marked the elevation of the possible over the actual, of the fanciful over the factual. Their crucial innovation—one that laid the foundations for Robert's art—was to make ruins valuable not as traces of a fading past but rather as playful signifiers of an absent signified.

"You who wish to become an architect, begin by being a painter," wrote Ledoux in 1804. A similar pronouncement could easily have been made by his friend Robert, whose picturesque aesthetic so inspired Ledoux.[62] The statement underscores the legacy of the generation of the 1740s. Although trained as architects, sculptors, and painters, together these artists questioned the boundaries between their disciplines. They excelled in the production of painterly architectural fantasies and multimedia festival structures—works that foreshadowed garden *fabriques.* Such interdisciplinarity, along with the *pensionnaires'* proclivity for the graphic arts, went against the grain of academic doctrine, which held painting to be the highest art form. At a time when printmaking was absent from the Académie's curriculum, the *pensionnaires* experimented with the medium in the studios of the foremost practitioners of topographical prints, Vasi and Piranesi. Under the influence of the architect-etcher Piranesi, these *pensionnaires* cast themselves as "painter-architects" and "painter-etchers," and in their art of *archéofiction,* Rome itself was transformed into "a sort of imaginary capital."[63]

Therein lies the distinctiveness of this formative episode in the reception of antiquity: namely, that for a brief period in mid-eighteenth-century Rome the aesthetic uses of ruins reflected in equal measure a consciousness of monumental duration and a will toward dematerialization. The mobilization of ruin imagery to this latter effect is exemplified in the *pensionnaires'* contribution to the Chinea. In 1738, French students began taking part in this festival by designing the *macchine* that were the basis for (and were literally consumed in) the celebrations' fireworks displays, as well as participating in the production of engravings that transcribed (with varying degrees of accuracy) the festivities. Following the discoveries of Herculaneum and Pompeii, architectural antiquity became a moving force in the festival's "ephemeral splendors": the *macchina* designed in 1747 by Le Lorrain featured, according to the engraving that he produced after the event, a circular Corinthian temple—of the sort that may be seen "by the seaside at Baiae"—atop a vast staircase, housing a sculpture of Venus, framed by obelisks and decorated with statues of ancient figures who offer libations before burning altars (fig. 10). Two years later, Petitot took as the unprecedented subject of his *macchina* for the Chinea a recent archaeological event: the discovery of the remains of the amphitheater at Herculaneum, which he "very, very conjecturally restored."[64]

Fig. 10. Louis-Joseph Le Lorrain (French, 1715–59)
Macchina (machine) for the Chinea festival with the Temple of Venus Genetrix, 1747, engraving, 35.8 × 47.1 cm (14⅛ × 18½ in.)
Los Angeles, Getty Research Institute

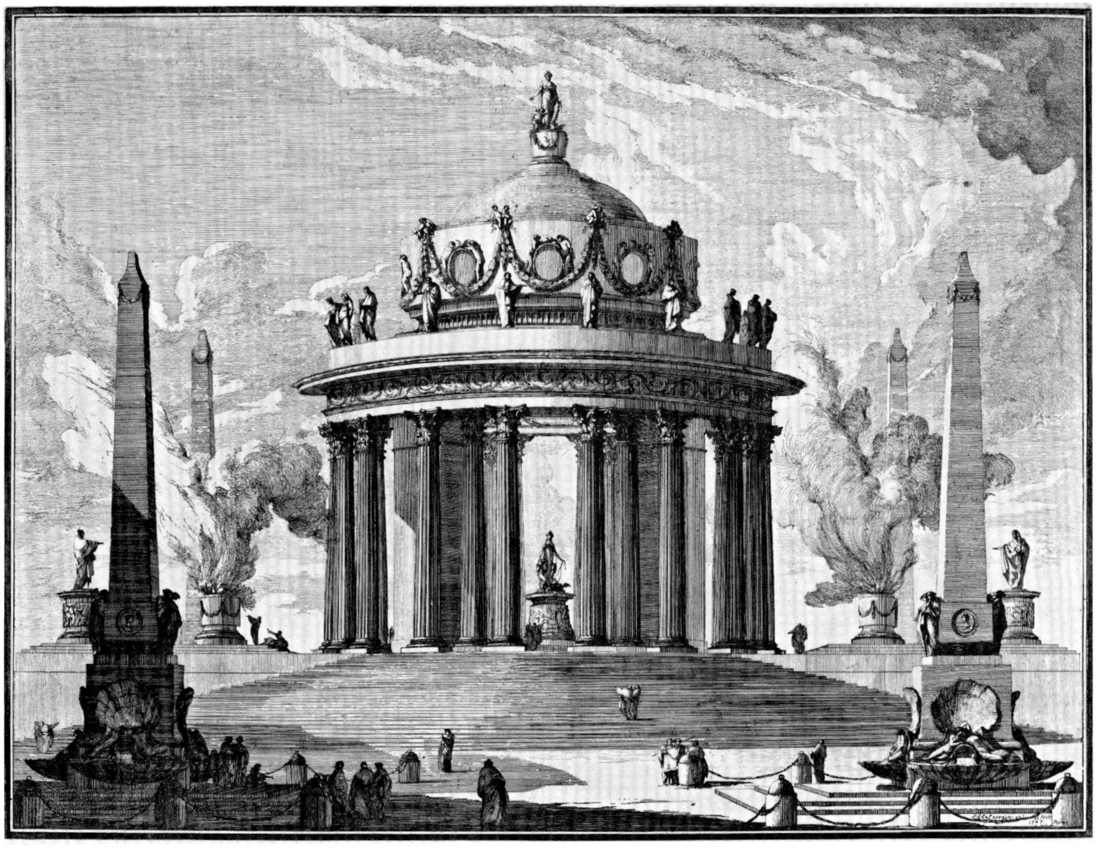

Like the creation of architectural fantasies, participation in the Chinea offered a creative outlet to a restive population of *pensionnaires* who relished the seemingly perpetual spectacle of Rome's festival culture.[65] It also permitted them to reverse academic truisms. The art of the Piranésiens revealed an intuitive belief that the more fragile the subject, and the less reducible to typology, the better. As Joseph Rykwert suggests, the ephemeral structures devised by the *pensionnaires* resembled suspended friezes at a time when "the antique fragment torn from the vast corpse of the past" was deemed the only truly authentic embodiment of antiquity, in distinction to "the more systematic remains." The cult of "the particular example," the "eccentric capital," the "extravagant molding," the "tangible . . . antiquity-object" incompatible with the "antiquity-idea" coincided with the deflation of the Classicist myths—of tradition based, it now seemed, in fraudulence—that had governed the study of architecture.[66] The disturbing realities of ancient buildings exposed in Antoine Desgodets's *Édifices antiques de Rome* (1682), as well as in studies such as Johann Bernhard Fischer von Erlach's *Entwurff einer historischen Architectur* (1725), which emphasize the eclecticism of architectural models, challenged the ideals of Classicism. In this way, the disenchantment of Classical decorum emboldened a "non-iconic vision" of architecture, associated most notably, as we shall see, with the reason-defying compositions of Piranesi.[67]

The singular and unpredictable, then, presented themselves as totems of authenticity. It is thus not surprising that an imagery of found objects—of chance encounters with antiquity's remnants—pervades the work of the Académie's *pensionnaires*. The frontispiece to *Suite de ruines d'architecture*—published by the architect Gabriel Pierre Martin Dumont, who resided at the Palais Mancini from 1742 to 1746—presents a compendium of randomly accrued remains: a tomb, a frieze, a statue, decaying column segments, and architectural ruins (fig. 11). Though densely assembled, these antiquities represent disparate pasts, and the very improbability (indeed, artificiality) of their reunion functions as a signpost for a facticity alien to Classicism's norms and standards. The identification of ruins as outlaws from a tame and regulated order is hyperbolized in this series' engravings, which employ chiaroscuro to heighten the sense of a subject impenetrable to the workings of reason. Dumont's view, for instance, of an artist occupying a majestic ruin and copying from an antique statue—one situated beside an assortment of decaying capitals and a lone frieze—valorizes the notion of an engagement with antiquity unmediated by convention (fig. 12).

Of course, the very insistence upon the virtues of an unforeseen and, better yet, scarcely comprehensible confrontation with antiquity would itself devolve into convention. In a gouache by Charles-Louis Clérisseau, who resided at the Académie from 1749 to 1753, the ceiling of a monumental portico has been shattered, yet a funerary tomb remains remarkably preserved in its niche (fig. 13). Lowly peasants bearing bundles and a child interacting playfully with a dog create an overall sense of happenstance and of the accidentally seen, securing the scene's claims to a kind of truth telling. Even the statue at left is cropped, enacting the mobile gaze of the eighteenth-century flâneur. Clérisseau specialized in such effects. His most famous commissions included the creation, in the 1760s, of a "ruin room" at the convent of Santa Trinità dei Monti—a chamber painted in trompe l'oeil to resemble a "cella of a temple

Fig. 11. Gabriel Pierre Martin Dumont (French, 1720–91)
Suite de ruines d'architecture
From Gabriel Pierre Martin Dumont, *Suite de ruines d'architecture*, in idem, *Recueil de plusieurs parties d'architecture de différents maîtres tant d'Italie que de France* (Paris, 1765), frontispiece

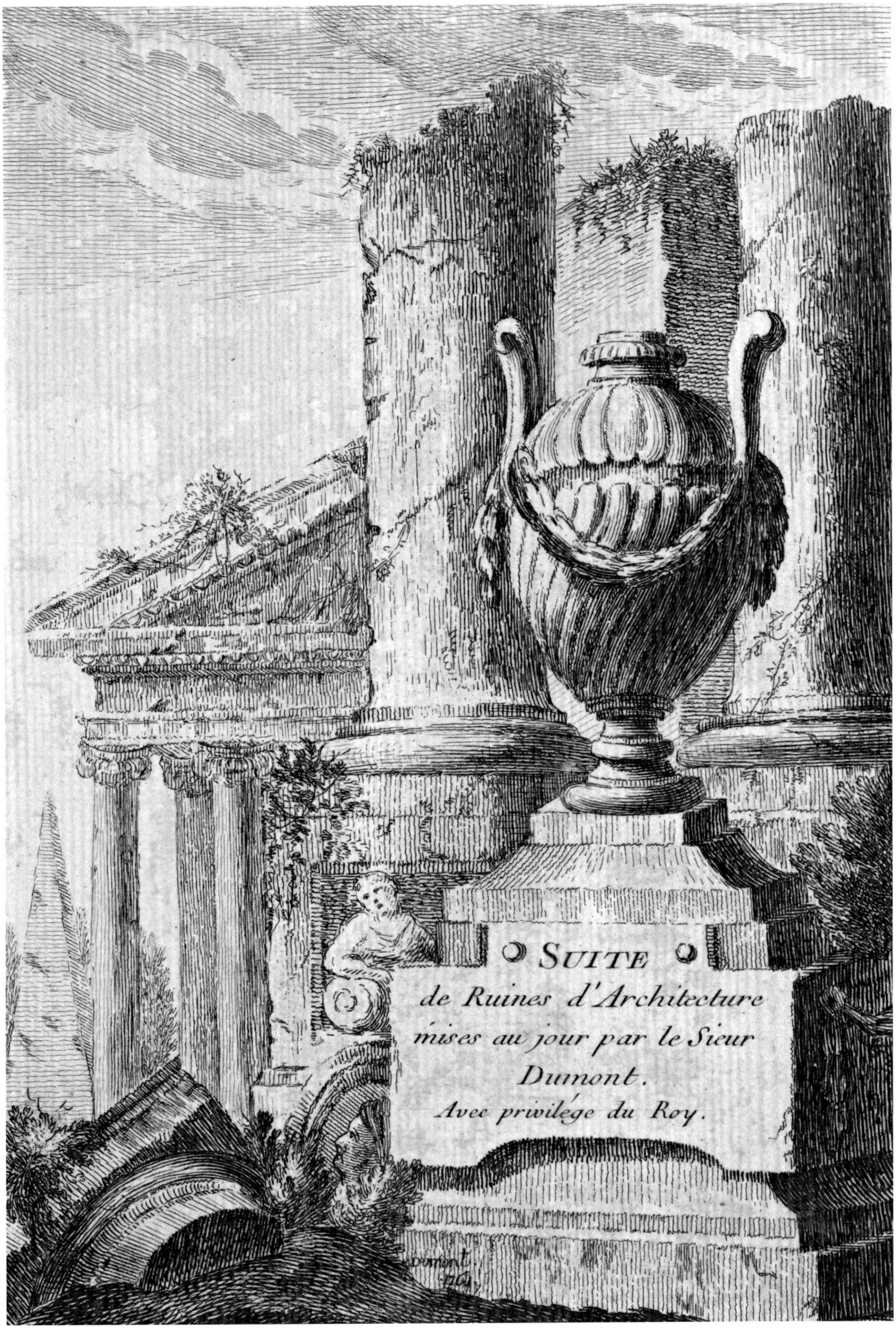
SUITE
de Ruines d'Architecture
mises au jour par le Sieur
Dumont.
Avec privilége du Roy.

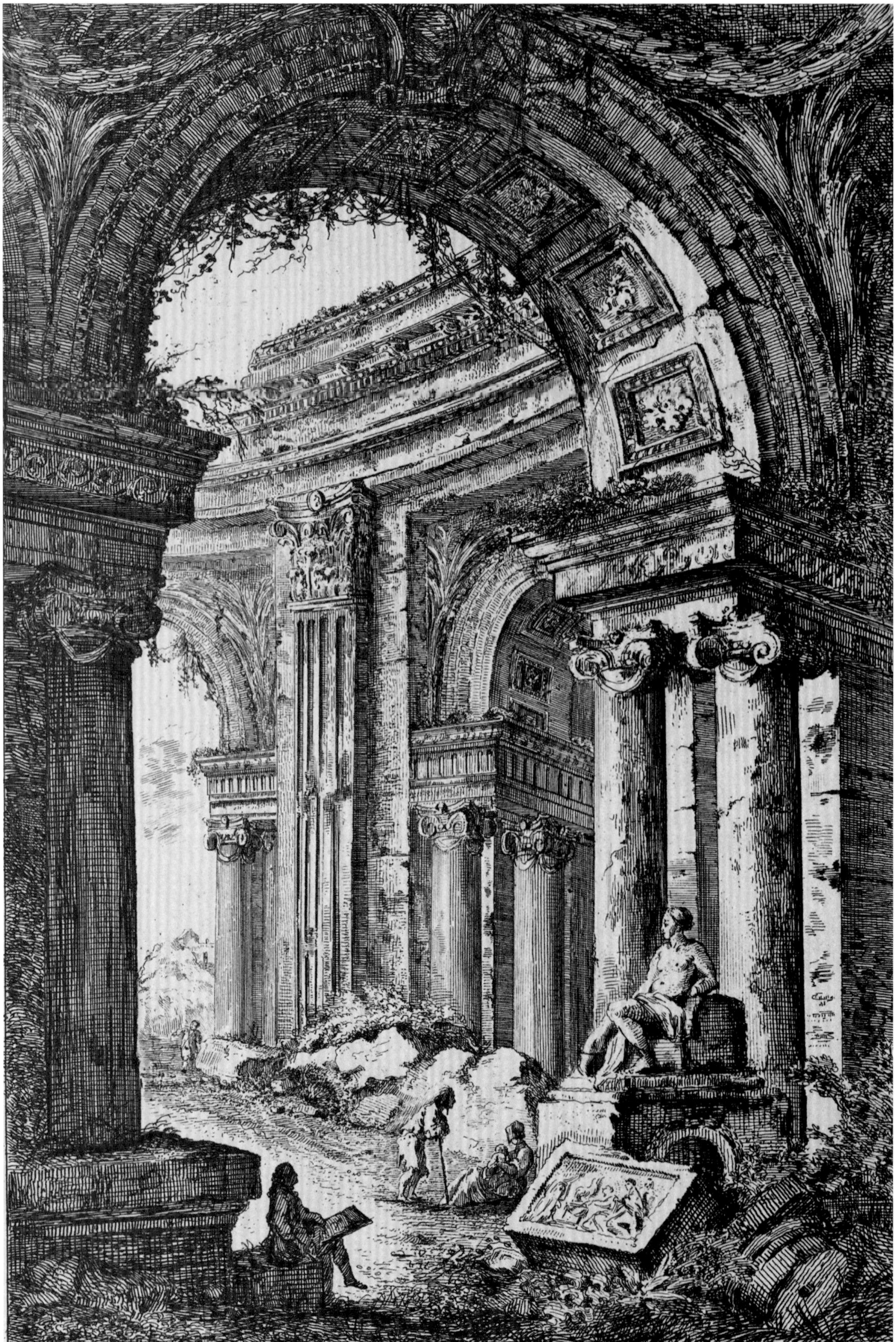

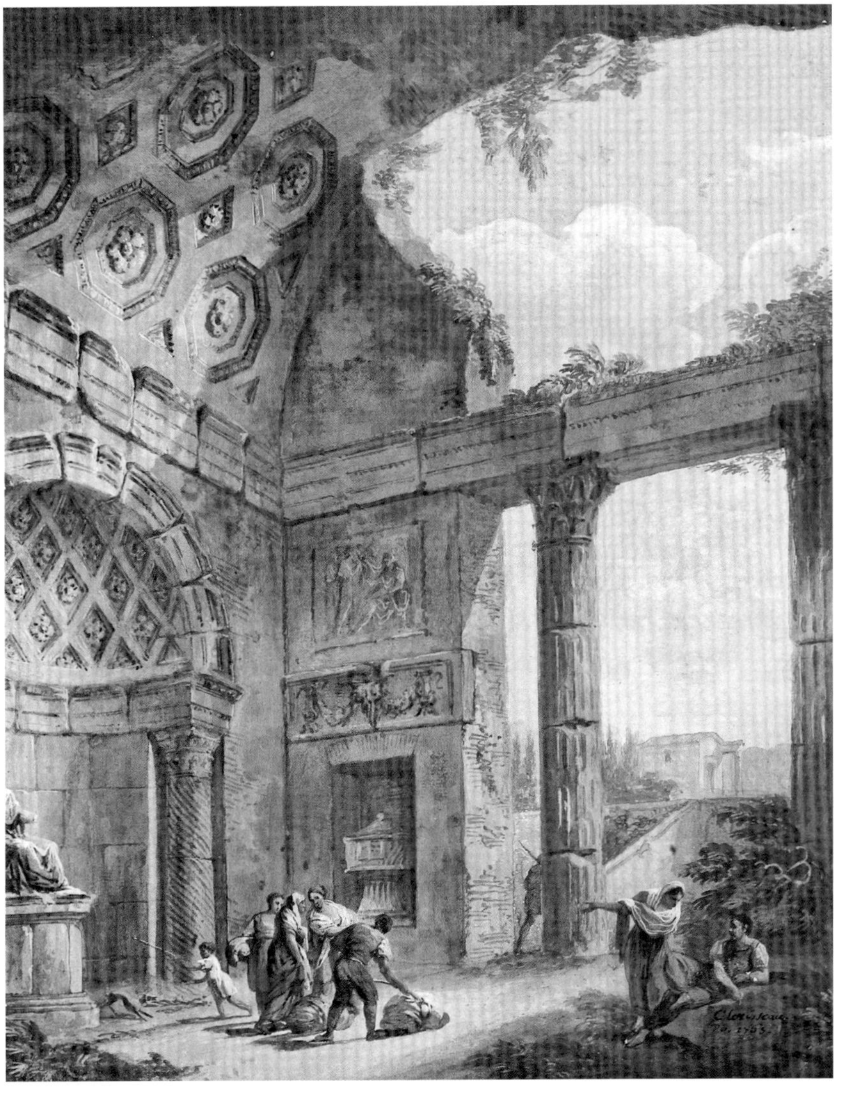

Fig. 12. Gabriel Pierre Martin Dumont (French, 1720–91)
Artist Sketching a Statue in a Ruin
From Gabriel Pierre Martin Dumont, *Suite de ruines d'architecture,* in idem, *Recueil de plusieurs parties d'architecture de différents maîtres tant d'Italie que de France* (Paris, 1765)

Fig. 13. Charles-Louis Clérisseau (French, 1722–1820)
Figures in a Vaulted Portico, 1763, gouache, 47 × 36.5 cm (18½ × 14⅜ in.)
Present location unknown

adorned with antique fragments that have escaped the ravages of time." A frustrated architect, Clérisseau became—like Robert—a sought-after decorator, designing fashionable interiors for such wealthy Parisian patrons as the notary Alexandre-Balthazar-Laurent Grimod de La Reynière.[68]

Catalysts of artistic innovation inasmuch as they deviated from Classicism's expectations, antiquity's remains lived on as commodified exemplars of nonconformity. Not only do the *fabriques* designed for *jardins à la mode* make this clear. The later decades of the eighteenth century marked the intersection of *anticomanie* and advances in print technology.[69] In 1772, the printmaker Jean-François Janinet invented a technique for duplicating the effects of watercolor and wash drawings, thus contributing to the escalating market for color prints. Three years later, he inaugurated a series of wash manner prints featuring views of Roman villas and ruins after Clérisseau, Panini, and Robert (fig. 14).[70] The commercial possibilities of partnering with printmakers skilled in the art of color prints attracted such second-tier architectural landscape painters as Pierre-Antoine Demachy, who collaborated with the printmaker Charles-Melchior Descourtis on a series of views, including *Views of the Environs of*

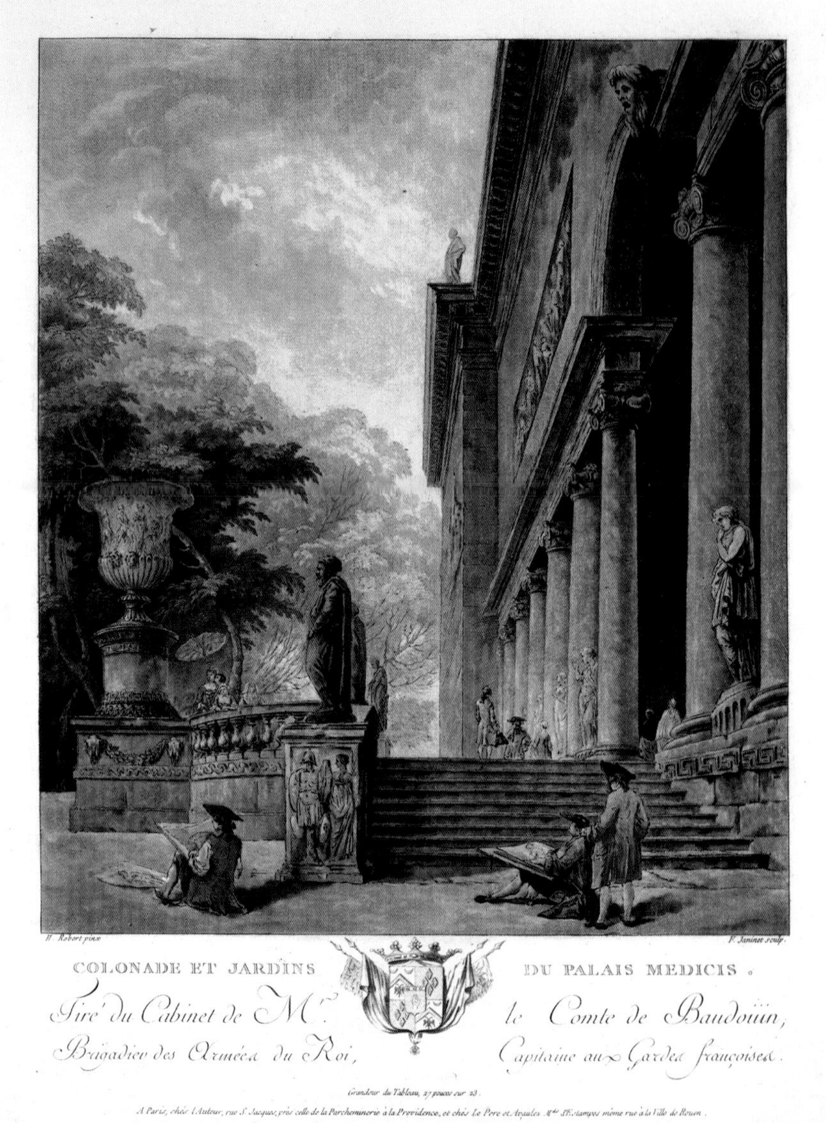

Fig. 14. Jean-François Janinet (French, 1752–1814), after Hubert Robert (French, 1733–1808)
Colonade et jardins du Palais Medicis (Colonnade and gardens of the Medici Palace), ca. 1776, etching and wash manner printed in colors, 29.1 × 24.4 cm ($11\frac{7}{16} \times 9\frac{5}{8}$ in.)
Washington, D.C., National Gallery of Art

Fig. 15. Jean-François Janinet (French, 1752–1814), after Jean-Henri-Alexandre Pernet (French, ca. 1763–after 1789)
XVI° vue de la Grece (Sixteenth view of Greece), ca. 1800, etching and wash manner printed in colors, 21.2 × 14.1 cm ($8\frac{3}{8} \times 5\frac{1}{2}$ in.)
Paris, Bibliothèque nationale de France

Rome (1784), despite the fact that Demachy had never traveled to Italy.[71] His student Jean-Henri-Alexandre Pernet was another painter of ruins who teamed up with accomplished printmakers. Janinet published color prints after Pernet's *Roman Ruins,* along with several compositions entitled *View of Greece.* Like Demachy, Pernet never made the trip to Italy, let alone Greece, and his unapologetically fanciful capricci synthesized elements from Piranesi's etchings and the Roman works of Fragonard and Robert. As seen in his *XVI° vue de la Grece,* such views capitalized on the taste for mysterious forms and unexpected perspectives (fig. 15). The print presents a wild scenography of exploding trees and massive temples dripping with foliage. The colonnade's oblique recession is a device borrowed from Piranesi. A fantastical funerary monument seizes the attention of passersby, who gesticulate in wonder. No doubt the decorative force of the print compensated for the derivative character of such effects.[72]

The tradition of responding to ruins through prints featuring imaginary views dates to the Renaissance, when northern European artists visiting Rome struggled to

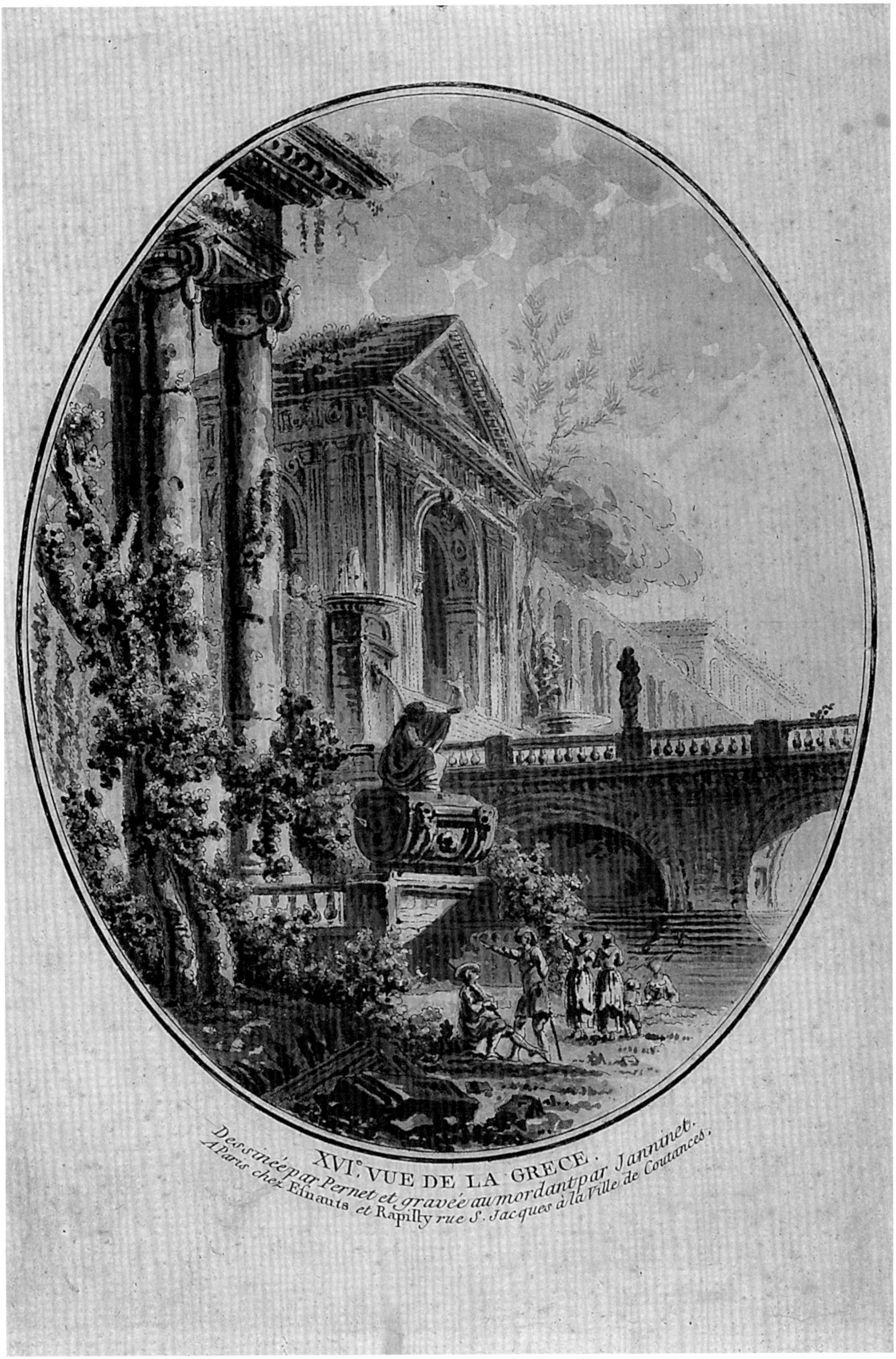
XVI.e VUE DE LA GRECE.
Dessinée par Pernet et gravée au mordant par Janninet.
A Paris chez Esnauts et Rapilly rue S. Jacques à la Ville de Coutances.

come to terms with the city's chaotic remains. As Margaret McGowan has suggested, the substitution of fictive landscapes for the rubble-strewn spaces of Rome constituted one attempt among many to mediate the city's disorienting reality. From engravings after Leonard Thiry's fanciful ruins to even the unruly hybridity of Jacques Androuet du Cerceau's ornament etchings, the subjugation of Rome's heterogeneous terrain to the modern printing press revealed an impulse (albeit conflicted) to catalog and control.[73] In the latter half of the eighteenth century, by contrast, imaginary views of Classical landscapes asserted the notion that the freewheeling exercise of the artist's imagination, far from compromising the integrity of the past, offered the ultimate tribute to the greatness of the ancients. That they did so marked the impact of Piranesi. Having arrived in Rome in 1740, at a moment when opportunities for building commissions were scarce, the Venetian etcher immersed himself in a world of his own making. He argued—in the very name of antiquity—that imaginative conjecture surpassed accurate representation: "An artist, who would do himself honour... must not content himself with copying faithfully the ancients, but studying their works he ought to shew himself of an inventive, and, I had almost said, of a creating Genius." For Piranesi, the "creative adaptation" of past models accorded more with the spirit of the ancients than the "slavish imitation" of their works.[74] As he states in his *Prima parte di architetture e prospettive* (1743), "These speaking ruins have filled my spirit with images that accurate drawings... could never have succeeded in conveying." Piranesi's polemical writings, along with his own spectacular architectural fantasies, gave the imprimatur of "honour" to French artists whose capricci reiterated the authenticity of the fictive (or the inauthenticity of the "accurate") with varying degrees of earnestness.[75]

Piranesi wielded his conviction in caprice so as to denounce the limitations of modern imaginations. The heroic grandeur and ornamental exuberance on view in his *Prima parte*—exemplified, for instance, in his *Imperial Mausoleum* (fig. 16)—implicitly condemned the sterility of Rome's current building culture, with its indifference to the lessons of the ancients and discouragement of experimentation. Absolute complexity on a massive scale reflected Piranesi's reaction—in publications such as *Le antichità romane* (1756) and *Della magnificenza ed architettura de' romani* (1761)—against the rise of a Greco ideal of naturalism and simplicity. As in his frontispiece to the second volume of *Le antichità romane* (fig. 17), the etcher celebrated the extravagance of Rome's material culture through his own fearlessly original compositions. Piranesi's *Campo Marzio dell'antica Roma* (1762)—a work that fantastically reconstructed the Campo Marzio under the late empire—revealed his contempt for Johann Joachim Winckelmann's argument that Roman art, with its love of license, represented a debasement of the purity and perfection of the Greeks (see fig. 46). Identifying himself with his subject, Piranesi defended his recourse to fantasy: "I am rather afraid that parts of the Campus that I describe should seem figments of my imagination and not based on any evidence.... But before anyone accuses me of falsehood, he should, I beg, examine the ancient [marble] plan of the city... and he will find that the ancients disobeyed the strict rules of architecture just as much as the moderns."[76]

For Piranesi, the capriccio's remoteness from the order of necessity, its lack of transparency to "evidence" and "rules," made it the marker of a radical honesty.

Fig. 16. Giovanni Battista Piranesi (Italian, 1720–78)
Imperial Mausoleum
From Giovanni Battista Piranesi, *Prima parte di architetture e prospettive*, pl. 3, from the third edition of *Opere varie di architettura prospettive grotteschi antichità sul gusto degli antichi romani* (Rome, 1750)

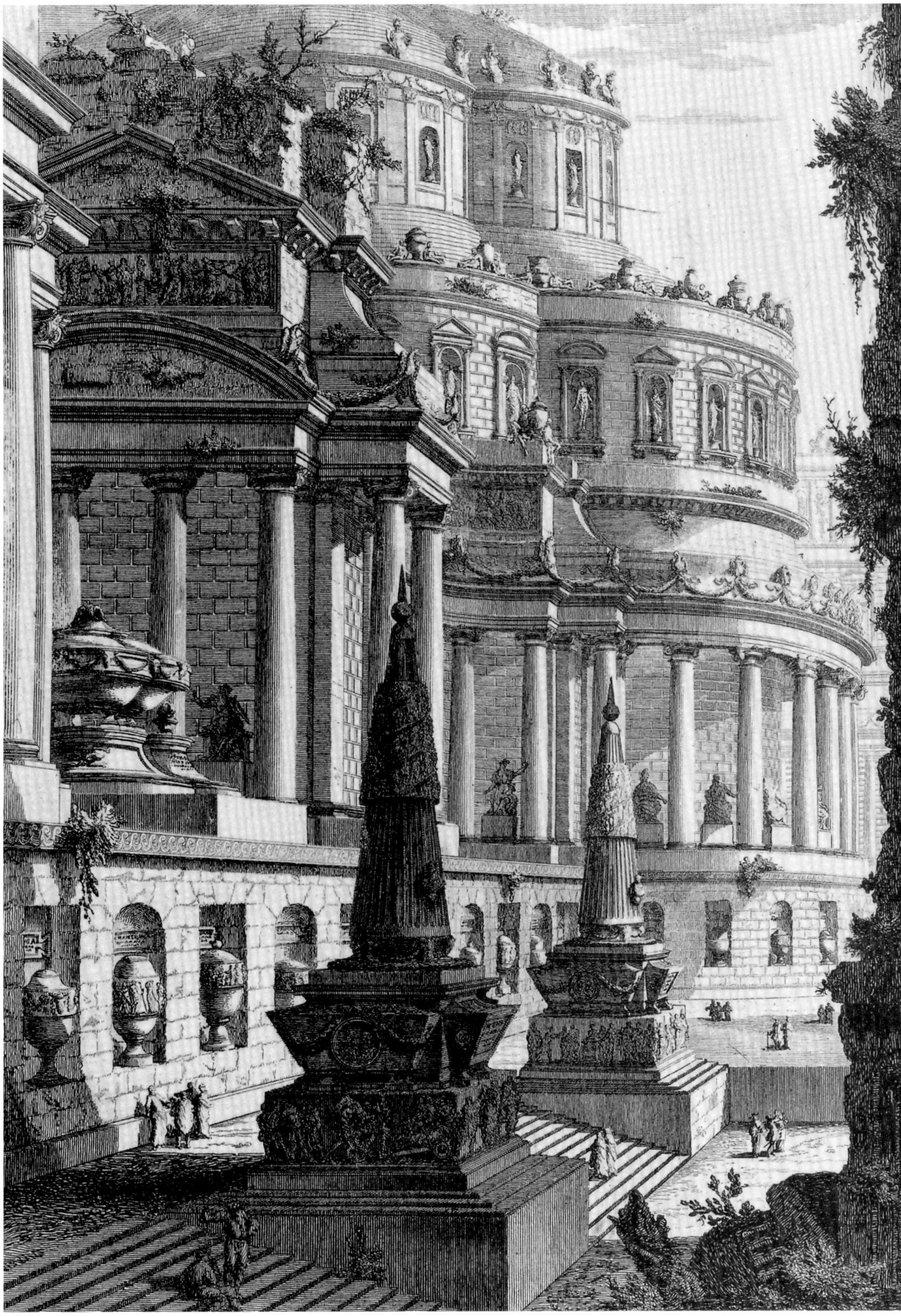

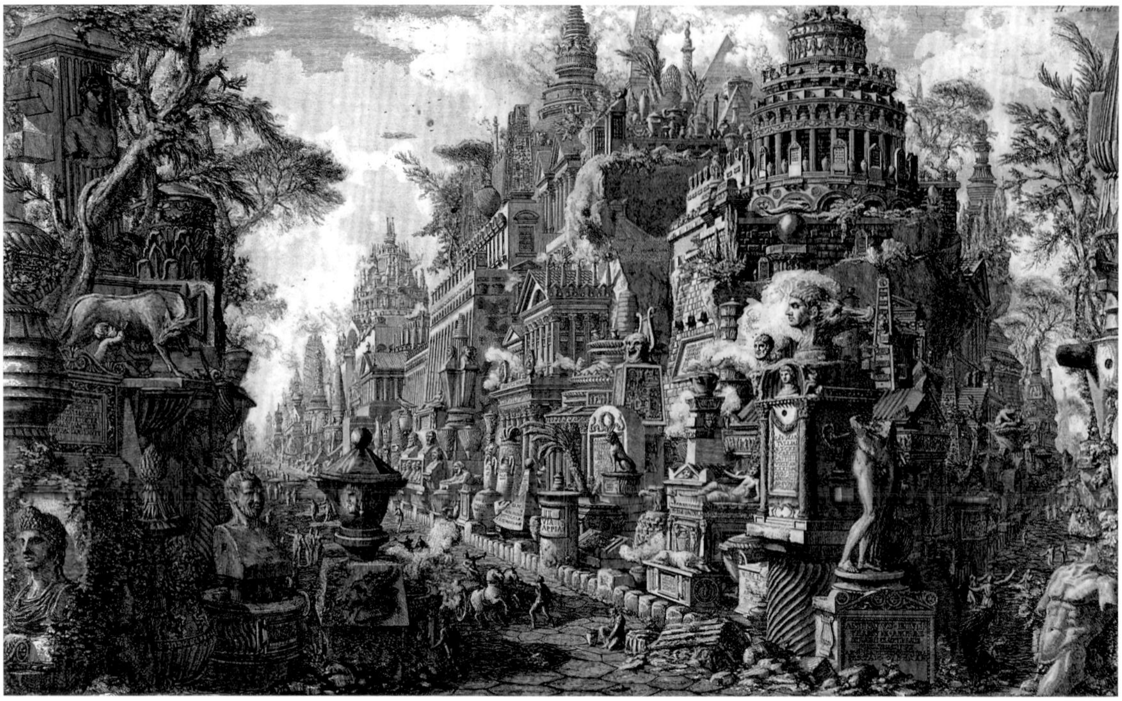

Fig. 17. Giovanni Battista Piranesi (Italian, 1720–78)
Imaginary Tombs on the Via Appia
From Giovanni Battista Piranesi, *Le antichità romane,* vol. 2 (Rome, 1784), frontispiece

Such an argument aimed to discredit the French Enlightenment belief that architecture had its basis in what Marc-Antoine Laugier described as "fixed and unchangeable laws"—in "principles . . . founded on simple nature." As Laugier claims in his *Essai sur l'architecture* (1753), all "the splendors of architecture ever conceived" originated in man's first dwelling, the primitive hut ("The pieces of wood set upright have given us the idea of the column"). Only the parts "essential to the composition of an architectural Order . . . are the cause of beauty," he maintains, while those that have been "added by caprice cause every fault."[77] In his *Parere su l'architettura* (Opinions on architecture), Piranesi debunks the notion that architecture is anything other than sheer unadulterated artifice: "Austerity, reason, and imitation of huts are all incompatible with architecture . . . [which] . . . consists of ornaments that are all extraneous."[78]

According to Manfredo Tafuri, Piranesi's abolition of the difference between structure and ornament, between the essential and the extraneous, brought architecture to the brink not of regeneration but of crisis. The proof, for Tafuri, of Piranesi's avant-garde will to negate the coherence of architecture (and to prophesize a "society . . . liberated from . . . values") exists in the violently fragmentary and disarticulated spaces featured in *Carceri d'invenzione* (Prisons of the imagination).[79] Their imagery of architectural contortion externalizing the torments of enchained prisoners, the *Carceri* demonstrate that the most fantastical of Piranesi's capricci are also the most chilling (see figs. 47, 57, 59). The etcher chose the theme of the prison as a vehicle for the capacities of the unfettered imagination—an irony that sets in relief the dark side of play. To advocate extremes of imaginative rule-breaking was to invoke a reign of inconstancy and idiosyncrasy—the law of lawlessness.

Though the intensity of Piranesi's etchings was hardly matched in the capricci produced by his contemporaries at the Académie, the *pensionnaires* of the

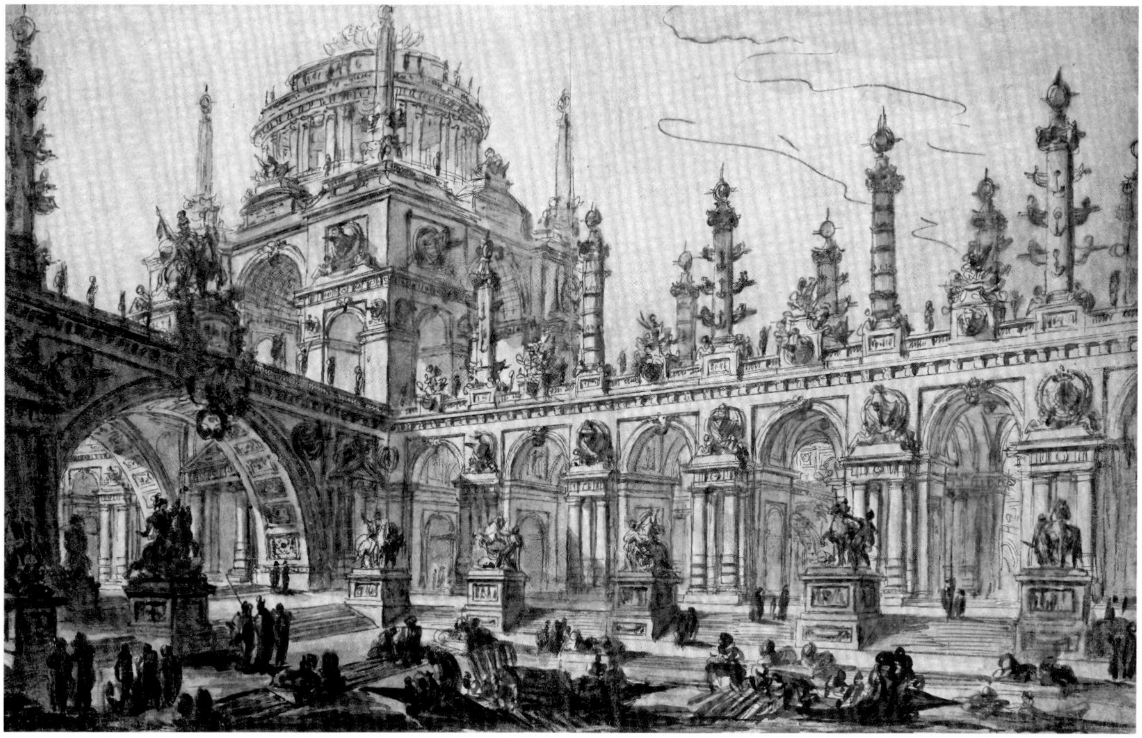

Fig. 18. Charles Michel-Ange Challe (French, 1718–78)
Architectural Fantasy, n.d., pen, brown ink, gray and black wash, 42.9 × 66.6 cm (16⅞ × 26¼ in.)
New York, Metropolitan Museum of Art

1740s embraced the vanguard logic of the Venetian's hostility to rules, his resistance to a codified language of architecture. As if in flight from all facets of constrictive tradition, the Piranésiens occupied the margins and lowest precincts of cultural production—graphic work and ephemeral architecture—and consequently created little that was meant to last. Challe, who spent the final years of his life attempting to translate Piranesi's writings, fell deeply under the spell of the etcher's architectural fantasies. Among Challe's contributions to the genre is a drawing featuring an extravagantly ornate port, festooned with rostral columns (fig. 18).[80] Challe's virtuoso use of the brush to evoke the furious movement of boats and people manifests the compulsion of painterly architecture to dissolve fixity. Like festival architecture, "asserting the superiority of the ephemeral over the permanent," Challe's fantasies repel the limits of the possible, thus ensuring that meaning will never ossify, because it will never cohere.[81]

The *pensionnaire* who was most receptive, however, to the dystopian underside of the capriccio—to the prospect of inhabiting an utterly artificial universe—was the architect-etcher Jean-Laurent Legeay. His etchings and drawings of the 1750s and 1760s evoke the Mannerist aesthetic of Piranesi's *grotteschi*—fantasies that hark back to the savagery of Salvatore Rosa and the inscrutability of Giovanni Battista Tiepolo's *Scherzi di fantasia* (Playful fantasies) series. An etching from Legeay's series of 1768, *Tombs,* typifies the doom-laden quality of his capricci (fig. 19). Jagged branches frame a monumental tomb decorated with statues of captive women. Legeay tended to situate the viewer in the vaguely subterranean depths of a primitive landscape and to overlay his surfaces with a dense web of hatching, thus creating a sense of both claustrophobia and vertigo. A similar effect of entrapment characterizes an architectural fantasy that Legeay executed in pen, ink, and watercolor, likely in the late 1750s (fig. 20).[82]

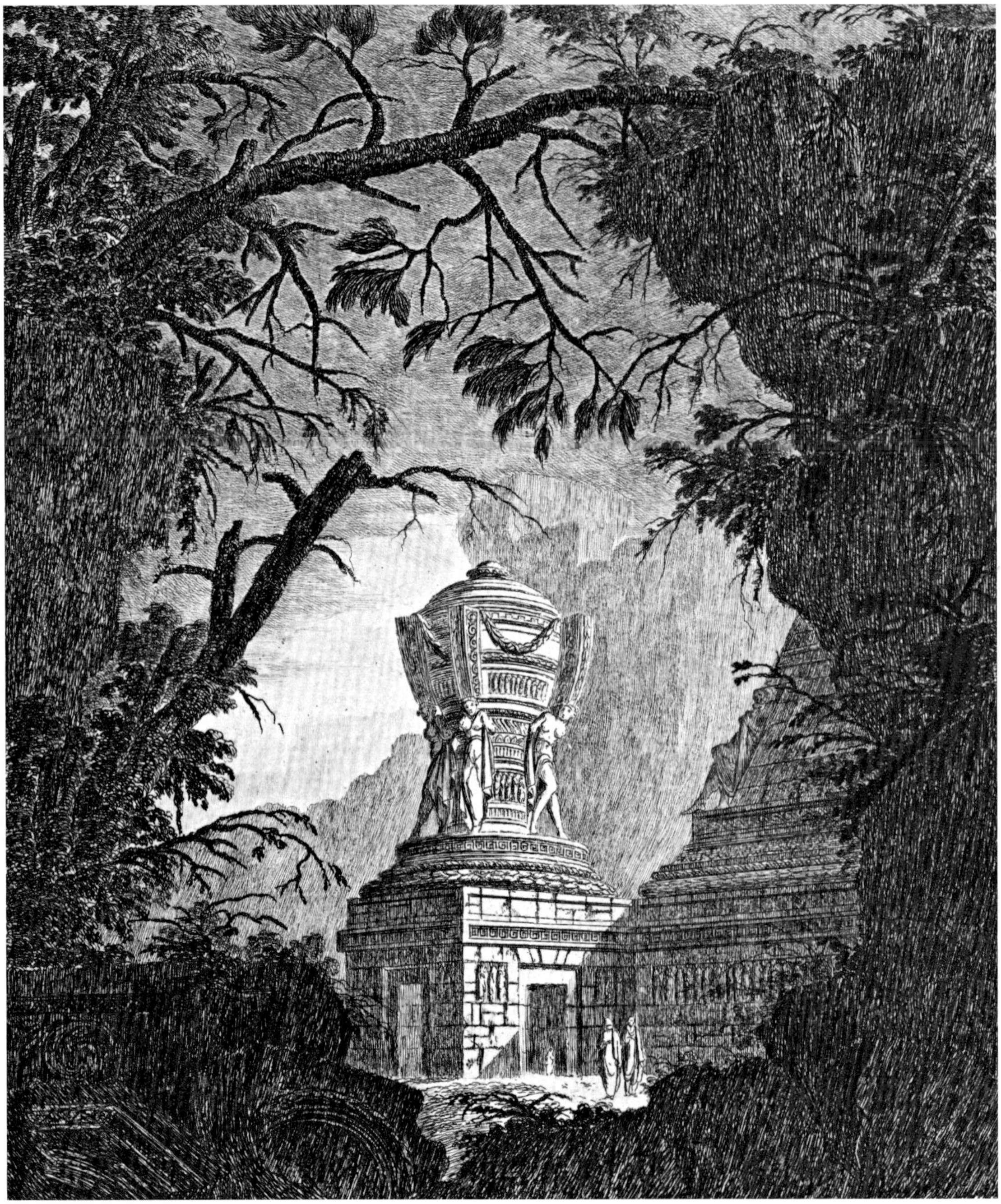

Fig. 19. Jean-Laurent Legeay (French, 1710–86)
Monumental Tomb with Tree Branches
From Jean-Laurent Legeay, *Collection de divers sujets de vases, tombeaux, ruines et fontaines, utile aux artistes* (Paris, 1770)

Mysterious shadows fall across a landscape made airless by the congested assembly of so many monuments—including the central funerary structure with its grimacing sphinxes; an abundance of columns, arches, and antiquities; and a variation on the tomb of Nero at upper left. The obscured ground-plane appears to buckle under the weight of cultural detritus. The edifice at left, with its dangling lantern, hanging chains, and barred windows, recalls the prison imagery that circulated through the repertoire of early eighteenth-century scenographers.[83] In keeping with the logic that Piranesi elaborated in his *Carceri* of 1761, Legeay's capricci put forth a sense of constriction founded in imaginative excess.

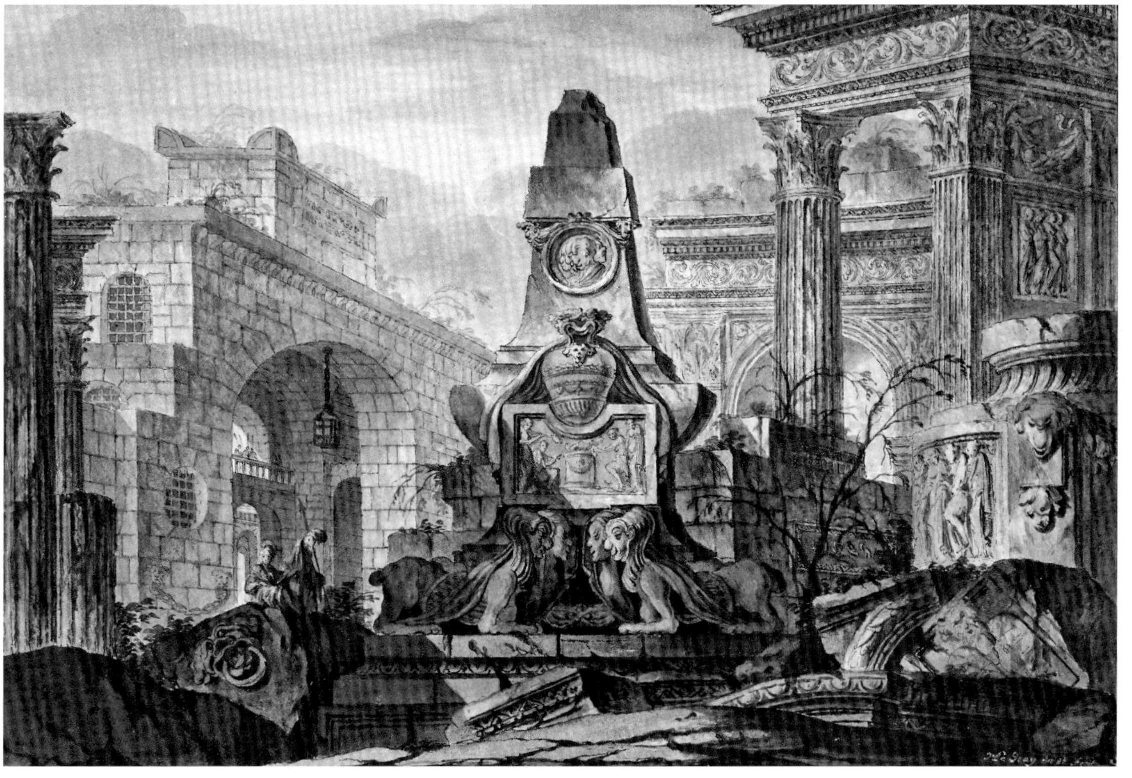

Fig. 20. Jean-Laurent Legeay (French, 1710–86)
Architectural Fantasy, n.d., pen, ink, and watercolor on paper, 19 × 27.4 cm (7½ × 10¾ in.) Cambridge, Fitzwilliam Museum

Legeay's macabre and stifling fantasies underline the resonance of Piranesi's capricci for a dissatisfied generation of French artists—as well as the profound irony that, for these *pensionnaires,* rigorous inventiveness spelled the foreclosing of possibility. Piranesi's command to venerate the irrationally outlandish, though heeded by his French followers, did not result in more heroic attempts at world-making. It did, however, coincide with the rapid expansion of the art and antiquities trade, with *anticomanie's* colonization of far-flung exotica, and with the grand tour's promotion of a taste for "the marvelous," "the strange," "the singular," and "the astonishing."[84] By asserting a hierarchy in which the inassimilable trumped the typical, Piranesi effectively issued a clarion call to a marketplace that thrived on novelty.[85] It is difficult, in this light, not to equate the experimental prowess showcased in Piranesi's *Imaginary Tombs on the Via Appia* with a kind of pathology (see fig. 17). Spectacular innovation is the prerequisite for infinite fragmentation. The sheer variety of antiquities, shattering the page like so many shards, makes of the image a ruin. The etching stands as a concentrated meditation on the fate of antiquity in an age of mechanical reproduction—when the dissemination of prints had the effect of commodifying precisely the ruins that Piranesi meant to auraticize.[86]

Though vindicating eclecticism, the image lays bare the complexity of navigating an order in which structure has been superseded by ornament, "truth" by "falsehood," and original causes by random effects. The page's *horror vacui* leaves the viewer with no choice but to scan its monuments, trophies, statues, tombs, altars, and hieroglyphs in piecemeal fashion, never to resolve its dense network of fragments into an integrated whole. Piranesi's staging ground for the artist's liberated imagination plunges the viewer into a mode of apprehension that is necessarily partial, halting, and, in the end, violently curtailed. In effect, the work issues a straightforward statement about the brutality of the precarious order it conjures.

It seems appropriate that one of the most famous testaments to Piranesi's legacy appears in Thomas De Quincey's description of the opium-induced hallucinations recounted to him by his friend Samuel Taylor Coleridge. The poet's visions unfold within a terrifyingly unresolved architecture straight out of Piranesi's prisons, and wandering the endless succession of stairways is the unfortunate etcher himself, forever "groping his way upward."[87] De Quincey's *Confessions of an English Opium-Eater* (1821) reflects Piranesi's influence not merely on the production of cultural forms but—just as important—on the shaping of a mentality. Consistent with De Quincey's remembrance, Piranesi's impact—not unlike opium—proved potentially mind altering. Thus, for the architect John Soane, the danger of Piranesi's example lay not simply in his having succumbed to the "bewitching siren" of "novelty" and the "charms" of "variety." Given Piranesi's acute sensitivity to the remains of Classicism, Soane writes, his aesthetic choices could be interpreted only as products of a confused mind:

> That men unacquainted with the remains of ancient buildings should indulge in licentious and whimsical combinations is not matter of surprise, but that a man who had passed all his life in the bosom of classic art, and in the contemplation of the majestic ruins of ancient Rome... a man who had given innumerable examples how truly he felt the value of the noble simplicity of those buildings, that such a man, with such examples before his eyes, should have mistaken confusion for intricacy, and undefined lines and forms for classical variety, is scarcely to be believed; yet such was Piranesi.[88]

Soane feared, and the Romantics intuited, that Piranesi's defiance of Classicism augured a dangerous kind of self-oblivion. Such worry may be taken as evidence of a perception that the *retour à l'antique,* far from shoring up Classicism's principles, was unleashing a force field for fictions. Indeed, Piranesi's precedent legislated the complicity of the aesthetic of ruins in a reversal of values—one that subjugated a diachronic order of immanent truths to a synchronic one of chaotic superfluity.

This aspect of the ruin aesthetic—its abjuring of significant content—returns us to Robert's *Game of Dice amidst Roman Ruins* (see fig. 1). In associating ruins with game playing, Robert accentuated what structuralists have described as the posteriority of the act of play. For the linguist Émile Benveniste (as for Claude Lévi-Strauss), noting the origins of games of chance in ancient divinatory practices, play constitutes structure as opposed to sense: "In play only the ritual survives and all that is preserved is the *form* of the [mysterious rite], in which each element is re-enacted time and again. But what has been forgotten or abolished is the myth, the meaningfully worded fabulation that endows the acts with their sense and their purpose."[89] Similarly, Roger Caillois characterizes game playing as hostile to its original source: "Without doubt," he writes, "secrecy, mystery, and even travesty can be transformed into play activity, but it must be immediately pointed out that this transformation is necessarily to the detriment of the secret and mysterious, which play exposes, publishes, and somehow *expends.*"[90]

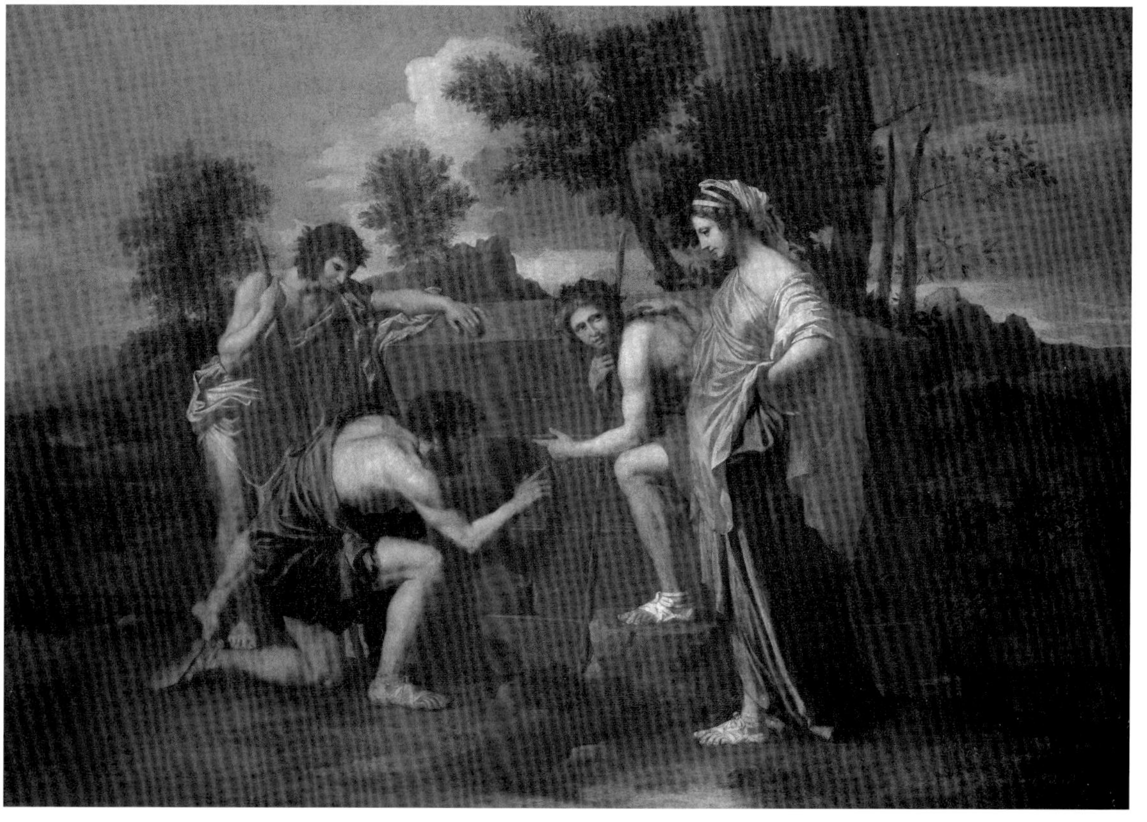

Fig. 21. Nicolas Poussin (French, 1594–1665)
Arcadian Shepherds,
ca. 1638–40, oil on canvas,
85 × 121 cm (33½ × 47⅝ in.)
Paris, Musée du Louvre

Robert's *Game of Dice* not only thematizes but also appears to carry out this transformative work of play. A candidate for the source that the *Game of Dice* demystifies, or "*expends,*" presents itself in Poussin's *Arcadian Shepherds,* the primal scene of deixis, so to speak, and a painting that—hidden away at Versailles but widely, if inaccurately, reproduced—was as famous in Robert's day as it was elusive (fig. 21).[91] The central dice-thrower in Robert's watercolor—replete with blue drapery, bended knee, and pointed finger—assumes the pose of Arcadia's bearded shepherd, transforming the game of chance into a shambolic reinterpretation of Poussin's allegory of transience. Robert has substituted for Arcadia's disquieting tomb the improvised gaming table, and for the shepherds' solemn attempt to decipher meaning the gamblers' pregnant pause over the dice. Disguising the components of Poussin's landscape and draining them of their original function, the watercolor stages the reconfiguration of a mysterious object from the past into a site of chance and potentiality. The painting's incarnation of total absorption—the monument modeling the integrity of the picture plane, the heroically proportioned figures exemplifying concentration—gives way to Robert's aesthetic of precariousness. Death-haunted Arcadia and the injunction to remember are thus transmuted into the gambler's paradise and the bliss of self-forgetting. It is as a whimsical expression of latecoming, then, that we may interpret the watercolor, with its game of chance founded on the ruins of a world whose surfaces have long since traded in the traces of meaningful indexicality for picturesque accident. "You have the technique, but you lack the ideal," chides Diderot in his *Salon de 1767.*[92] The comment aptly summarizes Robert's distance from Arcadia.

Ex Parvo, Multum

We have been tracking the emergence of a new order, so as to arrive at the following coincidence: that between the ruin aesthetic's breach of Classicism and what Pocock describes as the shift from continuity to contingency. "Under continuity," writes Pocock,

> we may see society describing itself as perpetuating its usages and practices, transmitting its different forms of authority and, in these and other ways, maintaining its legitimacy.... Under the heading of contingency, however, we become aware of other and less institutionalized phenomena. We are in the domain of fortune, as it used to be called: of the unpredictable contingencies and emergencies which challenge the human capacity to apprehend and to act, and which may appear either exterior or interior to the institutional structure of society.... When time is the dimension of continuity, the institutional structure is seen as successfully creating its own time—though if it is fully successful in doing so, this will by no means be the same as creating its own future, but rather ensuring that no future ever comes into existence. When time is the dimension of contingency, the structure is seen as striving to maintain itself in a time not created by it, but rather given to it by some agency, purposive or purposeless, not yet defined.[93]

Belief in "a secular and historical future" had its corollary in what I have described above as a post-Arcadian conception of ruins. For obvious parallels may be drawn between the rise of an aesthetic valorization of unforeseeable outcomes over the transmission of authority, and the demise of the social hierarchy's "institutional structure" in the wake of increased access to wealth. Thus the ruin aesthetic's deviation from Classicism could be appreciated in distinctly political terms, as Diderot demonstrates in his review of Robert's paintings at the Salon of 1767:

> Well, well, the powerful men of the earth who believed they built for the ages, who erected such superb residences for themselves, and who in their folly anticipated an uninterrupted series of descendants, heirs to their names, their titles, and their opulent way of life, nothing remains of their work, of their enormous expenditure, of their grand visions but debris serving to shelter some of the most indigent and unfortunate members of the human race, much more useful as ruins than ever they were in their initial splendor.[94]

Diderot's use of decaying opulence as an image epitomizing the death of continuity need not be interpreted strictly as verification of the ruin's allegorical import. What I would like to suggest in the remainder of this chapter, rather, is that there existed an isomorphic link between a consciousness of contingency and the cult of ruins.

In an age hypnotized by natural disaster, ruins understandably stirred apocalyptic visions—exemplified, as we shall see in the next chapter, by Mercier's prophecies of earthquakes and conflagrations. However, catastrophism was also consonant with a widespread infatuation with risk. High-stakes gambling on life and fire insurance took off in the last years of the ancien régime. Financiers floated insurance companies as investment trusts on the Bourse de Paris, capitalizing on the lure of novelty and on a mass willingness to "exchang[e] present certainty for future uncertainty."[95] The gambling mania benefited not only the stock exchange but also the interests of the French state: in 1776, Louis XVI established the Loterie Royale de France to balm the budgetary wounds of the Seven Years' War and thereafter collected millions of livres in annual revenue with which to finance the national debt.[96]

Official sponsor of a culture of risk, the state peddled its debts through such popular ventures as annuities, or life-contingent incomes that expired upon the death of the person named in the contract. These functioned, in effect, as opportunities to bet on the lives of family members and strangers alike and, though considered morally suspect, were avidly purchased by the public. Robert himself made a small fortune investing in life-contingent contracts. The bank managed by Robert's client, Jean Girardot de Marigny, helped broker one of the most notorious outbreaks of the life-betting frenzy, one that culminated in international bereavement with the premature passing of one Pernette-Elisabeth Martin, on whose eight-year-old head rested two million livres in investments. Martin had been one of thirty Genevan female youths presented to the public as a sure bet, a subject whose longevity, favored by the laws of probability, would furnish investors with an abiding source of annual revenue from the French government.[97]

Robert's banking- and financier-class clients occupied the epicenter of risk. Most notable among the financial wizards who were enlisted by the state to reverse the tides of debt was Laborde. Born in Béarn, as he recounts in his memoirs, "in the most narrow mediocrity," Laborde amassed a vast fortune in maritime trade that he parlayed into a career in international banking.[98] In addition to being possibly the wealthiest individual in France by the time he was thirty, Laborde brandished impeccable credentials as a money manager along with unassailable creditworthiness in the eyes of European lenders. In 1758, the government enlisted him to secure a loan from Spain, and a year later he assumed the position of court banker. Thereafter, Laborde managed the vertiginous sums—hundreds of millions of livres between 1759 and 1765—that he personally borrowed from Cologne, Frankfurt, Hamburg, Brussels, and elsewhere and advanced to the French court. Laborde served the state just after the financial disaster of the Seven Years' War, at a time when the king's credit had evaporated. Beyond placing his own credit on the line and risking catastrophic ruin, Laborde embodied the credit of the nation, rendering his gambles inextricable from the fortunes of France.[99] In 1767, Laborde had himself replaced by the Caisse d'escompte (Discount bank), a private institution responsible for lending money to the Crown.

Behind Laborde's ascent of the echelons of power—he was also a member of the *Ferme générale,* the body of financiers who collected the nation's taxes in return for a share of the surplus over the sum guaranteed to the king—lay the court's policy of managing its debt by dissolving the difference between public finance and private capital. More broadly, his career reflected the destabilizing impact of money on the ancien régime's social hierarchy.[100] Though Laborde took pride in having overcome his humble origins against tremendous odds, the arrival at the French court of a low-born outsider with no family or institutional connections in Paris had a bombshell effect. In fact, it was Laborde's foreignness to the world of court intrigue that earned him Choiseul's approbation. The sheer improbability of Laborde's rise was a sign of what Guy Chaussinand-Nogaret describes as the triumph of a future-directed, capitalist outlook over the old, tradition-bound one of the high aristocracy. A noble, writes Chaussinand-Nogaret, "was defined by his lineage. His merit was inseparable from that of his ancestry, and the worth of his forebears underlay his own virtue. In one extreme sense he had no individual existence, no separate self. He was merely a link in an ancestral chain."[101] A "new kind of capitalist," Laborde recognized that his inauspicious beginnings enhanced his trustworthiness, effectively keeping him awash in credit. Ennobled at the age of thirty-one, he inscribed his crest with the phrase *Ex parvo, multum* (From little comes much).[102]

The expression may be taken as a canny reference not only to Laborde's unlikely trajectory but also to the mechanisms of credit that determined it. François Véron Duverger de Forbonnais, writing in the *Encyclopédie,* noted that one's credit was worth more to the extent that it rested on an "impression" of wealth. Whereas actual assets necessarily imposed a limit on one's credit, a widely shared sense of creditworthiness—however unfounded—could enable credit's expansion ad infinitum.[103] It is further instructive that the spirit of *Ex parvo, multum,* with its logic of destinies superseding origins, exerted a powerful aesthetic appeal. For it was in the eighteenth century that the willingness to give credence to values that were imagined rather than inherent, artificial rather than organic, emerged as an impulse that was at once economic and aesthetic. Thus Marc Shell asserts, "Credit, or belief, involves the ground of aesthetic experience."[104] Credit was only as valuable as it was imagined to be.

The allure of *Ex parvo, multum* first unveiled itself when Law instituted his Système, initiating the process whereby credit replaced money in the eighteenth century "as the principal medium of exchange."[105] The Scottish financier's plan to rejuvenate the French economy following the ruinous prodigality of King Louis XIV rested on his conviction that belief in the value of paper currency—in mere "sign money," or "symbolic money," as it was widely described—would generate national wealth.[106] To this end, Law oversaw the opening of the Banque générale (the future Banque royale) in 1716 and its union with the Compagnie des Indes four years later, thereby merging the new banknotes with the stock of the overseas trading company and driving up speculation in its shares. As Thomas Kavanagh has shown, the Law affair served as a gateway to the age of risk: it put in place "a new and deeply disruptive temporality of wealth," one that had everything to do with fear of and hope for a future radically distinct from the past.[107] The Système overturned the customary logic that credit be based in specie. It reflected the understanding that actual wealth was far less valuable than fortunes conjectured.

Law's creation of a viable credit economy sustained by public confidence necessitated a series of spectacular cognitive revisions. Investor confidence depended on reversing the (fact-based) perception that, as Jean-Baptiste Colbert stated, "the king has no credit" and that "one negotiates with him in the belief that he must declare bankruptcy."[108] Establishing the credibility of the king, not to mention the value of intrinsically worthless paper currency, thus required that the public forgo the lessons of the past in order to gamble on the potential windfall of the future. The Système failed when the public—following the machinations of Law's enemies—ceased to believe in it, and the dependence decades later on the Caisse d'escompte as a currency-issuing institution, rather than a national bank, was but one lingering symptom of the trauma that ensued. Nonetheless, by flooding the market with credit instruments,

Law—an "early and unrecognized champion of signifier over signified"—delivered stagnant sectors of the economy to unprecedented prosperity.[109] Moreover, his experiment entailed the transformation of French subjects into "members of the financial public." The effect of Law's Système, observed Voltaire, was "to instruct us" in what had previously amounted to "a hidden art, a sort of chemistry." Enfranchised into the financial life of the kingdom, the public now played a role in the shaping of fiscal policy. Yet perhaps the greatest payoff of the Système's "instruction" lay in preparing the public for the dramatic expansion of financial markets following the Law affair—particularly, the soaring growth of credit.[110]

As Emma Rothschild has shown, the story of credit in the eighteenth century is one "of intense emotion," and understanding credit's centrality to the century's momentous changes requires what she calls "an economic history of sentiments." The example to which she refers is Anne-Robert-Jacques Turgot's account of a credit crisis that shook the province of Angoulême in 1769 (an episode that coincided with Turgot's use of the term *capitaliste* in his *Réflexions sur les richesses* of that same year).[111] The "Angoulême affair"—one of "terror" and "a sort of vertigo," writes Turgot in his *Mémoire sur les prêts d'argent* (1770)—originated when a group of formerly bankrupt traders fabricated notes of credit to one another and delivered them to the town's bankers and "capitalists." Following the conspiracy's discovery, denunciations ensued: the bankers were accused of charging usurious interest rates; criminal complaints were lodged. The crisis ultimately provoked the "absolute discredit of all commerce in Angoulême" along with such broad repercussions as a national food shortage.[112]

At the center of Turgot's *Mémoire* is the problem of risk, which is identified along with time as among the essences of economic life. Turgot describes how interest and exchange rates are subject to ever-changing values, circumstances, and opinion, varying "from one man to another."[113] The crisis, pitting traders in high-risk industries against bankers vulnerable to the ruinous charge of usury, exposed the conditions of insecurity under which "capitalists" labored. The episode revealed economic life to be a passionate affair, in which ratiocination and calculation could rapidly be overtaken by sentiment and imagination. Commenting on the marriage of false witness with histrionic emotions, one resident of Angoulême wondered: "Is there anything of which men are not capable, once they allow themselves to be carried away by the torrents of their passions?"[114] The event presented a microcosm of the market's cultivation of frenetic, individual beliefs at the cost of a stable, reasoned consensus. In short, capitalism fostered delirium.

As a narrative about the dangerous circulation of fictions, the Angoulême story highlights the connections between the use of paper credit and the rise of the novel in the eighteenth century.[115] Sandra Sherman writes that, as a purely textual phenomenon, credit operates like fiction: both produce "signs without referents, ciphers with no payoff"; in short, credit "misrepresents." The rumor-induced hysteria unleashed in Angoulême mirrors credit's mode of generating "a kind of dissipative narrative, a discourse in which the originary *situs* of debt retirement ultimately evaporates." And like its literary counterpart, credit appealed to the mind's eye; Archibald Hutcheson notes of the South Seas bubble that "imagined" overtook "intrinsick" value, to which it was opposed.[116] In credit's very lack of transparency lay its perverse appeal: Daniel Defoe deplores credit's fictive character yet finds beguiling its "resistance to empirical address." Credit seized the imagination, suggesting that the expansion of credit markets incorporated the public into a shared aesthetic exercise. Credit occasioned the pleasure of "epistemological decay." In this way, it "forced the mind into a *creative* mode: imagining the future."[117] The growth of credit went hand in hand, then, with an aesthetic appreciation of what decomposition made possible. Resting as it did on the substitution of imaginative gains for empirical losses, credit, we might add, found its aesthetic analogue in the ruin.

For ruins exemplified the playful possibilities of dematerialization precisely at a time of growing reliance on disembodied media of exchange and increasing abstraction in monetary life. The pleasure of ruins involved "the nullification of the signified"—escape from the confines of predetermined experience and the consequential embrace of "a universe of uncertainty."[118] The homology between the vogue for ruins and an orientation toward risk may be gleaned from Charles-François de Lubersac de Livron's description of the Monceau garden of Louis Philippe, duc d'Orléans, also known as the duc de Chartres. The picturesque retreat's artificial *fabriques* included a crumbling castle that masqueraded as an ancient château, and Lubersac remarked that the structure had "a little too much the air of a property seized long ago and of which the proprietor submits to the creditors and the bailiffs."[119] This perception of the ruin as repossessed property—as instantiation of unforeseeable returns—likely had little to do with the duc de Chartres's sizable gambling debts, which he would soon seek to reverse by undertaking an ambitious speculative development project around his Paris property.[120] The comment is illuminating, though, insofar as it implicates the ruin within an economy of chance, and more specifically within the vicissitudes of credit.

It is in Diderot's *Salon de 1767* that the conception of the ruin as a figure of radical reversal is most forcefully expressed. The critic lavishes praise on a canvas by Robert featuring the remains of the palace of Pope Julius II converted into a stable (fig. 22). In the painting, coffered vaults are juxtaposed with stacks of hay, marble columns with wooden ladders. Diderot pronounces the work a "sublime mixture of grandeur, opulence, and dereliction" and enthusiastically lists its transgressions: "The rustic accoutrements of a cottage amid the debris of a palace! The temple of Jupiter, the residence of Augustus transformed into a stable, a hayloft! The place in which the fates of nations and kings were decided... what is it now? A country inn, a farm."[121] Significantly, the passage reprises Montesquieu's excited summation, in *Les lettres persanes,* of the upheavals witnessed half a century earlier in France, under Law's Système: "The nobility is ruined! the State is in chaos! the classes are in confusion! Everywhere you look there are nobodies getting to the top!"[122] The frisson of fortune's wild unpredictability infuses both Montesquieu's furious sketch of financial ruin and Diderot's ekphrastic response to Robert's desecrated castle. Montesquieu's economic terror is thus sublimated into Diderot's aesthetic pleasure. The recurrence reveals the extent to which the ruin itself—in the spirit of *Ex parvo, multum*—functioned as a vehicle of sublimation: it helped naturalize the depreciation of what was stable and continuous by investing contingency with supreme aesthetic value.

"People of Betique, do you want to be rich? Imagine that I am very rich, and yourselves too. Convince yourself each morning that your fortunes have doubled overnight. Then get up and, if you have creditors, pay them with what you have imagined and tell them to imagine in turn."[123] So intones the villainous progeny of

Fig. 22. Jean-François Janinet (French, 1752–1814), after Hubert Robert (French, 1733–1808)
Remains of the Palace of Pope Julius, 1775, etching and wash manner printed in colors, 29.1 × 24.5 cm (11½ × 9⅝ in.)
Rouen, Musée des beaux-arts

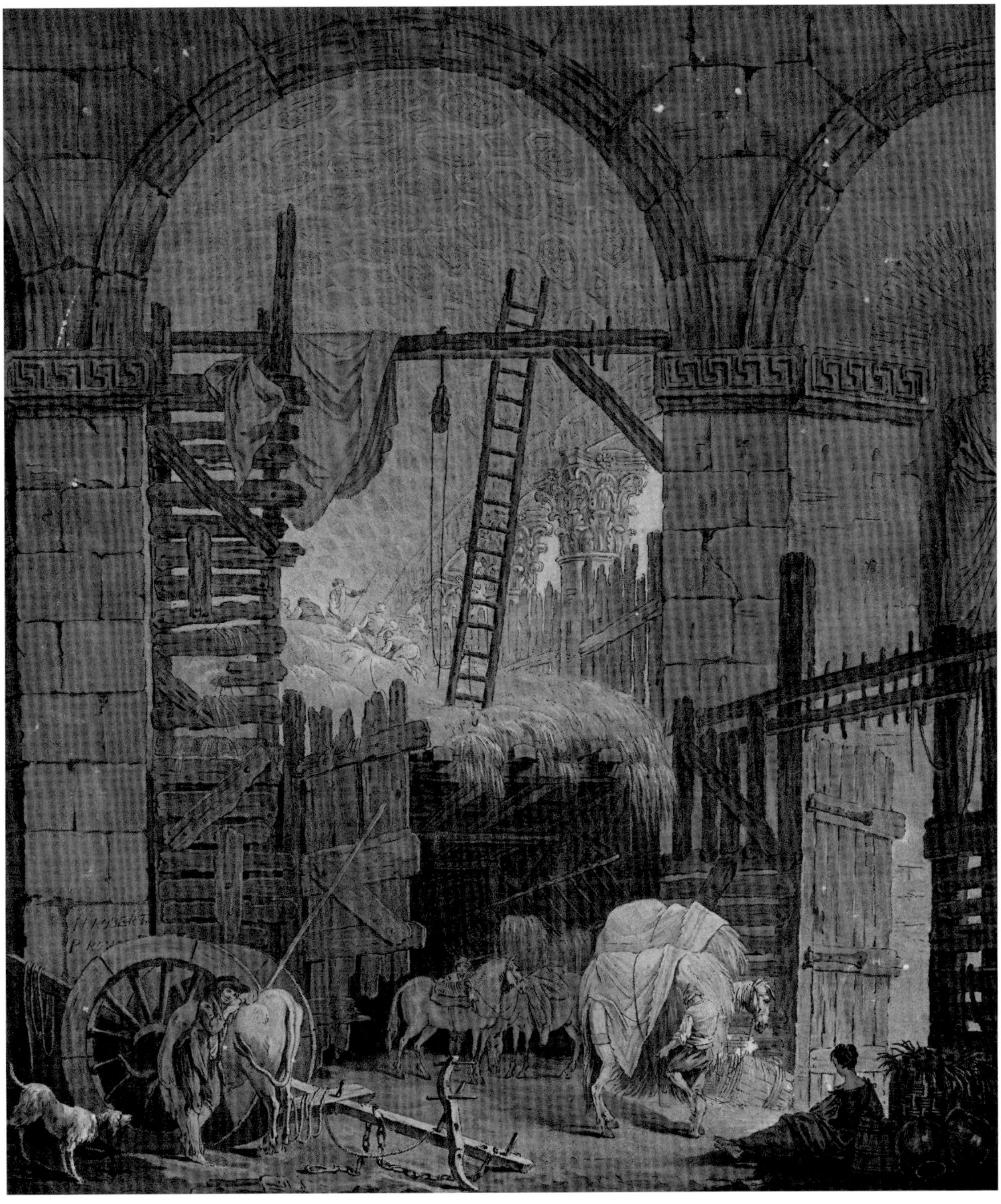

the god of wind in Montesquieu's *Lettres persanes,* in an episode satirizing the illusions perpetrated by the use of credit. Like other critics of "the papered century," Montesquieu equated financial instruments with works of fiction. Denounced by Defoe as a "chimera," and likened by Voltaire to "commerce of the imagination," credit was condemned not only for sustaining the illusion of wealth but also for veiling a reality of debt.[124] The credit economy muddled the distinction between profits and losses, Montesquieu observed: it created "confusion between a circulating paper that represents money or a circulating paper that is the sign of the profits a company has made or will make in commerce, and a paper that represents a debt."[125] Credit injected uncertainty into the present, and disrupted the linear passage of time by conflating yesterday's debts and tomorrow's earnings. Suspended, then, between plenitude and possibility, between past value and future returns, credit exhibited precisely the condition that is the hallmark of the ruin. For it was in the eighteenth century that ruins gained recognition as "configurations of ongoing decline *and* growth, decomposition *and* recomposition, erosion *and* accretion"—as unstable sites of temporal fluctuation. And just as credit was subject to external factors and existed only on the order of opinion and belief—that is, in absolute porousness to the "unpredictable contingencies and emergencies" of "fortune"—so was the ruin an object of wonder for its symbiotic relationship with nature and exigency.[126]

Montesquieu's wind god, in his final, desperate plea, declares, "Citizens . . . I see that you are the richest nation on earth; but to make your fortune complete, allow me to take away half of what you possess."[127] Ruins, like credit, extended to the imagination the future-oriented pleasures of the constitutively unfinished. As emblems of certainty in retreat, ruins offered initiation into a modern era of risk. Thus when Walter Benjamin wrote that games of chance "paved the way for empathy with exchange value," he just as readily could have described the eighteenth-century cult of ruins.[128]

NOTES

1 Denis Diderot, "Salon of 1767," in *Diderot on Art,* ed. and trans. John Goodman (New Haven: Yale Univ. Press, 1995), 2:219.

2 Diderot, "Salon of 1767," 2:212.

3 Anne-Claude-Philippe, comte de Caylus, "Discours du Comte de Caylus sur les dessins" (7 June 1732), *Revue universelle des arts* 9 (1859): 318; cited in George P. Mras, "Literary Sources of Delacroix's Conception of the Sketch and the Imagination," *Art Bulletin* 44, no. 2 (1962): 105.

4 Edmund Burke, *A Philosophical Enquiry into the Origin of Our Ideas of the Sublime and Beautiful,* ed. Adam Phillips (Oxford: Oxford Univ. Press, 1990), 70; cited in Wendelin A. Guentner, "British Aesthetic Discourse, 1780–1830: The Sketch, the *Non Finito,* and the Imagination," *Art Journal* 52, no. 2 (1993): 41.

5 Friedrich Melchior, Freiherr von Grimm, "Réflexions sur les effets qu'ont les différents arts sur notre imagination à propos de la *Dissertation sur la tragédie,* par D. Hume," *La correspondance littéraire, philosophique et critique, 1er January–15 June 1760,* ed. Sigun Dafgård (Stockholm: Uppsala, 1981): 2:3; and Diderot, "Salon of 1767," 2:219.

6 On gambling in eighteenth-century France, see esp. John Dunkley, *Gambling: A Social and Moral Problem in France, 1685–1792* (Oxford: Voltaire Foundation at the Taylor Institution, 1985); Francis Freundlich, *Le monde du jeu à Paris: 1715–1800* (Paris: A. Michel, 1995); Olivier Grussi, *La vie quotidienne des joueurs sous l'ancien régime à Paris et à la cour* (Paris: Hachette, 1985); and Thomas M. Kavanagh, *Enlightenment and the Shadows of Chance: The Novel and*

the Culture of Gambling in Eighteenth-Century France (Baltimore: Johns Hopkins Univ. Press, 1993). Jennifer D. Milam has recently argued for the inherently playful character of eighteenth-century aesthetics; see her *Fragonard's Playful Paintings: Visual Games in Rococo Art* (Manchester: Manchester Univ. Press, 2006).

7 Donald Crawford, "Nature and Art: Some Dialectical Relationships," *Journal of Aesthetics and Art Criticism* 42, no. 1 (1983): 52.

8 Diderot, "Salon of 1767," 2:206, 202, 206, 196–97.

9 Henri Bernardin de Saint-Pierre, *Études de la nature* (Paris: Deterville, 1804), 3:191.

10 Joachim du Bellay, *Antiquitez de Rome = Ruines of Rome,* English trans. Edmund Spenser (Binghamton, N.Y.: Center for Medieval & Early Renaissance Studies, 1994), 25. On the changed attitude toward ruins in the eighteenth century, see Roland Mortier, *La poétique des ruines en France: Ses origines, ses variations, de la Renaissance à Victor Hugo* (Geneva: Librairie Droz, 1974), 88–106. On pre-Enlightenment conceptions of ruin, see in particular Sabine Forero-Mendoza, *Le temps des ruines: L'éveil de la conscience historique à la Renaissance* (Seyssel: Éditions Champ Vallon, 2002); and Margaret M. McGowan, *The Vision of Rome in Late Renaissance France* (New Haven: Yale Univ. Press, 2000). See also the diachronic overview of the ruin theme in Hubert Burda, *Die Ruine in den Bildern Hubert Roberts* (Munich: Wilhelm Fink, 1967), 9–38. For a bibliographical essay on the literature on ruins, see Robert Ginsberg, *The Aesthetics of Ruins* (Amsterdam: Rodopi, 2004), 461–94.

11 Robert's debts to the Bamboccianti are discussed in Jean-François Méjanès, *Hubert Robert,* exh. cat. (Paris: Musée du Louvre, 2006), 9–10. My account draws on David A. Levine, "The Roman Limekilns of the Bamboccianti," *Art Bulletin* 70, no. 4 (1988): 569–89.

12 Levine, "Roman Limekilns," esp. 575–81.

13 Gerda Reith, *The Age of Chance: Gambling in Western Culture* (London: Routledge, 1999), 24–25.

14 Ingrid G. Daemmrich, "The Ruins Motif as Artistic Device in French Literature: Part I," *Journal of Aesthetics and Art Criticism* 30, no. 4 (1972): 453, 450. For a general account of the evolution of perceptions of the ruin in France, see Mortier, *Poétique.*

15 Reith, *Age of Chance,* 14. See the discussion of probability theory in Kavanagh, *Enlightenment,* esp. chap. 1. The quoted phrase is from Burke, *Philosophical Enquiry,* 66. The ruin's de-allegorization is discussed in Daemmrich, "Ruins Motif."

16 Reinhart Koselleck, *Futures Past: On the Semantics of Historical Time,* trans. Keith Tribe (Cambridge: MIT Press, 1985), 21–22.

17 Niklas Luhmann, *Risk: A Sociological Theory,* trans. Rhodes Barrett (Berlin: Walter de Gruyter, 1993), 43.

18 J. G. A. Pocock, "Modes of Political and Historical Time in Early Eighteenth-Century England," in idem, *Virtue, Commerce, and History: Essays on Political Thought and History, Chiefly in the Eighteenth Century* (1985; reprint, Cambridge: Cambridge Univ. Press, 1995), 98.

19 Reith, *Age of Chance,* 43.

20 Georges Bernier, *Hubert Robert: The Pleasure of Ruins,* exh. cat. (New York: Wildenstein, 1988), 6. The biographical sketch that follows draws on Jean de Cayeux with Catherine Boulot, *Hubert Robert* (Paris: Fayard, 1989), 21–41.

21 Mariette reports on Robert's formation and training with Slodtz in *Abecedario de P. J. Mariette . . . ,* ed. Ph. De Chennevières and A. de Montaiglon (Paris: J. B. Dumoulin, 1857–58; reprint, Paris: F. de Nobele, 1966), 4:413. On the sculptor, see François Souchal, *Les Slodtz, sculpteurs et décorateurs du roi (1685–1764)* (Paris: Edition É. De Boccard, 1967).

22 The possibility is noted in Paula Rea Radisich, *Hubert Robert: Painted Spaces of the Enlightenment* (Cambridge: Cambridge Univ. Press, 1998), 7. Alain-Charles Gruber reports on another instance of the painter following in the footsteps of the sculptor: in 1778, Robert was considered for the position of *dessinateur du cabinet du roi* with the Menus-Plaisirs (this post of designer of royal entertainments, including fireworks and festivals, was ultimately given to the architect Pierre-Adrien Pâris); see Alain-Charles Gruber, *Les grandes fêtes et leurs décors à l'époque de Louis XVI* (Geneva: Librairie Droz, 1972), 15. Gruber's

discussion underscores the close connections between Robert's genre of fantasy architecture and the design of festival décor.

23 Anatole de Montaiglon and Jules Guiffrey, eds., *Correspondance des directeurs de l'Académie de France à Rome avec les surintendants des Bâtiments* (Paris: Charavay frères [et al.], 1887–1912), 11:266, no. 5337 (Marigny to Natoire, 21 March 1759). Robert was one of approximately nineteen artists who received lodging at the Palais Mancini between 1752 and 1770 without having been awarded the Grand Prix. See Christian Michel, *Charles-Nicolas Cochin et l'art des lumières* (Rome: École française de Rome, 1993), 492.

24 On Robert's deviation from academic standards, see Méjanès, *Hubert Robert,* 7–8. The uncommon praise bestowed on Robert is noted in Henri Lapauze, *Histoire de l'Académie de France à Rome,* vol. 1, *1666–1801* (Paris: Libraire Plon, 1924), 282.

25 Montaiglon and Guiffrey, *Correspondance,* 10:394, no. 4916 (Natoire to Vandières, June 1752).

26 See *Charles-Joseph Natoire: Nîmes, 1700–Castel Gandolfo, 1777; Peintures, dessins, estampes et tapisseries des collections publiques françaises,* exh. cat. (Troyes: Musée des beaux-arts, 1977), 102–3; and Emile Dacier, "Natoire paysagiste," in "Mélanges offerts à M. Jules Guiffrey," special issue, *Archives de l'art français,* n.s., 8 (1916): 230–42. On Natoire's tenure, see Lapauze, *Histoire de l'Académie,* chap. 10.

27 Legrand notes that the two artists sketched together; he also records Vasi's comment to Piranesi: "Vous êtes trôp peintre, mon ami, pour être jamais graveur"; see Jacques-Guillaume Legrand, "Notice historique sur la vie et les ouvrages de G. B. Piranesi" (1801), *Nouvelles de l'estampe,* no. 5 (1969): 202, 194.

28 The longing among *pensionnaires* to travel outside the capital—to visit its environs, Naples, southern Italy, and Sicily—remained fervent, to Marigny's irritation. In 1755, the general director of the Bâtiments du roi withheld from the architect Marie-Joseph Peyre permission to undertake such a trip, claiming "the *pensionnaires* have enough training to complete in Rome during their three years of study"; seven years later Marigny requested that "our architects concern themselves more with things relative to our manners and customs than to the temples of Greece." See Montaiglon and Guiffrey, *Correspondance,* 11:87–88, no. 5099 (Marigny to Natoire, 30 April 1755) and 11:437–38 (Marigny to Natoire); cited in Laura Mascoli, "Le 'Journal du voyage en Italie' de l'abbé de Saint-Non," *Dix-huitième siècle,* no. 21 (1989): 436.

29 The abbé's comment is in Jean-Claude Richard de Saint-Non, "Journal ou notes sur un voyage fait en Italie," in idem, *Panopticon italiano: Un diario di viaggio ritrovato, 1759–1761,* ed. Pierre Rosenberg with Barbara Brejon de Lavergnée (Rome: Edizioni dell'Elefante, 1986), 122–23.

30 Cayeux, *Hubert Robert,* 45–46.

31 See Joseph Disponzio, "Introduction," in Claude-Henri Watelet, *Essay on Gardens: A Chapter in the French Picturesque,* trans. Samuel Danon (Philadelphia: Univ. of Pennsylvania Press, 2003). On the artist's relationship with Watelet and Marguerite Le Comte, see Cayeux, *Hubert Robert,* 65–67. On Robert at Moulin Joli, see Jean de Cayeux, *Hubert Robert et les jardins* (Paris: Editions Herscher, 1987), 91–93.

32 On details of the private academy and its significance for the painter's subsequent career in garden design, see Cayeux, *Hubert Robert,* 143–48; and Méjanès, *Hubert Robert,* 13–14. On Robert's commission to help renovate the gardens at Versailles, see Susan B. Taylor, "*Ut Pictura Horti:* Hubert Robert and the Bains d'Apollon at Versailles" (Ph.D. diss., University of Pennsylvania, 1990). On Robert as a garden designer and the place of gardens in his art, see Cayeux, *Hubert Robert et les jardins;* and Günter Herzog, *Hubert Robert und das Bild im Garten* (Worms: Wernersche Verlagsgesellschaft, 1989).

33 Jean-Claude Richard de Saint-Non, *Voyage pittoresque; ou, Description des royaumes de Naples et de Sicile* (Paris: Imprimerie de Clousier, 1781–86), 2:vi, 1:81, 2:5.

34 Friedrich Johann Lorenz Meyer, *Les tableaux d'Italie,* trans. Elisabeth Chevallier (Naples: Centre Jean Bérard, Bibliothèque de l'Institut français de Naples, 1980), 209; cited in Elisabeth Chevallier, "Les fouilles d'Herculaneum vues par les voyageurs du XVIIIe siècle,"

in Elisabeth Chevallier and Raymond Chevallier, *Iter Italicum: Les voyageurs français à la découverte de l'Italie ancienne* (Geneva: Slatkine, 1984), 33, 35.

35 Geoffrey Scott, *The Architecture of Humanism: A Study in the History of Taste* (Garden City, N.Y.: Doubleday, 1954), 70; cited in Jean H. Hagstrum, *The Sister Arts: The Tradition of Literary Pictorialism and English Poetry from Dryden to Gray* (Chicago: Univ. of Chicago Press, 1958), 158.

36 On Robert's production at Méréville, see Jean de Cayeux, "Hubert Robert, dessinateur de jardins, et sa collaboration au parc de Méréville, d'après des documents inédits," *Bulletin de la Société de l'histoire de l'art français* (1968): 127–33; Cayeux, *Hubert Robert et les jardins;* Olivier Choppin de Janvry, "Méréville," *L'oeil,* no. 180 (1969): 30–40, 83, 96; Simone de Lassus, "Les fabriques de Méréville et de Jeurre," *L'information de l'histoire de l'art,* no. 1 (1975): 32–36; and Simone de Lassus, "Quelques détails inédits sur Méréville," *Bulletin de la Société de l'histoire de l'art français* (1976): 273–87.

37 Cayeux, *Hubert Robert et les jardins,* 50, 116–17.

38 See McGowan, *Vision of Rome,* esp. 94–96, 148–59.

39 Watelet, *Essay on Gardens,* 23. On the significance for Watelet of Étienne Bonnot de Condillac's *Traité des sensations* (1754), see Disponzio, "Introduction," 14–15. For a succinct account of the impact of the new sciences on garden theory, see Michel Baridon, "Garden of the Perfectibilists: Méréville and the Désert de Retz," in John Dixon Hunt and Michel Conan, eds., *Tradition and Innovation in French Garden Art: Chapters of a New History* (Philadelphia: Univ. of Pennsylvania Press, 2002), 121–34.

40 Hubert Robert to Jean-Joseph de Laborde, 7 August 1786, Bibliothèque d'art et d'archéologie Jacques Doucet, Paris, MS 1099.

41 Cited in Simone de Lassus, "Essai sur les fabriques de jardins au XVIIIe siècle en Ile-de-France: 1736–1793" (Thesis [3rd cycle], Université Paris Sorbonne—Paris IV, 1985), 1:204. See also Lassus, "Fabriques de Méréville," 32–36; as well as Cayeux, *Hubert Robert et les jardins,* 102–12. Robert describes the site for the monument to Cook in his letter to Laborde of 7 August 1786. The quotation from Watelet appears in his *Essay on Gardens,* 26–27.

42 Alexandre de Laborde, *Description des nouveaux jardins de la France et de ses anciens châteaux, mêlée d'observations sur la vie de la campagne et la composition des jardins = Description of the Modern Gardens and Ancient Castles in France = Beschreibung der neuen Gärten und alten Schlösser in Frankreich* (Paris: Imprimerie de Delance, 1808), 107.

43 Sophie Le Ménahèze, *L'invention du jardin romantique en France, 1761–1808* (Neuilly-sur-Seine: Éditions Spiralinthe, 2001), 177.

44 Louis Carrogis de Carmontelle, *Jardin de Monceau, près de Paris, appartenant à son Altesse Sérénissime monseigneur le Duc de Chartres* (Paris: Delafosse, 1779), x. It is, in part, a testament to the garden's aesthetic of changeability that Carmontelle depicted Méréville and other picturesque estates in his "transparencies"—the scrolling miniature transparent panoramas that he began producing in 1782 and that may be considered precursors to the motion picture. See Laurence Chatel de Brancion, *Carmontelle's Landscape Transparencies: Cinema of the Enlightenment* (Los Angeles: J. Paul Getty Museum, 2007), esp. chap. 6.

45 Baridon, "Garden of the Perfectibilists," 122. For a general account of French picturesque gardens, see the relevant essays in Michel Baridon, *Les jardins: Paysagistes, jardiniers, poètes* (Paris: R. Laffont, 1998); Jurgis Baltrušaitis, "Gardens and Lands of Illusion," in idem, *Aberrations: An Essay on the Legend of Forms,* trans. Richard Miller (Cambridge: MIT Press, 1989); Dora Wiebenson, *The Picturesque Garden in France* (Princeton: Princeton Univ. Press, 1978); and *Jardins en France, 1760–1820: Pays d'illusion, terre d'expériences,* exh. cat. (Paris: Caisse nationale des monuments historiques et des sites, 1977).

46 Watelet, *Essay on Gardens,* 50–51, 26.

47 Watelet, *Essay on Gardens,* 39–40. Similarly, Jean-Marie Morel details the enjoyable effects of the "fracas and violence" of flowing water in his *Théorie des jardins* (Paris: Pissot, 1776; reprint, Geneva: Minkoff Reprint, 1973), 118. Rocks, Morel notes in his chapter on the subject, are "almost always accompanied by the fall of torrents and cascades" (178).

48 Watelet, *Essay on Gardens,* 41.

49 The Temple de la Philosophie was likely meant as the antithesis of William Kent and Lord Cobham's Temple of Modern Virtue at Stowe; the latter was illustrated, along with Stowe's Temple of Ancient Virtue, in *Stowe: A Description of the Magnificent House and Gardens of the Right Honourable Richard, Earl Temple, Viscount and Baron Cobham,...,* new ed. (London: Printed for John Rivington, B. Seeley & T. Hodgkinson, 1763). Unlike its counterpart—a completed structure based on the Temple of Vesta at Tivoli—the Temple of Modern Virtue was a sham ruin, a "satiric vision of the present." The Temple de la Philosophie, by contrast, "suggests progress rather than decay, hope rather than despair"; see Elizabeth Wanning Harries, *The Unfinished Manner: Essays on the Fragment in the Later Eighteenth Century* (Charlottesville: Univ. Press of Virginia, 1994), 92.

50 On Robert's role at Ermenonville, as well as his views of the garden, see Cayeux, *Hubert Robert et les jardins,* 93–101.

51 On the coupling of binary elements in Robert's landscapes, see Stéphanie Thuilliez, "Les quatre éléments dans l'oeuvre d'Hubert Robert," in Hervé Brunon, Monique Mosser, and Daniel Rabreau, eds., *Les éléments et les métamorphoses de la nature: Imaginaire et symbolique des arts dans la culture européenne du XVIe au XVIIIe siècle; Actes du colloque international de l'Opéra de Bordeaux (17–21 septembre 1997)* (Bordeaux: William Blake, Art et Arts, 2004), 325–35.

52 Barbara Maria Stafford, *Voyage into Substance: Art, Science, Nature, and the Illustrated Travel Account, 1760–1840* (Cambridge: MIT Press, 1984), 4.

53 Ernst Cassirer, *The Philosophy of the Enlightenment,* trans. Fritz C. A. Koelln and James P. Pettegrove (Princeton: Princeton Univ. Press, 1951), 295, 297, 279, 293. On the dissolution of Classical aesthetics in the eighteenth century, see Wladyslaw Folkierski, *Entre le classicisme et le romantisme: Étude sur l'esthétique et les esthéticiens du XVIIIe siècle* (Cracow: Académie polonaise des sciences & des lettres, 1925); André Fontaine, *Les doctrines d'art en France: Peintres, amateurs, critiques, de Poussin à Diderot* (Paris: H. Laurens, 1909); and Annie Becq, *Genèse de l'esthétique française moderne: De la raison classique à l'imagination créatrice, 1680–1814,* 2 vols. (Pisa: Pacini, 1984).

54 Cassirer, *Philosophy of the Enlightenment,* 301, 325, 324.

55 "Lettre sur les tableaux tirés du Cabinet du roy et exposées au Luxembourg depuis le 24 octobre 1750," *Collection Deloynes: Collection de pièces sur les beaux-arts imprimées et manuscrites (1673–1808)* (Paris: Bibliothèque nationale de France, 1980), 52:100–101, no. 1428; cited in Édouard Pommier, "Postface," in Jean-Baptiste-Pierre Lebrun, *Réflexions sur le muséum national, 14 janvier 1793,* ed. Édouard Pommier (Paris: Réunion des musées nationaux, 1992), 86. Echoing Cassirer, Pommier writes that in the Luxembourg exhibition as in the garden, "The artworks are nothing but instruments of a spectacle that informs, diverts, refreshes, astonishes. They disappear behind the images they've produced" (87).

56 Pommier, "Postface," 88.

57 Watelet further notes that the "frightening, sentimental, or emblematic type of garden...may command a few moments of admiration, but the effect does not last long." In truth, however much he valorizes the effects in the garden of "mystery," "surprise," and "chance," Watelet's statement that the principle of the picturesque is "to combine constantly elements that arouse our curiosity and compel us to move about with elements that fix our attention and invite us to linger" can be taken as evidence of his desire to temper fluctuation with stasis. See Watelet, *Essay on Gardens,* 43, 34, 50. On this score, see the interpretation of "subjectivism" as a symptom of "historical pessimism" in Henry Vyverberg, *Historical Pessimism in the French Enlightenment* (Cambridge: Harvard Univ. Press, 1958), 111–15. According to Vyverberg, whereas "classical aesthetics, devoted to fixed principles and standards, had defined progress in terms of increasing efficiency in the use of established techniques," the new aesthetics—exemplified in Dubos's *Réflexions critiques sur la poésie et sur la peinture*—emphasized climate ("the fleeting vagaries of time and place") as the prime determinant of cultural production. Consequently, "there could result no conception of simple or linear progress or decadence in the arts, but only a kaleidoscopic picture of cyclical or fluctuating development."

58 Watelet, *Essay on Gardens,* 55. Thus we learn in a letter that a bridge Laborde had commissioned for Méréville no longer interested him and that Robert hoped to sell it to "some proprietor of an English garden." The episode is suggestive of the transience of *fabriques* in a luxury economy. See Robert to Laborde, 25 June 1789.

59 Jacques-Antoine Dulaure, *Nouvelle description des environs de Paris...* (Paris: Lejay, 1786), 1:v; cited in Le Ménahèze, *Invention,* 49. My discussion of the garden as an extension of the fashion industry draws on her observations.

60 See Villa Medici, *Piranèse et les Français, 1740–1790,* exh. cat. (Rome: Edizioni dell'Elefante, 1976); as well as the essays in Georges Brunel, ed., *Piranèse et les Français: Colloque tenu à la Villa Médicis, 12–14 mai 1976* (Rome: Edizioni dell'Elefante, 1978). Since the eleventh century, a *chinea* (an obsolete Italian word for "white horse") along with a monetary tribute had been offered to the papacy by the ambassadors extraordinary of the ruling house of the two Sicilies. In the eighteenth century, the annual Festa della Chinea marked this display of fealty with fireworks as well as a procession. Like the collective activity of the Piranésiens, the Chinea festivities were short-lived: considered by the king of Naples as a wasteful relic of feudalism, the practice came to an end in 1788. See John E. Moore, "The Chinea: A Festival in Eighteenth-Century Rome" (Ph.D. diss., Harvard University, 1992), as well as his "Prints, Salami, and Cheese: Savoring the Roman Festival of the Chinea," *Art Bulletin* 77, no. 4 (1995): 584–608.

61 These *pensionnaires* remained almost uniformly committed to creating large-scale public works. Unable to reconcile their grandiose aspirations with the realities of private patronage, a number of them took court positions only to be plagued by charges of megalomania. See Chantal Gastinel-Coural, "Un dessin de Michel-Ange Challe pour la pompe funèbre de Louis XV en l'Église abbatiale de Saint-Denis," in Maria Teresa Caracciolo, ed., *Hommage au dessin: Mélanges offerts à Roseline Bacou* (Rimini: Galeria, 1996), 490–99; Christian Elling, "Le séjour romain de Nicolas-Henri Jardin," in Georges Brunel, ed., *Piranèse et les Français: Colloque tenu à la Villa Médicis, 12–14 mai 1976* (Rome: Edizioni dell'Elefante, 1978), esp. 191–92; Gilbert Erouart, "Jean-Laurent Legeay: Recherches," in Brunel, *Piranèse et les Français* (this note), 200–212; and Gilbert Erouart, *L'architecture au pinceau: Jean-Laurent Legeay, un piranésien français dans l'Europe des lumières* (Milan: Electa, 1982). On these artists' influence on Neoclassicism, see, for example, John Harris, "Le Geay, Piranesi and International Neo-Classicism in Rome, 1740–1750," in Douglas Fraser, Howard Hibbard, and Milton J. Lewine, eds., *Essays in the History of Architecture Presented to Rudolf Wittkower* (London: Phaidon, 1967), 181–96; and Emil Kaufmann, *Architecture in the Age of Reason: Baroque and Postbaroque in England, Italy, and France* (Cambridge: Harvard Univ. Press, 1955).

62 Claude-Nicolas Ledoux, *L'architecture considérée sous le rapport de l'art, des moeurs et de la législation* (Paris: Imprimerie de H. L. Perronneau, 1804), 1:112–13; cited in Erouart, "Jean-Laurent Legeay," 206. Robert's influence on Ledoux is signaled in Anthony Vidler, *Claude-Nicolas Ledoux: Architecture and Social Reform at the End of the Ancien Régime* (Cambridge: MIT Press, 1990), 45 and passim.

63 The rise of the "painter-architect" or "architect-painter" is discussed, along with the metamorphosis of Rome, in André Chastel, "Préface," in Villa Medici, *Piranèse et les Français, 1740–1790,* exh. cat. (Rome: Edizioni dell'Elefante, 1976), 15. The term *archéofiction* appears in Georges Brunel, "Introduction," in Villa Medici, *Piranèse et les Français* (this note), 29. On the "painter-etcher," see Victor I. Carlson, "The Painter-Etcher: The Role of the Original Printmaker," in Victor I. Carlson and John W. Ittmann, eds., *Regency to Empire: French Printmaking, 1715–1814,* exh. cat. (Baltimore: Baltimore Museum of Art, 1984), 25–27.

64 Joseph Rykwert, *The First Moderns: The Architects of the Eighteenth Century* (Cambridge: MIT Press, 1980), 361–62.

65 The *pensionnaires'* participation in a culture of masquerades, carnivals, religious processions, and other festive events is detailed by the artist Michel-Barthélemy Hazon (1722–1818). Extracts from his correspondence in 1746 are published in Louis de Launay, *Une grande famille de savants: Les Brongniart* (Paris: G. Rapilly, 1940), 170–94.

66 Rykwert, *First Moderns,* 364.

67 Thus Jacques-François Blondel's insistence that students of architecture receive a solid training in French Classicism before traveling to Rome, lest they return corrupted; see Jean-Marie Pérouse de Montclos, "Piranèse, les Français et le classicisme international," in Georges Brunel, ed., *Piranèse et les Français: Colloque tenu à la Villa Médicis, 12–14 mai 1976* (Rome: Edizioni dell'Elefante, 1978), 421. The disillusionment caused by such studies is described in Werner Szambien, *Symétrie, goût, caractère: Théorie et terminologie de l'architecture à l'âge classique 1550–1800* (Paris: Picard, 1986). The quotation is from Daniel Rabreau, "Des scènes figurées à la mise en scène du monument urbain: Notes sur le dessin 'théâtral' et la création architecturale en France après 1750," in Brunel, *Piranèse et les Français* (this note), 446.

68 Legrand, "Notice historique," 218; translated in Thomas J. McCormick, *Charles-Louis Clérisseau and the Genesis of Neo-Classicism* (Cambridge: MIT Press, 1990), 103. See also McCormick's discussions of the "ruin room" (103–12) and of Clérisseau as decorator (163–78).

69 On the "revolution" in color printing, see Judith C. Walsh, "Ink and Inspiration: The Craft of Color Printing," in Margaret Morgan Grasselli, Kristel Smentek, and Judith G. Walsh, *Colorful Impressions: The Printmaking Revolution in Eighteenth-Century France,* exh. cat. (Washington, D.C.: National Gallery of Art, 2003), 23–33.

70 See Ef-105 (5)-Fol, Cabinet des estampes, Bibliothèque nationale de France.

71 Victor I. Carlson and John W. Ittmann, eds., *Regency to Empire: French Printmaking, 1715–1814,* exh. cat. (Baltimore: Baltimore Museum of Art, 1984), 270, no. 96.

72 On the little that is known of this artist, see Cara D. Denison, Myra Nan Rosenfeld, and Stephanie Wiles, *Exploring Rome: Piranesi and His Contemporaries,* exh. cat. (New York: Pierpont Morgan Library, 1993), 201, no. 115.

73 On the tension between an appreciation of the modern advances of the printing press and the awareness stirred by ruins that modernity was not necessarily superior to antiquity, see McGowan, *Vision of Rome,* 130–31.

74 As noted by Andrew Robison, *Piranesi, Early Architectural Fantasies: A Catalogue Raisonné of the Etchings* (Washington, D.C.: National Gallery of Art, 1986), 12. The quotation is from Giovanni Battista Piranesi, *Diverse maniere d'adornare i cammini...* (Rome: Generoso Salomoni, 1769), 33.

75 Piranesi appears to have been the first artist to identify his architectural fantasies as caprices; see Alice Jarrard, "The Architectural Caprice, 'Historiciz'd,'" in Guillaume Peureux, ed., *Le caprice* (Rennes: Presses Universitaires de Rennes, 2004), 172. The quotation is from Dorothea Nyberg, ed., "Original Text of *Prima parte* and English Translation," in *Giovanni Battista Piranesi: Drawings and Etchings at Columbia University,* exh. cat. (New York: Avery Architectural Library/Department of Art History & Archaeology, Columbia Univ., 1972), 115–18; cited in John Wilton-Ely, "Introduction," in Giovanni Battista Piranesi, *Observations on the Letter of Monsieur Mariette...,* trans. Caroline Beamish and David Britt (Los Angeles: Getty Research Institute, 2002), 3; Wilton-Ely's essay—to which my account is indebted—surveys Piranesi's publications and their contributions to the Greco-Roman debate. The main works alluded to in this chapter include *Prima parte di architetture e prospettive* (Part one of architecture and perspectives; 1743); *Opere varie di architettura...* (Various works of architecture...; 1750); *Le antichità romane...* (The antiquities of Rome...; 1756); *Invenzioni capric di carceri...* (Fanciful images of prisons...; 1745), reissued as *Carceri d'invenzione...* (Prisons of the imagination...; 1761); *Della magnificenza ed architettura de' romani...* (On the magnificence and architecture of the Romans...; 1761); *Il Campo Marzio dell'antica Roma...* (The Campo Marzio of ancient Rome...; 1762); and *Osservazioni sopra la lettre de Monsieur Mariette...* (Observations on the letter of Monsieur Mariette...; 1765).

76 Giovanni Battista Piranesi, "Al chiarissimo signore, Sig. Roberto Adam," in idem, *Il Campo Marzio dell'antica Roma* (Rome, 1762), [xi]; translated in Wilton-Ely, "Introduction," 27.

77 Marc-Antoine Laugier, *An Essay on Architecture,* trans. Wolfgang and Anni Herrmann (Los Angeles: Hennessey & Ingalls, 1977), 3, 11–12.

78 Giovanni Battista Piranesi, "Opinions on Architecture," in idem, *Observations on the Letter of*

Monsieur Mariette..., trans. Caroline Beamish and David Britt (Los Angeles: Getty Research Institute, 2002), 104.

79 Manfredo Tafuri, *Architecture and Utopia: Design and Capitalist Development,* trans. Barbara Luigia La Penta (Cambridge: MIT Press, 1987), 18. See also Manfredo Tafuri, "'The Wicked Architect': G. B. Piranesi, Heterotopia, and the Voyage," in idem, *The Sphere and the Labyrinth: Avant-Gardes and Architecture from Piranesi to the 1970s,* trans. Pellegrino d'Acierno and Robert Connolly (Cambridge: MIT Press, 1987), 25–54. Tafuri's account concerning the architectural impossibility of Piranesi's *Carceri* extends observations made in Ulya Vogt-Göknil, *Giovanni Battista Piranesi: Carceri* (Zurich: Origo Verlag, 1958).

80 See Mary L. Myers, *French Architectural and Ornament Drawings of the Eighteenth Century,* exh. cat. (New York: Metropolitan Museum of Art, 1991), 40–41, no. 24.

81 William Alexander McClung, "A Place for a Time: The Architecture of Festivals and Theaters," in Eve Blau and Edward Kaufman, eds., *Architecture and Its Images: Four Centuries of Architectural Representation,* exh. cat. (Montreal: Centre canadien d'architecture, 1989), 99. McClung encourages a reading of ephemeral constructions as architectural fantasies, writing that festival architecture was "deliberately incomplete," that it "permitted, indeed encouraged, the indecorous combination or synthesis of forms," and that it "challenge[d] the spectator to reject the authority of the merely actual and to inhabit for a significant moment the realm of the possible" (87, 95, 107).

82 Erouart, *Architecture au pinceau,* 82; 80; 229, no. 135; 217, no. 51.

83 See, for example, Robison, *Piranesi,* 16–17, figs. 11–14.

84 Chloe Chard, *Pleasure and Guilt on the Grand Tour: Travel Writing and Imaginative Geography, 1600–1830* (Manchester: Manchester Univ. Press, 1999), 4.

85 This dimension of Piranesi's production—its inadvertent complicity with the logic of the market—is signaled by Tafuri, who notes, for example, the cynical reaction of James Barry to the argument for eclecticism advanced in the *Diverse maniere:* "A book by the Cavalier Piranesi has just been published, written... for the purpose of condemning the Greeks.... But this purpose conceals something more equivocal than may easily be believed: merchants often indulge in double dealing, and he has accumulated an enormous quantity of various marbles which he would be happy to sell. Given, however, that no one would ever take them for objects of Greek origin, for a very obvious reason, the renewal and the sharpening of old prejudices against the Greeks prove to be a useful contribution towards facilitating the sale of his collection. This is the purpose of his book, published as a kind of publicity announcement"; Tafuri, *Sphere and the Labyrinth,* 52; cited in Jonathan Scott, *Piranesi* (New York: St. Martin's Press, 1975), 243–44.

86 The relevance of Walter Benjamin's "The Work of Art in the Age of Mechanical Reproduction" (1936) to the print culture of eighteenth-century antiquarianism is posited in Dana Arnold and Stephen Bending, "Tracing Architecture: The Aesthetics of Antiquarianism," *Art History* 25, no. 4 (2002): 421.

87 Thomas De Quincey, *Confessions of an English Opium-Eater and Other Writings,* ed. Barry Milligan (London: Penguin, 2003), 78.

88 John Soane, "Lectures on Architecture," in David Watkin, *Sir John Soane: Enlightenment Thought and the Royal Academy Lectures* (Cambridge: Cambridge Univ. Press, 1996), 603; cited in Wilton-Ely, "Introduction," 82, no. 123.

89 Claude Lévi-Strauss, "Mythe et oubli," in Julia Kristeva et al., *Langue, discours, société: Pour Émile Benveniste* (Paris: Éditions du Seuil, 1975), 299; cited in Giorgio Agamben, *Infancy and History: On the Destruction of Experience,* trans. Liz Heron (New York: Verso, 2007), 78.

90 Roger Caillois, *Man, Play and Games,* trans. Meyer Barash (Urbana: Univ. of Illinois Press, 2001), 4.

91 The painting spawned a veritable industry of misleading prints and erroneous descriptions in the eighteenth century. See Richard Verdi, "On the Critical Fortunes—and Misfortunes—of Poussin's 'Arcadia,'" *Burlington Magazine* 121, no. 911 (1979): 95–107. Robert's court appointments as designer of the king's gardens at Versailles and as keeper of the king's

pictures at the museum likely permitted him to see the painting firsthand. Poussin's painting also helped inspire the vogue for tombs in gardens. See Le Ménahèze, *Invention*, 101.

92 Diderot, "Salon of 1767," 2:198.

93 Pocock, "Modes of Political and Historical Time," 92.

94 Diderot, "Salon of 1767," 2:217.

95 Lorraine Daston, *Classical Probability in the Enlightenment* (Princeton: Princeton Univ. Press, 1988), 117. On insurance and other gambits in the financial industry, see the following by Jean Bouchary: *Les manieurs d'argent à Paris à la fin du XVIIIe siècle*, 3 vols. (Paris: Librairie des sciences politiques et sociales, 1939–43); *Les compagnies financières à Paris à la fin du XVIIIe siècle*, 3 vols. (Paris: Marcel Rivière, 1940–42); and *L'eau à Paris à la fin du XVIIIe siècle: La Compagnie des eaux de Paris et l'entreprise de l'Yvette* (Paris, Marcel Rivière, 1946). See also Herbert Lüthy, *La banque protestante en France: De la révocation de l'Édit de Nantes à la révolution* (Paris: SEVPEN, 1961), esp. 2:369–727; and George V. Taylor, "The Paris Bourse on the Eve of the Revolution, 1781–1789," *American Historical Review* 67, no. 4 (1962): 951–77.

96 Daston, *Classical Probability*, 144

97 Lüthy, *Banque protestante en France*, 2:464–69; see also George Alter and James C. Riley, "How to Bet on Lives: A Guide to Life Contingent Contracts in Early Modern Europe," *Research in Economic History* 10 (1986): 1–53. On Robert's investments, see Claude Gabillot, *Hubert Robert et son temps* (Paris: Librairie de l'art, 1895), 238.

98 Yves-Réné Durand, "Mémoires de Jean-Joseph de Laborde, banquier de la cour et fermier général," *Bulletin de la Société de l'histoire de l'art français* (1968–69): 115. See François d'Ormesson and Jean-Pierre Thomas, *Jean-Joseph de Laborde, banquier de Louis XV, mécène des lumières* (Paris: Perrin, 2002). On the banker's friendship with Robert, who was arguably his favorite artist, see 140–43. (Laborde owned Elisabeth-Louise Vigée-Lebrun's portrait of Robert, today in the Musée du Louvre.)

99 In a letter of 2 March 1761 to Choiseul, Laborde alludes to the untenability of his position: "I believe that a good citizen should always aspire to make himself useful... it's a pleasure that I relish and that I can relish without agreeing to accumulate million upon million, difficulty upon difficulty and risk upon risk for my honor." Archives de la Maison Noailles; cited in D'Ormesson and Thomas, *Jean-Joseph de Laborde*, 61.

100 See William Doyle, *Venality: The Sale of Offices in Eighteenth-Century France* (New York: Clarendon Press, 1996), as well as the cases detailed in Yves Durand, *Les fermiers généraux au XVIIIe siècle* (Paris: Presses universitaires de France, 1971).

101 Guy Chaussinand-Nogaret, *The French Nobility in the Eighteenth Century: From Feudalism to Enlightenment*, trans. William Doyle (Cambridge: Cambridge Univ. Press, 1985), 4. For more recent considerations of the French nobility's place in an evolving economy, see Gail Bossenga, "The Patrimonial State, Markets, and the Origins of the French Revolution," in Kevin Lee Cope and Scott Paul Gordon, eds., *1650–1850: Ideas, Aesthetics, and Inquiries in the Early Modern Era* (New York: AMS Press, 2005), 11:443–509; see also Jay M. Smith, ed., *The French Nobility in the Eighteenth Century: Reassessments and New Approaches* (University Park: Pennsylvania State Univ. Press, 2006).

102 D'Ormesson and Thomas, *Jean-Joseph de Laborde*, 13, 47.

103 François Véron Duverger de Forbonnais, "Crédit," in Denis Diderot and Jean Le Rond d'Alembert, *Encyclopédie; ou, Dictionnaire raisonné des sciences, des arts et des métiers* (Paris: Briasson [et al.], 1754–72), 4:445–46.

104 Marc Shell, *Art and Money* (Chicago: Univ. of Chicago Press, 1995), 73. Scholars of economic literary theory have argued not only that "economic theory is the repressed truth of aesthetics" but "that the reverse is also true"; see Mary Poovey, "Aesthetics and Political Economy in the Eighteenth Century: The Place of Gender in the Social Constitution of Knowledge," in George Levine, ed., *Aesthetics and Ideology* (New Brunswick, N.J.: Rutgers Univ. Press, 1994), 80.

105 Thomas Manley Luckett, "Credit and Commercial Society in France, 1740–1789" (Ph.D. diss., Princeton University, 1992), 7.

106 Such designations were standard in the eighteenth century. See Richard T. Gray, "Buying into Signs: Money and Semiosis in Eighteenth-Century German Language Theory," in Martha Woodmansee and Mark Osteen, eds., *The New Economic Criticism: Studies at the Intersection of Literature and Economics* (London: Routledge, 1999), 95–113.

107 Kavanagh, *Enlightenment,* 86, 69. On the Law affair, see Edgar Faure, *La banqueroute de Law, 17 juillet 1720* (Paris: Gallimard, 1977); see the bibliography on the Système, 691–722. See also Lüthy, *Banque protestante en France,* vol. 1, chap. 3; and Paul Harsin, *Les doctrines monétaires et financières en France du XVIe au XVIIIe siècle* (Paris: F. Alcan, 1928), pt. 5.

108 Jean-Baptiste Colbert, "Mémoire" (1 October 1659), in idem, *Lettres, instructions, et mémoires de Colbert,* ed. Pierre Clément (Paris: Imprimerie impériale, 1861–82), 7:181; cited and translated in Thomas E. Kaiser, "Money, Despotism, and Public Opinion in Early Eighteenth-Century France: John Law and the Debate on Royal Credit," *Journal of Modern History* 63, no. 1 (1991): 5.

109 Kavanagh, *Enlightenment,* 88.

110 Kaiser, "Money, Despotism, and Public Opinion," 4, 27. Voltaire's statement—cited and translated on page 27—is from Voltaire, *Oeuvres complètes de Voltaire,* ed. Louis Moland (Paris: Garnier Frères, 1877–85), 22:359–60. On the explosion of credit following the Law affair, see Philip T. Hoffman, Gilles Postel-Vinay, and Jean-Laurent Rosenthal, *Priceless Markets: The Political Economy of Credit in Paris, 1660–1870* (Chicago: Univ. of Chicago Press, 2000). As the authors conclude, the legacy of the Law affair was not the failure of financial innovation but rather the empowerment of notaries whose skillful mediation between borrowers and lenders ensured the vitality of the private credit market.

111 Emma Rothschild, "An Alarming Commercial Crisis in Eighteenth-Century Angoulême: Sentiments in Economic History," *Economic History Review* 51, no. 2 (1998): 269, 289.

112 Anne-Robert-Jacques Turgot, *Mémoire sur les prêts d'argent,* in *Oeuvres de Turgot et documents les concernant,* ed. G. Schelle (Paris: F. Alcan, 1913–23), 3:161–62; cited and translated in Rothschild, "Alarming Commercial Crisis," 269, 272.

113 Turgot, *Mémoire,* 179; cited and translated in Rothschild, "Alarming Commercial Crisis," 273.

114 A.-F. Robin, "Recueil secret des pièces intéressantes concernant la révolution arrivée dans le commerce de banque de la ville d'Angoulême, et les persécutions suscitées aux banquiers en 1769," ed. Abbé Mazière, *Bulletin de la Société archéologique et historique de la Charente* 8, 9 (1918): 23; cited and translated in Rothschild, "Alarming Commercial Crisis," 276.

115 See Martha Woodmansee and Mark Osteen, "Taking Account of the New Economic Criticism: An Historical Introduction," in idem, eds., *The New Economic Criticism: Studies at the Intersection of Literature and Economics* (London: Routledge, 1999), 3–50. Poovey, contesting the division between literature and economics, states that monetary instruments constituted literary genres in and of themselves, in Mary Poovey, *Genres of the Credit Economy: Mediating Value in Eighteenth- and Nineteenth-Century Britain* (Chicago: Univ. of Chicago Press, 2008).

116 Sandra Sherman, *Finance and Fictionality in the Early Eighteenth Century: Accounting for Defoe* (Cambridge: Cambridge Univ. Press, 1996), 16–17; the statement from Hutcheson, cited on p. 30, is from Archibald Hutcheson, *A Collection of Calculations and Remarks Relating to the South Sea Scheme and Stock, Which Have Been Already Published* (London, 1720), 63.

117 Sherman, *Finance and Fictionality,* 37, 27.

118 The phrases are used, respectively, in Tafuri, *Sphere and the Labyrinth,* 49; and Emma Rothschild, *Economic Sentiments: Adam Smith, Condorcet, and the Enlightenment* (Cambridge: Harvard Univ. Press, 2001), 2.

119 Charles-François de Lubersac de Livron, *Discours sur les monumens publics de tous les âges et de tous les peuples connus* (Paris, 1775), lviii; translated in David L. Hays, "'This is not a *jardin anglais*': Carmontelle, the Jardin de Monceau, and Irregular Garden Design in Late-Eighteenth-Century France," in Mirka Beneš and Dianne Harris, eds., *Villas and Gardens in Early Modern Italy and France* (Cambridge: Cambridge Univ. Press, 2001), 302.

120 Edouard Fournier, "Le Palais-Royal et ses environs," in Fedor Hoffbauer, ed., *Paris à travers les âges: aspects successifs des monuments et quartiers historiques de Paris depuis le XIIIe siècle jusqu'à nos jours* (Paris: Firmin-Didot, 1875–1882), 2:39–44.

121 Diderot, "Salon of 1767," 2:206–7.

122 Charles-Louis de Secondat, baron de Montesquieu, *Les lettres persanes* (1721); translated by C. J. Betts in *The Persian Letters* (London: Penguin Books, 1993), 245.

123 Charles-Louis de Secondat, baron de Montesquieu, *Les lettres persanes;* translated in J. Robert Loy, *The Persian Letters* (New York: World, 1961), 308; cited in Kavanagh, *Enlightenment,* 84.

124 Johann G. Büsch, *Sämtliche Schriften über Banken und Münzwesen*... (Hamburg: C. E. Bohn, 1801), 221; Daniel Defoe, *The Chimera; or, The French Way of Paying National Debts Laid Open*... (London: Printed for T. Warner..., 1720); Voltaire, *Oeuvres historiques,* ed. René Pomeau (Paris: Gallimard, 1957), 1311; all cited in Shell, *Art and Money,* 66, 68.

125 Charles-Louis de Secondat, baron de Montesquieu, *The Spirit of the Laws,* trans. Anne M. Cohler, Basia Carolyn Miller, and Harold Samuel Stone (Cambridge: Cambridge Univ. Press, 1989), 418. On the confusion in the eighteenth century between credit and money, see Charles Rist, *History of Monetary and Credit Theory from John Law to the Present Day,* trans. Jane Degras (New York: Augustus M. Kelley, 1966), 31–98.

126 The quotations are from Nick Yablon, "The Metropolitan Life in Ruins: Architectural and Fictional Speculations in New York, 1909–1919," *American Quarterly* 56, no. 2 (2004): 336; and Pocock, "Modes of Political and Historical Time," 92, respectively.

127 Montesquieu, *Persian Letters* (Betts), 258.

128 Walter Benjamin to Theodor Adorno, 9 December 1938, in Theodor Adorno et al., *Aesthetics and Politics,* translation edited by Ronald Taylor (London: NLB, 1977), 140; cited in Hal Foster, *Compulsive Beauty* (Cambridge: MIT Press, 1995), 151.

CHAPTER 2
Scenes from Hell

> This . . . Capitol, eternal like the city, and this city, eternal like its founder—these, in earlier times, had made an impression on the mind of the Romans which it would have been desirable to preserve.
>
> —Charles-Louis de Secondat, baron de Montesquieu (1748)[1]

> I know what it costs to establish a new religion.
>
> —Claude-Nicolas Ledoux (1775)[2]

Soon after his return to Paris in 1765 following a decade in Rome, Robert—possessed of a *ruiniste*'s affection for menaced forms—assumed the role of chronicler of the city's demolitions and disasters. Sketchbook in hand, he returned repeatedly to the charred remains of the hospital at the Hôtel-Dieu, which burned in 1772, and he caused a sensation at the Salon of 1781 with pendant works featuring the fire that had recently ravaged the Opéra (figs. 23, 24).[3] He painted explosive views of church demolitions, which occurred with some frequency after 1787, when the Église des Saints-Innocents and its overcrowded cemetery were condemned (see figs. 36, 37). Such works reflect the emergence of an aesthetic interest in catastrophe—one that developed alongside, and at times seems nearly interchangeable with, the cult of ruins. Diderot's review of Robert's paintings in 1767 abounds with signs of the affinity between the two, as when the critic observes the effect of the setting sun upon Robert's view of a dilapidated Roman palace, and promptly imagines the Salon bursting into flames—consumed, he writes, by "a large nearby conflagration that threatened the entire building." Diderot was hardly unique in associating the "poetics of ruins" with the appeal of "ravages and rubble."[4] Bernardin de Saint-Pierre ponders the existence in humankind of a "taste for destruction" before launching into a vivid account of the spectacle of Neronian Rome in flames.[5] The author's musings appear in his "Plaisir de la ruine," and it was perhaps inevitable that in the age of the Lisbon earthquake, and of the discovery of antiquity's buried cities, ruins were invested with ideas not only of duration but also of disruption: that is, with what Burke describes as the startling effects of "the sudden and unexpected."[6]

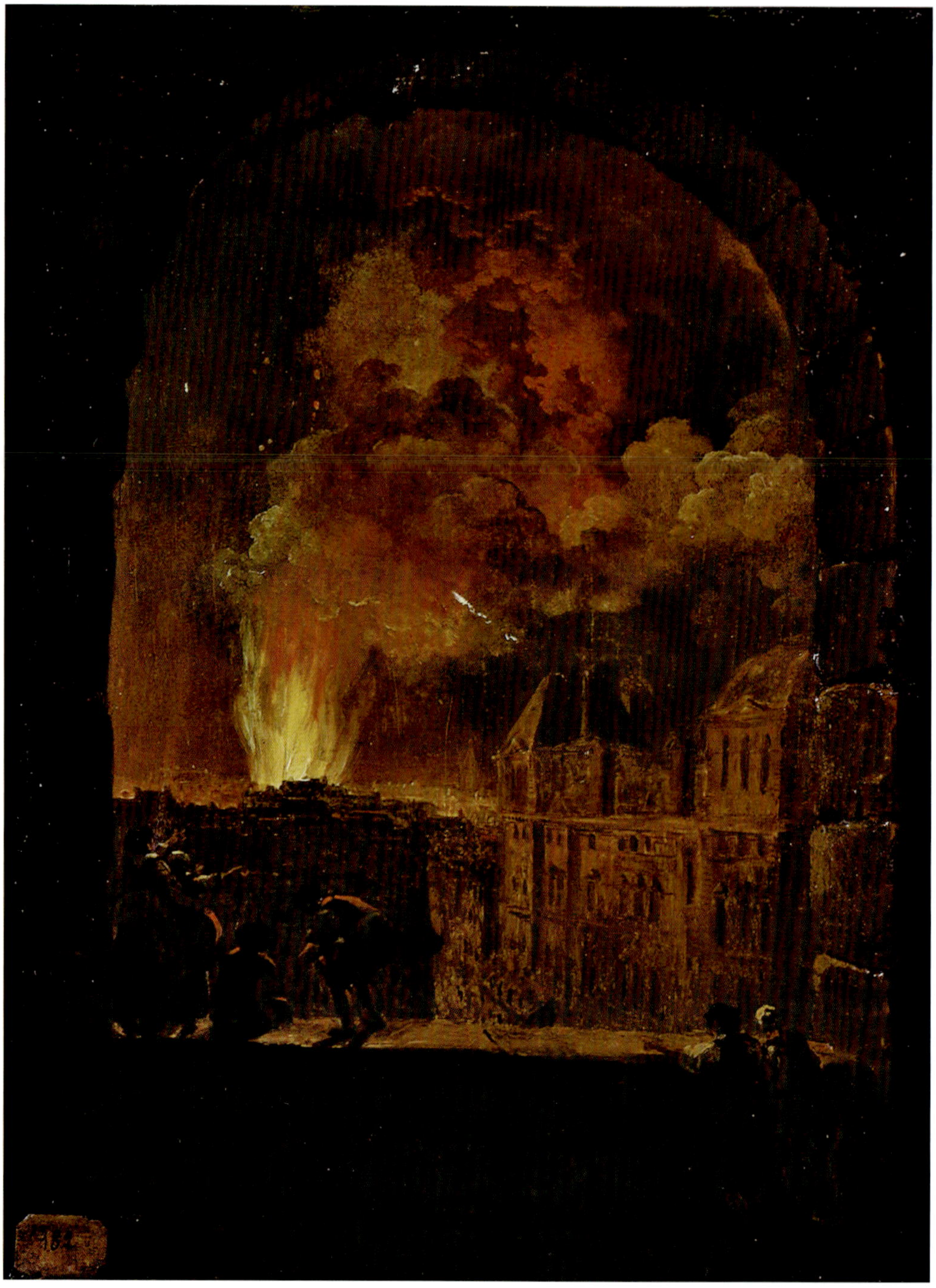

Fig. 23. Hubert Robert (French, 1733–1808)
Fire at the Opéra of the Palais-Royal, Viewed from a Crossing in the Louvre, 1781,
oil on panel, 32 × 24 cm (12⅝ × 9½ in.)
Paris, Musée de l'Opéra

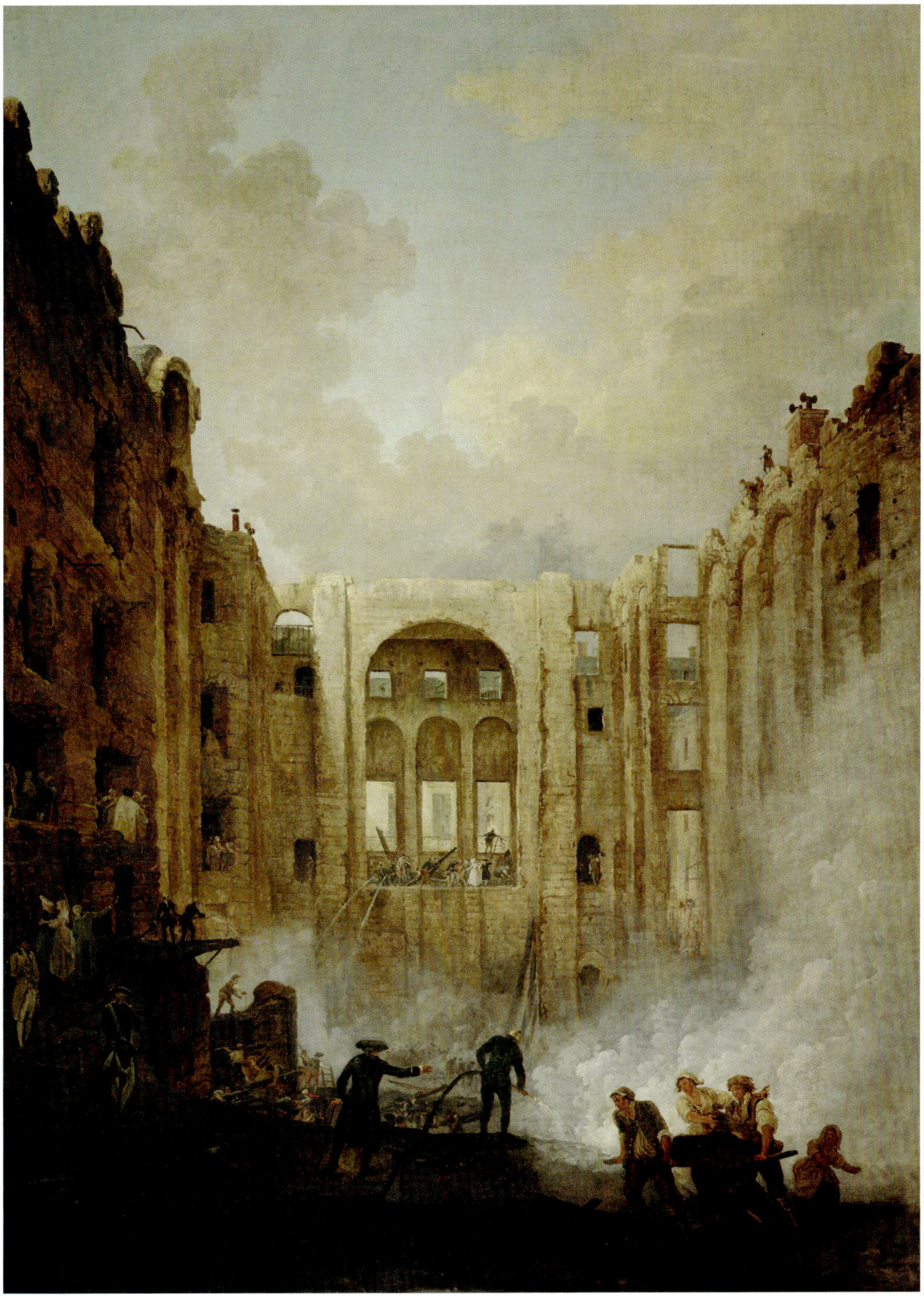

Fig. 24. Hubert Robert (French, 1733–1808)
Interior of the Opéra of the Palais-Royal the Day after the Fire, 1781, oil on canvas, 171 × 126 cm (67⅜ × 49⅝ in.)
Paris, Musée du Louvre

Robert's disaster scenes capitalized on the pleasures of unpredictable destruction—pleasures reflective of the appetite for the sublime and, as indicated in Bernardin de Saint-Pierre's reverie, of the pastime of turning antiquity's calamitous events into sources of delectation. More specifically, such artworks reveal the hold over Parisian imaginations exercised by visions of Pompeii-esque cataclysm at a time when the French capital was preparing itself for modernization. Returning from Rome, Robert encountered a disaster-prone city whose perpetual redevelopment was largely financed by his risk-courting patron class. He painted his views of the capital's ruins during a period when the creation of capacious boulevards, Neoclassical monuments, and new quarters (*nouvelles villes*) gave Paris the look of an endless construction site, and when apprehensions of a "building epidemic" intersected with fantasies of the city's end.[7] As shall be discussed, Robert's paintings basked in the association between volatile urban transformation and the ascendancy of a speculative economy. The climate of recklessness in which they were produced was one saturated with imaginings of Paris's ruin, as well as with meditations on the downfalls of capitals past. Though inasmuch as they inevitably promoted submission to an order of uncertainty, such imaginings were as complicit in the consolidation of risk culture as they were resistant to it.

Robert's dramatic views of disaster invite attention to his own entrepreneurial instincts. At a time when the circulation of town planning initiatives left Parisians well versed in the economic, aesthetic, and hygienic necessity of urban improvement, the painter recognized in the changing face of the city a subject worthy of grand-scale, publicly exhibited paintings.[8] Moreover, far from neutralizing the novelty value of such subjects, Robert exploited it—as demonstrated in the case of his pendants featuring the destroyed Opéra. The paintings garnered attention for their startling subject matter and sloppy handling—not to mention their considerable selling price: Girardot de Marigny—the banker and soon-to-be head of the Caisse d'escompte (the institution that introduced bank notes into general circulation)—purchased the pair for 100 louis (2,400 livres) each. As François Métra, writing in the *Correspondance secrète,* recounted, "Robert has well painted and still better sold two fires at the Opéra that have attracted everyone's attention." Two princes were reportedly competing for the canvases when they found themselves outbid by Girardot. Robert "wants to be paid in the way he executes," the chronicler explained dryly: "Of all the painters, he's the quickest."[9]

Robert's hurried execution of the paintings within six weeks of the fire that destroyed the Opéra, and just in time for the exhibition, was not lost on critics. As Antoine Renou, in an effort to make sense of the work's compositional errors, put it: "Robert undoubtedly believed that this moment should be rendered as rapidly as it was perceived."[10] The first view, featuring the fire as viewed through a window in the Louvre—where Robert was then lodging—presented distortions of scale so exaggerated as to arouse laughter: according to one commentator, the dwarfed figures, shown ogling at the faraway spectacle, wore the dress of Italian peasants, prompting him to allege sarcastically that the canvas depicted the Opéra's demise from a distance of several thousand miles (see fig. 23). The critic went on to mock the painting's theatrically dark palette, before dismissing the second view—displaying the Opéra as it appeared the day after the fire—as an unbearable "mess of debris" (see fig. 24). The indignation aroused by the sight of the ruined monument was perhaps best expressed by a writer for the *Mercure de France* who, after condemning the first painting ("no truth in the color, no clarity in the architecture"), castigated the subject matter of its pendant. Describing a "carcass of a building... with no decoration, badly drawn figures... and lots of white smoke," the exasperated critic demanded, "Why would [such] details occupy a distinguished artist?"[11]

With few exceptions (including one critic who declared Robert to have "perfectly rendered the beautiful horror"), the critics panned the pendants as outrageous subversions of academic convention. The subject of contemporary catastrophe belonged to the lowly medium of the documentary print, not to the elevated precincts of painting—thus the *Mercure*'s bewildered response: "Is *this* the stuff of painting?"[12] Most of all, the works detracted from the otherwise progressive tenor of that year's Salon. Mouffle d'Angerville, reviewing the exhibition for the *Mémoires secrets,* hardly had Robert's pendants in mind when he reported that the "siècle de Louis XVI" was off to a most promising start. The critic's confidence in the "restoration of the arts" rather reflected the concentration of state-commissioned, large-scale history paintings—works by the Académie's precocious newcomers, David, François-Guillaume Ménageot, François-André Vincent, Jean-Simon Berthélemy, and Joseph-Benoît Suvée. As David's *Belisarius* and Ménageot's *Leonardo Dying in the Arms of Francis I* made resoundingly clear, the public could expect that the future of the arts lay in the masterful transmission of meaningful narratives from the past.[13]

In their own way, Robert's views of the Opéra similarly recovered a version of history, but one as ominous and unwelcome as the narratives commemorated by David and his generation were moving and instructive. The Italian dress worn by the figures in his *Fire at the Opéra* compounds the scene's resemblance to a modern-day version of Vesuvius. The precedent of monumental antiquity infuses his *Interior of the Opéra* (see fig. 24), a massive structure reminiscent—with its cavities, blind arches, and crenellated stones that prematurely crumble—of a Roman ruin. The elegant curiosity seekers at left recall grand tourists admiring the ruins of the Eternal City, an effect that is even more pronounced in a drawing Robert executed of the same subject (fig. 25). The painter's perfunctory record of contemporaneity thus also appears to be a palimpsest of the distant past, eerily accelerated into the present.

A preliminary sketch he produced of the Opéra's interior, moreover, suggests that Robert labored to ensure that the final painting would stir ideas of ancient ruin unmediated by transcendent morality tales (fig. 26). In the sketch, the two men transporting a cadaver from the ashes evoke, in their gravity, the bearers of Phocion's corpse in Poussin's famous painting. Étienne Baudet had produced an engraving of the painting in 1684, and Robert (whose debts to Poussin were explored in the previous chapter) may have had the *Landscape with the Funeral of Phocion* in mind when he conceived the vignette (fig. 27). If so, he subsequently extricated himself from the source: in his final painting, the corpse-bearers—who appear distinctly less dignified here than in the sketch, due in part to the addition of a distraught woman and child—no longer exit the scene stage right, as their counterparts in *Phocion* do. (Additionally, the white sheet in Robert's sketch has given way to a brown one in the painting—an effect that distinguishes the cadaver from the smoky backdrop, while also undermining its resemblance to Poussin's Athenian hero.) The sympathetic bystanders in the foreground of the sketch—figures who inject the tragedy with meaning

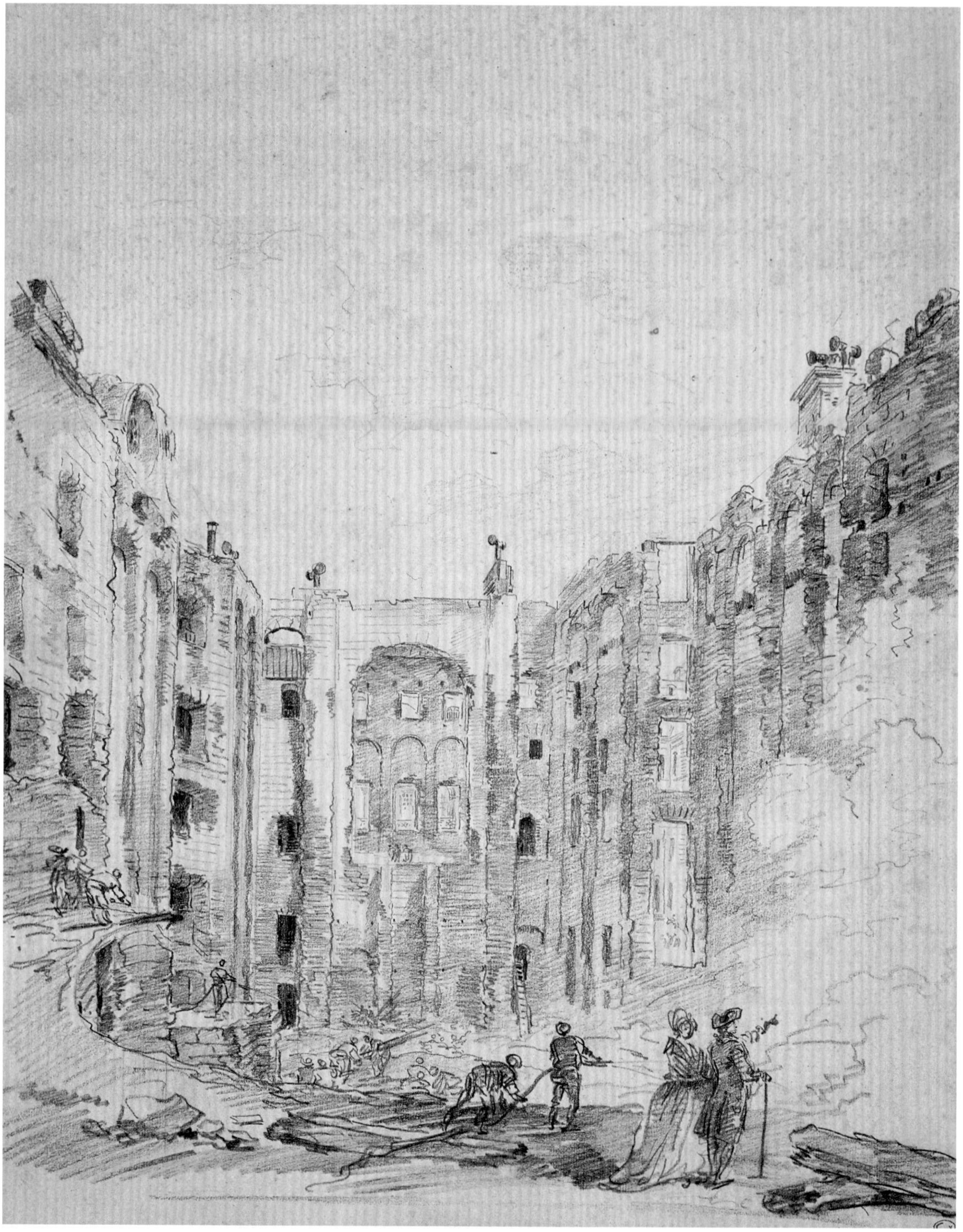

Fig. 25. Hubert Robert (French, 1733–1808)
Ruins of the Opéra after the Fire of 1781, 1781, black chalk on ivory laid paper, 46.3 × 36.3 cm (18¼ × 14¼ in.)

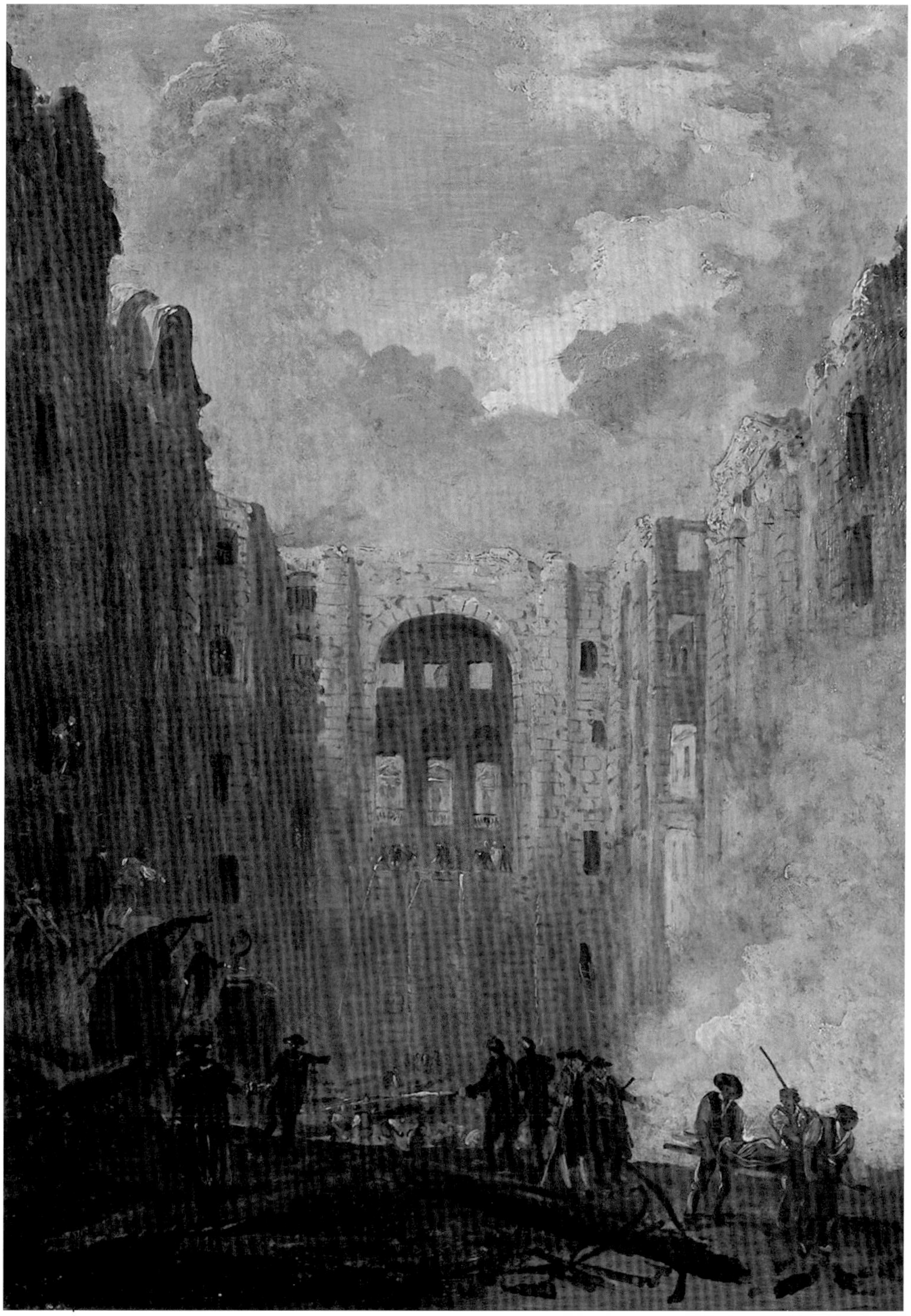

Fig. 26. Hubert Robert (French, 1733–1808)
Interior of the Opéra of the Palais-Royal after the Fire, 1781, oil on panel, 32 × 24 cm (12⅝ × 9½ in.)
Paris, Musée de l'Opéra

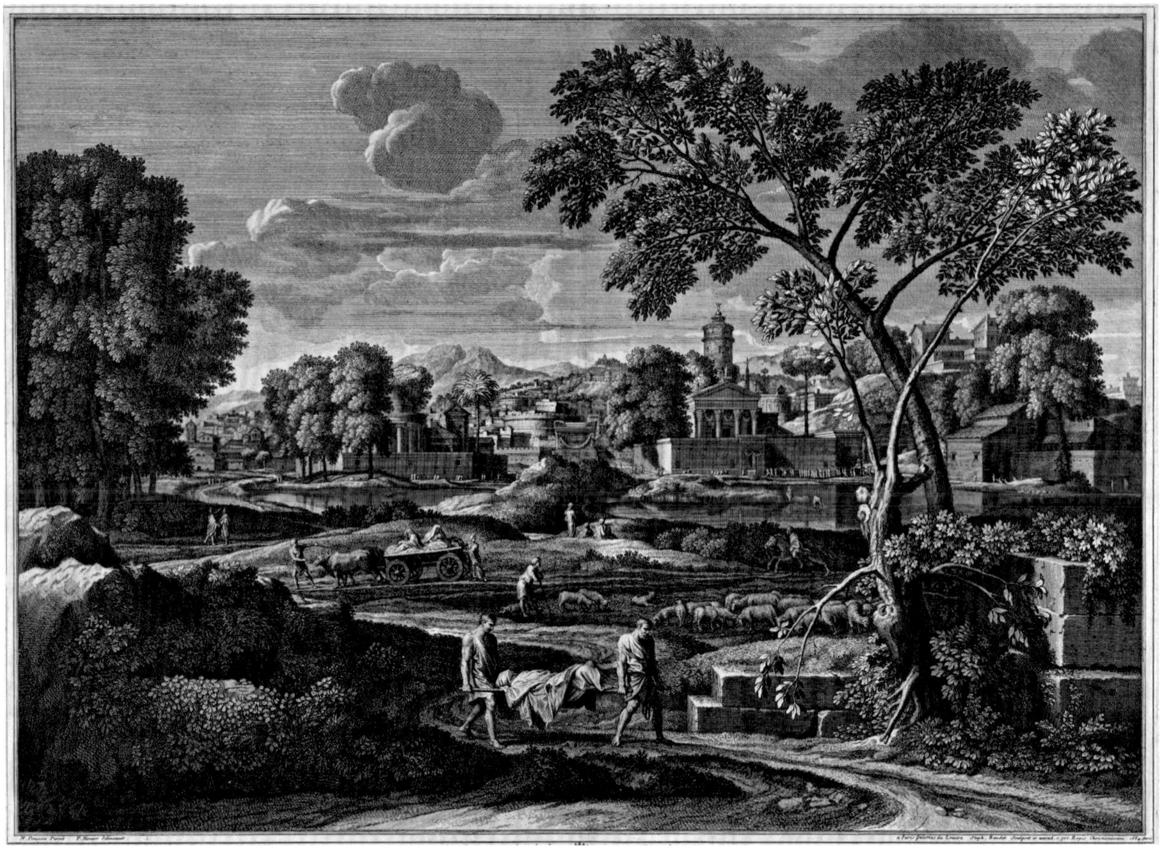

Fig. 27. Étienne Baudet (French, ca. 1638–1711), after Nicolas Poussin (French, 1594–1665)
Landscape with the Funeral of Phocion (1648), 1684, engraving, 57.2 × 75.7 cm (22½ × 29¾ in.)
Los Angeles, Getty Research Institute

by compelling pity in the beholder—are excluded from the painting. In their place, ungainly protagonists deflect, rather than attract, attention, for the true subject of Robert's work is the curiosity of the Opéra's destruction; it is not the rescue workers with whom the viewer identifies but rather the various onlookers shown peering at the disaster scene from the windows and heights of the ruin. The effect is to travesty history painting by substituting for its immutable ideals the senselessness of "sudden and unexpected" destruction.

In so doing, Robert's pendants forced acknowledgment of the perverse extent to which antiquity's grip on modern imaginations loosened that of Classicism. The *anticomanie* emblematized by the artworks answered to a craving not for high-minded subjects but rather for narratives of Vesuvian disaster—one that fed on fantasies of urban debacle. Although from the outcry over the canvases, one would hardly guess that eviscerated European capitals were becoming something of a leitmotif, sounding the age's penchant for the sublime. In his *Salon de 1767*, for example, Diderot imagines Paris decimated by fire: "The spectacle of Paris in flames would horrify you.... This terrible conflagration, in which men, women, children ... all perished, overwhelms you; you flee, you avert your gaze, you close your ears to the screams." And yet, observes the critic, "after a certain lapse of time you'd enjoy strolling through the ashes."[14] Similarly, Bernardin de Saint-Pierre—picturing the sight of the fire set by Nero ("those long flames that, in the middle of the night, lick the heavens")—remarks that "great destruction" pleases, for "our soul, being in movement, loves all extraordinary emotions." A few years later, in a memoir written about his trip to Italy, Charles-

Marguerite-Jean-Baptiste Mercier Dupaty described a giant conflagration at Saint Peter's Square—a "magnificent" event, though entirely fictive.[15]

Such lurid accounts took their cue from Burke's *Philosophical Enquiry into the Origin of Our Ideas of the Sublime and Beautiful,* available in French translation since 1765. Burke's study explores the power exerted over the imagination by the sublime, defined as "whatever is fitted . . . to excite the ideas of pain . . . danger . . . [and] terror." From literary depictions of the wrath of God to the mysteries of Stonehenge, the sublime incited fear tinged with rapture. Suggests Burke, the enjoyment of beholding disaster was divinely ordained, for being drawn to the misfortune suffered by others served to reinforce the "bond of sympathy." In this way, Burke seeks to explain why "terror is a passion which always produces delight when it does not press too close," and why, as Diderot too would recognize, "there is no spectacle we so eagerly pursue, as that of some uncommon and grievous calamity"—a point he illustrates vividly:

> This noble capital, the pride of England and of Europe, I believe no man is so strangely wicked as to desire to see destroyed by a conflagration or an earthquake, though he should be removed himself to the greatest distance from the danger. But suppose such a fatal accident to have happened, what numbers from all parts would croud to behold the ruins, and amongst them many who would have been content never to have seen London in its glory?[16]

Catastrophe, then, functioned as the ultimate medium for an aesthetic category whose distinctiveness Voltaire succinctly captured: "To build is beautiful, but to destroy is sublime."[17] As Mercier noted, "The sublime . . . accompanies great disasters, calamities, floods that batter and crush the human species . . . the burning of cities, earthquakes." So too, as his writings suggest, did a fascination with the sublime betray a growing sense of doom: "Thebes, Tyr, Persepolis, Carthage, Palmyra, are no more. These cities that stood proudly on the globe, whose grandeur, power and solidity seemed to promise almost eternal duration have left hardly a trace of the places they occupied." Will it be "an earthquake," Mercier continues, "a flood . . . a fire that will annihilate" Paris? Natural disasters, he concludes, "are nothing" compared with the man-made ones that threaten to level "populous cities."[18]

Such dire prognostications abounded in the last decades of the century. They did so, moreover, at a time when catastrophe emerged as "one of the great growth industries."[19] The period witnessed a vogue for artificial volcanoes (followed by earthquakes)—terror-inducing *fabriques* that testified to the cultivation of pastimes geared toward converting dread into pleasure. Chambers's influential *Dissertation on Oriental Gardening* of 1772 cemented a fad for what he describes as "terrible" gardens, where "large volumes of flame" emanated from "deep caverns" and "subterranean habitations."[20] Volcanoes, along with fires and scenes of hell, appeared in Philippe de Loutherbourg's celebrated optical spectacle, the Eidophusikon, which had its London premiere in 1781. At the same time, Vesuvius—which remained in a near constant state of eruption from 1770 to 1790—became a major tourist attraction. Robert thus painted his *Opéra* views in a culture marked by an ever-more-extravagant taste for "the eruptive sublime."[21] And seen from a certain perspective, his blatantly theatrical pendants not only exhibit but also appear to make light of the mounting desire to recreate primordial chaos. It is tempting to interpret the first of his views in particular as a tongue-in-cheek tribute to a contemporary impulse to bring Pompeii to Paris. With its volcanic imagery, the painting recalls the sensational moonlit views of the erupting volcano produced by Vernet's pupil Pierre-Jacques Volaire whose masterful draftsmanship Robert could only parody.

Robert's pendants suspended seriousness; the laughter of the critics confirmed as much. Yet, in addition to derisive banter, the paintings also provoked a genuine discomfort, as revealed by the *Mercure de France* review. Devoid of the naturalism of Volaire as well as of the epic content of Vernet's celebrated shipwreck scenes, Robert's canvases frankly confessed the self-sufficiency of disaster as a subject matter—its power to arrest the beholder regardless of the presence of heroes and villains. What is more, their very artifice plainly captured the manufactured quality of "catastrophilia." Robert was well placed to appreciate the commodification of natural disaster, and it is worth considering that, in poking fun at the gloomy fixation on calamitous scenarios, he was equally ironizing his own production. For one thing, as noted in the previous chapter, the painter was among several well-regarded artists to assist in the illustration of Saint-Non's *Voyage pittoresque; ou, Description des royaumes de Naples et de Sicile,* the inaugural volume of which appeared the year that Robert produced his pendants. The travel guide is strewn with hair-raising accounts of misadventure amidst southern Italy's recently discovered disaster sites. Robert's contributions included a view of Vesuvius erupting—executed in absentia (!)—featuring the tower of lava exploding into the heavens and onto the page, menacing the text as well as the minute figures shown cavorting at the base of the mountain (fig. 28). The vignette illustrates a colorful tale by the narrator, recounting his near death experience touring the volcano.[22] Epitomizing the spirit of the *Voyage pittoresque* were the compositions of the painter-printmaker Desprez, who supplied more than 130 images, the majority of which appealed to a fondness for the ghoulish and the occult. One such view imaginatively depicts the Temple of Isis in Pompeii "as it would have appeared in the year A.D. 79 at the time that it was destroyed by the eruption of Vesuvius" (fig. 29). The dramatic frontality of the temple positions the viewer center stage in a scene of ecstatic and mysterious ritual, while overhead the darkened sky already hints at the impending disaster. The artist employed the newly developed technique of color mezzotint, the invention of which allowed printmakers to mine painting's "animated characteristics," its capacity to "give . . . life," and indeed, Desprez's achievement of painterly chiaroscuro heightens the work's effect of bone-chilling immediacy. In this same spirit of transgressing the border between past and present, the ruins of Pompeii and Herculaneum stir the narrator to imagine the unearthing in two thousand years' time of a buried provincial city on French soil.[23]

When Robert, then, exhibited his pendant views of the Opéra in 1781, he did so in a cultural climate mesmerized by antiquity's disaster sites. At around the same time that subscribers received the first installment of the *Voyage pittoresque,* Sylvain Maréchal began issuing his eight-volume work, *Les antiquités d'Herculanum,* which explicated the artworks and rituals of "our ancestors."[24] The ancient past was made newly proximate for an audience eager to commune with its traumatized forebears. Of course, Robert was not the only witness of the fire at the Opéra who was reminded of A.D. 79: "Imagine my surprise," declared Réstif de La Bretonne, recounting his

Fig. 28. Hubert Robert (French, 1733–1808); engraved by Carl Guttenberg (German, 1743–90) *Vue de la sommité et du crater du Vesuve, au moment de la derniere eruption arrivée le 8. d'août 1779. à 9. heures du soir* (View of the summit and crater of Vesuvius in the last eruption on 8 August 1779 at nine o'clock in the evening) From Jean-Claude Richard de Saint-Non, *Voyage pittoresque; ou, Description des royaumes de Naples et de Sicile,* vol. 1 (Paris, 1781), 208

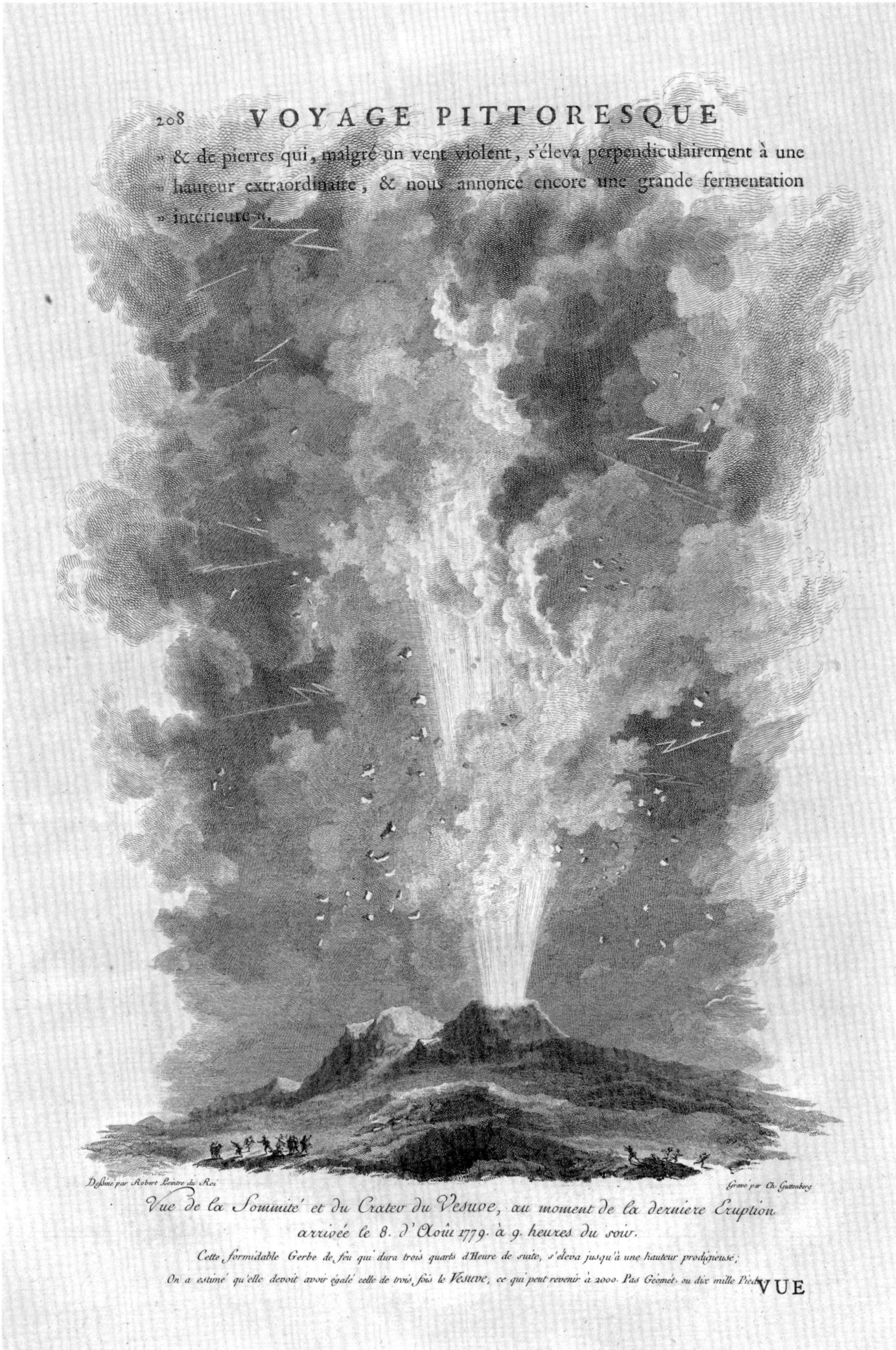
208 VOYAGE PITTORESQUE
» & de pierres qui, malgré un vent violent, s'éleva perpendiculairement à une
» hauteur extraordinaire, & nous annonce encore une grande fermentation
» intérieure ».
Dessiné par Robert Peintre du Roi
Gravé par Ch. Guttenberg
Vue de la Sommité et du Cratere du Vesuve, au moment de la derniere Eruption
arrivée le 8. d'Août 1779. à 9. heures du soir.
Cette formidable Gerbe de feu qui dura trois quarts d'Heure de suite, s'éleva jusqu'à une hauteur prodigieuse;
On a estimé qu'elle devoit avoir égalé celle de trois fois le Vesuve, ce qui peut revenir à 2000. Pas Géomét. ou dix mille Pieds.
VUE

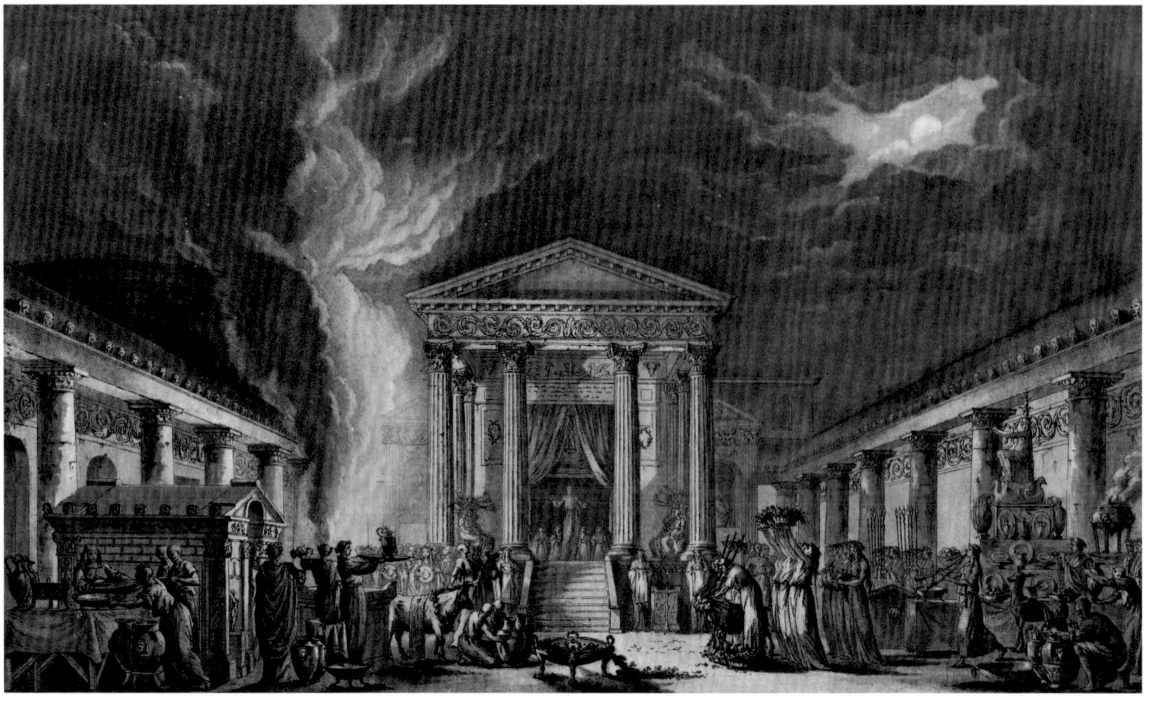

Fig. 29. Louis-Jean Desprez (French, 1743–1804)
Temple of Isis in Pompeii as It Would Have Appeared in the Year A.D. 79 at the Time That It Was Destroyed by the Eruption of Vesuvius
From Jean-Claude Richard de Saint-Non, *Voyage pittoresque; ou, Description des royaumes de Naples et de Sicile,* vol. 2 (Paris, 1782), no. 75

evening walk, "at seeing a bright and terrible blaze rising in the middle of town!... I have never seen a more exact replica of Vesuvius or Etna.... The fire was a horrifying sight.... What power nature has, in this terrible element! How fearsome a blazing volcano must be!" Réstif proceeded to describe an exchange he overheard between two passersby, discussing—in the vernacular language of popular science—what he called "an apt truth." As one man patiently explained to the other, given the growing disequilibrium in the universe between fire and water, "the conflagration of the entire globe" was only a matter of time.[25]

If Robert's pendants denaturalized the attraction to sublime calamity, Desprez's *Temple of Isis,* more than portraying fear over the end of the world, served to activate it: the engraving played at abolishing the interval of centuries separating the ancients from the moderns, so as to place viewers in the psychic space formerly occupied by the residents of Herculaneum and Pompeii. Desprez's image may well have been influenced by a historiography on ancient religion that included Nicolas-Antoine Boulanger's seminal volume, *L'antiquité dévoilée par ses usages* (Antiquity unveiled through its customs; 1766). The study concerned the lasting effects of the memory of primordial disaster—namely, the flood—on human behavior, and specifically on the propensity for religious belief. Along with George-Louis Leclerc de Buffon and John Locke, David Hume and Paul Henri Dietrich, baron d'Holbach, Boulanger sought to disenchant the foundations of religion by demonstrating to readers that the passions driving their faith—terror, superstition, and dread of an unknown future—were remnants of a psyche battered by ancient cataclysm.[26] Given that religion, according to Boulanger, originally served to alleviate the traumatic memory of catastrophic events while promising protection from them in the future, the enactment of religious ritual in Desprez's print renders the calamity to come all the more tragic. It is ironic that the interest in antiquity's fear-driven occult practices—exemplified in

Desprez's print—may have had roots in sympathetic accounts, like Boulanger's, of primitive terror as "the true portal to our history." ("I saw written in nature," professes Boulanger, "that man was thrown into profound turmoil by his misfortunes; I saw that he trembled; I saw that he became sad, melancholy and religious to an extreme; I saw that he conceived a total disgust for this unfortunate world.")[27] Whereas the aesthetic of sublime destruction valorized terror as the most powerful of emotions, Boulanger's study endeavored to demystify disaster along with the religion to which it gave rise.

An engineer who reputedly took note of the earth's primordial scars while cutting roads through the eastern region of the kingdom, Boulanger claimed to have uncovered the material origins of religion. Describing the volcanic eruptions and flooding that besieged the planet, he showed that "there was nothing in the mind which had not previously been in the senses—not even Hell—and there had once been a Hell on earth."[28] Naturally, the primitives, delirious with terror, had turned to religion—that "institution of mysteries," writes Boulanger, that made man "forget his frightening chimeras and mournful preoccupations," thus transforming a traumatized order into a social one. For "all peoples who have been deprived of mystery" have "remained errant, ferocious . . . savage and barbarous." Liberating primitive peoples from their "troubles and fears," "fables . . . civilize[d]" them.[29]

Boulanger and his fellow philosophes instructed their readers, as Holbach put it, that "the objects and ideas capable of exciting them most violently had no reality at all and were only words devoid of meaning, phantasms born of ignorance and altered by a sick imagination."[30] And yet, however much Boulanger strove to emancipate his readers from the shackles of superstition, his palpable sympathy for his shell-shocked subjects laid bare an ambivalence about the future—a suspicion that the Enlightenment belief in progress was potentially no less irrational than belief in the gods. Hume, too, expressed doubt about humankind's ability to tolerate, without turning to religion, the enmeshed sentiments of hope and fear that dominated existence. Such narratives as theirs implicitly questioned civilization's linear advance.[31] They raised the prospect that on the other side of modern rationality lay the primitive's unhinging capacity for terror.

Indeed, Boulanger's discoveries had the inadvertent effect of narrowing the gap between the ancient and the modern, for studies like his helped fuel a kind of millenarian identification with the victims of primordial cataclysm. According to Mercier, invoking "an uninterrupted tradition" of natural disaster—from the flooding of oceans to the eruptions of volcanoes—the mind was imprinted with "the terrors of ancient upheavals," much as the earth bore "visible and profound traces of ruins and devastations." The chronicler's writings echoed popular belief—fed by a scientific literature on the earth's perishability—in the imminence of the end of the world. In his *Tableau de Paris,* Mercier describes the sense of savage fright that overtook the city in 1784, when the Académie des sciences circulated evidence supporting the rumor that a comet would strike the planet, and Parisians—"pale and melancholy"—rushed to the confessionals.[32] The episode points up the possibility that acquainting modern subjects with their tormented antecedents served not to disabuse them of supernatural belief but rather to strengthen it.

Boulanger's study, in its inability to pry rationality from regressive impulses—the archaic character of supernatural belief from its productive role in the civilizing

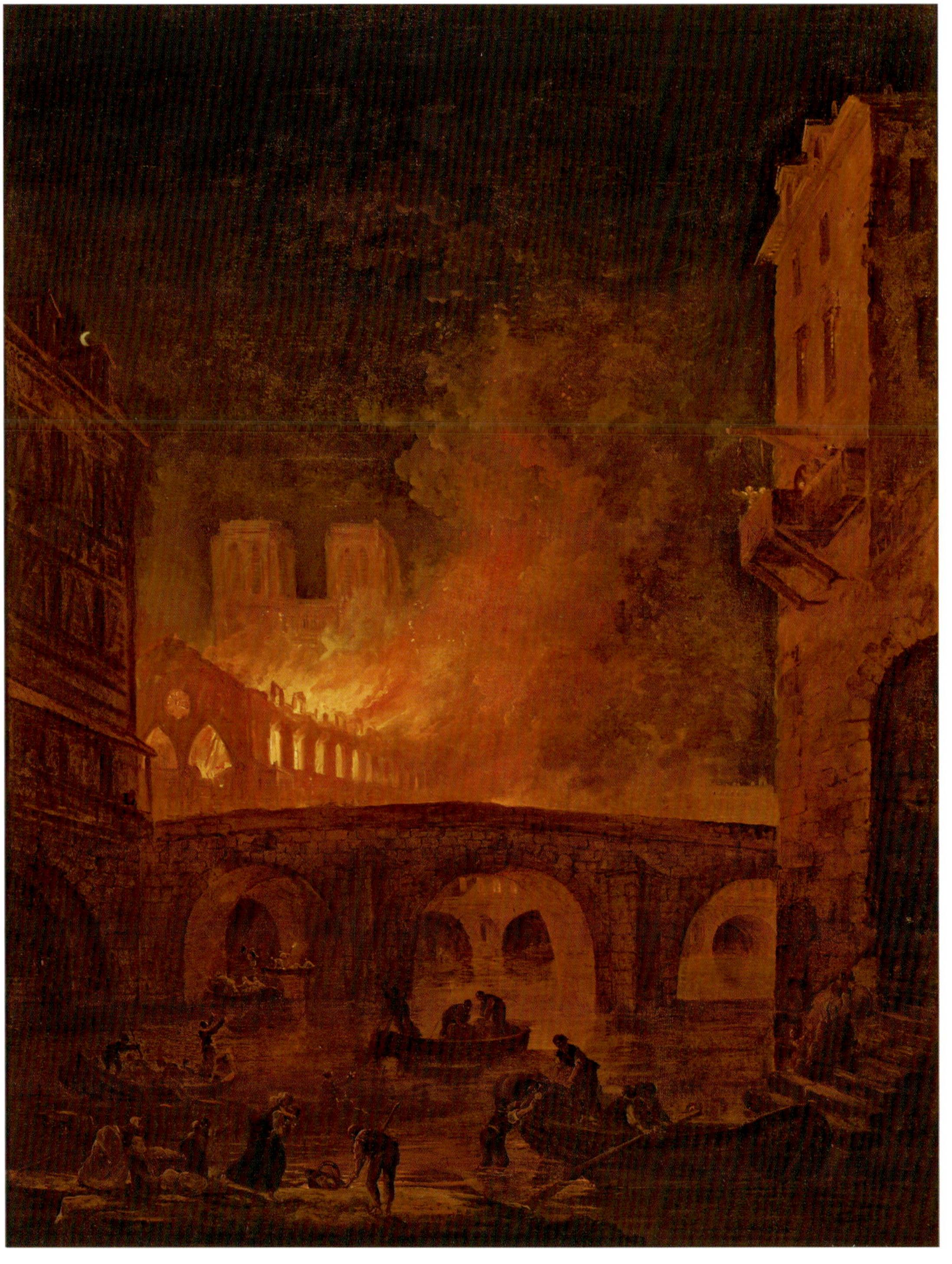

Fig. 30. Hubert Robert (French, 1733–1808)
The Fire at the Hôtel-Dieu in Paris, 1772, 1773, oil on canvas, 145 × 109 cm (57⅛ × 42⅞ in.)
Stockholm, Nationalmuseum

process—exhibited a predicament that may similarly be tracked in Robert's disaster scenes. For what evidently interested the painter in the subject of modern-day calamities was their tendency to trigger the memory of catastrophes past: his *Interior of the Opéra* (see fig. 24) appears to capture on the one hand a local disaster imperiling the Louvre and the neighboring Palais-Royal and on the other hand the reincarnation of Vesuvius. Similarly, his *Fire at the Hôtel-Dieu in Paris* (fig. 30) offers a view at once of the conflagration suspended above the Seine's Petit Pont and, ineluctably, of the apocalypse replete with the River Styx—thereby tapping into what Bernard Groethuysen, describing the lingering image of hell, calls the "last remnant among the worldly of a constantly shrinking religious experience."[33]

Robert's disasters appear to have addressed themselves, then, as much to the sophisticated skeptic as to the believer within the nonbeliever. In contradistinction to the feverish, proto-Romantic morbidity of Desprez, his paintings play simultaneously at inciting terror and dispelling it. Thus in his view of the burning hospital, the fire—set back in space and theatrically framed by two buildings—is contained, however momentarily, by a kind of rote application of the conventions of harmonious composition. In Robert's *Fire at the Opéra*, an exaggerated distance separates the viewers from the disaster site. Such works recall the origins of ancient terror if only to neutralize the threat of its resurgence, thus affirming the evolved status of the modern subject—his remoteness from the traumatized condition of Boulanger's primitives. And yet, Robert's paintings, in resurrecting the ghosts of the past, nonetheless flirted

Fig. 31. Hubert Robert (French, 1733–1808)
The Burning of Rome, 1773, oil on canvas, 73.4 × 94.9 cm (28⅞ × 37⅜ in.)
Frankfurt am Main, Städel Museum

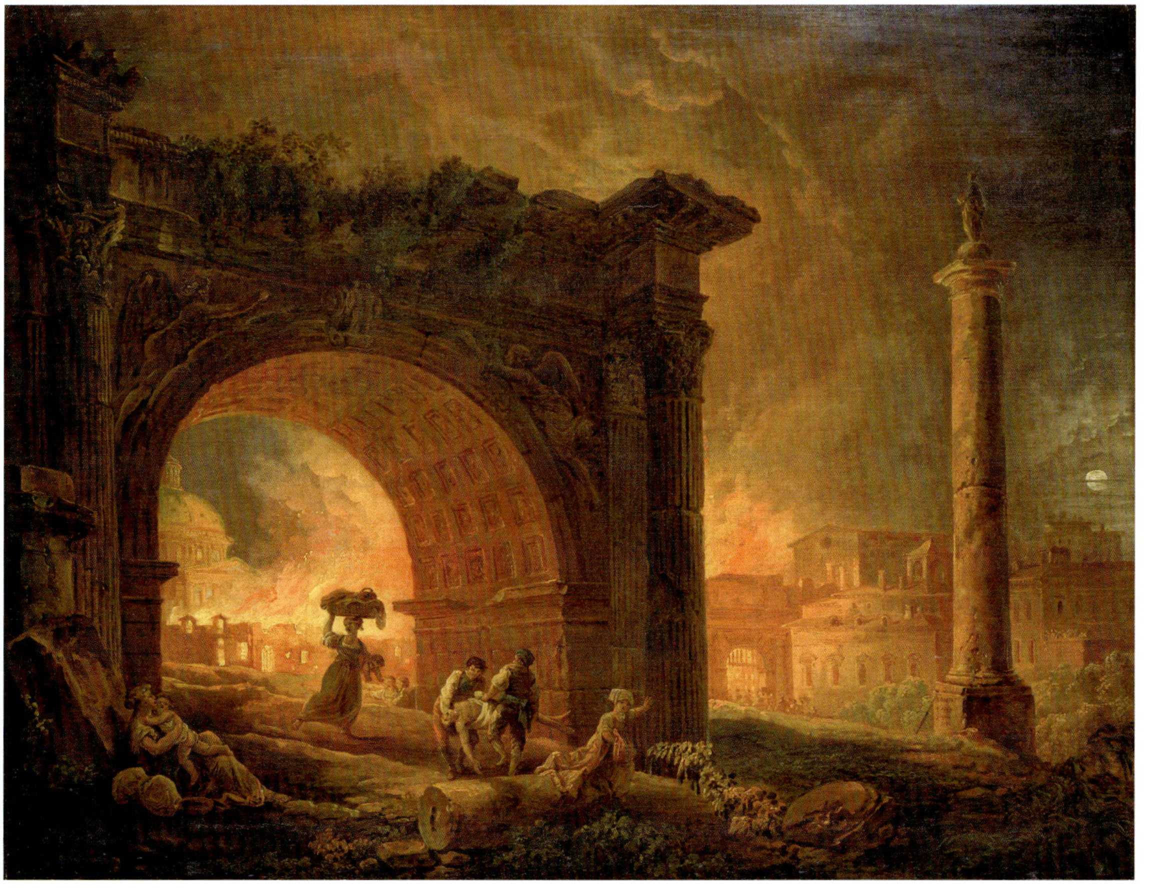

with the possibility that the modern capital was falling victim to some ancient pattern of destruction. It is notable that at the Salon of 1785, the painter exhibited pendant canvases, *The Burning of Rome* and *The Ancient Monuments of France,* a coupling that distinguished the two capitals while also fusing them suggestively under the sign of calamity. Similarly, Robert's *Burning of Rome* of 1773 was executed soon after his view of the burning hospital at the Hôtel-Dieu in Paris and was evidently inspired by it (fig. 31).[34] Such works underscored the divide between contemporary delight and primitive dread. As intimations of cyclical destruction, however, they also put forth the disquieting suggestion that modern Paris was channeling antiquity's dark side.

Regression and Its Discontents

Adding to the suspense sustained in Robert's conflagration paintings—between submission to and triumph over the fate of the ancients, between civilization's reversal and its advance—were the dueling valences of fire in contemporary imaginations. Mercier wrote admiringly of fire as that which at once "conserves and devours," being at once "the force and life of the universe" and "the most violent, the most rapid destroyer of its forms."[35] The salutary yet destructive character of fire was widely discussed among advocates of urban renewal in Paris. Fire posed a persistent and grave danger in the capital: outbreaks are routinely recorded in the diary kept (from 1764 through 1789) by the bookseller Siméon-Prosper Hardy, and fire twice destroyed the Opéra during the course of the century.[36] Yet according to urban reformers, Parisians were equally endangered by an overall climate of filth, stench, and refuse, compounded by a densely built and chaotically organized center. So treacherous seemed conditions in the capital that advocates of rebuilding it wistfully invoked the potential upside of its annihilation by fire. The police chief Nicolas Delamare recounted with approval Nero's burning of Rome, which led to the building of wider and more magnificent streets. Similarly, Voltaire, writing in 1749, enthusiastically narrated the dramatic improvements made to London following the fire of 1666, and dreamt of the "superb" and "magnificen[t]" city that could be built, if only Paris would burn. A few decades later, Mercier, opining that "everything of grandeur is the result of accident," concluded: "One can't deny that fires have been useful for the embellishment of the city."[37]

Indeed, partisans of change welcomed conflagration as a catastrophic event that nonetheless expedited the work of reform, and the perceived virtue of fire as an efficient tool of progress ought not to be divorced from the gleeful tone of a painting like Robert's *Fire at the Hôtel-Dieu* (see fig. 30). By the middle of the century, Paris was conceived as a sick patient, with obstructed arteries and a circulatory system ridden with toxins, and no small amount of blame for the city's deteriorating condition was placed on the hospital. Situated at the center of the city on the banks of the Seine, the hospital, site of five conflagrations during the eighteenth century, was feared to be more than just a fire hazard. The notoriously overcrowded institution was criticized for the soaring death rate of its patients, as well as for contaminating the air and water of the city. The engineer Pierre Patte and a host of lawyers, doctors, and Physiocrats urged a reform of the hospital system that would begin with its relocation.[38] An example of poor urban planning as well as indifference to the public welfare, the hospital—administered for six centuries by an order of Augustinian nuns—embodied the antithesis of the aims of the Enlightenment. The fire of 1772 created an opportunity to both reform the hospital and beautify the capital—as the architect Bernard Poyet demonstrated in a proposal to rebuild the institution on the city's periphery, by the Île des Cygnes, in the magnificent form of a modern-day Coliseum.[39] Financial supporters of the (failed) movement to relocate the hospital included Robert's patrons Girardot de Marigny, who purchased his *Opéra* views, and the banker Laborde. Needless to say, such civic involvement often followed as much from the moneymaking opportunities created by urban improvement as from enlightened concern.[40]

Heightening fire's capacity to generate a pleasurable sort of terror, then, was its colossal potential to advance, even while threatening, the general good. What critics condemned as Robert's incorporation of "thankless [*ingrats*] subjects" into the space of the Salon thus found its legitimacy in the public utility of catastrophe.[41] Significantly, the celebratory treatment of fire in Robert's paintings—the imparting of a positive charge to the violence of negation—accorded with the logic of *embellissement.* Despite connoting the addition to the city of decorative features, embellishment gradually came to signify their subtraction. Urban reform manifestos such as Patte's, listing the innumerable blights of the capital—houses piled pell-mell one upon the other, narrow and tortuous streets causing perpetual traffic congestion and endangering pedestrians, a lack of direct routes from one place to the next preventing the efficient circulation of goods and people—present embellishment as a euphemism for mass demolition. Though it bore obvious associations with visual concerns, embellishment increasingly functioned as the science of the invisible, specifically of air quality, circulation, and hygiene.[42] Despite being hailed as an instrument of progress, embellishment crystallized, in the eyes of the architect Jean-Louis Viel de Saint-Maux, the two-faced nature of urban reform.

In his *Lettres sur l'architecture des anciens et celle des modernes* (1787), Viel refutes the promise of urban reform to deliver the city to a progressive and rational future. Reform, he argues, resulted from a misguided philosophy of architecture that had been in place for centuries. Bitterly contrasting the ancient cult of monuments with the modern delight in demolition, Viel concludes that Paris is fundamentally hostile to the principles of architecture. In ancient times, he explains, monuments were venerated as sources of "instruction and happiness." Guarantors of agricultural fecundity—mediating not only between the heavens and the earth but between the sciences and the arts—they preserved like an "indelible book" the traces of human progress and the "inseparable connections" (*rapports inséparables*) that bound together all aspects of society. Severing the links that monuments once held intact, and willfully obscuring the "symbolic spirit" of ancient edifices, the moderns had reduced architecture to an art of empty imitation, befitting a society devoid of fixed principles. Only by misrepresenting the achievements of the ancients had modernity propagated the myth of its superiority. Alienated from its roots, architecture contentedly recycled the forms of antiquity bereft of all substance. Urban reform—in its enthusiasm for dismantling the capital's edifices—reflected the character of a nation recoiling from its past. No architect, Viel declares, had yet proposed a plan for urban improvement that did not first require "razing Paris." Monuments, he laments, are demolished even before they are completed. The fashion for ruins, he adds, only confirmed the extent to which demolitions had become a national pastime.[43] The observation brings Viel's *Lettres* into dialogue not only with Patte's sweeping agenda for reform but also with Bernardin de Saint-Pierre's meditation, in his "Plaisir de la ruine," on the "taste for destruction."

According to Viel's vitriolic assessment, the ruination of the capital's monuments was synonymous with modernity's conversion of all things "solid" into their opposites. Foremost among the casualties was the integrity of architecture. Art's "essence," writes Viel, lay in its "disinterest," and its "enemy" in "cupidity." Yet today's artists, overturning that noble dictum, exploit architecture as an instrument of enrichment. Architects, Viel notes, have rendered monuments "subject[s] of speculation, without considering the society for which they are built, nor the posterity" that will inherit them. Thus had the art of architecture fallen prey to the corrosive effects of capitalist Paris, "perhaps the most difficult city in the world" for those who wish to remain "virtuous."[44] Beneath the reformer's veneer of modern rationality lurked market-induced delirium, and masquerading behind the reformist rhetoric of public utility were the private interests of the speculator.

Viel's text, for all its eccentricities, provides a revealing assessment of the encroachment of the market economy into the domain of architecture. The author's perceptions were not misplaced. In the second half of the century, dwindling public funds created opportunities for private enterprise, and the involvement of commercial developers in important building projects sparked widespread criticism. Real estate investments soared in the wake of the Seven Years' War and the American War of Independence, buoyed by the expansion of the credit market, as well as by the availability of capital that had been previously applied toward war financing.[45] Commentators described a *manie de bâtir* that, according to Mercier, resulted by 1785 in no less than a third of the city being built or reconstructed over the previous thirty-year period: "Huge blocks of dwellings rise from the ground as if by magic and new districts of the most magnificent houses take shape," he writes. "The building mania gives an air of grandeur and majesty to the city.... The speculators cry out for the contractors who, with a plan in one hand and a contract in the other, bring balm to the hearts of the capitalists."[46] As demonstrated in the interdependency of credit rates and construction activity, the Paris real estate market evidenced the vitality of speculative society.[47] Together, speculative development and urban reform sent land values soaring. Guidebooks and maps illustrating the capital—published with ever-increasing frequency—were rapidly rendered obsolete by the pace of construction. Transformations on a seemingly daily basis left the city perpetually "unrecognizable," noted the *Journal de Paris* in 1787, the year that Viel published his *Lettres sur l'architecture.*[48]

For Viel, the subjugation of the art of architecture to profit interests meant more than the decline of the profession; it represented the final expiration of the "revelation"—expressed in the monuments erected by the ancients—"that lets man know, *your faculties are the work of the Eternal.*"[49] For modern Parisians were cognizant only of market fluctuations. Treating the city's edifices not as invaluable portals to the past but rather as dispensable obstacles to the future, urban reform materialized the depreciation of certitudes and stability. By Viel's logic, the vogue for ruins epitomized the desacralization of monuments.

With his *Lettres,* Viel took his place in a trajectory of Paris critics who wrote despairingly of the dangerous liaison between art and money. That the architect confined a great many of his critical observations to the notes indicates less their diminishing significance than a diminishing need to restate the obvious. Viel's grumblings about the corrupting effects of commerce echo the thunderous denunciations launched in the middle of the century against mondaine dissoluteness by the critic Étienne La Font de Saint-Yenne. In his *Réflexions sur quelques causes de l'état présent de la peinture en France* (1747), La Font identified in the commercial interests of moneyed classes a threat to the values of a morally upright public sphere. More specifically, he condemned the Rococo interior as a lair of commodity culture and decried its deleterious effects on art production—namely, the emasculation of the heroic and "prime genre of history painting."[50] Like Viel four decades later, La Font perceived the marginalization of virtue from art as symptomatic of a topsy-turvy order. Writes Katie Scott, La Font opposed the Rococo's "specular values (of desire, gain, duplicity, emptiness, of something in nothing)"—manifest in the *hôtel*'s mirrored interiors as well as in François Boucher's licentious paintings—to the Salon's (as yet unrealized) potential to uplift the public with paintings featuring historically exemplary narratives. In its irrationality and trickery, Rococo art, La Font insinuates, bore the traces of "the inhumanity of opulence" and the "omnipotence of credit," just as surely as its financier-class patrons remained, in public lore, despised personifications of gluttony following the John Law affair.[51] In 1747, La Font's immanent political critique of a state overrun by the influence of financiers—from policy to arts patronage—counted precisely upon this association.

Such criticism reverberates in the reception of Robert's paintings, and particularly in Métra's comment that Robert wished "to be paid in the way that he executes." It is appropriate that Robert's art, like Boucher's before it, drew accusations of monetary motivation, and even of commercial corruption. For though Robert immersed himself for a decade in Roman antiquity, his paintings (albeit to a far lesser extent than his friend Fragonard's) testify to the endurance of the Rococo. The work of a *ruiniste* with a specialty in decorative ensembles ("It was very fashionable and grand to have one's salon painted by Robert," noted Elisabeth-Louise Vigée-Lebrun), his production both recalls and corrects the designs of Jacques de Lajoue and Gilles-Marie Oppenord (figs. 32, 33).[52] Ensconced in Robert's time-laden landscapes, the ornamental devices of his antecedents, divested of their weightlessness, become properly monumental: ruins are inflated to grandiose proportions and endowed with historical majesty, in keeping with the Neoclassical turn—and, more specifically, with the interests of an elite intent on distancing itself from the taint of prodigality by staging its subscription to the values of antiquity and simplicity.[53] Nonetheless, it was undoubtedly part of the painter's great appeal that in updating and rescripting elements of the Rococo—his signature offering of peasants gallivanting amidst ruins was his answer to Watteau's *fête galante*—Robert extended its lifeline.

Traces of a Rococo aesthetic of playfulness and ephemerality appear in a number of Robert's urban ruins. The cotton puffs of smoke shown enveloping the right foreground of Robert's *Interior of the Opéra* and the candied hues of what may be a view of the burning Opéra (fig. 34) recycle the pastel palette of the Rococo along with Boucher's signature froth—as if the enchantments of the aristocratic *hôtel* had escaped their confines to run rampant in the streets of Paris.[54] The theatricality of the scene—a study in tropical pink and velvety gray gusts of billowing

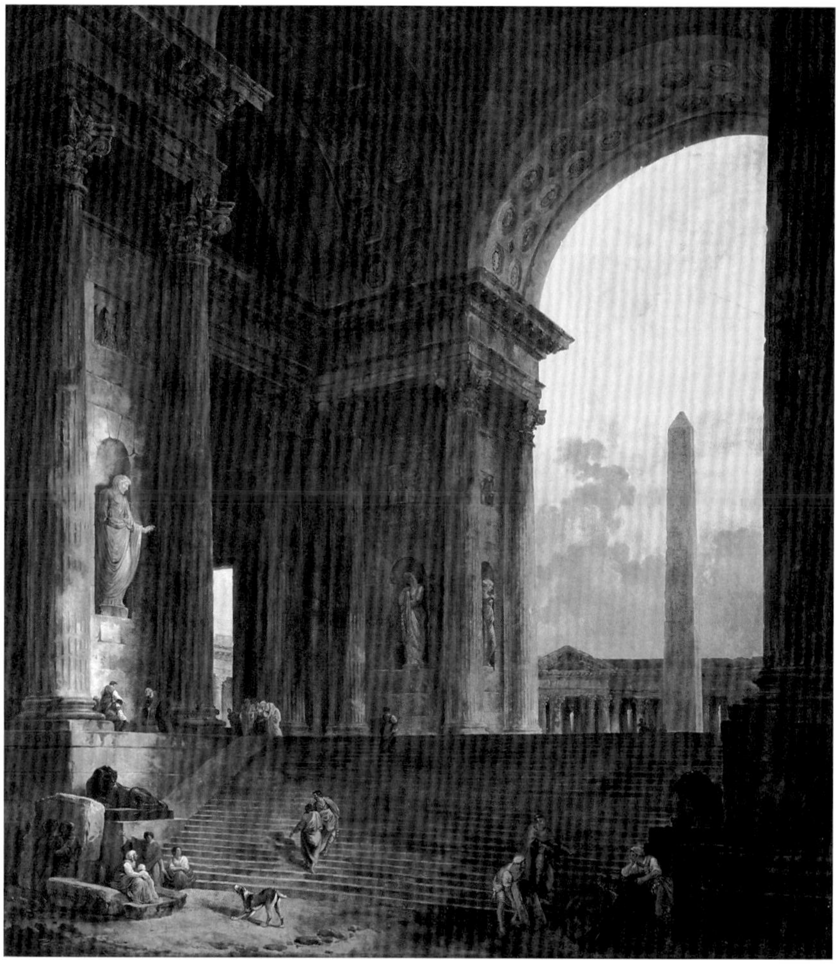

Fig. 32. Hubert Robert (French, 1733–1808)
The Obelisk, 1787/1788, oil on canvas, 255.6 × 223.5 cm (100⅝ × 88 in.)
Chicago, Art Institute of Chicago

Fig. 33. Gabriel Huquier (French, 1695–1772), after Gilles-Marie Oppenord (French, 1672–1742)
Designs for *salons*, ca. 1748, etching, 28.2 × 46.6 cm (11⅛ × 18⅜ in.)
Paris, Bibliothèque nationale de France

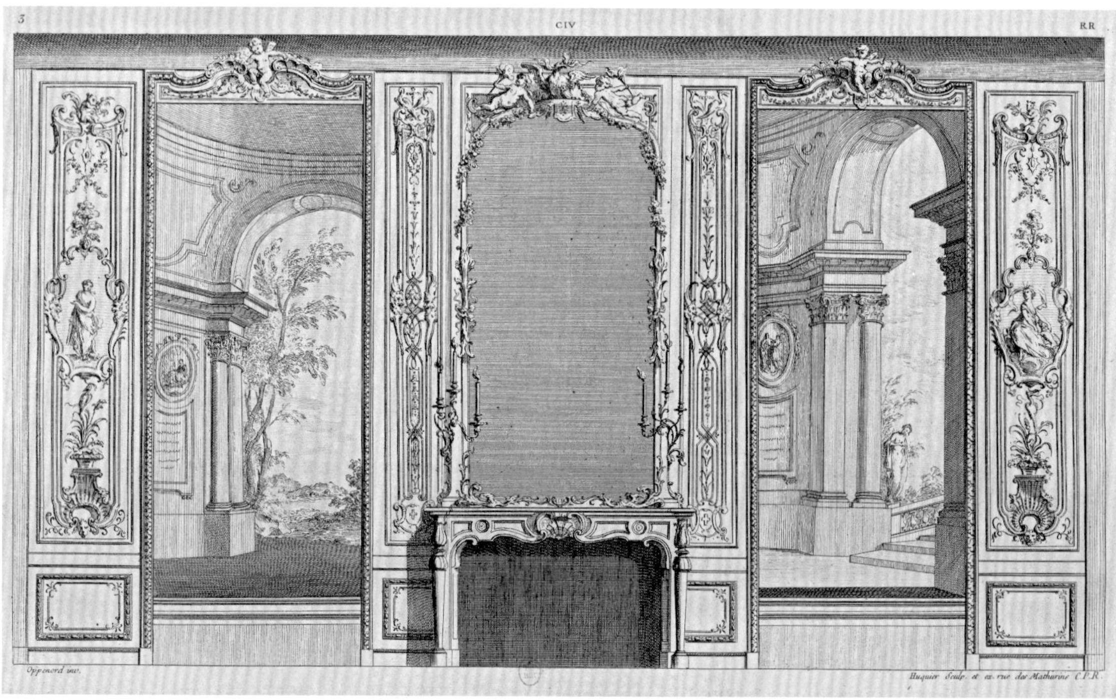

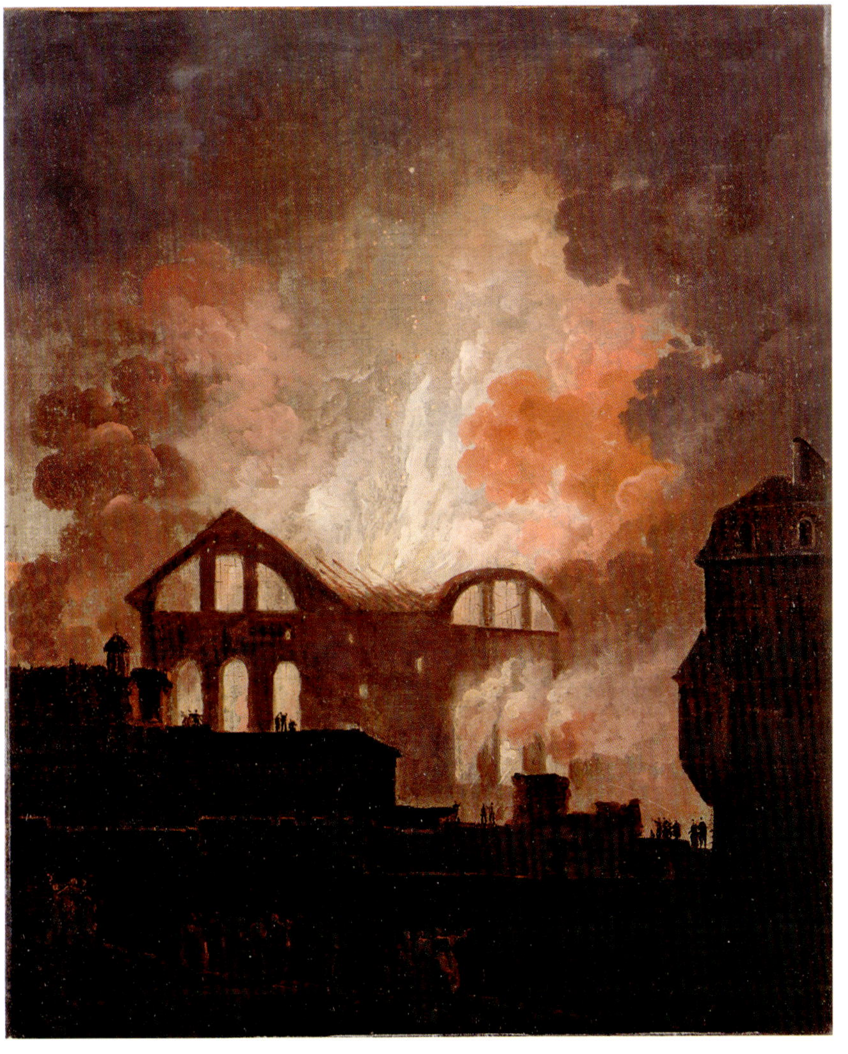

Fig. 34. Hubert Robert (French, 1733–1808)
The Burning of the Opéra at the Palais-Royal, ca. 1781, oil on canvas, 75 × 57 cm ($29\frac{1}{2} \times 22\frac{3}{8}$ in.)
Pau, Musée des beaux-arts

smoke—recalls the pyrotechnic extravaganzas of Baroque scenography. The luminous color field saturating the monument's skeletal structure underscores the transience of the moment. In both its form and subject matter, the painting offers itself as a virtuoso performance in the *non-finito,* forever arresting the specter of volcanic metamorphosis.

If Robert's standard paintings of landscapes with ruins discipline the Rococo ornament by segregating natural and architectural components (fig. 35), then the opposite could be said of his view of the conflagration. The painting—an exercise in bewitchment—features a world ruled by caprice rather than decorum. Conceptually akin to the Rococo grotesque's invasion of the center by what was once marginalized, its undoing of narrative purposiveness by gratuitous happenstance, Robert's disasters and demolitions collapse the distinction between inside and outside, between the built order and senseless chaos. Such pictures reveal the elasticity of the genre of ruins that Robert made his own, while also turning the genre on its head: in them, one witnesses the sensational reversal of Simmel's claim that the ruin's destruction "is not something senselessly coming from the outside but rather the realization of a tendency inherent in the

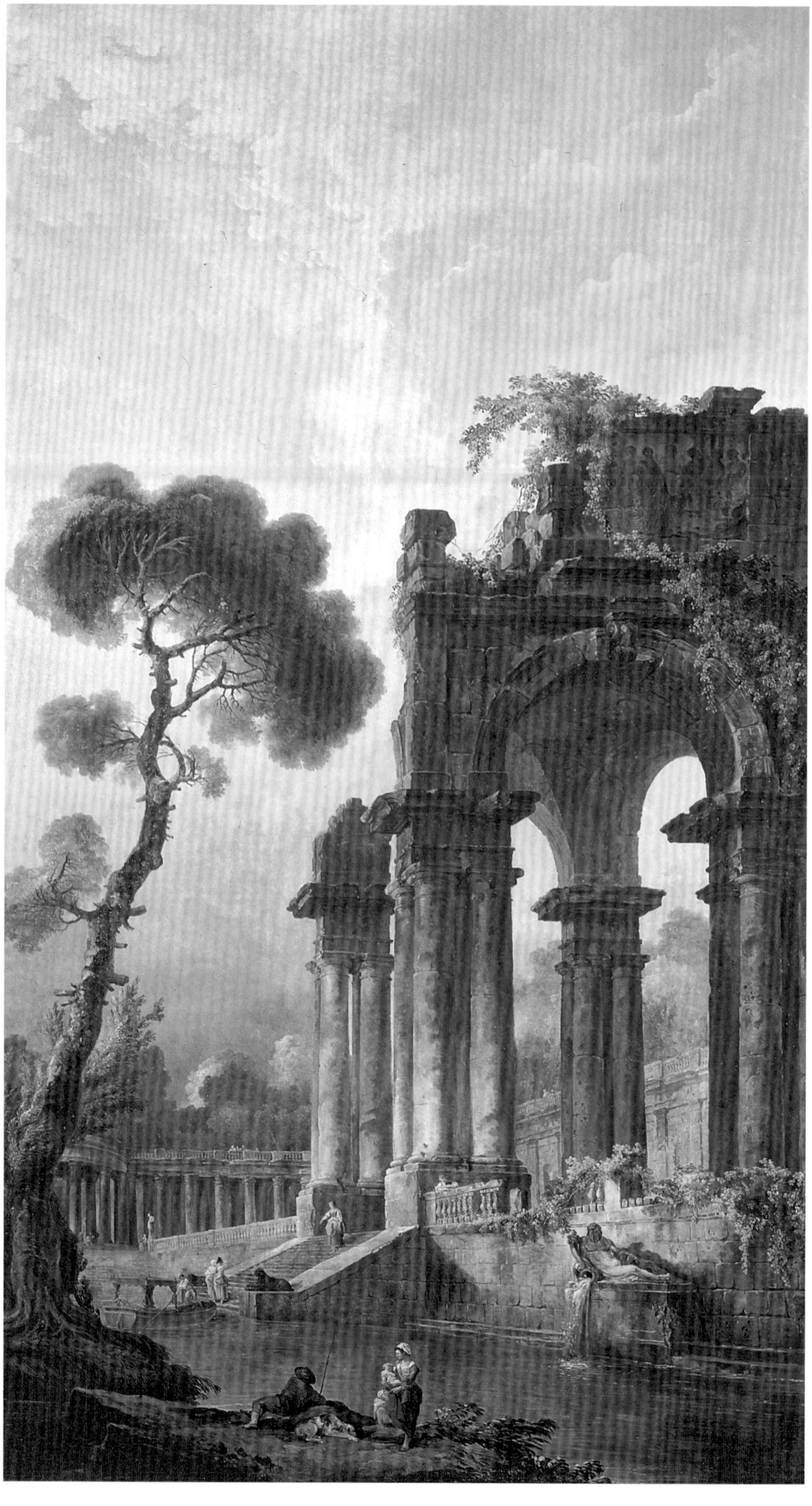

Fig. 35. Hubert Robert (French, 1733–1808)
Ruins by the Water, 1779, oil on canvas, 263 × 199.5 cm (103½ × 78½ in.)
Moscow region, Museum-Estate Arkhangelskoye

deepest layer of existence of the destroyed."[55] In overwriting architecture's tendencies toward decline with the thrill of spectacular accident, Robert inflates the artifice, and diminishes the pathos, of his subjects.

For Robert, the city's performances in inconstancy inspired recourse to what La Font condemned as a style suited to "a nation avid for anything new."[56] What is notable about this resurgence of the Rococo is that it took place at a moment when the lessons of Régence profligacy were being taken to heart—especially as they pertained to real estate. The building spree of Robert's day harked back to the one witnessed in the first decades of the century; it was *les grands* fleeing Versailles who turned Paris into a veritable capital.[57] Significantly, construction in the faubourgs incited concern in Robert's time as it did during the Régence, not only over the difficulties of feeding an expanding population but also over the relentless sprawl of opulence. Luxury, it was feared, contained the seeds of ruin. Thus Germain Brice, whose *Description de la ville de Paris* saw fourteen editions between 1684 and 1752, sounded an alarm that would be echoed by Viel and other critics of urban expansion, when he likened development to a death sentence: "The city of Paris," he worried in 1725, following the demolition of its ramparts, could very well "extend to infinity and, in the course of time, suffer the sad misfortune of those famous and superb cities that were destroyed by immoderate luxury and by extreme grandeur, such as Thebes, Memphys, Babylon, Heliopolis, Palmyra, Persepolis, Leptis [Magna], and even Rome."[58] The building industry was seen as firmly tethered to private interest and, more specifically, to the wild unpredictability of the market. As Jean-Aymar Piganiol de La Force recalled in his guidebook to the capital, "Never had so much building gone on in Paris and in the *Fauxbourgs* than during the minority of Louis XV . . . as paper money took the place of gold and silver everyone strove to give permanence to his fortune, and buildings sprang up everywhere."[59]

Piganiol's explanation of an earlier era's frenzied construction activity calls attention to the congruence between architectural and economic transformations in the city. His publication—appearing four decades after the events it described—proved particularly timely. In associating the capital's grand new quarters with the flow of "paper money," Piganiol registers the sense of both solidity and fragility that haunted the building mania. His account implicitly submits that construction compensated for the absence of gold. Yet in Piganiol's day as during the Régence, the building frenzy proved as impervious to "permanence" as did paper itself. The infusion of money into the real estate market, coextensive with the credit boom, had the effect of transforming the urban fabric into "fictitious capital," or an asset premised upon the expectation of future revenue.[60] Fears of the city's downfall—beginning with Brice's warning of disastrous, mass self-deception—were the inevitable byproducts of the illusions propagated by paper.

Robert executed his disaster and demolition paintings at a time when the operations of speculative development deepened two distinct but related anxieties: first, that the bursting of the real estate bubble would precipitate widespread ruin, and second, that degenerate aesthetic pastimes were complicit in the trickery of the market. The latter worry—which had roots in the gravely pessimistic portrait of French culture offered in Rousseau's *Discours sur les sciences et les arts* (1750) and in La Font's argument that *le style moderne* was a scourge that needed to be contained—resurfaces in Viel's observation that the taste for ruins went hand in hand with the decreasing esteem in which a commercial culture held its edifices. It is tempting to cast his assertion as a useful bit of ekphrasis, particularly insofar as Robert's patrons included some of the city's most prominent real estate speculators. And interpreted through the coloration of Viel's assessment, Robert's urban ruins appear all the more consonant with the upheavals to which speculative finance subjected the urban terrain. Exercises in hyperbolic spectacle, his disaster scenes, by this logic, euphemized the "nightmare of a commodity economy."[61]

Significantly, Robert's burning monuments bore associations not only with the lofty category of the sublime but also with the nightmarish economic scenarios entertained by critics of the gambling mania. Sharing Viel's conviction that the roots of modern decadence had been planted centuries earlier, Jean Dusaulx asserts in his history of gambling—*De la passion du jeu depuis les temps anciens jusqu'à nos jours* (1779)—that the city's vices marked age-old habits of depravity. The current climate, however, manifested a consciousness of chance (*hasard*) that "influences... all circumstances of private life" no less than it did "commerce and the operations of finance," which adopted risk as a founding principle. Like the English, he laments, "we think only of lucre." Meanwhile, state-sponsored lotteries—"ruining the people in order to someday provide it with a hospital bed"—exploited the gambling mania. Dusaulx's reading of Tacitus had convinced him that the mores of Parisians were little different from those of the ancient Romans, and, ominously, that the rage for gambling recalled the "last convulsion" of the Roman Empire.[62]

Dusaulx portrays Paris as reveling in its own violent vicissitudes, and he does so through recourse to the imagery of conflagration. Gambling was associated with fire, for the presence of *lampions* that lured passersby into clandestine casinos: "Flaming pots set the Paris night ablaze," observes one visitor to Paris. Dusaulx notes that, following the Law affair, gamblers sought out the game in the "blazing foyers" of brothels, illuminated by fires. Several of the capital's gambling houses, he states, went by the name of "Hell."[63] The import of this imagery also informed the reaction against fireworks displays, which Enlightenment critics disparaged as alchemical pageants in which huge amounts of money literally went up in smoke and as comparable to gambling for their wasteful frivolity. Fittingly, variations on Dusaulx's argument resounded in 1785, following the introduction of fire insurance as a speculative venture: critics argued that, far from promoting security, the insurance scheme—an extension of the gambling mania—would compel subscribers to burn down their homes and businesses, thus further igniting a culture of "fear" and "risk."[64]

Profligate Paris as one giant gaming table, an arena for the wickedly changeable, as opposed to the permanently upright: this was the vision of the city that critics like Viel and Dusaulx put forth. And it was one that Robert's views of urban destruction would appear to corroborate. For on the one hand, such paintings mirrored a radical reformist imagination—one that identified "disappearance" with "progress," and "debris" with the coming of a "new city" dreamed of by "virtuous visionaries."[65] On the other hand, Robert's scenes of catastrophe vivified the commodification of Paris real estate by capturing the city's monuments at their most volatile moments of transformation. How appropriate, then, that Robert's paintings—and specifically his views of raging conflagrations—laid waste to academic decorum: exalting the "sudden and unexpected," his flayed structures signal the collusion between the sublime and an economic drive to annihilate "the stationary." As suggested by Dusaulx's criticism, such paintings extended to viewers the thrills of a high-stakes gamble—or rather, they stimulated the "pleasures of surprise" that Montesquieu associated with gambling and games of chance.[66]

Of course, part of the point of the paintings is their packaging of "surprise"—their effect of counteracting, while glorifying, inconstancy. In Robert's *Fire at the Opéra,* the blinding eruption could not be more at odds with—nor less mediated by—the cold stone presence of the window frame. The architectural device, mimicking the pictorial medium, calls attention to the taming of the episode into the object of a view. With its slapstick staging of the obligatory distance from danger—a precondition of the Burkean sublime—the painting pulls the curtain from its own mechanics. Yet consequently, the beholder who partakes of the opportunity to spectate upon the drama of destruction is invited to dwell on the painting's assurance of a safe and stable viewing position as itself another performance.

In so foregrounding their own impulse to theatricalize, such paintings underscore the need they evidently meant to fill. To treat the city's unmaking as stagecraft was, among other things, to make light of—thereby minimizing—its disorienting impact. Robert's views of church demolitions in particular trumpet the degree to which the fetishization of the city as a theater of suspense displaced less pleasurable reactions to the "surprise" of destruction. These events became increasingly routine in the second half of the century, when urban reformers endeavored to rid the capital of what were perceived as its decrepit medieval eyesores. Robert's depictions of the subject shun sentimentality in favor of showcasing the built environment's gratification of a desire to "exchang[e] present certainty for future uncertainty."[67] In one such view featuring the demolition of an unidentified church, Robert has captured the rubble in midair, and the audience that has gathered to witness the event anticipates the monument's collapse with both excitement and dread (fig. 36). The two men at center who bravely approach the wreckage are framed at right by the captivated yet tremulous couple shown clinging to a pillar and at left by women and children who are at once tempted and terrified by the spectacle. Whether the gesticulating figure beside them is urging them to overcome their fears and behold the destruction, or admonishing them to step back, is unclear—and intentionally so, for the true subject of the work is the disabling of the capacity to disassociate promise from menace. Similarly, in his painting featuring the demolition of the Église Saint-Jean-en-Grève (on land that was sold to a private citizen for a few hundred thousand livres), onlookers marvel at the explosion of the decaying fourteenth-century monument, while at right, three minuscule figures take flight (fig. 37).

To be fair, church demolitions—like conflagrations—were evidently something of an attraction; indeed, the architect Louis François Petit-Radel, who was entrusted with the demolition, boasted the skill of knowing how to level a Gothic church in ten minutes flat and proudly exhibited diagrams of his technique at the Salon of 1800.[68] Precisely for their scenographic effects and distortions of scale, Robert's paintings bore the patina of an age captivated by spectacles of progress and reversal alike—with the one often kindling expectations of the other. Thus if the artist turned urban destruction into theater, he did so by dramatizing the real obscurity of the imminent future.

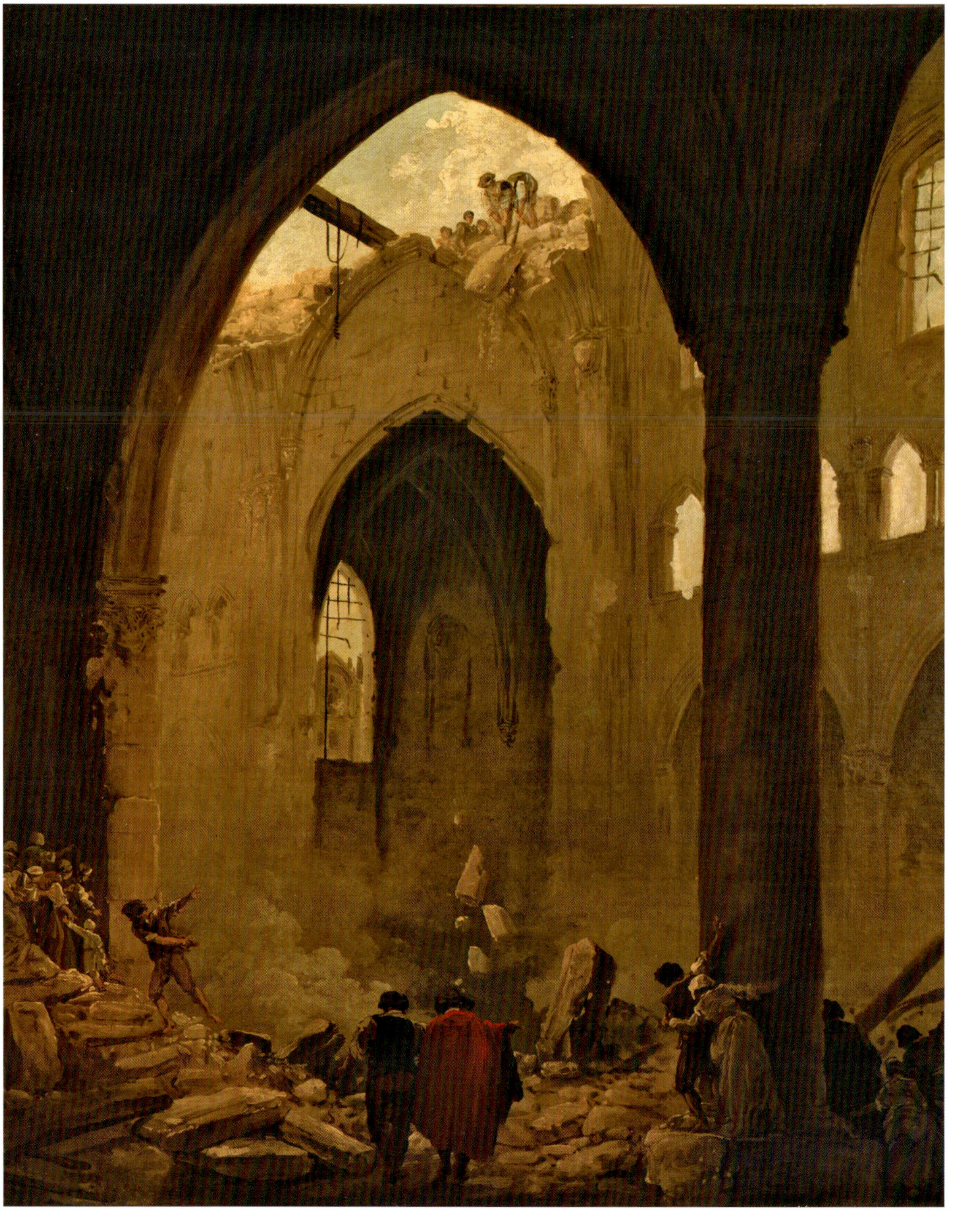

Fig. 36. Hubert Robert (French, 1733–1808)
Demolition of a Church,
ca. 1787, oil on canvas,
87 × 69 cm (34¼ × 27⅛ in.)
Moscow, Pushkin Museum of Fine Arts

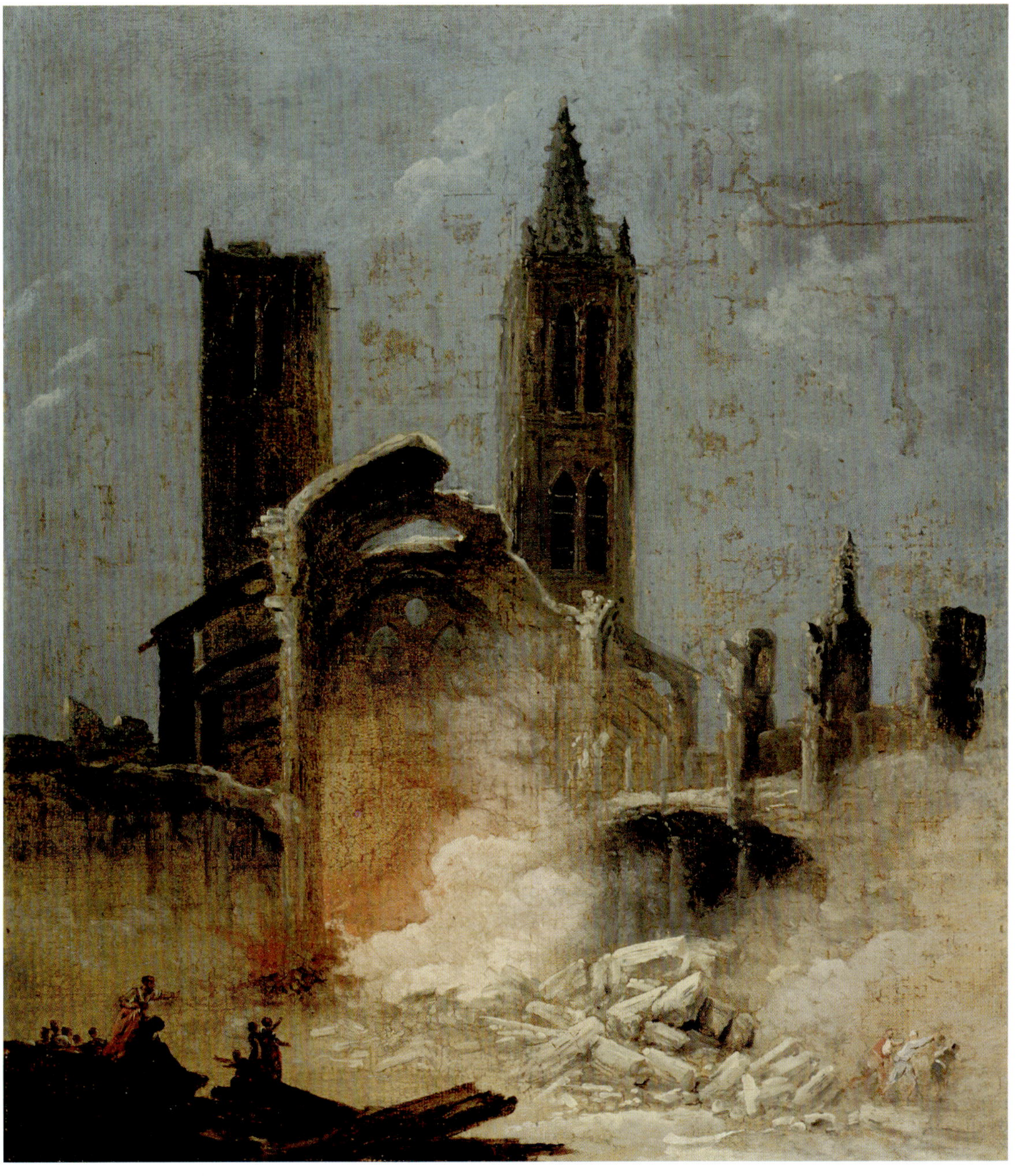

Fig. 37. Hubert Robert (French, 1733–1808)
Demolition of the Église Saint-Jean-en-Grève in 1800,
1800, oil on canvas,
62 × 53.5 cm (24⅜ × 21⅛ in.)
Paris, Musée Carnavalet

Enchanted City

In paintings such as *The Fire at the Hôtel-Dieu in Paris* and the Frankfurt version of *The Burning of Rome,* both executed in 1773, Paris and Rome morph into each other. That same year, Robert produced *The Construction of the École de Chirurgie* (School of surgery) *in 1773,* a work that similarly blurs the boundary between the two cities (fig. 38). As Cayeux observes of the painting, "What better resembles a ruin than an unfinished edifice?"[69] Robert's canvas features the triumphantly Neoclassical monument designed by Jacques Gondoin enveloped in sunlight and scaffolding. The Classical grandeur of Gondoin's façade is but one of the ways in which Rome is invoked. The courtyard is strewn with concrete and marble slabs, and the presence of two strolling monks in the central foreground reinforces the illusion of a Roman structure in partial ruin. So too do the workers—shown variously completing the relief, resting by the wagons, and preparing the limestone at right—resemble modern-day Romans restoring an ancient monument.

The painting, moreover, has precedent in a study Robert produced while in Rome, one displaying his attraction to subjects that straddled the not yet complete and the already dilapidated: *The South Façade of the Palazzo Poli with the Trevi Fountain under Construction,* executed in red chalk while the artist was a *pensionnaire* (fig. 39). The page features the fountain laden with ladders and carpentry tools, the sculpture draped in canvas, the basin unfinished. The empty site, one of picturesque

Fig. 38. Hubert Robert (French, 1733–1808)
The Construction of the École de Chirurgie in 1773, 1773, oil on canvas, 63 × 79.5 cm (24¾ × 31¼ in.)
Paris, Musée Carnavalet

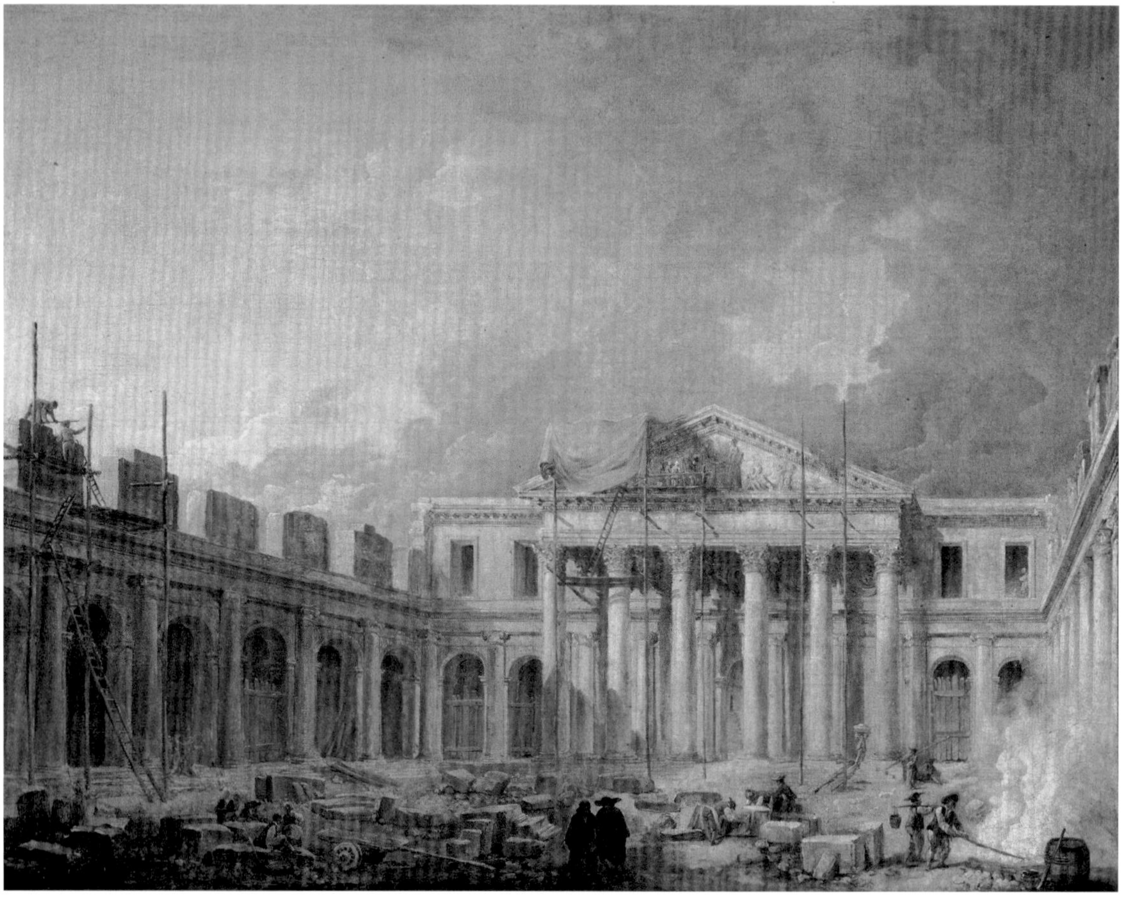

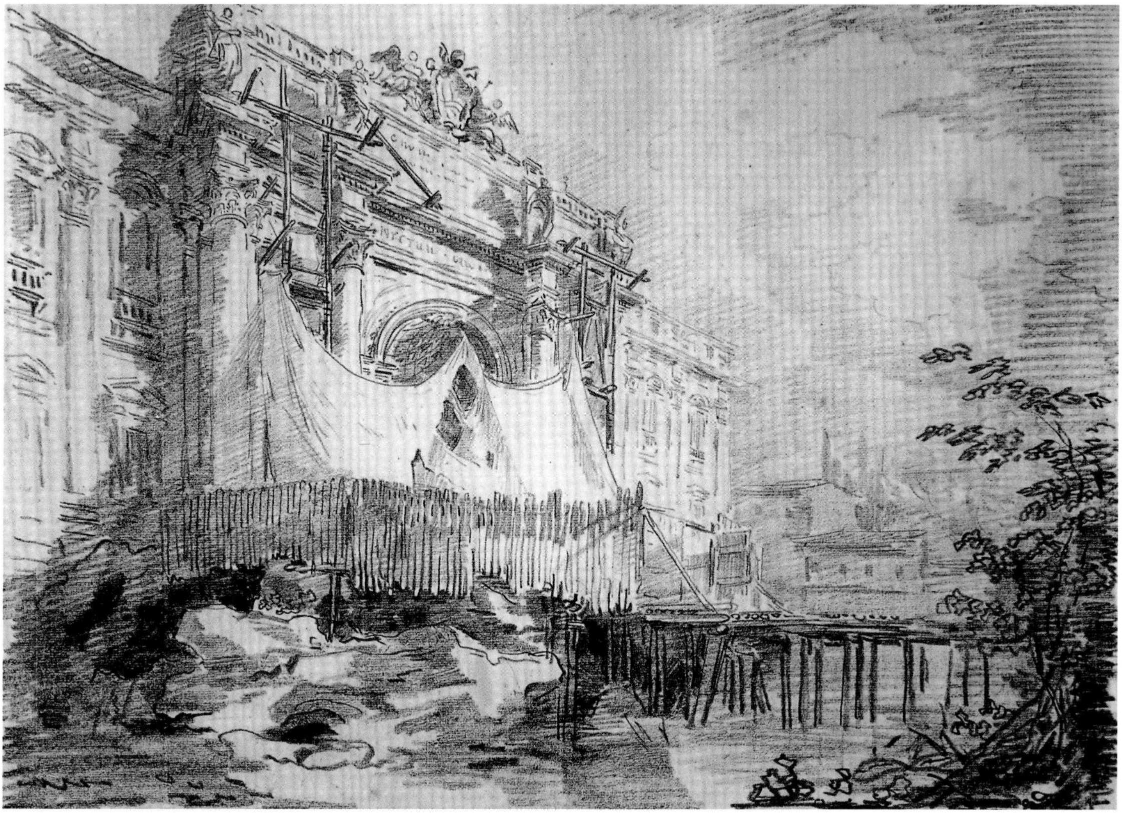

Fig. 39. Hubert Robert (French, 1733–1808) *The South Façade of the Palazzo Poli with the Trevi Fountain under Construction,* ca. 1760–62, red chalk on white laid paper, 32.3 × 44.7 cm (12¾ × 17⅝ in.) New York, Pierpont Morgan Library

dereliction, hesitates between anticipation and abandonment. (Properly so, given the belated completion of the ancient fountain in 1762, 122 years after Pope Urban VIII first commissioned Gian Lorenzo Bernini to redesign it.)[70] In Robert's drawing, the delicately rendered edifice hovers in a state of semi-erasure—an effect pronounced in the pale and softly rendered passage of the façade at left. Juxtaposed with the vigorous hatching in the left foreground—reiterated in the scaffolding—as well as with the savage eruption of plant life that darkens the corner at right, the fountain appears all the more to fade into the page.

In Robert's view of a decade later, Gondoin's École de Chirurgie, with its Corinthian-temple front, is as commanding as it is translucent. The sun-drenched monument radiates massiveness along with an effect of derealization. The encroaching presence of foliage in the drawing of the Trevi Fountain is here replaced by smoke from the burning lime, its vapor at once contrasting with and melting into the structure's luminous surface. Robert thus enforced a kind of premature ghostliness upon an unfinished edifice that would epitomize the progressive use of antique architectural examples for modern ends: from the school's amphitheater—modeled after Greek counterparts and featuring a coffered half-dome reminiscent of the Roman Pantheon—to the imposing colonnade that lined the street, Gondoin's monument incarnated a "modern secular temple of medicine." The commission itself, moreover, reflected the status of Paris as a world capital of the medical arts.[71]

Suffused with the promise of Classical continuity as well as the portent of decay, Robert's *École de Chirurgie* retains the suspense of his disaster and demolition scenes, while inverting their logic. Just as these latter works embraced calamity as a source of unforeseen opportunity (for future reconstruction, as well as for aesthetic pleasure), so does Gondoin's nearly completed monument threaten to devolve into ruin. The painting may be compared to Jean-Baptiste Maréchal's whimsical view of 1786 of the *hôtel* built by Ledoux for the Opéra dancer Marie-Madeleine Guimard (fig. 40). With its Ionic columns and sculptural frieze celebrating the muse of dance, the *hôtel* exemplified the city's aspirations toward Neoclassical splendor. Maréchal's drawing features the edifice in a celestial setting, graced by a chorus of goddesses at right, and, overhead, putti bearing laurel wreaths. Inscribed "Maison de Mlle Guimard, rue de la Chaussée d'Antin par Ledoux," the drawing doubles as an advertisement for one of the city's most fashionable quarters. Yet the cloud-swept landscape, consistent with Mercier's description of the "magic" of the building industry, hints that the appearance of grandeur is one of spectacle without substance. The drawing well emblematized its subject, for by 1786, the *hôtel* had fallen victim to the financial reversals suffered by one of Guimard's protectors, and its enchanted quality quickly withered. Such transience, in truth, was unavoidable, for actresses were prohibited from inheriting or bequeathing property.[72] As a representation of the former *hôtel* of a controversial patron, Maréchal's drawing would appear to have little in common with Robert's painting of a public monument, and yet both artworks draw attention to the paradox whereby the very sumptuousness of the city's new edifices seemed to herald their evanescence. The similarity is apt, for building projects commissioned by the fiscally struggling state were subject to the same risks as those undertaken in the private sphere.

Robert's painting and Maréchal's drawing alike thus treat the city's prosperity—evinced in the accelerated pace of construction, the swift metamorphosis of Paris into a new Rome—as potentially ephemeral, and indeed, the capital's transformations incited pride as well as disquiet. Mercier marveled at the enormous changes wrought by the building boom while worrying about the sort of future they augured. He filled his *Tableau de Paris* with descriptions of the city as a site teetering between

Fig. 40. Jean-Baptiste Maréchal (French, act. 1779–1824)
House of Mademoiselle Guimard, rue de la Chaussée-d'Antin, Ledoux, 1786,
pen and wash, 10.7 × 20.1 cm (4¼ × 8 in.)
Paris, Bibliothèque nationale de France

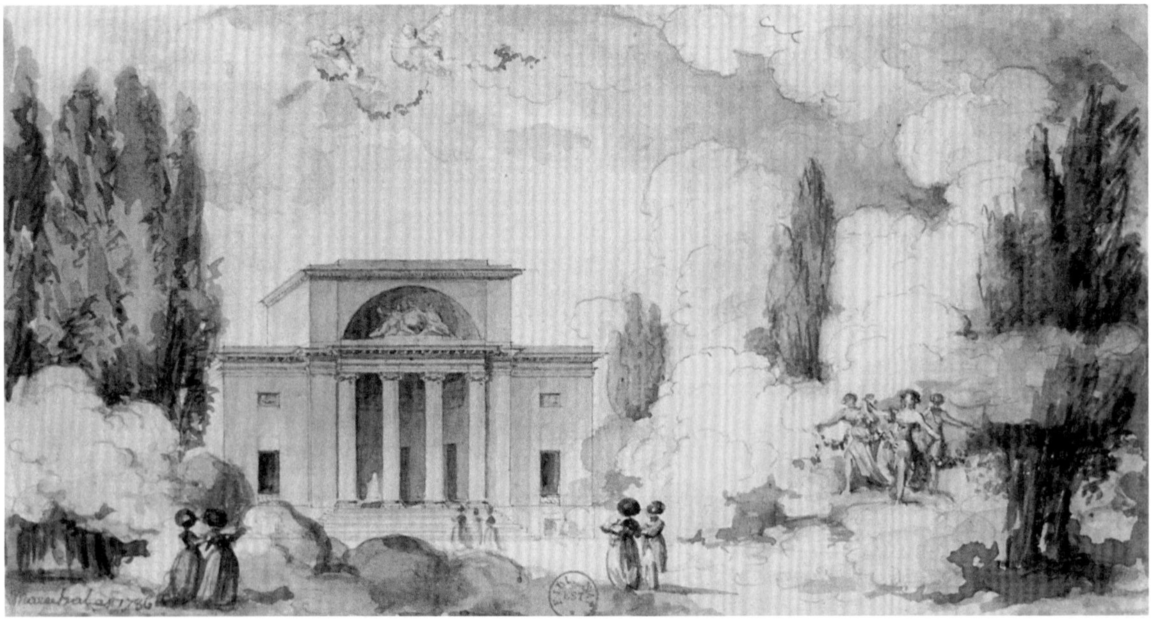

opulence and decadence, between wealth and bankruptcy. The construction frenzy heralded at once magnificence and ruin. Châteaux, he writes, rise from the earth at the speed of asparagus, and last for "the space of a moment. Everywhere one sees nothing but houses and châteaux for sale. These places where... *luxe* has deployed its ruinous fantasies... are bought at low prices, and demolished by the same workers who constructed them, and who resell the materials to other fools, equally tormented by the building mania." An expanding real estate bubble clouded judgment, disabling investors from distinguishing between profits and losses. Access to new financial instruments, observes Mercier elsewhere in his chronicles, ensured the dangerous spread of the "gambling frenzy."[73] Similarly, because the construction boom was sustained by the rampant growth of credit, today's new buildings threatened to become tomorrow's ruins.[74]

In a recent study, Sonenscher shows that such presentiments were driven by an awareness of the Janus-faced nature of credit—the ease with which it enabled economic prosperity, while at the same time catalyzing the potential for expansive debt.[75] Tellingly, in contemporary parlance the expression *à credit* denoted "the lack of a solid foundation," and the operations of credit were compared, in the *Encyclopédie,* to a building on fire.[76] Credit cloaked the city's future in uncertainty. And what is especially significant about the reliance on credit instruments is that it prompted nervous commentators to forecast the repetition of an ancient cycle of decline and fall.[77] The worry, voiced by Brice and Mercier alike, that Paris would go the way of antiquity's vanished cities—that the capital's growth would precipitate its destruction—reflected credit-based perception of the uncertain margin between riches and ruin.

Such a worry underscores the usefulness of designating Robert a transitional figure between the Rococo and the Neoclassical and of attending to the overlap of the categories in his city views. In different ways, his *École de Chirurgie* and his disaster scenes alike may be interpreted in light of a failure of confidence in the city's future that translated into a distrust of the distinction between transience and solidity. Thus the architect Blondel feared that the current climate of speculative building would revive the decadence of the Rococo and corrupt the principles of his art. What critics of the changing built environment suspected, in effect, was that *le bon goût* (the "good taste" synonymous with Neoclassicism) masked a "ruinous" disorder.[78] Viel, for one, saw his as an age of "incertitude."[79] Yet "incertitude," as we have seen, was equally treated as a basis for aesthetic enjoyment, as witnessed in Robert's penchant for suspenseful subjects.

If any painter harbored inside knowledge of the shaky foundations of the capital's new grandeur—of the conditions of risk subtending the construction of a Neoclassical city—it was Robert. His patrons included the city's most enterprising land developers, foremost among them Laborde. In 1769, the banker leased the city's swampy northern terrain from the impoverished religious order of the Mathurins, thereby launching the Chaussée d'Antin. (It was this quarter that Viel and other critics of urban sprawl had in mind when they deplored the loss of the city's agricultural resources—in this case, the market gardens formerly tended by the Mathurins.) The comte d'Artois (Louis XVI's brother)—whose *folie* at Bagatelle (itself the product of a gamble) Robert helped decorate in the 1780s—initiated an unsuccessful endeavor the previous decade to develop a *nouvelle ville* in proximity to the Champs-Élysées.

Another client, Marie-Gabriel-Florent-Auguste de Choiseul-Gouffier, pulled off a coup along the rue neuve Saint-Augustin, undertaking a massive development operation financed by twelve Nantean creditors and a team of Belgian bankers.[80] Robert occupied the same social and professional orbit as the architects who engaged in property speculation in addition to building *hôtels* in the capital's new quarters. His paintings decorated Laborde's *hôtel* on the rue d'Artois, as well as the homes of residents of the faubourg Poissonnière (such as the notary Charles-Nicolas Duclos-Dufresnoy) and other quarters built on speculation. His *Fire amidst the Principal Edifices of Rome* hung in the *hôtel* that Jean-François-Thérèse Chalgrin designed for Charlotte-Christine-Antoinette de Lenoncourt, the marquise de Langeac, built in the Champs-Élysées with the help, it appears, of profits from land speculation. The painter's close relationships with debt-ridden architects and financiers—along with hapless nobles (like Langeac, whose business dealings reduced her to near ruin, as well as his patron Choiseul, who was forced to auction off his art collection and try his own hand at property speculation)—made him aware of the alacrity with which fortunes changed.[81] When Robert furnished his clients with decorative panels specially designed for their *hôtels,* it was doubtless with the knowledge that nothing was permanent. He was likely cognizant, moreover, of the effects of fluctuations in the city's real estate market on his paintings. In 1777, for instance, news circulated of the sale of "un grand Hôtel" in the faubourg du Roule, decorated with "Tableaux de Robert faits pour les places."[82]

Robert would thus have been well aware of the consequences on the urban terrain of a speculative economy. What is more, his tendency to conflate the monuments of Paris with those of Rome arguably reveals his perception not only of the flourishing of risk but of its manifestations on the level of style. For the painter's return from Rome coincided with a series of ill-fated building ventures—projects whose fruits had been designed to connote the enduring power of monumental antiquity. Examples include the Halle au Blé (Grain market) of 1766, built by Nicolas Le Camus de Mézières to resemble a Roman amphitheater, and the Comédie Française, completed in 1782 by Charles De Wailly and Marie-Joseph Peyre and evocative of

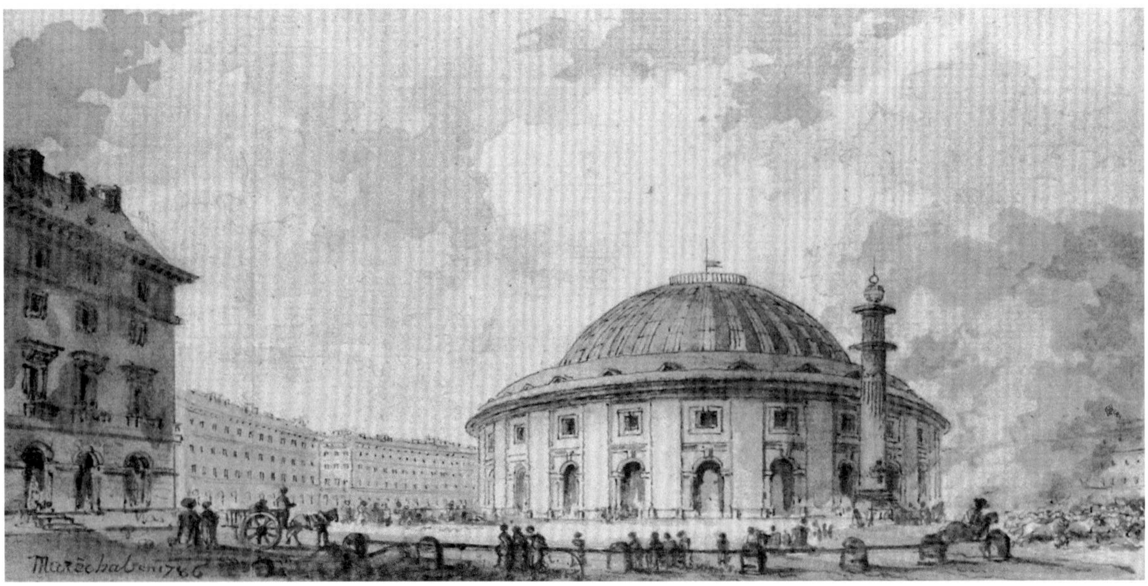

Fig. 41. Jean-Baptiste Maréchal (French, act. 1779–1824)
Halle au Blé and rue de Viarmes, 1786, pen and wash, 10.2 × 20.2 cm (4 × 8 in.)
Paris, Bibliothèque nationale de France

a Classical temple (fig. 41). The public was scandalized that such works had been entrusted to private developers, who were accused of exploiting the opportunity to raise land values at the cost of serving the civic ideals embodied by both monuments. In the financial failure of the projects, critics saw an allegory of decadence: "Limitless luxury," predicted La Font, "will inevitably bring about the total ruin of this State."[83]

It is striking that such harbingers of a replay of downfall were inspired by construction projects, for to impart to new buildings the aspect of antiquity's monuments was to invite faith in their longevity. Consider the case of the Colisée. The monstrous feat was reputedly spearheaded by Robert's benefactor, Choiseul, whose favored architect, Louis-Denis Le Camus, was charged with its design.[84] The enormous vauxhall, recalling the massive designs of Piranesi, was built to resemble an ancient temple—redolent for one commentator of the festival culture of the Greeks and Romans—and to hold as many as forty thousand visitors.[85] It closed in 1779 after eight years, already in a state of dilapidation and with hundreds of creditors left unpaid. Within five years, France's Coliseum was demolished. "One can only admire the madness of the authors of such a project, and the still greater madness of those who furnished funds for the execution," noted Louis Petit de Bachaumont. For his part, Mercier—scoffing at the rapid demise of the Colisée, in sad contrast to its ancient namesake—perceived in the debacle further proof of the doomed condition of the capital's building industry.[86] Such derision was well targeted, for the naming of the Colisée, in addition to honoring the venue with a Classical pedigree, likely represented a vain attempt to assure the credibility of a risky speculative venture.

In his history of urbanism, Pierre Lavedan reserves a special category for speculators as animators of development—incited, he writes, by "the lure of money" to be had "not in conservation but in transformation. In principle, the speculator is always on the side of movement."[87] However politically charged, the adoption in Paris of a Classical architectural vocabulary, in displaying the triumph of continuity over contingency, disavowed what in reality often amounted to a high-risk gamble. In referencing Piranesi's Rome, a building like the Colisée served to counteract apprehensions that the disorders of the credit economy—what Pocock characterizes as its "hysterical fluctuations" as well as "the changeable," "the unpredictable"—would be let loose upon the built environment.[88] Ledoux's borrowings from the etcher worked to similar effect, as illustrated in the Hôtel Thélusson (fig. 42). The residence he created (with Robert's help) for the widow of a Swiss banker in the Chaussée d'Antin was part of a speculative operation in which the architect doubled as agent, designing and managing the adjacent lots. Framing the *hôtel* was a monumental Doric arch, reminiscent of antiquity's triumphal, half-buried arches, such as the one at the Circo di Massenzio, and indebted to Piranesi. Writes Anthony Vidler, Ledoux employed the arch as a "grand aesthetic gesture" to raise the value of terrain that was "otherwise known as marshy, unstable, and difficult to build on."[89] In effect, the scenography discredited the possibility that the splendid properties of the Chaussée d'Antin would descend straight back into the swamp from which they had so miraculously emerged.

"Chalgrin, Ledoux and Brongniart are currently the three most popular architects in Paris, where houses are to be seen springing up as if by magic," noted the architect Poyet in 1775. For commentators of the period, the Chaussée d'Antin—a quarter summoned into existence by "le moderne Midas," as Diderot dubbed Laborde—

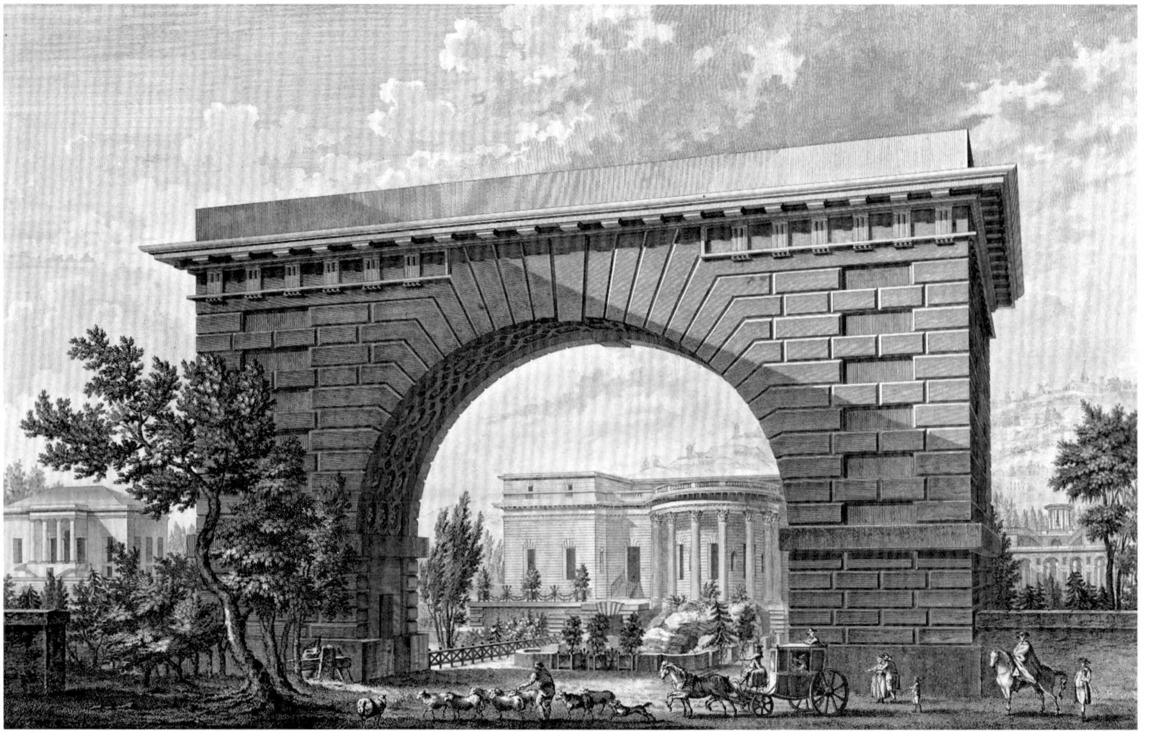

Fig. 42. **Claude-Nicolas Ledoux (French, 1736–1806)**
Perspective View of the Entry to the House of Madame de Thélusson
From Claude-Nicolas Ledoux, *L'architecture considerée sous le rapport de l'art, des moeurs et de la législation,* vol. 2 (Paris, 1847), pl. 165

was a place of dreamlike irreality.[90] According to the architect Jacques-Guillaume Legrand, the "enchanted aspect" of the Hôtel Thélusson recalled the myth of Amphion's lyre and the architecture that its music magically conjured. No doubt the sense of fantasy pervading the Chaussée d'Antin had something to do with the socioeconomic status of its residents—primarily "usurers," "extortionists," and "speculators," as Mercier described them. (They included the financier Maximilien Radix de Sainte-Foix, whose mismanagement of the comte d'Artois's money earned him the nickname "sans foi.") Like the schemes with which they lured a public credulous in all "money matters," the houses erected by these "magicians" of the financier class appealed to a "love of the marvelous," as did the quarter's sprawling picturesque gardens.[91] Descriptions of the quarter—with its "play" of water upon the "variegated terrain," the "happy" interchange between nature and architecture—lend credence to Fredric Jameson's proposal that the practice of land speculation can be said to breed its own aesthetic style. Isaac de Pinto might readily have been reflecting on the materialization of conditions of wealth in the Chaussée d'Antin, in a book endorsing the establishment of a national bank in France: the author, whose own speculations bankrupted him in 1763, invokes the "magic of credit" in distinctly picturesque terms, characterizing the circulation of money as that which "cascades."[92]

The picturesque possibilities engendered, then, by the Chaussée d'Antin's marshy terrain, with its literal "lack of a solid foundation," added to its air of "magic" and to the notion that the quarter, in all its unlikely majesty, was casting a kind of spell on the city. After all, as Viel observes, Paris "loves . . . nothing solid." The pithy remark returns us to a subject personal to Robert. It appears in a note to a discussion in which Viel reveals his distaste for the sorts of magic tricks perpetrated by fashioners of picturesque landscapes. More specifically, the objects of Viel's disapproval are the ruins ornamenting *jardins à l'anglaise.* "Several supposed artists have made entire edifices in the form of ruins," comments Viel, "as if modern constructions don't fall to ruin quickly enough; as if we weren't accustomed to seeing them collapse even before they are finished."[93] Throughout the city, he continued, buildings were destroyed in advance of their completion, in order to be reconceived anew, while brand-new edifices were already beginning to crumble. To conflate the city's poorly constructed buildings with the sorts of artificial ruins that appeared in gardens was to underscore a larger point about the decline of architecture—one similarly made by Mercier. The chronicler, convinced that the city's built order was no more stable than its economy, predicted that shoddy carpentry would bring down any building erected in the past thirty years, and in a century's time, every house would disintegrate.[94] Viel's statement, though, more specifically bespeaks an architect's sensitivity to the aesthetic manifestation of the logic of speculation—the responsiveness of artistic form to capitalism's "colonisation of the future."[95] However perversely, fake ruins naturalized the spirit of untimely obsolescence in which modern buildings were ostensibly erected. The implication is that artificially decaying structures functioned as picturesque apologias for the hastened expiration of the capital's edifices, as well as for the sullied status of architecture in a climate of frenzied speculation. In sum, the consumption of ruins evidenced a city entranced by the signs of its own impermanence.

Viel's disdain for ruins was thus convergent with as well as shaped by his attitude toward commercial enterprise. The latter, it is worth noting, rendered moot the distinctions between unfinished structures, prematurely decaying edifices, and instantaneously destroyed buildings. All three posed possibilities for profitable reconstruction, making them valuable commodities in the speculative economy. What they shared was a hypothetical value superior to that of intact monuments. Accordingly, if the aesthetic of ruins affirmed this commercial hierarchy of values, then Robert's scenes of demolition and catastrophe constituted a natural subcategory of the genre, and not only because they tapped so emphatically into the "taste for destruction." Disaster sites posed investment opportunities—none more so than the Opéra's ruin. At the time that Robert exhibited his views of the destroyed monument, businessmen in partnership with architects—both from the painter's milieu—were already scheming to rebuild it at a profit.[96]

Viel's discussion, then, brings into focus the pressures that the speculative economy placed on the cult of ruins. For if ruins, as we saw in the previous chapter, pleased as figures of chance and irresolution, then the growing value ascribed in financial life to "transformation" as opposed to "conservation" rendered their appreciation as such problematic. Thus Diderot, who enjoyed in ruins qualities similar to those found in incomplete sketches, also identified Robert's lack of finish with commercial machinations. According to the critic, Robert's facile handling of paint evidenced a greed for luxe and a love of gain. "If this artist continues to sketch," Diderot warns in his *Salon de 1771,* "he will lose the practice of finishing, his head and his hand will become libertine.... He wishes to earn his ten louis in the morning; he is ostentatious, his wife is a woman of fashion, he must work fast, but he will lose his talent." In closing, Diderot advises the painter: "Get in the habit of finishing, Mr. Robert, and when you have gotten it, Mr. Robert, it will not cost you much more to make a painting than a sketch."[97] Diderot's criticism paved the way for oft-repeated observations linking Robert's rapidity of execution with impatience "to be paid." Just as speculators were accused of sacrificing the general welfare in pursuit of personal wealth, Robert's pendants at the Salon of 1781 appeared to betray the public values sanctified in history painting for the sake of self-enrichment. Métra's insinuation that commercial interests had infiltrated Robert's practice and Viel's hostility toward the vogue for ruins need hardly be considered the final word on the painter's predilections in order to be taken seriously as nods to the exploitation of disaster in aesthetic and financial life alike.

It remains the case, however, that Robert, alone among the city's view painters, mined the capacity of the unfinished—an ever-more-prominent characteristic of urban life—to grip the imagination. Jean-Baptiste Lallemand, a *vedutista* who trained in the company of Robert and Piranesi in Rome and shared their zeal for fantastical ruins, churned out staid and classicizing city views. Demachy, a ruin and view painter whose canvases were unfavorably compared to Robert's, incorporated dry (though not necessarily faithful) transcriptions of the reconstruction of the Louvre colonnade and the demolitions of churches into his architectural landscape repertoire. In opposition to Robert's bravura painterly performances, Demachy's views were feats of restraint and precision, showcasing the skills less of a painter than of a printmaker (thus Diderot's contemptuous recommendation that he "destroy his brushes") (fig. 43).[98] Robert was neither the first nor the only painter to discover in the changing cityscape a commanding subject. Yet he appears uniquely to have registered the double-sided perceptions occasioned by Paris, where tremulous invocations

Fig. 43. Pierre-Antoine Demachy (French, 1723–1807)
The Clearing of the Colonnade of the Louvre, 1764, oil on canvas, 41 × 51.5 cm (16⅛ × 20¼ in.)
Paris, Musée Carnavalet

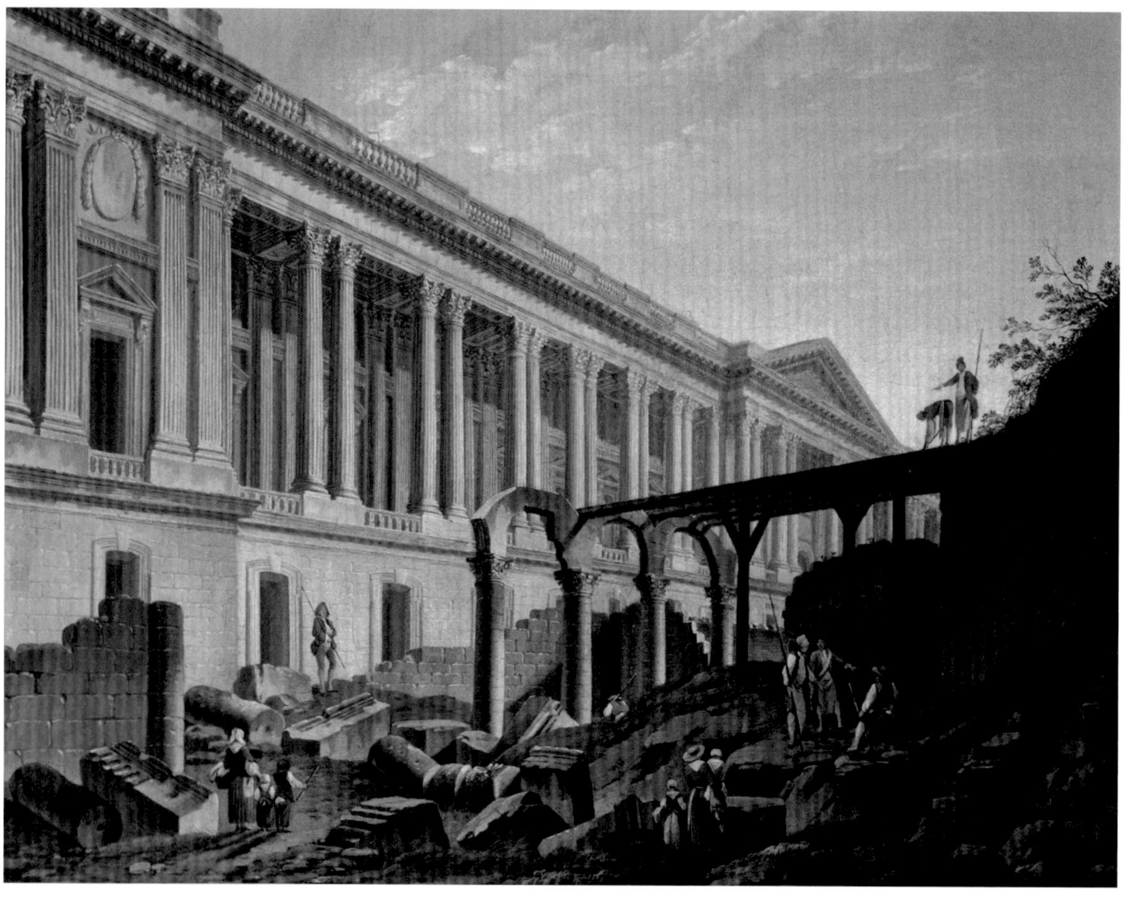

of antiquity's discredited capitals competed with hopeful recreations of ancient magnificence, and fears of draining the city's resources vied with the exhilarating promise of the building spree. Such recognition, to say the least, enabled the artist to cater to the pleasures of the unfinished, as Grimm describes: "The more [the artist] leaves to the [viewer's] imagination, the more he is sure to affect him violently."[99] Robert's suspenseful scenes thus revealed the inscrutability of the fate of the city to be the ultimate sublime subject. They verified, however farcically, that the most enticing of aesthetic experiences were also those that corroborated the logic of a risk economy.

Time of Hell

Taken together, Viel's portrait of urban corruption, Diderot's diatribe against Robert's commercial instincts, and the critical reactions to the capital's frenzied speculative development create a powerful backdrop to key attributes of the painter's disaster scenes: specifically, his aversion to finish and his absorption in the process of Fortuna overtaking the built environment, aesthetic orientations grounded in a widespread perception that the capital was hurtling full-speed toward some mysterious and ominous future. My interest lies not in arguing that Robert's views of a volatile cityscape were consubstantial with the "perpetual motion quest" of speculative society.[100] It is rather in making sense of the theatricality with which his works trafficked in the kinds of enchantments that were thought to presage the capital's downfall. That is, if the marvelous new quarter emerging "as if by magic" in the Chaussée d'Antin compelled a kind of belief in the usurious conjuration of something from nothing, then Robert's enraptured glorifications of destruction invested the city's sudden deficits with supreme aesthetic value—yet, as noted, they did so with prominent artifice. From the staged character of a painting like *Fire at the Hôtel-Dieu* (see fig. 30) to the concentrated exuberance of his church demolitions, Robert's art reveals a compulsion to treat the city as an immanently manageable theater of "astonishment," to appropriate Burke's term.[101] Such works, viewed in this light, point to the compensatory role played by the sublime as both the expression and appeasement of terror.

The sublime, writes Thomas Weiskel, "revives as God withdraws from an immediate participation in the experience of men."[102] The statement yields ironic insight into Robert's hellish images of the city—paintings that commune with the theme of divine retribution. His view of the ruined Opéra's interior (see fig. 24) is a case in point. Under the gaze of the onlookers above, the wreckage resembles not only an archaeological site but an inferno as well, from which they—the blessed—have been spared. It is difficult not to read a kind of wry Christian symbolism in the painting: Robert has packed his disaster scene with absurdly literalist versions of a sacral iconography, from the wood in the foreground configured as crosses to the multitudes of miniature "men of sorrows" who wrap their arms around charred beams, lugging and dragging them. (These workers are stationed in the central pit of the ruin, just beneath the figures in the central foreground, where their stooped forms rhyme with the curve of the overhanging hose.) Still more evocative of the Passion is the scarcely visible worker—parallel to the picture plane, at the far end of the structure and in the center of the canvas—who, framed by a small crowd of onlookers, bears his long, wooden weight at a low-lying diagonal. Robert has further embedded the painting with motifs of salvific passage. Through the frame of the far, rectangular window at right, parallel to the picture plane, barely perceptible figures—rendered with a series of impressionistic brushstrokes—appear to ascend a ladder. Still more literally, the hosing of fire with water reiterates the transubstantiation-like conversion of one material substance into another.

Robert's invocations of divine reckoning, however roguish, were symptomatic of a preoccupation with the intimacy between spiritual belief and a fixation on calamity. It is thus useful to recall Boulanger's excavation of the connection between the two in *L'antiquité dévoilée,* which focuses on the means whereby religion replaced an unmanageable fear of future catastrophe with "a salutary fear"—mixed with hope—over the soul's immortality. Through ancient festival rites, the people were socialized, and "misfortune and misery" turned into their opposites. Occurring at the end of a season or agricultural period—at the temporal interstices when primal terror over impending cataclysm was most likely to surface all festivals, Boulanger observes, commemorated the flood, while obliterating its memory: even as these mysterious celebrations symbolically reenacted the original events of destruction, their source was kept secret from the people. During these days of mystery, a sensibility of indifference to fate was institutionalized: "All worldly concerns . . . were banished; no longer were there Tribunals to punish the guilty"; schools ceased to instruct, and the government did not function. Anarchy reigned, and all social distinctions were dissolved. In short, "everyone behaved as if they had no concern for the future." Strikingly, Boulanger cites as evidence of such a respite from anxiety the people's custom, during the festival period, of engaging in the play of "dice and . . . all the games of chance that the police normally proscribed."[103]

In the process recounted by Boulanger, whereby the primal traces of devastation are retained and sublimated at the service of generating a happy and orderly society, games of chance assume a formative role: an atavistic dread of the future is overcome through institutions of play, through socialized surrender to an uncertain fate. In Boulanger's account, play serves as a means of overcoming a previous trauma. As in Caillois's treatment of the subject, reviewed in the previous chapter, play operates in homeopathic fashion, internalizing—so as to disable—elements of its mysterious and frightening precedent. As Johann Jakob Bachofen writes, "All games have a mortuary character." At ancient funeral ceremonies, he notes, games of chance marked the absorption of the ghost—an "unstable signifier"—into the stabilizing realm of ritual.[104]

This connection between play and death—and the channeling into games of chance of a fear of mortality—has been further explored by scholars of gambling. Lorraine Daston has shown that probability theory first emerged as a means of calculating mortality statistics. Kavanagh has pointed to "a profound complicity between probability theory's concerted emasculation of chance and our own continual rejection from consciousness of any real sense of our impending death." Given the link, he continues, between "chance, the less than certain, and the gamble of death," to embrace chance in the form of gambling—to reject the reasoned abstractions of probability theory—is on some level to gamble with one's own mortality.[105]

For their very proximity to death, games of chance enabled, in Boulanger's account, the substitution of pleasure for panic. Robert's paintings of urban disasters, executed in a climate teeming with apocalyptic prognostications and remembrances of the annihilation of civilizations past, suggest that the sublime served a similar function. Just as antiquity's religious rites turned sources of trauma into modes of enchantment, the sublime made volatility and decay—hallmarks of the speculative economy—consumable. It did so, moreover, at a time of critical transition—when the church found its monopoly on credulity challenged by the increasingly powerful and equally mysterious institution of the market; when the civilizing process, that is, once more demanded a kind of supernatural faith. Not unlike the "institution of mysteries" described by Boulanger, the market—sustained by the "magic of credit"—fostered its own religion of hope-fear: as Simmel observes, the decline of religious belief coincided with the "growing spiritualization of money" and with a mystical faith in the alchemy of capital.[106] Robert, captive witness to the demolitions of churches at the secular altar of profit, properly recognized the sublimity of his subjects, even as his choreographed maneuvers winked at their occurrence "as if by magic."

It is for this reason that Boulanger's text offers such a useful foil to Robert's paintings. The "unveiler" of antiquity believed as much in the sacrosanct values of Enlightenment rationality as in the basic human appetite for the marvelous. "I saw written in nature": with these words, Boulanger proceeds to recover the repressed "portal to our history." *L'antiquité dévoilée* acknowledges the inevitability of supernatural belief even as its own longing is for a world more transparent. Thus one detects in Boulanger's project a kind of nostalgia—if not for the enchantments of the ancient world, then for its fading legibility. A similar observation may be made of the sublime. The dazzling impenetrability of smoke, flames, and debris characterizing Robert's destruction scenes marked the obvious relish with which he brought a Burkean imagery of the "dark, uncertain, confused" to bear on Paris.[107] Yet it was perhaps with a secret earnestness that he also made an increasingly "unrecognizable" city recognizable, lending it, however fleetingly, the familiar visage of Pompeii, of Rome, of Hell.

NOTES

1 Charles-Louis de Secondat, baron de Montesquieu, *Considerations on the Causes of the Greatness of the Romans and Their Decline,* trans. David Lowenthal (Indianapolis: Hackett, 1999), 98.

2 Claude-Nicolas Ledoux to Charles-André de Lacoré, 24 August 1775, Archives du Doubs, C 40; cited in Commission du vieux Paris, *Ledoux et Paris* (Paris: Rotonde de la villette, 1979), 33.

3 The whereabouts of the first of these two pendants are unknown; the work is reproduced in Claude Gabillot, "L'incendie de l'Opéra en 1781 et les tableaux de Hubert Robert," *Gazette des beaux-arts* 9 (1913): 26–36. The painting appears to have differed little from the oil study now in the Musée de l'Opéra (see fig. 23).

4 Denis Diderot, "Salon of 1767," in John Goodman, ed. and trans., *Diderot on Art* (New Haven: Yale Univ. Press, 1995), 2:208, 197.

5 Henri Bernardin de Saint-Pierre, *Études de la nature* (Paris: Deterville, 1804), 3:184–85.

6 Edmund Burke, *A Philosophical Enquiry into the Origin of Our Ideas of the Sublime and Beautiful,* ed. Adam Philipps (Oxford: Oxford Univ. Press, 1990), 57, 76. On Robert's Paris views, see Louis Réau, "Hubert Robert, peintre de Paris," *Bulletin de la Société de l'histoire de l'art* (1927): 207–27; Bernard de Montgolfier, "Hubert Robert, peintre de Paris au Musée

Carnavalet," *Bulletin du Musée Carnavalet,* nos. 1–2 (1964): 2–35; and Paula Rea Radisich, "Hubert Robert's Paris: Truth, Artifice, and Spectacle," *Studies on Voltaire and the Eighteenth Century* 245 (1986): 501–18.

7 The phrase is from Jacques-Denis Liégeon, "Exposition du projet d'un nouvel hôtel pour MM. les Comédiens français," 28 November 1769, Archives nationales, O^1 846, no. 10.

8 Robert's *Festivities at the Pont de Neuilly,* featuring the bridge at the moment of its much-heralded completion by the engineer Jean-Rodolphe Perronet, is a case in point (though the whereabouts of the canvas are unknown, a sketch hangs in the Musée Carnavalet). On the interest aroused by the work, see Bernadette Fort, ed., *Les Salons des "Mémoires secrets" 1767–1787* (Paris: École nationale supérieure des beaux-arts, 1999), 143. On urban reform, see esp. Isabelle Backouche, *La trace du fleuve: La Seine et Paris, 1750–1850* (Paris: École des hautes études en sciences sociales, 2000); Nicholas Papayanis, *Planning Paris before Haussmann* (Baltimore: Johns Hopkins Univ. Press, 2004); and Béatrice de Andia, ed., *L'urbanisme parisien au siècle des lumières* (Paris: Action artistique de la ville de Paris, 1997). For an overview of building enterprises, see Allan Braham, *The Architecture of the French Enlightenment* (Berkeley: Univ. of California Press, 1980).

9 François Métra, *Correspondance secrète, politique et littéraire* (London: John Adamson, 1775–93), 12:83. See also Gabillot, "L'incendie de l'Opéra." The details of the fire are recounted in René Farge, "L'incendie de l'Opéra en 1781," *Bulletin de la Société d'iconographie parisienne* (1908): 9–26.

10 [Antoine Renou], "Suite l'examen d'une critique du Salon," *Journal de Paris,* no. 267 (24 September 1781): 1076.

11 These comments were recorded, respectively, in *Pique-nique convenable à ceux qui fréquent-ent le Sallon, préparé par un aveugle* (1781): 16–17; and "Exposition des Ouvrages de Peinture, Sculpture et Gravure au Sallon du Louvre, année 1781," *Mercure de France* (6 October 1781): 29; reprinted as *Mercure de France* (Geneva: Slatkine Reprints, 1971), 121:328.

12 *Réflexions joyeuses d'un garçon de bonne humeur sur les tableaux exposés au sallon en 1781;* cited in Claude Gabillot, *Hubert Robert et son temps* (Paris: Librairie de l'art, 1895), 128. On Robert's pendants as violations of the hierarchy of genres, see Sabine Weicherding, "Faut-il brûler l'Opéra? Hubert Robert et l'incendie de l'Opéra de 1781," in Thomas W. Gaehtgens et al., eds., *L'art et les normes sociales au XVIIIe siècle* (Paris: Éditions de la maison des sciences de l'homme, 2001), 477–92. The quotation from the *Mercure de France* is translated in Radisich, "Hubert Robert's Paris," 501.

13 Fort, *Salons des "Mémoires secrets,"* 220. On the significance of these paintings and the revitalization of a national school of history painting, see Thomas E. Crow, *Painters and Public Life in Eighteenth-Century Paris* (New Haven: Yale Univ. Press, 1985), chap. 6, esp. 197–209.

14 Diderot, "Salon of 1767," 100.

15 Bernardin de Saint-Pierre, *Études de la nature,* 185; Charles-Marguerite-Jean-Baptiste Mercier Dupaty, *Lettres sur l'Italie, en 1785* (Lausanne: Jean Mourer, 1796), 238–43.

16 Burke, *Philosophical Enquiry,* 36, 42–44.

17 Voltaire, "La guerre civile de Genève," *Oeuvres de Voltaire,* ed. Adrien-Jean-Quentin Beuchot (Paris: Firmin-Didot Frères, 1833), 12:292.

18 Louis-Sébastien Mercier, *Mon bonnet de nuit* (Neufchâtel: Imprimerie de la Société typographique, 1784), 2:147; idem, *Tableau de Paris,* new ed. (Amsterdam, 1782–88), vol. 4, chap. 355, pp. 299–300, 305.

19 Neil MacGregor, "Le voyage pittoresque de Naples et de Sicile," *Connoisseur* 196, no. 788 (1977): 132.

20 William Chambers, *Dissertation on Oriental Gardening* (Dublin: Wilson, 1773), 27–28; cited in Christopher Thacker, "The Volcano: Culmination of the Landscape Garden," *Eighteenth-Century Life* 8, no. 2 (1983): 76.

21 See Iain McCalman, "Magic, Spectacle, and the Art of de Loutherbourg's Eidophusikon," in Ann Bermingham, ed., *Sensation and Sensibility: Viewing Gainsborough's Cottage Door* (New

Haven: Yale Center for British Art, 2005), 181–97, 209–11. See Kevin Salatino's discussion of "the eruptive sublime" in idem, *Incendiary Art: The Representation of Fireworks in Early Modern Europe* (Los Angeles: Getty Research Institute, 1997), 54–76.

22 Jean-Claude Richard de Saint-Non, *Le voyage pittoresque; ou, Description des royaumes de Naples et de Sicile* (Paris: Imprimerie de Clousier, 1781–86), 1:208–10. The episode is recounted in MacGregor, "Voyage pittoresque," 133.

23 *Le pour et le contre* 17 (1739): 268; translated in Kristel Smentek, "An Exact Imitation Acquired at Little Expense: Marketing Color Prints in Eighteenth-Century Paris," in Margaret Morgan Grasselli, Kristel Smentek, and Judith G. Walsh, *Colorful Impressions: The Printmaking Revolution in Eighteenth-Century France,* exh. cat. (Washington, D.C.: National Gallery of Art, 2003), 10; Saint-Non, *Voyage pittoresque,* 2:56.

24 Sylvain Maréchal, *Les antiquités d'Herculanum avec leur explications en françois* (Paris: David, 1780), 1:iii.

25 Réstif de La Bretonne, *Les nuits de Paris; or, The Nocturnal Spectator: A Selection,* trans. Linda Asher and Ellen Fertig (New York: Random House, 1967), 162–64.

26 On this subject, see Frank E. Manuel, *The Eighteenth Century Confronts the Gods* (New York: Atheneum, 1967), esp. 128–241.

27 Nicolas-Antoine Boulanger, *L'antiquité dévoilée par ses usages; ou, Examen critique des principales opinions, cérémonies, et institutions religieuses et politiques des différens peuples de la terre* (Amsterdam: M. M. Rey, 1766), 5.

28 Manuel, *Eighteenth Century,* 215. See the sketch of Boulanger's biography in "Extrait d'une lettre écrite à l'editeur sur la vie et les ouvrages de M. Boulanger," in Boulanger, *Antiquité dévoilée,* iii–vi.

29 Boulanger, *Antiquité dévoilée,* 149.

30 Paul Henri Dietrich, baron d'Holbach, *Système de la nature*... (London [Amsterdam], 1770), 1; translated in Manuel, *Eighteenth Century,* 231.

31 See Manuel's discussion of this subject in *Eighteenth Century,* 3–12, 177–83, 225. Hume explores the "mixed passions" of hope and fear in his *Dissertation on the Passions,* which was published along with his *Natural History of Religion* in 1757. In section 8 of the latter study, Hume writes that the "active imagination of men" and the power played by their "hopes and fears" ensured that "the principles of religion have a kind of flux and reflux in the human mind." David Hume, *A Dissertation on the Passions; The Natural History of Religion: A Critical Edition,* ed. Tom L. Beauchamp (Oxford: Clarendon Press, 2007), 58.

32 Mercier, *Mon bonnet de nuit,* 1:5; idem, *Tableau de Paris,* vol. 3, chap. 227, p. 84. Discussed in Henry F. Majewski, "Mercier and the Preromantic Myth of the End of the World," *Studies in Romanticism* 7, no. 1 (1967): 4–5.

33 Bernard Groethuysen, *The Bourgeois: Catholicism vs. Capitalism in Eighteenth-Century France,* trans. Mary Ilford (New York: Holt, Rinehart & Winston, 1968), 67.

34 The pendants were purchased by the Russian prince Paul Petrovitch (then traveling in France pseudonymously as the "comte de Nord"). Musée de Valence, *Hubert Robert et Saint-Pétersbourg: Les commandes de la famille impériale et des princes russes entre 1773 et 1802,* exh. cat. (Paris: Réunion des musées nationaux, 1999), 120, no. 14. Cayeux notes the relationship between *The Fire at the Hôtel-Dieu in Paris* and *The Burning of Rome* in Jean de Cayeux with Catherine Boulot, *Hubert Robert* (Paris: Fayard, 1989), 207.

35 Mercier, *Mon bonnet de nuit,* 1:11.

36 Siméon-Prosper Hardy, *Mes loisirs: Journal d'événements tels qu'ils parviennent à ma connaissance,* ed. Maurice Tourneux and Maurice Vitrac (Paris: A. Picard, 1912).

37 These examples are taken from Nicolas Delamare, *Traité de police,* 2nd ed. (Paris: Chez M. Brunet, 1719–38), 4:9–10; translated in Papayanis, *Planning Paris,* 37; Voltaire, *Des embellissements de Paris,* in Mark Waddicor, ed., *The Complete Works of Voltaire* (Oxford: Voltaire Foundation, Taylor Institution, 1994), 231–32; and Mercier, *Tableau de Paris,* vol. 1, chap. 88, p. 280. For another account of the symbolic dimension of the subject—one concerning fire as a sign of creative genius in the writing of Diderot and his contemporaries—

see Jacques Chouillet, "La métaphore du feu et son développement pictural de 1765 à 1781," in René Démoris, ed., *Les fins de la peinture* (Paris: Desjonquères, 1990), 19–27.

38 Pierre Patte, "Des embellissemens de Paris," in idem, *Monumens erigés en France à la gloire de Louis XV* (Paris, 1765), 212–13. On the movement to reform the hospital, see Marcel Candille, "Les projets de translation de l'Hôtel-Dieu de Paris hors de la cité," *Revue de l'assistance publique* vol. 7, no. 44 (1956): 743–52; vol. 8, no. 46 (1957): 239–63; no. 47, 343–59; no. 48, 433–49; Bruno Fortier, "Architecture de l'hôpital," in Michel Foucault et al., *Les machines à guérir: Aux origines de l'hôpital moderne* (Brussels: P. Mardaga, 1979); and Anthony Vidler, "Confinement and Cure: Reforming the Hospital, 1770–1789," in idem, *The Writing of the Walls: Architectural Theory in the Late Enlightenment* (Princeton: Princeton Architectural Press, 1987), 51–72. On the transition from aesthetic conceptions of the city to a discourse centered on the pathologies of urban life, see Emmanuel Le Roy Ladurie, "De l'esthétique à la pathologie," in Roger Chartier, Emmanuel Le Roy Ladurie, and Bernard Quilliet, *La ville des temps modernes: De la Renaissance aux révolutions* (Paris: Éditions du Seuil, 1998), 287–92.

39 On the circumstances of the fire—which ravaged the hospital from the early hours of 30 December until 9 January, when the flames abated—see Marcel Aubert, "L'Hôtel-Dieu et l'incendie de 1772," *Société d'iconographie parisienne* (1910): 13–24. Poyet's proposal is described in his *Mémoire sur la necessité de transférer et reconstruire l'Hôtel-Dieu de Paris...* (Paris, 1785).

40 Rondonneau de La Motte, *Essai historique sur l'Hôtel-Dieu de Paris...* (Paris: Nyon l'ainé, 1787), iii–vi. In 1788, the firm formerly associated with Girardot attempted unsuccessfully to administer a high-interest loan to finance the hospital's relocation. See Marcel Rouff, "Une grève de gagne-deniers en 1786 à Paris," *Revue historique,* no. 105 (1910): 340–41; and Radisich, "Hubert Robert's Paris," 510–11.

41 Fort, *Salons des "Mémoires secrets,"* 240.

42 Patte, "Des embellissemens de Paris." On embellishment, see Jean-Marc Dudot et al., *Le devoir d'embellir: Essai sur la politique d'embellissement à la fin de l'ancien régime* (Nancy: CEMPA, 1978). That embellishment marked the prioritization of science over the realm of the visible is reflected in Nicolas Goulet's statement, "If the proposed site of embellishment is an unhealthy environment...the most splendid buildings will not make [it] more beautiful." In Nicolas Goulet, *Observations sur les embellissemens de Paris et sur les monumens qui s'y construisent...* (Paris: Chez l'auteur, 1808), 2–3. See Antoine Picon's account of the role of embellishment in the crisis of Classical architectural theory in *French Architects and Engineers in the Age of Enlightenment,* trans. Martin Thom (Cambridge: Cambridge Univ. Press, 1992), chap. 8. See also Françoise Choay, *The Rule and the Model: On the Theory of Architecture and Urbanism,* ed. Denise Bratton (Cambridge: MIT Press, 1997), esp. chap. 5. For an alternative account of urbanism, one disputing the marginalization of visual concerns, see Rodolphe el-Khoury, "Polish and Deodorize: Paving the City in Late-Eighteenth-Century France," *Assemblage* 31 (1996): 6–15.

43 Jean-Louis Viel de Saint-Maux, "Septième lettre sur l'architecture des anciens," in idem, *Lettres sur l'architecture des anciens et celle des modernes* (Geneva: Minkoff Reprint, 1974), 3, 7, 9, 6, 21, 10, 58n30, 34, 23.

44 Viel de Saint-Maux, "Septième lettre," 58n30, 19–20, 56nn24–25.

45 See Pierre Pinon, Patricia Boniface, and Patrick Gullon, *Lotissements spéculatifs et formes urbaines: Le quartier de la Chaussée d'Antin à la fin de l'ancien régime* (Paris: Bureau de la recherche architecturale, École d'architecture de Paris—La defense, 1986).

46 Mercier, *Tableau de Paris,* vol. 1, chap. 88, pp. 277–78 (for the first part of the quotation), vol. 8, chap. 635, p. 191 (for the second); translated in Michel Gallet, *Stately Mansions: Eighteenth Century Paris Architecture* (New York: Praeger, 1972), 4.

47 See Philip T. Hoffman, Gilles Postel-Vinay, and Jean-Laurent Rosenthal, *Priceless Markets: The Political Economy of Credit in Paris, 1660–1870* (Chicago: Univ. of Chicago Press, 2000), 156–57. "Between 1770 and 1789," the authors write, "net private indebtedness in Paris

climbed 533 million livres, or 28 million a year." Every year, the credit market funded the acquisition of 12 million livres' worth of "private assets," primarily "the buildings produced by Parisian developers." On speculative society, see J. G. A. Pocock, "Modes of Political and Historical Time in Early Eighteenth-Century England," in idem, *Virtue, Commerce and History: Essays on Political Thought and History, Chiefly in the Eighteenth Century* (1985; reprint, Cambridge: Cambridge Univ. Press, 1995), 91–102.

48 "Each day sees new buildings constructed, new streets opened, new quarters and new squares formed." "Prospectus d'un ouvrage intitulé, *Annales Municipales*... par M. Ameilhon...," *Journal de Paris,* supplement to no. 46 (15 February 1787): 201.

49 Viel de Saint-Maux, "Septième lettre," 7.

50 Étienne La Font de Saint-Yenne, *Réflexions sur quelques causes de l'état présent de la peinture en France,* in René Démoris and Florence Ferran, eds., *La peinture en procès: L'invention de la critique d'art au siècle des lumières* (Paris: Presses de la Sorbonne nouvelle, 2001), 91; translated in Melissa Hyde, *Making Up the Rococo: François Boucher and His Critics* (Los Angeles: Getty Research Institute, 2006), 92.

51 Étienne La Font de Saint-Yenne, *Sentimens sur quelques ouvrages de peinture, sculpture et gravure, écrits à un particulier en province* (Paris, 1754), 138; translated in Katie Scott, *The Rococo Interior: Decoration and Social Spaces in Early Eighteenth-Century Paris* (New Haven: Yale Univ. Press, 1995), 254.

52 Elisabeth-Louise Vigée-Lebrun, *Souvenirs;* translated by Gerard Shelley as *The Memoirs of Mme Elisabeth Louise Vigée-Le Brun, 1755–1789* (London: John Hamilton, 1926), 159. I use the term *Rococo* out of convenience, despite the term's coinage well after the demise of the style it (disparagingly) named; on the neologism's coinage, see Hyde, *Making up the Rococo,* 9–12. Robert's vast art collection included works by Watteau, Jean-Baptiste Pater, his friend Fragonard, and above all Boucher. See the "Catalogue des tableaux... de la vente après décès du Cabinet d'Hubert Robert," in Gabillot, *Hubert Robert,* 256–71. In addition to copying from the work of Boucher, Robert may have taken drawing lessons from him. See Cayeux, *Hubert Robert,* 88–89, 130.

53 Robert's patrons were forthright on this point. The letters the painter exchanged with Laborde (discussed in the previous chapter) concerning plans for Méréville express their common interest in *simplicité.* Similarly, Pierre-Augustin Caron de Beaumarchais, writing to Robert in 1790, communicates his desire for a decorative ensemble that will harmonize with "the simple and antique manner of [his] salon," as well as his fear of being "reproached with luxe." The letter, in a private collection, is cited in Cayeux, *Hubert Robert,* 270; and Radisich, *Hubert Robert,* 14.

54 The subject of this view is debatable. It is possible that the work is a caprice, although the building's thermal windows were typical of theaters (Christophe Leribault, curator formerly at the Musée Carnavalet, personal communication, 2006). Notably, Watteau's follower Nicolas Lancret absorbed the fire motif into his repertoire of erotic subjects. See, for instance, Georges Wildenstein, *Lancret* (Paris: G. Servant, 1924), pl. 4; and Elise Goodman-Soellner, "Nicolas Lancret's 'Le miroir ardent': An Emblematic Image of Love," *Simiolus: Netherlands Quarterly for the History of Art* 13, nos. 3–4 (1983): 218–24.

55 Georg Simmel, "The Ruin," in Kurt H. Wolff, ed., *Essays on Sociology, Philosophy, and Aesthetics* (New York: Harper & Row, 1965), 263.

56 La Font de Saint-Yenne, *Réflexions,* 93; translated in Hyde, *Making Up the Rococo,* 79n90.

57 Scott, *Rococo Interior,* 147.

58 Germain Brice, *Description de la ville de Paris et de tout ce qu'elle contient de plus remarquable,* ed. Pierre Codet (9th ed., Paris: Libraires associés, 1752; reprint, Paris: Librairie Minard, 1971), 1:115. The ramparts were demolished and replaced by boulevards between 1685 and 1705. Viel's warnings about the city's expansion appear in his "Septième lettre," 20, 56n25.

59 Jean-Aymar Piganiol de La Force, *Description historique de la ville de Paris et de ses environs* (Paris: Libraires associés, 1765) 1:25; translated in Scott, *Rococo Interior,* 147.

60 David Harvey (following Karl Marx), *The Limits to Capital* (London: Verso, 1999), 367; my use of the phrase draws on points made by Fredric Jameson in "The Brick and the Balloon: Architecture, Idealism and Land Speculation," *New Left Review* 228 (1998): 25–46.

61 Gilles Deleuze and Félix Guattari, *Anti-Oedipus: Capitalism and Schizophrenia* (Minneapolis: Univ. of Minnesota Press, 1998), 186. On eighteenth-century theories of the decadence of the arts, see Christian Michel, *Charles-Nicolas Cochin et l'art des lumières* (Rome: École française de Rome, 1993), 299–336.

62 Jean Dusaulx, *De la passion du jeu depuis les temps anciens jusqu'à nos jours* (Paris: Moutard, 1779), 91, 97, 101, 95.

63 As reported by the marquis d'Argenson in *Journal et mémoires* (Paris: Renouard, 1859–67), 2:93; cited and translated in Thomas M. Kavanagh, *Enlightenment and the Shadows of Chance: The Novel and the Culture of Gambling in Eighteenth-Century France* (Baltimore: Johns Hopkins Univ. Press, 1993), 31. Dusaulx's comments appear in his *De la passion du jeu,* 87–89.

64 Jacques-Pierre Brissot de Warville, *Dénonciation au public d'un nouveau projet d'agiotage...* (London, 1786), 21. On this controversy, see Robert Darnton, "L'idéologie à la Bourse," in *Gens de lettres, gens du livre,* translated from the English by Marie-Alyx Revellat (Paris: Editions Odile Jacob, 1992), 86–98. On the discourse against fireworks, see Werner Oechslin and Anja Buschow, *Architecture de fête: L'architecte metteur en scène,* translated from the German by Marianne Brausch (Brussels: Pierre Mardaga, 1984), 27.

65 André Corboz, *Peinture militante et architecture révolutionnaire: À propos du thème du tunnel chez Hubert Robert* (Basel: Birkhäuser, 1978), 45.

66 Charles-Louis de Secondat, baron de Montesquieu, *Essai sur le goût* (1757), ed. Charles-Jacques Beyer (Geneva: Librairie Droz, 1967), 80. "Capitalism... never can be stationary," writes Joseph A. Schumpeter in *Capitalism, Socialism and Democracy* (New York: Harper & Row, 1976), 82–83.

67 Lorraine Daston, *Classical Probability in the Enlightenment* (Princeton: Princeton Univ. Press, 1988), 117.

68 On this church and the circumstances of its demolition, see H. Lemoine, "L'Église Saint-Jean-En-Grève: Ses cimetières et sa démolition," *Bulletin de la Société de l'histoire de Paris et de l'Île-de-France* 49 (1922): 71–76.

69 Cayeux, *Hubert Robert,* 208.

70 Cara D. Denison, Myra Nan Rosenfeld, and Stephanie Wiles, *Exploring Rome: Piranesi and His Contemporaries,* exh. cat. (New York: Pierpont Morgan Library, 1993), 175, no. 97.

71 See, respectively, Barry Bergdoll, *European Architecture, 1750–1890* (Oxford: Oxford Univ. Press, 2000), 65; and Braham, *Architecture of the French Enlightenment,* 137–45.

72 Tanis Hinchcliffe, "Gender and the Architect: Women Clients of French Architects during the Enlightenment," in Louise Durning and Richard Wrigley, eds., *Gender and Architecture* (Chichester: Wiley, 2000), 127. On the lavish homes designed for actress-courtesans, see Kathryn Norberg, "Goddesses of Taste: Courtesans and Their Furniture in Late-Eighteenth-Century Paris," in Dena Goodman and Kathryn Norberg, eds., *Furnishing the Eighteenth Century: What Furniture Can Tell Us about the European and American Past* (New York: Routledge, 2007), 97–114.

73 Mercier, *Tableau de Paris,* vol. 10, chap. 776, pp. 54–55. See also, for example, his chapter entitled "Louis d'or," 9:147–49.

74 On borrowing as a recipe for ruin, see Nicolas Le Camus de Mézières, *Le guide de ceux qui veulent bâtir* (Paris: Chez l'auteur, 1781), 6–13.

75 Michael Sonenscher, *Before the Deluge: Public Debt, Inequality, and the Intellectual Origins of the French Revolution* (Princeton: Princeton Univ. Press, 2007).

76 Laurence Fontaine, "Antonio and Shylock: Credit and Trust in France, c. 1680–c. 1780," *Economic History Review,* n.s., 54, no. 1 (2001): 40. The reference to fire appears in François Véron Duverger de Forbonnais, "Crédit," in Denis Diderot and Jean Le Rond d'Alembert, *Encyclopédie; ou, Dictionnaire raisonné des sciences, des arts et des métiers* (Paris: Briasson [et al.], 1754–72), 4:447.

77 Sonenscher, *Before the Deluge,* 1–21.

78 Richard Cleary, "Romancing the Tome; or, An Academician's Pursuit of a Popular Audience in 18th-Century France," *Journal of the Society of Architectural Historians* 48, no. 2 (1989): 149. See also Jacques-Antoine Dulaure's characterization of antique austerity as a "fashion" in his *Nouvelle description des curiosités de Paris* (Paris: Lejay, 1787), 1:120–21. Viel similarly remarks that the style of the "innovators, so fateful for all the arts, will last no longer than the century whose end approaches." In the same pamphlet he denounces Ledoux for his "ruinous enterprises." *Décadence de l'architecture à la fin du dix-huitième siècle* (Paris: Perronneau, 1800), 8–9; cited in Emil Kaufmann, *Three Revolutionary Architects, Boullée, Ledoux, and Lequeu* (Philadelphia: American Philosophical Society, 1952), 458nn347–48.

79 Cited in Kaufmann, *Three Revolutionary Architects,* 457.

80 See François D'Ormesson and Jean-Pierre Thomas, *Jean-Joseph de Laborde: Banquier de Louis XV, mécène des lumières* (Paris: Perrin, 2002), 150–65, on the banker's real estate speculations, as well as Pinon, Boniface, and Gullon, *Lotissements spéculatifs,* on the speculative operations of Ledoux, Belanger, and De Wailly. On the comte d'Artois's building ambitions, see Valérie-Noëlle Jouffre, "Le quartier du Roule et les spéculations aux Champs-Elysées," *Cahiers du Centre de recherches et d'études sur Paris et l'Ile-de-France* 18 (1987): 49–60. On Robert's paintings at the Bagatelle, see Radisich, *Hubert Robert,* chap. 4. As Radisich notes, d'Artois accrued massive debt in order to win his 100,000-franc wager with Marie Antoinette that the palace could be built in a two-month period (81). On Robert's relationship with the comte de Choiseul-Gouffier, see Cayeux, *Hubert Robert,* 109. On Choiseul-Gouffier's land speculations, see Natacha Coquery, *L'hôtel aristocratique: Le marché du luxe à Paris au XVIIIe siècle* (Paris: Publications de la Sorbonne, 1998), 253–74.

81 On Robert's collaborations with Ledoux, see, for instance, Michel Gallet, *Les architectes parisiens du XVIIIe siècle: Dictionnaire biographique et critique* (Paris: Mengès, 1995), 305. On Robert's friendship with Alexandre-Théodore Brongniart (who designed Robert's country home in Auteuil), see *Alexandre-Théodore Brongniart, 1739–1813: Architecture et décor,* exh. cat. (Paris: Musées de la ville de Paris, 1986), 276–77; and Cayeux, *Hubert Robert,* 300–301. It should be noted that the king's negligence in issuing payments to the architects in his employ was likely a factor in their turn to speculative enterprise (despite the Académie's prohibitions on such activity). Such cases are compiled in Gallet, *Architectes parisiens.* Laborde's *hôtel* reputedly contained fourteen works by Robert; see Ferdinand Boyer, "Les collections et les ventes de Jean-Joseph de Laborde," *Bulletin de la Société de l'histoire de l'art français* (1961): 142. On the development of the faubourg Poissonnière, see Pascal Etienne, *Le faubourg Poissonnière: Architecture, élégance et décor* (Paris: Délégation à l'Action artistique, 1986). The extensive dealings in real estate of the marquise de Langeac are discussed in Jouffre, "Quartier du Roule," 53–54. On Choiseul's collection, see Emile Dacier, "La curiosité au XVIIIe siècle: Choiseul collectionneur," *Gazette des beaux-arts* 36 (1949): 47–74. On the plan hatched by Laborde to raise Choiseul's property values, see Ferdinand Boyer, "Un lotissement à Paris au XVIIIe siècle: De l'Hôtel de Choiseul à la Comédie Italienne," *La vie urbaine* 4 (1962): 241–60.

82 Cayeux cites this advertisement in *Hubert Robert,* 170.

83 On the ancient models upon which the Halle au Blé and the Comédie Française were based, see Braham, *Architecture of the French Enlightenment,* 100, 109. On the speculation involved in both projects, see, respectively, Françoise Boudon, "Urbanisme et spéculation à Paris au XVIIIe siècle: Le terrain de l'Hôtel de Soissons," *Journal of the Society of Architectural Historians* 32, no. 4 (1973): 267–307; and Daniel Rabreau and Monika Steinhauser, "Le théâtre de l'Odéon de Charles De Wailly et Marie-Joseph Peyre, 1767–1782," *Revue de l'art* 19 (1973): 8–49. La Font's comment appears in Piganiol de La Force, *Description historique de la ville de Paris,* 3:494–95; translated in Richard Wittman, *Architecture, Print Culture, and the Public Sphere in Eighteenth-Century France* (New York: Routledge, 2007), 183.

84 Choiseul's rumored involvement (no definitive evidence of his role in the operation has been found) is discussed in John Goodman, "'Altar against Altar': The Colisée, Vauxhall Utopianism and Symbolic Politics in Paris (1769–77)," *Art History* 15, no. 4 (1992): 444.

85 Goodman notes the precedent of Piranesi in "'Altar against Altar,'" 458n23. The comparison with antiquity is made in Georges-Louis Le Rouge, *Description du Colisée, élevé aux Champs-Élysées sur les dessins de M. Le Camus* (Paris: Le Rouge, 1771); cited in Jules Guiffrey, "Livret de l'exposition du Colisée" (1776), in idem, *Divers salons du dix-huitième siècle* (Nogent-Le-Roi, France: Jacques Laget, 1996), 74.

86 Louis Petit de Bachaumont et al., *Mémoires secrets pour servir à l'histoire de la république des lettres en France, depuis MDCCLXII jusqu'à nos jours; ou, Journal d'un observateur,* 24 May 1771 (London: J. Adamson, 1783–89), 5:268. Mercier's remarks appear in *Tableau de Paris,* vol. 3, chap. 214, pp. 32–33. The failure of this state-sponsored gamble is discussed in Robert M. Isherwood, *Farce and Fantasy: Popular Entertainment in Eighteenth-Century Paris* (New York: Oxford Univ. Press, 1986), 149–60.

87 Pierre Lavedan, *Histoire de l'urbanisme,* vol. 27, *Renaissance et temps modernes* (Paris: Henri Laurens, 1941), 182.

88 Pocock, "Modes of Political and Historical Time," 99.

89 See the discussion of the Hôtel Thélusson in Wend von Kalnein, *Architecture in France in the Eighteenth Century,* trans. David Britt (New Haven: Yale Univ. Press, 1995), 240. Braham notes in *Architecture of the French Enlightenment,* 188–89, that the main house's projecting salon recalled the Temple of Vesta at Tivoli, familiar from Piranesi's *Vedute di Roma.* Robert helped select the decorative pattern for the walls of the interior; Commission du vieux Paris, *Ledoux et Paris,* 38. Vidler's account is in his *Claude-Nicolas Ledoux: Architecture and Social Reform at the End of the ancien régime* (Cambridge: MIT Press, 1990), 60. On Ledoux's speculative activities in the quarter, see Pierre Pinon, "Lotissements spéculatifs, formes urbaines et architectes à la fin de l'ancien régime," in Monique Mosser and Daniel Rabreau, eds., *Soufflot et l'architecture des lumières* (Paris: École nationale supérieure des beaux-arts, 1986), 178–91.

90 Poyet's statement is cited and translated in Kalnein, *Architecture in France,* 240. On critical responses to the Hôtel Thélusson, see Commission du vieux Paris, *Ledoux et Paris,* 38. The appellation appears in Denis Diderot's "Salon de 1769," in idem, *Salons,* ed. J. Seznec and J. Adhémar (Oxford: Clarendon, 1957–67), 4:65.

91 In Charles-Paul Landon et al., *Annales du Musée et de l'école moderne des beaux-arts* (Paris: C. P. Landon, 1806), 6:19; cited in Commission du vieux Paris, *Ledoux et Paris,* 40. On the characterization of Sainte-Foix as "faithless" (by Auguste-Marie-Raymond, comte de La Marck), see Musées de la ville de Paris, *Alexandre-Théodore Brongniart,* 45. Mercier's comments appear in *Tableau de Paris,* vol. 7, chap. 557, p. 89; vol. 9, p. 104; vol. 2, chap. 191 ("Amour du merveilleux").

92 Jameson, "Brick and the Balloon," 26. On the picturesque elements, I quote from Jacques-Guillaume Legrand and Charles-Paul Landon, *Description de Paris, et des ses édifices...* (Paris: C. P. Landon, 1806), vol. 2, pt. 4, p. 4. On the fusion of the natural with the built, see Michael Dennis, *Court and Garden: From the French Hôtel to the City of Modern Architecture* (Cambridge: MIT Press, 1986), chap. 5, esp. 141. Pinto's discussion appears in Isaac de Pinto, *Traité de la circulation et du crédit...* (Amsterdam: Chez Marc Michel Rey, 1771), 33, 47.

93 Viel de Saint-Maux, "Septième lettre," 23, 58n30.

94 Mercier, *Tableau de Paris,* vol. 8, chap. 638, pp. 206–7.

95 Anthony Giddens, *Modernity and Self-Identity: Self and Society in the Late Modern Age* (Stanford, Calif.: Stanford Univ. Press, 1991), 111.

96 On the illicit venture between the architect Samson-Nicolas Lenoir (Robert's fellow academician in Rome, as well as a seasoned real estate speculator) and the royal minister Denis-Pierre-Jean Papillon de La Ferté, see Réné Farge, "Autour d'une salle d'Opéra: Un haut fonctionnaire de l'ancien régime, Papillon de la Ferté," *Annales revolutionnaires* 5 (1912): 1–22, as well as Nina L. Dubin, "Robert des Ruines," *Cabinet* 20 (2006): 92–97. On the role played by the Opéra in the capital's building spree, see Daniel Rabreau, "L'Opéra au centre de l'urbanisme parisien: Notes sur les projets de reconstruction de l'Opéra entre le Louvre et les Tuileries (1781–1800)," in idem, *L'Opéra au XVIIIe siècle: Actes du colloque* (Aix-en-Provence: Université de Provence / Marseille: Diffusion, J. Lafitte, 1982), 345–78.

97 Denis Diderot, "Salon de 1771," in idem, *Salons,* ed. J. Seznec and J. Adhémar (Oxford: Clarendon, 1957–67), 4:189; translated in Radisich, *Hubert Robert,* 5. Jean Chatelus also attends to the significance of Robert's speedy execution in "Quelques réflexions sur les peintres et l'argent à Paris au XVIIIe siècle," in Pierre Goubert, ed., *La France d'ancien régime: Études réunis en l'honneur de Pierre Goubert* (Toulouse: Société de démographie historique et éditions privat, 1984), 1:134.

98 Diderot, "Salon of 1767," 2:208. The withering assessments of Demachy that appeared in the pages of *Mémoires secrets* as well as in Diderot's criticism have overshadowed the painter's respectability in his day as a master of perspective (a subject he taught at the Académie royale). See Bernard de Montgolfier, "La démolition de l'Église des Saints Innocents vue par De Machy," *Bulletin du Musée Carnavalet* 25, no. 2 (1972): 27–30; as well as Marianne Roland Michel, "The Clearance of the Colonnade of the Louvre: A Study Arising from a Painting by De Machy," *Burlington Magazine* 120, no. 906 (1978): i–vi. See also her catalog entry on the artist in Villa Medici, *Piranèse et les Français, 1740–1790,* exh. cat. (Rome: Edizioni dell'Elefante, 1976), 114–20.

99 Frederic Melchior, Freiherr von Grimm, "Réflexions sur les effets qu'ont les différents arts sur notre imagination à propos de la *Dissertation sur la tragédie,* par D. Hume," *La correspondance littéraire, philosophique et critique, 1er janvier–15 juin 1760,* ed. Sigun Dafgård (Stockholm: Uppsala, 1981), 2:1–2.

100 The phrase comes from Lincoln Steffens, "The Modern Business Building," *Scribner's Magazine* 22 (1897): 46; cited in Nick Yablon, "The Metropolitan Life in Ruins: Architectural and Fictional Speculations in New York, 1909–1919," *American Quarterly* 56, no. 2 (2004): 317.

101 Burke, *Philosophical Enquiry,* 53.

102 Thomas Weiskel, *The Romantic Sublime: Studies in the Structure and Psychology of Transcendence* (Baltimore: Johns Hopkins Univ. Press, 1986), 3.

103 Boulanger, *Antiquité dévoilée,* 56–57.

104 Johann Jakob Bachofen, "An Essay on Ancient Mortuary Symbolism" (1859), in idem, *Myth, Religion, and Mother Right: Selected Writings of J. J. Bachofen,* trans. Ralph Manheim (Princeton: Princeton Univ. Press, 1992), 38; cited in Giorgio Agamben, *Infancy and History: On the Destruction of Experience,* trans. Liz Heron (London: Verso, 2007), 89, 92.

105 Daston, *Classical Probability in the Enlightenment,* 126. Kavanagh elaborates on her discussion in *Enlightenment,* 26–28.

106 Simmel further argues that "exchange is a form of socialization." Georg Simmel, *The Philosophy of Money,* trans. David Frisby (New York: Routledge, 1990), 198, 175.

107 Burke, *Philosophical Enquiry,* 55.

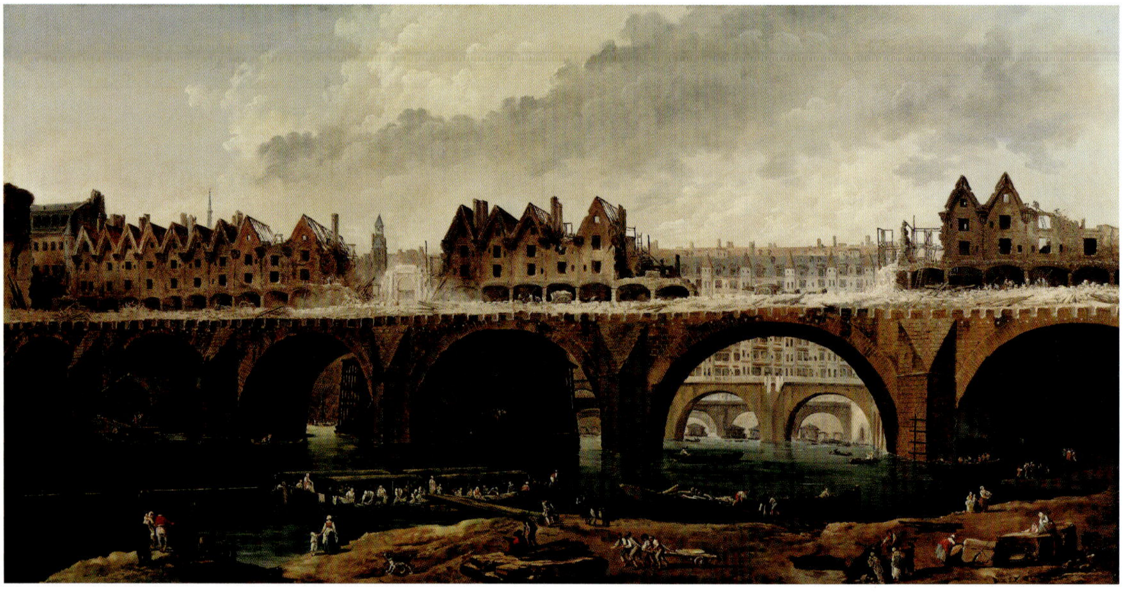

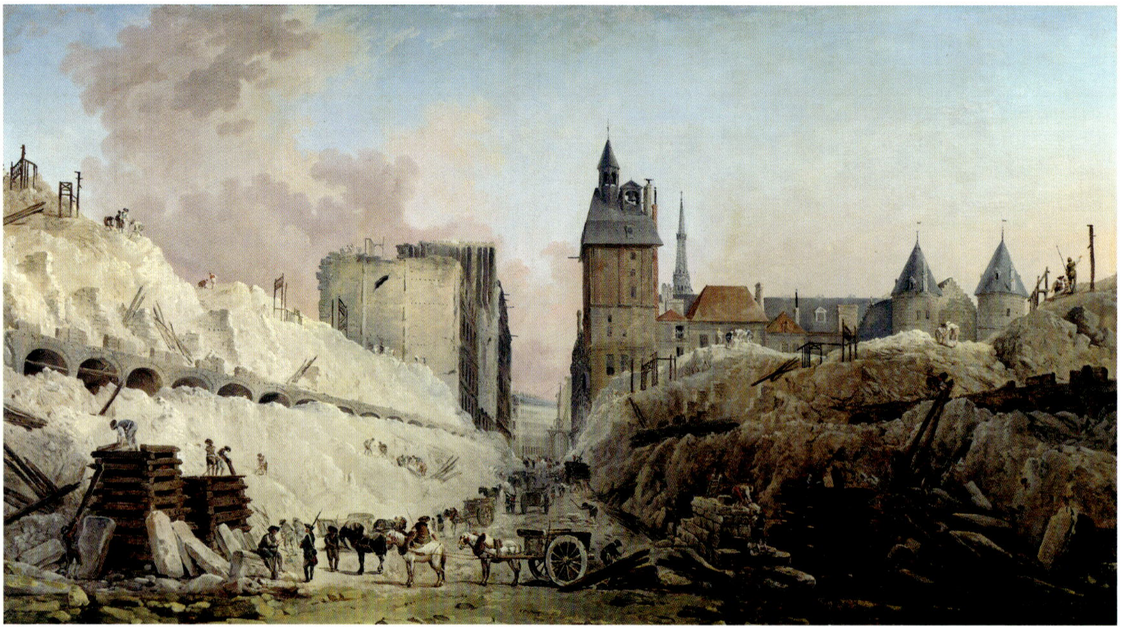

CHAPTER 3
anti-edifice

> Let us imagine the impossible: let us imagine that the world—sickened though it is by everything that does not change from day to day—were gracefully to accept your monotony; what would architecture then become?
>
> —Giovanni Battista Piranesi (1765)[1]

Between 1786 and 1809, the city of Paris executed one of the most ambitious undertakings in the history of the capital's embellishment: the demolition of the houses lining the Seine's bridges. The wooden structures—vestiges of medieval planning—had crowded the Pont Notre-Dame since the sixteenth century and the Pont-au-Change and Pont Marie since the seventeenth, and their removal had long been championed as a touchstone of urban reform. The houses—"hideous" blights on "beautiful bridges," wrote Voltaire—impeded the city's vistas, as well as the circulation of goods, pedestrians, and clean air:[2] so contended the innumerable embellishment proposals that began appearing in the middle of the century, authored by men such as Guillaume Poncet de La Grave and Jean-Baptiste-Jacques Élie de Beaumont, both lawyers and members of Parlement; the engineer Patte; and the geographer Jaillot, all of whose initiatives treated the river as the lifeblood of the capital, to be safeguarded from all obstructions.[3] Such projects took the renovation of the Seine's bridges as the starting point for a comprehensive plan of reform whose aim was integration of city and river and whose totalizing ambition redefined the practice of urbanism. The clearing of the bridges reflected a conception of the city as a general entity, all of whose quarters could be made amenable to the imperatives of circulation. The culmination of decades of reform initiatives, the demolitions superseded in importance any building project in recent memory: "Preferable to all the monuments built in the last fifteen years," recalled Jean-Baptiste Pujoulx, "was the clearing of the ponts au Change and Notre-Dame. It is necessary to have seen these bridges and the neighboring quais overloaded with high, smoky hovels, to have an idea of the importance of this restoration, which was solicited for more than thirty years."[4]

Fig. 44. Hubert Robert (French, 1733–1808)
The Demolition of Houses on the Pont Notre-Dame in 1786, 1787, oil on canvas, 81 × 154 cm (31⅞ × 60⅝ in.)
Karlsruhe, Staatliche Kunsthalle Karlsruhe

Fig. 45. Hubert Robert (French, 1733–1808)
The Demolition of Houses on the Pont-au-Change, Paris, 1788, oil on canvas, 86.5 × 159.5 cm (34 × 62⅞ in.)
Paris, Musée Carnavalet

Robert captured the demolitions on the Pont Notre-Dame and Pont-au-Change in several paintings, works that, in their grand format and inflated scale, attest to the historic stature of the subjects (figs. 44, 45). As with the disaster and demolition views that preceded them, the paintings feature the houses in the course of demolition, so that Robert's sprawling landscapes of partial ruin confound Pujoulx's clarity of retrospection. This effect is particularly pronounced in the *Pont-au-Change,* for the identity of the subject as a fluvial structure is obscured by the painting's point of view: the artist has positioned himself in the middle of the street on the north end of the bridge, thus effacing the presence of the river (see fig. 45). In distinction to the chronicler Pujoulx, looking back at a fait accompli from a superior vantage point, Robert inscribes himself in an expansive and provisional present: in the *Pont Notre-Dame,* his is the tiny, red-draped figure occupying the center foreground, seated on a pile of timber, busily recording the sweeping events that inevitably exceed his minuscule sketchbook (see fig. 44).

Robert's treatment of the demolitions makes immediately apparent their sublime status. Evocations of the infinite abound: in the microscopic splinters of the *Pont Notre-Dame,* as well as in the cropping of the painting, which creates the illusion of arches continuing well beyond the canvas. The uncontainable character of the processes at hand, so vast as to overwhelm the picture frames, is asserted in the immeasurable chasm of the *Pont-au-Change* and in the oceanic heaps of rubble—suspended, like the Red Sea parted, along the sides of the painting—which seem poised to spill into the space of the viewer. Such dramatic compositional devices—the frontal bridge, the plunging perspective—were the stock-in-trade of Piranesi. The painter's debt to the etcher in his rendering of the city's ruins is revealing, for Piranesi's sublime vocabulary, as Tafuri suggests, may be considered an extension of his own engagement with urbanism.[5]

Tafuri interprets the *Campo Marzio* and the *Carceri* as expressions of a contemporary crisis in architecture (figs. 46, 47). In these works, the city as a site of formal magnificence—its architectural integrity preserving the values of history—is negated. The lack of distinction in the *Carceri* between interior and exterior spaces, its subjection of the rules of perspective to "randomness," and the *Campo Marzio*'s reduction of monuments to mere incidents within a "continuum of fragments" suggest the dissolution of the city itself "*as a place of Form.*"[6] Lewis Mumford similarly emphasizes the "steady loss of form" that characterized the early modern city, noting that "liquid capital proved to be a chemical solvent... ruthless in its clearance of historic institutions and their buildings": with the "replacement of the concrete market place of the medieval town by the abstract transnational market," the city was forcibly patterned after "a money-making economy that had no definable ends or purposes other than its own further expansion."[7] The *Ichnographia* of Piranesi's *Campo Marzio* champions the corrosion of limits: the sinuous body of the Tiber dissolves the built order, undoing the autonomy, debasing the authority, of Rome's monuments. In marshaling the flow of the river to destabilize architectural values, Piranesi's etching foreshadows the demolition operations that Robert would depict fifteen years later.[8]

Tafuri's account may fruitfully be brought to bear on the problems—both aesthetic and economic—raised by the demolitions along the Seine's bridges. No less than Piranesi, Robert, as a chronicler of the city's contemporary ruins, confronted the "crisis of the architectural object," allegorized in his images of urban monuments in various states of disintegration.[9] His *Pont Notre-Dame* and *Pont-au-Change* record a critical instance of the city annihilating its formal constraints at the service of

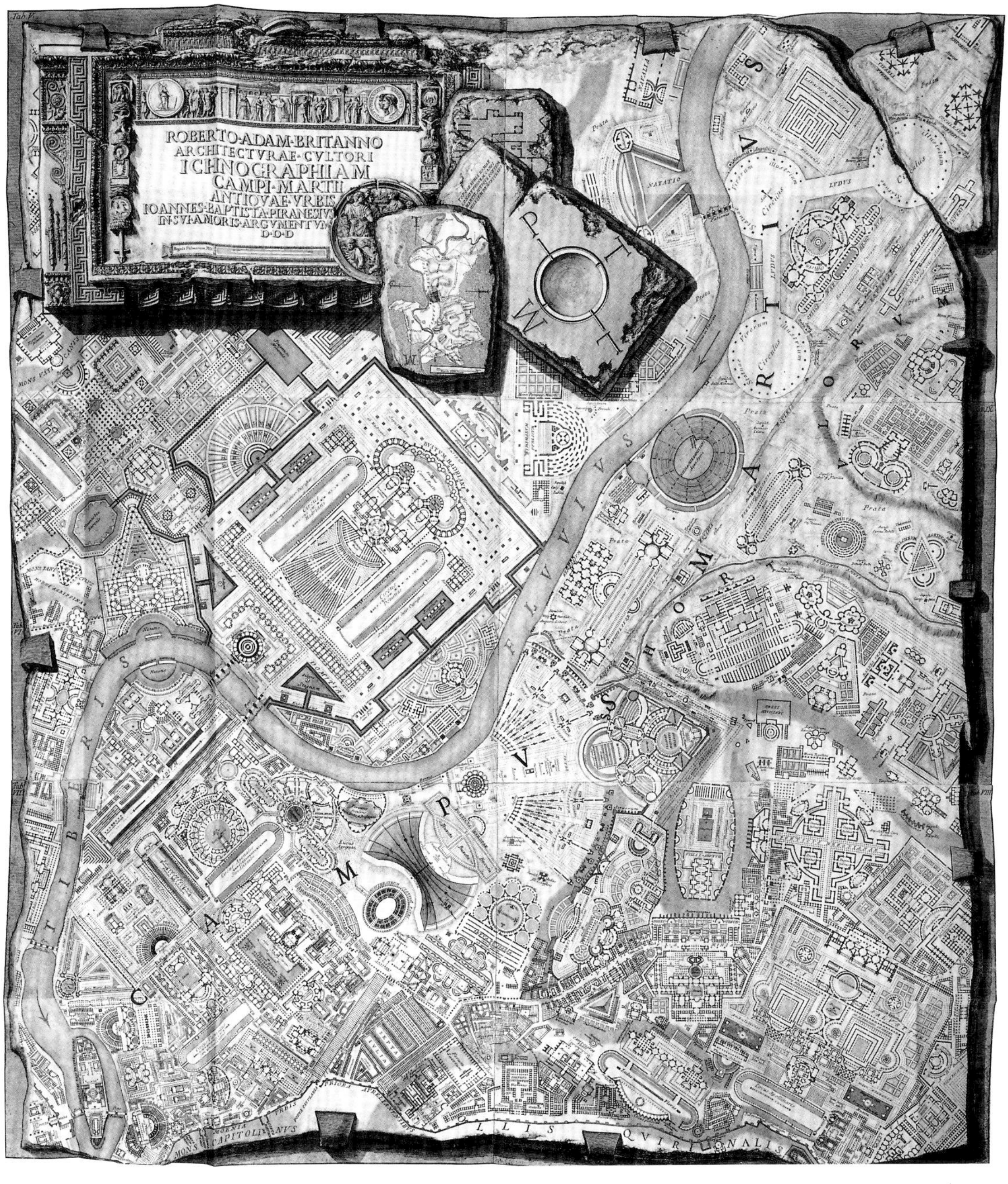

Fig. 46. Giovanni Battista Piranesi (Italian, 1720–78)
Ichnographiam Campi Martii
(Plan of the Campo Marzio)
From Giovanni Battista Piranesi, *Il Campo Marzio dell'antica Roma*... (Rome, 1762), pl. v

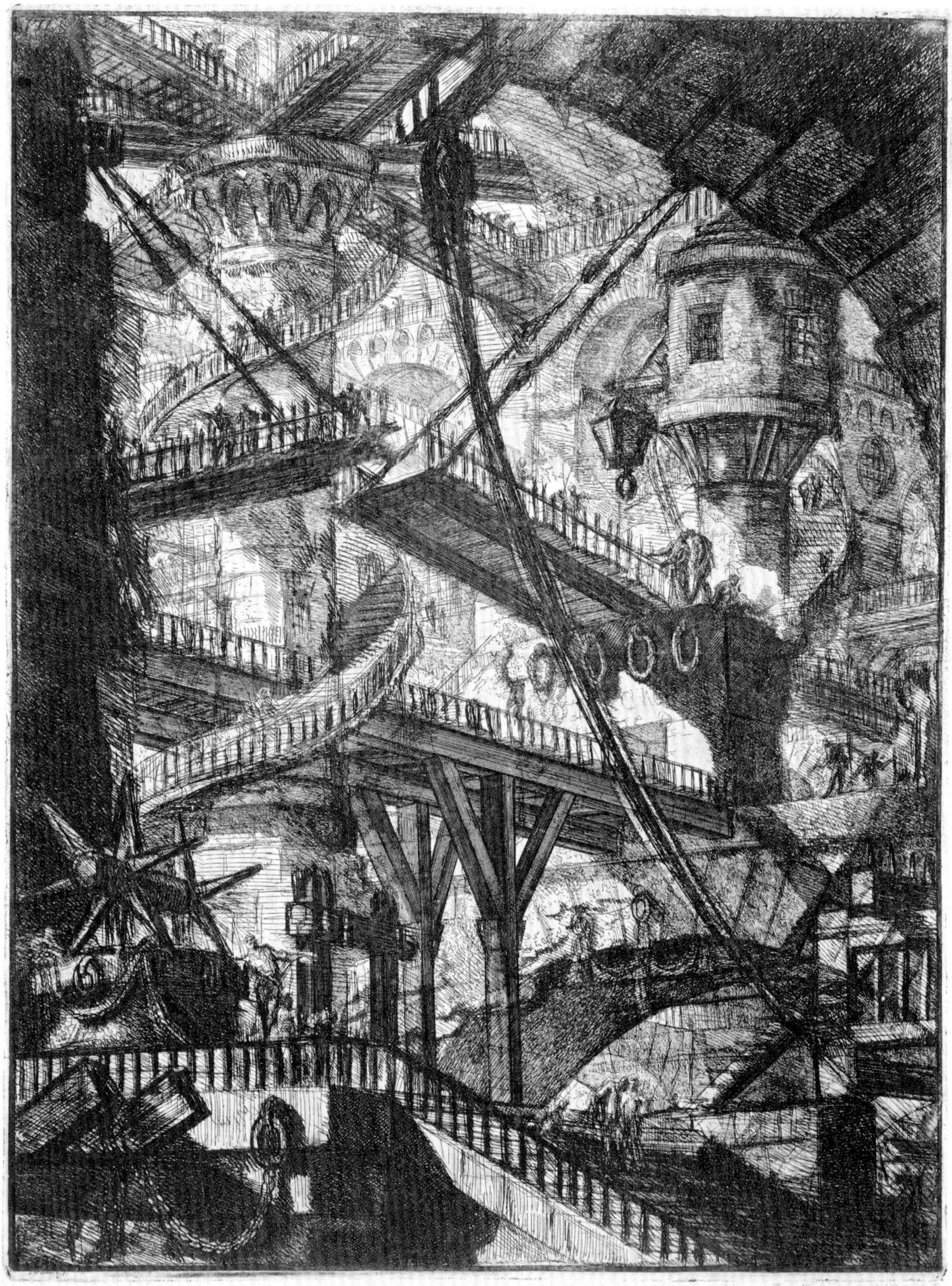

Fig. 47. Giovanni Battista Piranesi (Italian, 1720–78)
The Drawbridge (fifth state), no. VII in the *Carceri d'invenzione* series, after 1778, etching, 55 × 41 cm (21⅝ × 16⅛ in.)
Los Angeles, Getty Research Institute

unobstructed circulation. As such, Robert's hyperbolic figurations of urban sprawl reveal much about the ethos of eighteenth-century Paris urbanism. Beginning with Voltaire's essay of 1749, *Des embellissements de Paris,* the magnificence of a city was no longer perceived to reside solely in its monuments but rather in its overall infrastructure. "Essential to the beauty of a city," states Patte, "is that there be sufficient access from one quarter to the next, and all should be clear from the center to the circumference."[10] His own project for embellishment—in a capital whose planning appeared to have been the work of "chance alone," so that "entire quarters had practically no communication with one another"—lists, for brevity's sake, the few monuments to be safeguarded from demolition. "Embellishing" the city meant enhancing urban flow, as Pierre-Louis Moreau, official architect of Paris, demonstrated in his plan of 1769 to improve the city's navigability.[11] Moreau stipulated that the houses on the bridges be removed and the quais enlarged, that new public *places* and streets be created, and that the various building projects being planned throughout the city be considered in tandem with one another, so as to "render the course of the Seine both useful and agreeable throughout the whole of an immense city."[12]

Such pronouncements reveal the distance between the traditional definition of the city recorded in the *Encyclopédie*—"a collection of houses ... bounded by a common enclosure, usually of walls and moats," that is, "a space enclosed by ramparts"—and a new conception of the modern city as open and unbounded, suited to the uninhibited movement of people and commerce.[13] In his plan of 1756, Poncet de La Grave, of the French admiralty court, proposed the construction of additional canals and bridges, which, "being very essential for communication between different quarters, should be of the utmost importance in all projects made for the embellishment of Paris." The recommendation revealed the encroaching obsolescence of old uses of the city: Poncet mused that the construction of a bridge linking the Hôtel de Ville with the Nôtre-Dame cathedral would have the benefit of curtailing the winding procession undertaken on special occasions by the *prévot des marchands* (provost of the merchants), whose municipal power was ostentatiously displayed from quarter to quarter in the absence of a direct route between the two institutions.[14] The eclipse of the ceremonial aspects of the city by the priorities of circulation and functionality was further exhibited in the police chief Delamare's identification of the "paved street" as "the principal ornament of a city." By the end of the century, urbanists sought to reconstruct the city's sidewalks so as to link them with the national highway system.[15] It was one thing, of course, for paper proposals to extol the supreme value of overall circulation and of "a general plan." In reality, as Robert's paintings suggest, the particular would not be so easily relocated or expunged.

The *Demolition of Houses on the Pont Notre-Dame* (see fig. 44) juxtaposes a still vital culture on the brink of extinction with the rapid transformation unfolding on the bridge, where nearly half of the houses have vanished. Despite the momentous event taking place, the quotidian bustle of the river—though punctuated by the business of carting off building materials—continues uninterrupted. The laundresses, absorbed in their labor, take no note of the Piranesian landscape behind them—the towering arches of the Pont Notre-Dame, followed, in vertiginous succession, by the Pont-au-Change, Pont Neuf, and Pont Royale. The river remains a site of picturesque routine, the perseverance of which captivated the painter as much as the demolitions themselves did. In the Musée Carnavalet's version of the *Pont Notre-Dame,* the intractability of the built environment as a space of ritualized living is conveyed by the presence of chimney smoke at left, a detail bearing a kind of poignancy, insofar as it evokes the timelessness of fugitive habits (see fig. 63). In contrast to this feature's indexical relationship to the longue durée is the shimmering dust settling along the edge of the debris-strewn bridge, alighting upon the remains of a Classical portico, entryway to the water pump: thus does the perpetually repeatable vie with the passing instant. In light of such moments, the *Pont Notre-Dame* seems less a record of an occurrence than a palimpsest of disparate temporal traces, or an aggregation of differing modes of temporal perception. The city as a theater of fleeting optical effects—prophetic of the Impressionists' Paris—is juxtaposed with the city of ingrained, immemorial behaviors.

The painting, for all its emphatic attention to detail, is not easy to look at, which has in part to do with its formal structure. The picture is fractured by a seeming proliferation of perspectival possibilities, an effect of the elastic convexity of the bridge, as well as of the off-center point of view. There is no single subject here, but rather a multiplicity of details that extend beyond the canvas. Strikingly, no vista lies beyond the sequence of bridges, meaning there is no relief from the rapid pace of movement to which the eye submits, and the effect of the serial bridges is not to extend space but rather to contract it. It is, perversely, in the foreground, busy though it is with dispersed bits of information, that the eye seeks respite from the constricted space of the background. Thus are two worlds contrasted: the first defined by the serpentine crawl of the riverbank and by a human presence; the other, by the powerful bearers of architectonic order that rise up in superhuman succession. It was, evidently, the houses that formerly integrated these two realms, and with their demolition, Robert appears to paint a world bifurcated.

In confining attention to the foreground, Robert spotlights precisely an order of existence that advocates of embellishment sought to abolish. Not only did the engendering of a navigable city entail the removal of fishing boats and laundry barges, floating mills and water pumps, along with the houses themselves, which covered both bridges and embankments—it meant an end to the variegated life of the river, much of it dating from the Middle Ages. Overriding the diverse uses of the city's bridges—the luxury trade on the Pont Notre-Dame (where Edme-François Gersaint's shop, made famous by Watteau, was located), the artisanal services concentrated on the Pont Marie, the businesses of goldsmiths and money changers lining the Pont-au-Change—was the uniform pursuit of enhanced circulation. On 22 April 1769, royal approval of the demolition plans drawn up by Moreau officially put an end to a way of life that denizens of the city's bridges had known for generations. Residents of the Pont-au-Change in particular expressed fierce resistance to the loss of the bridge. It was their ancestors—established in the locale since the twelfth century—who had financed the building of the bridge, along with its houses, following the fire that destroyed it in 1621. The Pont-au-Change thus bound its residents in what they described as "un union inséparable."[16]

The demolitions occasioned a "trauma" in the city, prompting the mobilization of whole communities concerned to fight for more than a fair indemnity.[17] Prominent among the displaced were the dyers along rue de la Pelleterie, whose trade depended on proximity to the waters of the Seine. Their plea for greater compensation eloquently captured the impossibility of the economic lifeworld of the river to adjust to a new regime of circulation: "Our *ateliers* are not movable manufactories that can be placed where it is desirable, without deteriorating," they stated in a letter to the finance minister, Charles Alexandre de Calonne, in 1786, adding, "We are not merchants who can, without inconvenience, change boutiques or stores, by being accorded an indemnity of six months.... We are, as it were, attached to the same soil where we work."[18]

Robert's *Pont Notre-Dame* visualizes the rift between the river's time-honored use as a site of disparate activity and its new conception as a homogenized terrain: between the life of the Seine, synonymous with slowness, stasis, duration on the one hand, and the cultivation of a new order of speed on the other, one befitting a commercial society increasingly desirous of "communications immédiates."[19] Robert, as we have seen, was a painter notorious for his swiftness—nowhere more so than in his renderings of contemporary ruins, which necessarily required haste in execution. In the *Pont Notre-Dame,* a fragile balance between speed and stillness is sustained: the seriality of the bridges has the paradoxical effect of impeding flow, of hindering the river's recession into depth. Precisely this disavowal of distance, however—achieved by the quickness of the bridges' succession, by the illusion of their encroaching proximity to the picture plane, by the absence of a vista—creates the sensation of momentum. Reinforcing this effect is the speed with which the houses crumble, with which a fading world disintegrates. This is achieved with what appears to have been the single hair of a paintbrush, whose flight across the canvas is recorded in the luminous specks of white lining the arches. Interspersed with them, black ribbons of paint hover on the surface of the bridge, opaque indices of an accelerated moment.

In savoring such momentum, Robert revels in the limits of description, and, notably, it is the passages in the painting that most exemplify stillness, affording certainty in transcription, that bear traces of melancholy: the exalted specter of speed, the incalculable velocity of a moment captured, has as its inverse the tokens of death clustered in the right foreground of the river bank—the toppled statues that were formerly affixed to the houses and that now lie prostrate on the earth.[20] This detail, so unobtrusive as to be overlooked, is standard Robert fare, typical of his landscapes with ancient ruins as well as of his studies for the new Musée du Louvre, both of which traffic in anecdotal exchanges between living figures and inanimate sculptures. As displaced relics, however, the statues relate to the ruination at hand not only as picturesque accessories but also as prefigurations of the uprootings necessitated by the demolitions. Deracinated and projecting an aura of the uncanny, they concretize the symbolic economy of the picture, with its peculiar mixture of instantaneity and obsolescence—of the past and the premonitory. Their perpendicular arrangement echoing the interlocking forms nearby of planks and barges, the statues take their place in the riverbank's subtle network of relations, one that contrasts with the stark frontality of the bridges.

This sense of looming estrangement from a familiar urban landscape is magnified in Robert's *Demolition of Houses on the Pont-au-Change* (see fig. 45). In distinction to its pendant view, the Pont-au-Change is lined with houses that have already given way to heaps of rubble. Scattered laborers dismantle what is left of the structures and collect remnants of masonry and timber. On the right stand the medieval edifices of the Île de la Cité—the Tour de l'Horloge (visible as well behind the Classical portico in the *Pont Notre-Dame*); behind it, the spire of Sainte-Chapelle; and to the right, the towers of the Conciergerie—monuments exaggerated in scale, yet located at an improbably great distance from the minuscule figures in the foreground. The houses awaiting demolition are visible in the background at left. The windowless wall of the closest building bears an oblique tear across its gridlike surface, which registers uneasily like a rip in the picture plane itself.

A single, powerfully centralized perspective dominates the composition and yet, even more so than its pendant, the *Pont-au-Change* is a study in falteringly apprehended, irreconcilable contrasts: namely, between the boundless channel—punctuated by tidy stacks of masonry and leading resolutely to an ambiguous endpoint—and the impenetrable morass at its sides. These mounds, cast on the right in shadow, deflect attention. Rows of partially visible galleries, half-buried by debris, run parallel to, and reiterate, the central passageway. Particularly on the right, however, the vaulted structures, rather than extending the perspectival logic of the bridge, appear to flatten themselves against the picture plane. Not only is the sequestered nature of the mountainous heap rendered all the more precarious but the eye is left vainly attempting to stabilize the relationship between surface and depth. The tension between the two is amplified by the lack of correspondence between the puny laborers and the massive dimensions of the debris, entrapping the gaze in an endless to-and-fro struggle to synthesize part and whole, figure and ground.

Apart from the velocity of its perspective, the painting is infused with a kind of petrification; the immobilized stance of two horses in the center foreground lends the scene a friezelike stillness (thus affording respite to the roving gaze). This seems fundamentally a different landscape from that of the *Pont Notre-Dame,* for with the disintegration of the houses—indeed, the difficulty of apprehending the Pont-au-Change as a bridge at all—the city itself seems obliterated. Only the medieval edifices are distinguished from, though partially submerged by, the ruination, and they alone—incidents of specificity in a sea of general wreckage—stand as placeholders of urban history. For all that the demolitions are meant to distinguish progressive modernity from the past, little in Robert's picture attests to late eighteenth-century contemporaneity: the debris registers as vaguely postapocalyptic and, more eerily, as prehistoric. Like the horses marching back and forth, time appears to vacillate—an effect enhanced by the absence of the river: if the Seine functions in the *Pont Notre-Dame* as an embodiment of the eternal, of that which outlasts history's vicissitudes, its effacement here furthers the sense of temporal and spatial uncertainty.[21] The loss of the river also renders all the more unrelenting the painting's earthy monochrome, a characteristic already pronounced in its pendant. With both the *Pont Notre-Dame* and the *Pont-au-Change,* we have come a long way from the lushness of Vernet's river views, as well as from the cool blue clarity of Canaletto's London on the Thames.

"I know of nothing sublime which is not some modification of power," Burke states, and it is in relation to the powerlessness of the human witnesses to the demolitions, including the Lilliputian laborers who execute them, that the events depicted by Robert take on the quality of the sublime. The bridges, no longer inhabitable, seem immanently inhuman. Both paintings, in addition to conjoining "vastness of extent" and "the last extreme of littleness," deploy what Burke describes as an "uninterrupted progression" calculated to defy comprehension, for "the imagination cannot rise to any idea of infinity."[22] Indeed, it is in part the illusion of the Pont-au-Change's endless elasticity that impedes our comprehension of its identity.

Robert, like Piranesi before him, specialized in conjurations of infinity, recycling such motifs in his ruin paintings as the view of the endless corridor, lined by a continuous wall of columns.[23] In ways that differ from monumental antiquity, however, the Seine was an object of sublime imagining, designated by a new breed of urbanism as the key to unlimited economic potential: in the decades that preceded the demolitions, the most radical of aspiring urban planners entertained the possibility of a city without limits—a Paris connected by an endless series of waterways and ports to the world's oceans. In 1765, the engineer Claude-Siméon Passemant proposed transforming Paris into a seaport; he drew up plans to connect the capital to the Atlantic, envisioning the arrival of merchant vessels from as far away as America and Asia. Dissolving the limits to the city, as discussed in the previous chapter, raised the prospect of a greatly enlarged capital, according to critics who warned of the increased risk of famine.[24] A vast number of commentators, however, embraced the notion of a capital symbiotic with the flow of the river, and thus cleansed, literally and figuratively, of its toxins. In speaking of the demolitions as a "restoration," Pujoulx gave voice to a Rousseauist dream—prevalent in the discourse on planning—of redeeming the city by reconciling it with the principles of nature.[25] Similarly, Mercier, remarking that the "Seine remained hidden in the middle of the city by the unattractive and narrow houses" lining the bridges, called for the "return" to the city of its flow of air. Not unlike the Physiocrats, whose rhetoric of natural bounty helped legitimate commercial enterprise, urbanists—by subjugating the art of architecture to the priority of circulation—advanced the doctrine of laissez-faire.[26]

Robert's demolition views refrain from representing the considerable human costs of the affairs, the better, perhaps, to heighten expectation of the "restoration" to come. The paintings, as I have indicated, register the fact of disintegration—yet they do so at a distance. In this, they exhibit something of the will to abstraction that governed the enterprises—the readiness of commentators to overlook what the demolitions meant for those displaced by them in favor of enumerating their benefits to the general good. In keeping with this spirit of farsightedness, the most highly anticipated result of the undertakings was the panoramic prospect they would make available—"the magnificence of the view that will extend without obstacle on the entire course of the river in the interior of Paris," as the *prévôt des marchands* envisioned it.[27] The demolitions united the urban reformer's longing for unrestricted freedom of movement with what Stephan Oettermann describes as a "craving to experience the horizon" pervasive on the eve of the Revolution. Thus Mercier, dreaming in 1771 of a post-absolutist republican France, pictured the view from the city's naked bridges as he imagined it would appear in the year 2440: "What a prospect!... my view extended with pleasure along the vast course of the Seine."[28]

The demolitions denoted the desire for an outlook unclouded by the local and particular, and no longer anchored in the past, but directed instead toward the future. In a recent study, Richard Wittman underscores the role that bridges played in late eighteenth-century imaginings of "an escape from the social world embodied in the cityscape." The cleared bridge was "a space of movement and freedom, open to the sky and blissfully clear of an architectural heritage," "a space of anonymous, endless passage (such as the river below)." The appeal of such a site, he adds, lay in the disappearance of the community that formerly inhabited it, making it amenable to abstractions such as "humanity," "the nation," or the "image of a universal society."[29] Empowered to overlook the city from the heights of an empty bridge, the viewer—like the spectator of the nineteenth-century panorama—could partake of the "secularization of God's eye and the view from heaven."[30] No wonder Mercier remarks that there is nothing "as beautiful as the view from the middle of the Pont-Royal"—a bridge uncluttered by houses. Or, as Montesquieu observes: "The mind... abhors all limits... and thus one of its great pleasures is to take in a large and distant prospect. But this pleasure is not easily attained."[31]

Robert was prepared, then, to exclude the bridges' residents from his accounts of the demolitions—to sacrifice human specificity in favor of sublimity. Yet his canvases seem pointedly to suppress any hint of the panoramic prospect to come: weighted with debris, the landscapes, with their low viewpoints, foreshadow less the triumphant ascent to a "view from heaven" than the inexorable effects of gravity. The pink clouds of the *Pont-au-Change* and the blue river of the *Pont Notre-Dame* interrupt a bleak color scheme only to reinforce the inescapable condition of an earthbound built world. Limitlessness is posited yet also vaguely ironized, for the paintings at once flirt with the suggestion of the infinite and figure its abrupt cessation: the *Pont Notre-Dame* beckons the eye with the possibility of an endless succession of bridges, yet the proximity of the archways to the picture plane, as noted, disables spatial recession. Similarly, though the ruination lining the Pont-au-Change defies quantification, the painting's illusion of distance is undermined by the precisely rendered façade, at right, of the Conciergerie. The building's visible pattern of bricks furnishes the far with the look of the near. In short, an "uninterrupted progression" is at once courted and compromised. In much the same way that the still life of horses in the *Pont-au-Change* keeps the viewer from entering the landscape, the horizontally arranged statues on the riverbank in the *Pont Notre-Dame* serve as a reminder of (or more accurately, a substitute for) the particularities that the panoramic prospect meant to transcend.

The clearing of the bridges advanced a vision of the city for which, as Patte stated, no model existed—for no city had yet "sacrificed everything" for the sake of "the true well-being of man."[32] And yet, however much Robert emphasized the enormity of the operations, he also imparted to the subjects a sense of déjà vu. The composition of his *Pont-au-Change* bears a close formal resemblance, in fact, to a view of Rome that first appeared in a folio volume, *Les plus beaux édifices de Rome moderne,* published twenty-five years earlier by the French painter-printmaker Jean Barbault (fig. 48): the horses in the print's foreground, the tunnel-like perspective, even the distant form of an archway recur in Robert's painting, as does the character of desolation. Robert, whose print collection included views from Barbault's volume of 1761, *Les plus beaux monuments de la Rome ancienne,* would likely have been familiar with its sequel. *Rome moderne* was published in 1763 (posthumously, as the artist died a year earlier) by the French press on the Corso, Bouchard and Gravier, while Robert was residing in Rome.[33] Like Robert, Barbault was a disciple of Piranesi, and his *Veduta del Palazzo Sacchetti*—with its creeping shadows; vast, cloud-strewn sky; and decrepit idlers—reveals the influence of the etcher. So too does it bespeak a mid-eighteenth-century Frenchman's fascination with Rome's sprawling Baroque thoroughfares.

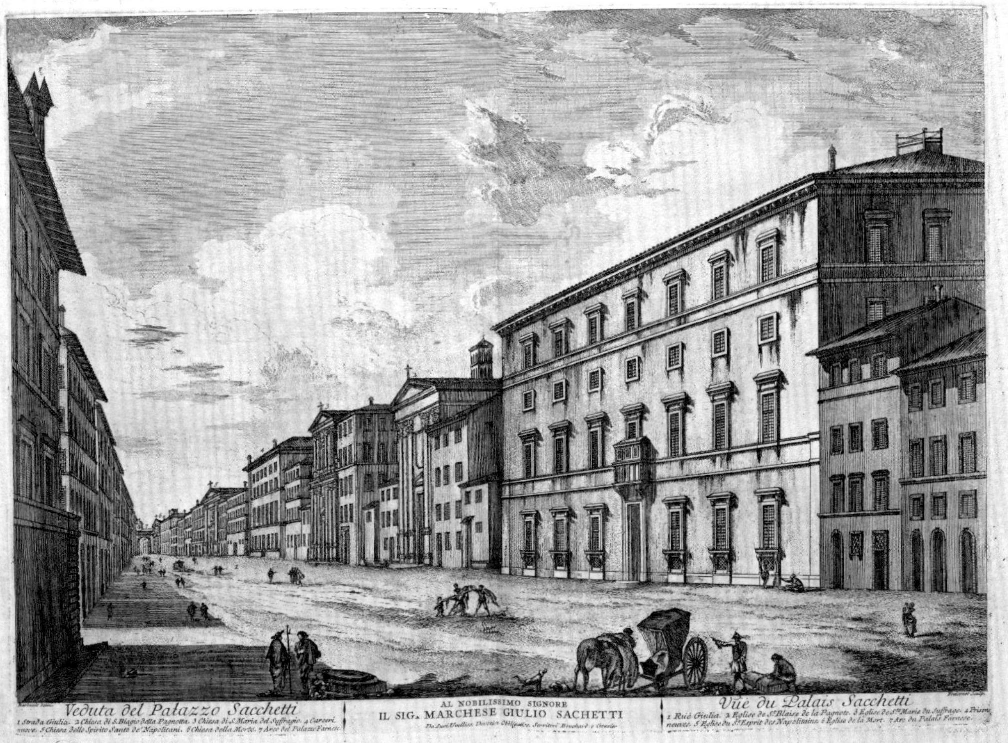

Fig. 48. Jean Barbault (French, 1718–62)
Veduta del Palazzo Sacchetti
From Jean Barbault, *Les plus beaux édifices de Rome moderne* (Rome, 1763), pl. 37

Despite taking as its titular subject the Palazzo Sacchetti, Barbault's print sequesters the building to the margins in order to accommodate the soaring perspective of the avenue, suggesting that though the monument may be beautiful, it is the street that is sublime.

What is arresting about Barbault's *Rome moderne*—what makes it an eerie preview of, or even, on some level, a postscript to, Robert's demolition views—is not only its belonging to the age of Burke. Barbault features Rome as a site not of concentrated activity but of dispersal, disavowing its virtual synonymousness with ritualized revelry ("Every evening in this city is a *fête publique,*" observed a French visitor in 1785).[34] Rome is effectively disciplined to a French Enlightenment conception of the city, one characterized by a distaste for precisely the sorts of mass festivities that Vasi, in his *Delle magnificenze di Roma antica e moderna* (1747–61), deemed central to the magnificence of the capital. Reducing congestion in urban quarters had become a priority of embellishment as early as the 1730s, when Delamare designated uncluttered access routes as instrumental to the operations of police circulation and surveillance. By the end of the century, as evidenced in the clearing of the Seine's bridges, the street was defined "as a site for traffic flow rather than neighborhood socializing."[35]

If Barbault exaggerated Rome's discomfiting emptiness, along with the agoraphobic experiences it generated, he did so with the understanding that part of the appeal of a city lay in its invitation to the urban dweller to pry pleasure from menace. With its cropped foreground edges, his *Palazzo Sacchetti* suggests a view enjoyed from the slightly elevated vantage point of a moving vehicle—thus catering to a taste for the thrilling dangers of rapid transit.[36] In the foreground of Barbault's print, a horse-drawn carriage is featured beside a coffin-shaped case, but the pairing—viewed as one in a series of meaningless vignettes—is more farce than tragedy. The picturesque column base at left, however, points to a consciousness not only of what was gained by the making of a modern city but also of what was lost, and, in this, the print bears further relation to Robert's painting. A peculiar statement in his book's introduction—one that Robert, it is tempting to think, may well have appreciated—informs readers that Barbault's dramatic "perspectives . . . compensate in some way for the injury of time that deprives us of the magnificence of ancient Rome."[37] The oddity of the declaration in a study devoted to modern Rome makes the sentiment all the more revealing. The implication is that the dream of a sublime metropolis, one that captured the imagination with the possibilities of unobstructed flow, reflected not only eager anticipation of the future but recompense for what no longer existed.

The Monuments of Kings

On 28 January 1787, the *Journal de Paris* printed a letter from the sculptor Pajou, the subject of which was the uncertain future of a work of art located on the Pont-au-Change. Executed by Simon Guillain, the monument—ensconced in an arcaded niche above a boutique—had occupied the northern extremity of the bridge since its inauguration in 1648. A bronze portrait ensemble of the young Louis XIV framed on a pedestal by his parents, Louis XIII and Anne of Austria, it featured the prince crowned by Fame, above a tympanum decorated with antique arms and the compressed bodies of four captive prisoners (fig. 49). In his letter, Pajou hailed the demolitions as a great public service and praised Parisians for their desire to propagate throughout the city "relief for suffering humanity; salubrity; and that air of grandeur" for which "our ancestors" had so little concern. "Public opinion has long proscribed

Fig. 49. ***Perspective View of the Pont-au-Change***
1750–1800, hand-colored copper engraving, 28.7 × 42.5 cm (11¼ × 16¾ in.)
Paris, Bibliothèque nationale de France

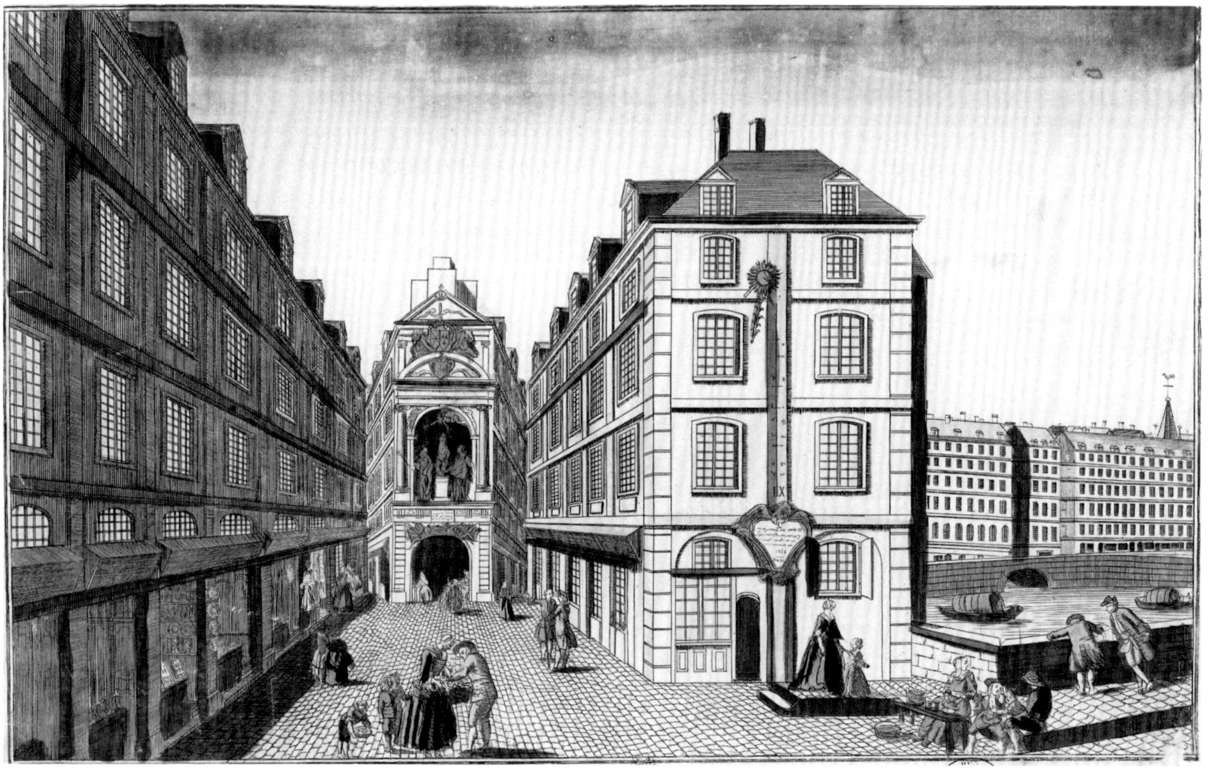

houses on bridges," he stated, "and these enormous burdens that have obstructed [city views] will disappear." However, "it being desirable to conserve the few monuments that it was necessary to displace," Pajou suggested that Guillain's "beautiful figures would very nicely decorate" the fountain at the Église Sainte-Eustache. To transfer them to that church would be to demonstrate, Pajou concluded, "that the same taste that has presided over the destruction of the houses presides also over the conservation of masterpieces."[38]

In a letter to the *Journal de Paris* on 15 February, a commentator named Alquier protested Pajou's logic. He noted that the residents of the Pont-au-Change had erected the monument in recognition of the royal favor the king had bestowed in granting them rights of residency. Today, urged Alquier, the fate of the monument should be decided in this same spirit of purposiveness. Hostile to the sculptor's seemingly arbitrary recommendation that the monument adorn the fountain at Sainte-Eustache, Alquier retorted that "surely the zeal of Mr. Pajou to conserve this monument has made him forget the *convenance* of his art": the portrait of the royal family, he declared, would simply not be suitable to "decorate a monument made in our day." The author concluded by proposing that the statues be placed at the Abbaye royale de Saint-Denis in the form of a mausoleum.[39]

Thus would Guillain's monument metamorphose, according to Alquier's solution, from a living testament of monarchical beneficence to a gateway for the dead. No less radical in its implications was Pajou's proposal to retain the monument in Paris. In 1778, Pajou, along with Robert, had been enlisted to take part in a committee on the planning of the Grande Galerie of the Louvre, future site of the national museum, and it appears to have been the proto-museological spirit of Pajou's suggestion that Alquier found so discomfiting. While a mausoleum at Saint-Denis, wrote Alquier, would "pay homage" to the monument, reinstalling Guillain's sculpture at a modern fountain at Sainte-Eustache would drain the work of its original meaning. Incarnating, in Alquier's words, the "benevolence of the king," the monument, once removed to the fountain and emptied of its former purpose, would henceforth appear as purely decorative. For Pajou, conversely, the historical value of the sculpture was of less interest than its status as a "masterpiece." Form, not content, justified its conservation and use as an object of embellishment. In the end, unable to form a consensus, the city removed the sculpture to a foundry, and more than half a century would elapse before its component parts—those that (narrowly) survived revolutionary iconoclasm—were reunited in the Louvre.[40]

The episode encapsulates the politics of embellishment on the eve of the Revolution—and more specifically, the breach between the symbolic language of kingship and urbanism's utilitarian vision of the city. However much it meant to commemorate the monarch, Alquier's proposal to exile the royal family from the heart of the capital, relocating it from the center to the margins, reveals the extent to which urban embellishment had extricated itself from the "cult of the king."[41] Commentators in the second half of the century refuted the notion of the capital as an extension of princely magnificence, pointing with dismay to the discrepancy between the opulence of the city's monumental order and the mass poverty of its residents. "There is no folly that lasts longer and elicits more attention than that executed in stone and in marble," proclaimed Diderot in 1760, frowning on the profligacy of monumentality.

"A bad work of literature passes and is forgotten; but a ridiculous monument lasts for centuries."[42] At a time that witnessed the defamation of royal monuments, Guillain's artwork embodied a bygone age—an outmoded view of the city as a theater of monarchical splendor: situated on the route that descended from rue Saint-Denis, the sculpture likely commemorated the royal entry into Paris. The goldsmiths established in the area had long participated in the fashioning of the ephemeral spectacles that celebrated the king's arrival, and the bronze monument appears to have functioned as a permanent version of the temporary structures that honored such occasions. Its removal illustrates what historians have cited as "the deficit of the visible" entailed by urbanism: a demotion of decoration, as well as of the royal figure, which resulted from a growing sense that monumentality, insofar as it impeded the flow of air, was toxic.[43]

The dismantling of Guillain's monument, along with the demolition of houses whose construction, according to commentators, the monarch should never have permitted, crystallized a turning point in the identity of the city—foregrounding the transformation of Paris "from a city of the king into a city of the bourgeoisie."[44] Christopher Prendergast, drawing on the distinctions between a capital and a metropolis, writes that by the late eighteenth century, Paris showed signs of transitioning from the former to the latter: "A capital is a political and cultural 'centre,' with the power and authority to dominate and protect a wider 'territory,' to keep in place a 'social hierarchy.'" A metropolis, in contrast, "'is not a centre and has no centre' and exists as an 'impersonal space of 'circulation' and 'exchange.'"[45] In *Le nouveau Paris* (1798), Mercier describes a city "dédéifié," (de-deified), but his reflections on the city's empty center—on the expiration of the capital as a space of symbolic form—predate the Revolution.[46] Paris had ceased to be a city of kings, observes the chronicler in his *Tableau de Paris,* when the court and clergy retreated to Versailles ("Ours are the only monarchs who live at a remove from their subjects"). Left behind was a capital strewn with defunct institutions. "The Louvre is empty," he writes, and "will never be finished, and the sovereign, I believe, has never spent twenty-four hours there." The clergy, like the king, was invisible, and in its absence the iconography of church façades appeared all the more indecipherable. As the literary historian Martial Poirson notes, the discomfort Mercier feels in the face of monuments that have ceased to signify gives way, in his vision of Paris in the year 2440, to the bliss of contemplating a city made empty. "I lost myself in grand and beautiful streets, properly aligned," Mercier writes.[47] As evinced in the chronicler's reveries, the city engineered by Georges-Eugène Haussmann—a city of *lieux de mémoire* giving way to vacant vistas—was one already imagined, even longed for, in the late eighteenth century.

Mercier's writings put forth the possibility that if urban embellishment amounted to an exorcism from the capital of the spirit of the king, so too did it serve as a kind of resacralization: belief in the emancipatory space of the void grew as the power of the monumental order withered. Little wonder that the architect Viel de Saint-Maux, whose rant against urban embellishment was reviewed in the previous chapter, so contemptuously characterized the hunger for a panoramic view. Writing in 1787, at the time of the demolitions on the bridges, Viel suggests sarcastically that citizens might as well be "oblige[d] to construct their houses on wheels," the better to accommodate the tireless pursuit of an agreeable prospect. The statement reflected Viel's disgust with the treatment of monuments as expendable items that could be moved hither and yon by artists determined "to build a new city"—the implication being that the reconfiguration of the capital would continue unabated, never to be declared finished.[48] That same year, the aspiring architect (and future royalist) Antoine-Chrysostôme Quatremère de Quincy similarly described the deterioration of a conservationist instinct as a kind of sacrilege.

Just as Pajou and Alquier were debating the relocation of Guillain's sculpture, Quatremère inaugurated his campaign—one that he would resume against the future Musée du Louvre—to ensure that monuments be preserved in the environments for which they had been intended. In a letter in the *Journal de Paris,* he addressed the fate of another monument threatened by its proximity to a demolition site: the Fontaine des Innocents (fig. 50). The quartier des Halles, where the fountain was located, had recently undergone extensive renovations, including the demolition of the Église des Saints-Innocents in 1787 and the replacement of the cemetery by a vegetable and herb market. The site's sole remaining relic was the Fontaine des Innocents, reportedly constructed by King Philip Augustus in the twelfth century to enclose the cemetery.[49]

For Quatremère, the uncertain fate of the fountain reflected the risk facing the "Monuments of Kings." Envisioning the monument "envelop[ed] in general ruin," he asks: "How is it... that a century enlightened in all its interests can commit against [God] an attack worthy of the barbarism of Goths" and threaten with "annihilation... a masterpiece of French sculpture?" Quatremère's diatribe is significant on several counts, among them his mobilization of the rhetoric that would soon resurface in his critique of the museum. Pommier underlines the brute precision of the language Quatremère employs in detailing the removal of the fountain from its rightful location: "démembrer, déplacer, dénaturer."[50] Writes Quatremère, "The intention [is to] dismember and carve up this fountain. I invite the friends of the arts to reflect, then,

Fig. 50. Jean-Nicolas Sobre (French, act. 1784–1802)
The Fountain of the Église des Saints-Innocents in 1787, 1787, pen, Chinese ink wash, and watercolor on paper, 25.5 × 42.5 cm (10 × 16¾ in.) Paris, Bibliothèque nationale de France

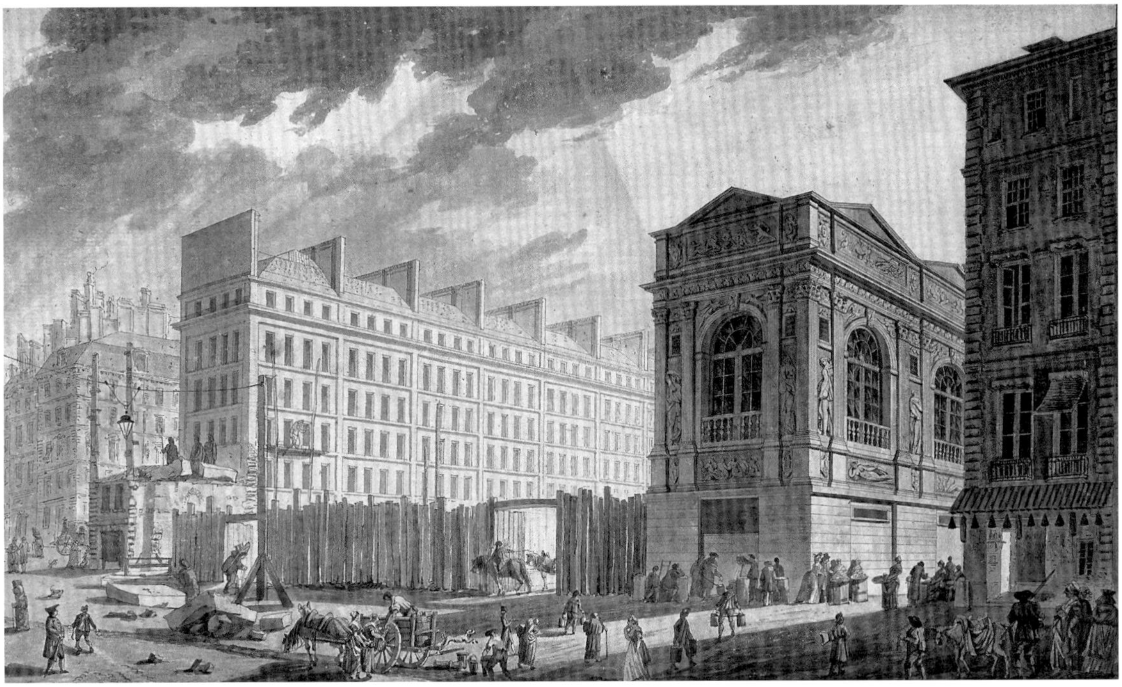

on the danger . . . of denaturing this monument . . . [should] the public good demand that it be displaced." Because the fountain's sculptures had been "designed [by Jean Goujon] for the place that they occupy," to extract them would be, in effect, to destroy them. In conclusion, Quatremère asks: "What would become of the history of the Arts if the edifices that contain the genius of each century, rather than acquiring as they age the public veneration that should render them sacred, were to find themselves condemned, like ephemeral productions of fashion, to appear one day, only to be replaced the next?"[51]

Quatremère's resounding finale contrasts the "public veneration" witnessed in the past to the current aversion to fixity. The temporality of monuments, he warns, is on the cusp of becoming indistinguishable from the ephemeral patterns of *la mode.* The closing analogy turned on a fundamental irony. For advocates of reform, a city cleared of its architectural obstacles and open to circulation was a city poised for "return" to its natural foundations. For Quatremère, in contrast, a city untethered from the monumental order was a city in limbo, doomed to perpetual cycles of demolition and displacement, of novelty and obsolescence.

The City as Capriccio

"Démembrer, déplacer, dénaturer": the terms denote the conditions by which monuments were assimilated to the urban marketplace. For Robert, the imperatives bred picturesque possibilities that he mined in a capriccio from about 1790, *The Pont Neuf* (fig. 51). An exercise in the poetics of temporal and spatial disjunction, the work features the capital's prized edifices—the "Monuments of Kings"—displayed imagina-

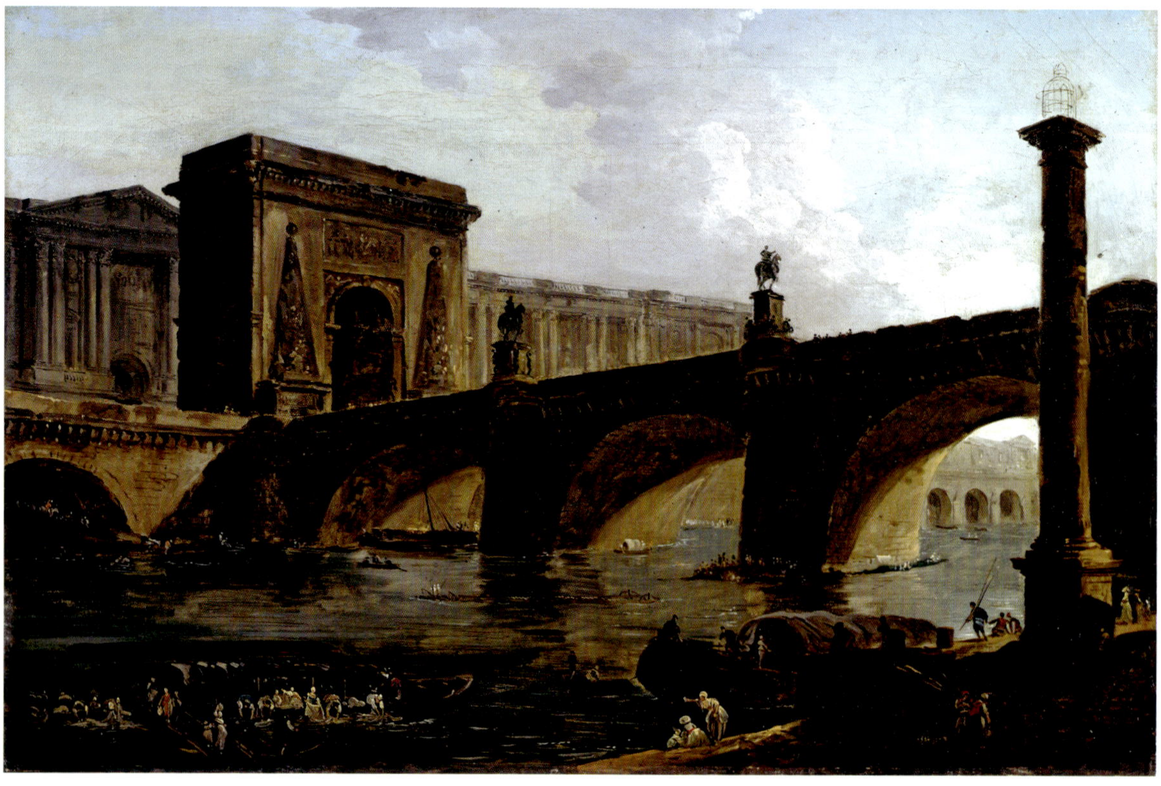

Fig. 51. Hubert Robert (French, 1733–1808)
The Pont Neuf, ca. 1790, oil on canvas, 43 × 55 cm (16⅞ × 21⅝ in.)
Epinal, Musée départemental d'art ancien et contemporain

tively around the central channel of the Seine. The Pont Neuf (inaugurated by King Henri IV in 1607), dividing the canvas along an oblique angle, is framed at right by the astrological column that Jean Bullant executed for Queen Catherine de Medici in 1572 (a monument that itself narrowly escaped destruction when the Hôtel de Soissons, where it formerly stood, was demolished in 1748).[52] Terminating the bridge at left is the triumphal gateway of the Porte Saint-Denis, built in 1672 to honor the military victories of Louis XIV. Behind it lies the Louvre colonnade, left unfinished by Claude Perrault in 1678; in the background, and barely perceptible, appear the Fontaine des Quatre Saisons—executed by Edmé Bouchardon on the rue de Grenelle in 1745—and the Pont Notre-Dame. The equestrian statues of Louis XV by Bouchardon, inaugurated at the Place Louis XV in 1763 (and left unfinished), and of Henri IV by Giambologna, installed at the center of the bridge in 1614, embellish the Pont Neuf at left and right, respectively. Minuscule figures line the bridge, and boats and barges—including a conveyor of laundresses in the left foreground—dot the translucent waters of the Seine. With its classicizing interest, the work presents itself as a paean to ancien régime edifices. As a capriccio, however, the painting submits its subjects to the very processes of deracination and disruption that Quatremère deemed hostile to the perpetuity of great monuments.

Robert's *Pont Neuf* was clearly a response to the numerous projects for the embellishment of the capital that centered on the Seine.[53] By congregating the city's disparate landmarks—effectively rendering them mobile—Robert treats the capriccio and the river as signs of each other's operations: the imaginative dislocations of the one are cleverly analogized with the capacities of the other as a medium of distribution. The capital's edifices, instead of obstructing flow, complement the motion of the river by behaving as vehicles of circulation: the Medici column repeats the function of the pier of the bridge behind it, the Porte Saint-Denis echoes the forms of the archways below, and the Louvre colonnade reiterates the horizontality of the quai. However uprooted, the monuments, united in their exemplarity of French Classicism, present no trace of a city "démembré." A study in consistency, the work—executed while the demolitions on the bridges were under way—wanders far from the frictions and divisions that characterized the *Pont Notre-Dame* and *Pont-au-Change.* Encompassing displacement and cohesion, Robert's capriccio demonstrates the power of the composite view to assimilate and make palatable the potentially inassimilable processes of the city's modernization.

In contradistinction to the previous paintings, the laws of gravity appear in the *Pont Neuf* to have been lifted: the defining feature of the work is its sketchy handling, its overall effect of imprecision, which renders the monuments as luminous and yielding as the waters of the Seine. Far from perpetuating the polarity between figure and ground exhibited in the demolition views, the *Pont Neuf* designates the surface as the all-absorbing object of attention. With its modest dimensions, the painting invites intimate study of its scintillating surface—of details ranging from the shimmery ripples of the Seine to the infinitesimal figures dotting the riverbanks, wading in the water and crowding the bridge. In their neutral earth tones, the monuments direct attention to the river as a field for the play of local color: to the turquoise streak lining the left edge of the interior of the arch at right, for instance; to the gleaming minions gathered on the adjacent sandbank; and to the furious white, red, and blue marks applied to the figures of laundresses in the left foreground. Such details, in their appetite for the fleeting, ascribe to the urban landscape the temporality of a perpetual present—as do the monuments, which, sundered from the pasts they formerly embodied, exhibit the values less of history than of immediacy. It would be inaccurate, however, to characterize the *Pont Neuf*—a fantasy of the city simplified—as a site of escape. If the work confines attention to the surface, it does so literally, by virtue of its claustrophobic composition. The abrupt angle of the Pont Neuf and the compression of the quai (at left) against the picture plane preclude spatial recession. The arch of the Porte Saint-Denis is as impenetrable as it is towering. Far from framing a vista, the cavities of the bridge, turned obliquely, offer a view of an architectural barrier.

Robert's *Pont Neuf* thus took its place in a lineage of capricci that blurred the distinction, as we saw in chapter 1, between mobility and constriction. As such, his painting registers the extent to which the terms of circulation and exchange informed the subject of urban embellishment. The worries voiced by Viel and Quatremère over the consequences of unfixing monuments from their original settings were not all that different from those articulated in the discourse on monetary theory: what troubled commentators in both domains was the transition from a "substantialist" theory of value to a "functionalist" one. As Richard Gray has shown, the manipulation by debt-ridden monarchs of national currencies, the use of credit instruments, and the fluctuating value of metal contributed in the eighteenth century to an awareness of money less as a thing of intrinsic value than as "a mere expedient of commerce and exchange." In keeping with this paradigm shift, it was recognized that just "as money condenses wealth into a more portable and useful form, so do words make knowledge more flexible and manageable." And just as language consisted of potentially misleading signs, so money, as we have seen, posed the dangers of "an economic edifice built without a foundation."[54]

The procedures of "démembrer, déplacer, dénaturer" that enabled circulation in the city, to Quatremère's dismay, also synopsized the substitution, in linguistic and financial practice, of abstractions for "things." Just as the historical import of a monument was deemed secondary to considerations of its impact on its surrounding quarter, so were words and money valuable purely as media of circulation dissociated from any intrinsic worth.[55] Gottfried Wilhelm, Freiherr von Leibniz, remarks on the efficiency, the accelerating function, of signs, relating the use of "notes" in "large trading centers" to the replacement of "things" by "signs, so that it is not necessary repeatedly to call to mind the thing every time it occurs." As a prerequisite to progress, the economy of signs could be as dangerously labyrinthine as it was liberating. Significantly, both John Locke and Étienne Bonnot de Condillac, recounting the dynamic of signs, describe the progress of human understanding in spatial terms. Writes Locke in 1690, words "interpose themselves so much between our understandings, and the truth which it [*sic*] would contemplate and apprehend, that, like the medium through which visible objects pass, the obscurity and disorder do not seldom cast a mist before our eyes, and impose upon our understandings."[56] Elsewhere, he depicts the association of ideas one to the next as "trains of motion . . . treading [along] a path," an image reiterated by Condillac, who likens signs to "chains to the different combinations of . . . ideas." For Condillac, "The use of signs is the principle which unfolds all our ideas," yet if reliance on signs was the key to advancing human knowledge, so did it result in "confusion" when the "source" of ideas was forgotten in the process.[57]

Robert's *Pont Neuf* playfully makes good on the promise of language as an *ars combinatoria,* a "sign-language on the basis of whose manipulation previously unknown truths could be discovered." The capriccio explores the "combinations... of ideas" that appear to the imagination, once signifiers of formerly fixed meaning are freed from their signifieds. It engaged the pleasures of random contiguity at a time when the arbitrary character of sign value was cause for alarm. Gray draws attention to the antithesis that made itself felt in the eighteenth century between ancient and modern systems of value: as opposed to traditional uses of currency, value in the modern age "becomes extrinsic and systematic"; importantly, it is this system that Robert valorizes by making it an expression for a kind of creative freedom.[58]

Capricci were ideally poised to register the eighteenth century's romanticization of and also its unease with circulation; as shall be discussed in the next chapter, those produced by Robert's instructor in Rome—Panini—were no exception. In the *Pont Neuf,* the genre's ability to bridge, so to speak, a "substantialist" and a "functionalist" theory of value is complicated by the painting's sketchy execution. The view hesitates, as we have seen, between monumentality and dissolution; Robert's liquid touch undermines the solidity of the edifices as volumetric subjects occupying three-dimensional space, thus melting the difference between city and Seine. The painter's reliance on atmospheric effects to convey a sense of mass and volume—evidenced in the pattern of light and shadow in the interior of the arches, and in the patch of sunlight on the column—renders the edifices less things of substance than optical events (fig. 52). The incompleteness of the sketch, its abnegation of depth for the sake

Fig. 52. Detail of fig. 51

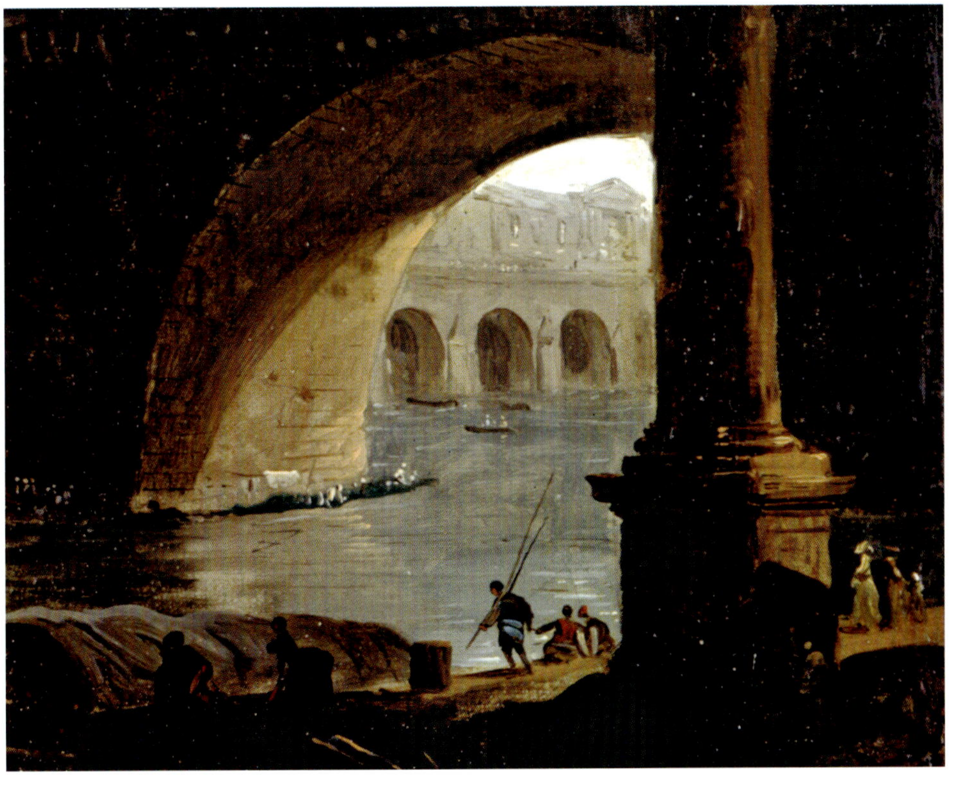

of sheer surface effect, thematizes the potential of the embellished city to devolve into a world unanchored.

The *Pont Neuf* was not the only imaginary view that Robert produced of the city's edifices. His *Monuments of Paris,* exhibited at the Salon of 1789, features the same subject (fig. 53). The capriccio was clearly in dialogue with the *Pont Neuf:* as in the latter work, the monuments include the Porte Saint-Denis stationed across from Bullant's column; in between them, in the background, appear the Louvre colonnade and to its right the Fontaine des Quatre Saisons. Also assembled are the Église Sainte-Geneviève, looming behind the Louvre; an equestrian statue of Louis XIV featuring the king in the guise of a Roman emperor; and the Fontaine des Innocents to its right. Approximately five times larger than the *Pont Neuf,* the *Monuments of Paris* has the dimensions of a history painting and was meant to be visible from a distance.

Its heroic scale precluding sketch-like imprecision, the *Monuments of Paris* performs a dramatic about-face from the *Pont Neuf.* Far from the latter's fantasy of the city's edifices as malleable decorations of a floating world, the publicly exhibited work endows them with the powerful solidity of ancient Roman monuments, rooted—despite the incongruity of their assembly—in the soil. The artist has ensconced his architectural subjects in a decaying, fragment-strewn landscape, one peopled by modern and ancient Romans alike. Darkened and worn by time—as exemplified by the slightly crumbling façade of the Porte Saint-Denis—the city's modern monuments are projected into the distant future. This effect is noteworthy given that at the time of the painting's execution, the dome of Sainte-Geneviève (a building that was favorably compared to the architecture of antiquity) remained unfinished, as did the Louvre colonnade, which has the appearance of emerging from the mounds of earth that partially

Fig. 53. Hubert Robert (French, 1733–1808)
The Monuments of Paris, 1788, oil on canvas, 117 × 175 cm (46⅛ × 68⅞ in.)
Montreal, Power Corporation of Canada Art Collection

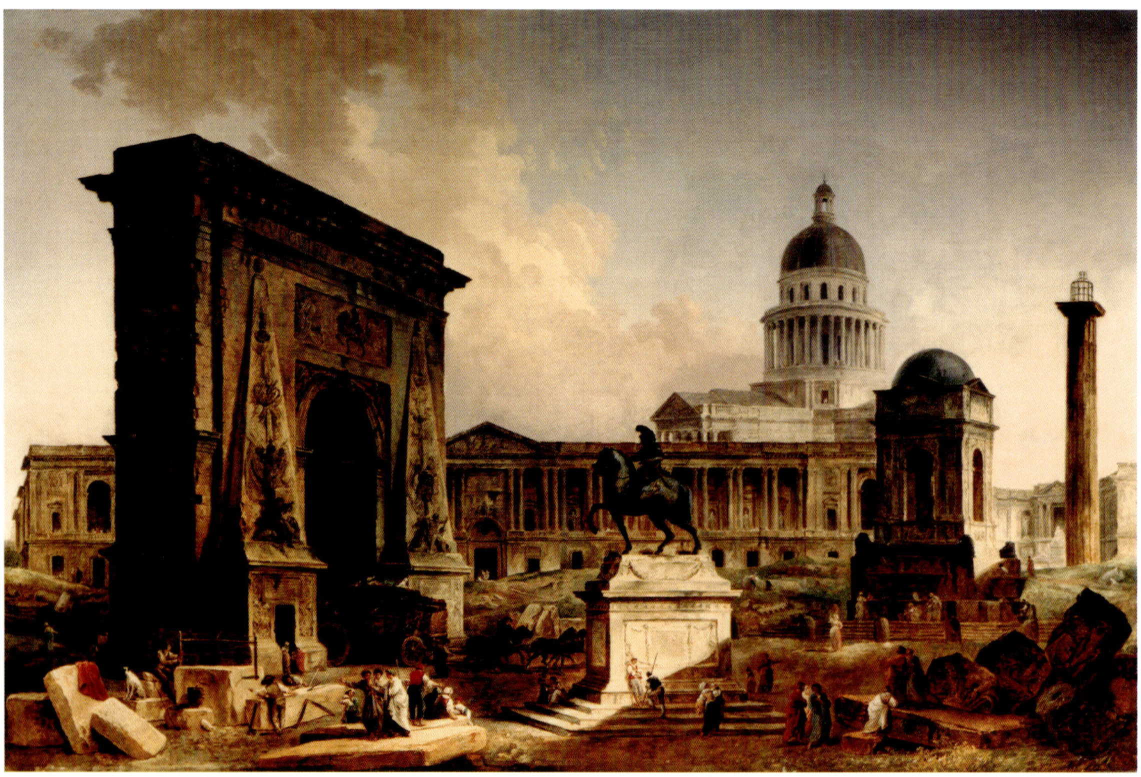

obscure it.[59] In representing these monuments in their completed form, as if in an outdoor museum or excavation site, Robert imbues his fictive landscape with its future tense. The painting thus repels—on the levels of both form and subject matter—the aesthetic of the unfinished employed in the *Pont Neuf.*

The *Monuments of Paris* was favorably reviewed in *L'année littéraire,* which distinguished the artist as setting a positive example for the future. Robert's painting, declares the critic, "has excited the greatest interest." The author continues, "If, among the engravers we could produce a Piranesi, a flood of prints could distribute [our] monuments throughout Europe, and the capital of France would have no dearth of admirers."[60] The call for a French Piranesi whose art would gratify national pride by showcasing Paris as the rival of Rome was one to which Robert emphatically responded: he exhibited the painting alongside a (now-lost) pendant, *Ancient Monuments of France*—featuring the relics of Roman antiquity on French soil. Thus celebrating the nation's ancient and modern monuments side by side, the canvases asserted that the edifices of Paris—like the Roman ones in Provence—would persist as national icons. The presence of laborers in the left foreground of the *Monuments of Paris,* cutting stone in preparation for a new building project, reinforces the work's message of continuity.

It is striking, however, that the impossible massiveness of Robert's subjects, in addition to ennobling them to the status of ancient edifices, heightens their resemblance to "refugees... after a cataclysm."[61] The impression conveyed by the vaguely postapocalyptic landscape—its topography reminiscent of an ancient archaeological site—is that only structures of mammoth proportions could have withstood the disaster that presumably laid waste to the city. That the monuments' hyperbolic presence betrayed a degree of defensiveness is suggested in part by the prominence of the Fontaine des Innocents. Months before the painting's completion, Quatremère had warned that the fountain's imperiled status spelled an end to the monumental order. As if to disavow such charges, Robert has restored to the recently "dismembered" monument the weight of history. Though, given the exhibition date of the work, it is tempting to associate the long-ago "cataclysm" evoked in the painting with the pending events of the Revolution. The canvas venerates the "Monuments of Kings," but so too does it present them as remnants of a vanished world.

It is in this sense that the painting reveals the consciousness not only of a landscape painter in the tradition of Panini but also of a curator-administrator, as Robert had been since 1784 at the Louvre. The monument—meaningfully included in Robert's painting—was then undergoing its transformation from abandoned royal palace to the nation's first museum. And, like museum objects, the "displaced" structures in Robert's painting invite interactions and interpretations no longer dictated by the terms of their original settings. The lowly figures and meditative viewers shown wandering amidst the structures have in essence inherited them; it is not the equestrian king who triumphantly passes through the gateway of the Porte Saint-Denis but a pack of peasants. The logic of embellishment, as we shall see in the next chapter, was one that extended to the museum. Just as relocating monuments served the interests of urban flow, so too did the museum function as a conduit of circulation: the artworks in its collection, dislodged from their original locations, were granted an abstraction that made them accessible to the public. Robert's services at the museum likely sensitized him to such parallels, just as they did his colleague Pajou, whose approach to the transferal of Guillain's royal monument reflected his own museum credentials.

Perhaps the sublime scale of Robert's monuments betrayed some vague and prescient discomfort with the paradigm of the museological that was creeping into the city under the guise of embellishment. For the painting, albeit by reducing the capital to a scattering of its landmarks, evidently aimed to reassure viewers that the monuments of Paris, like those of Rome, would endure in significance: that modernity would be the future's antiquity. To compare the work once more to the *Pont Neuf* is to recognize that the credibility of such a promise rested on the removal of the monuments from the banks of the river—indeed, on the effacement from the arid, rocky terrain of any trace of the Seine. The omission, made at a moment when the river supplanted the built order as the agent of a better future, is instructive. With it, Robert reinstates the imperatives of architecture as opposed to urbanism—of remembering as opposed to forgetting.

The allure of the latter, so powerfully associated with the Seine, found expression in the form of another futuristic work at the Salon of 1789: De Wailly's *Projet d'utilité et d'embelissement pour la ville de Paris* (fig. 54). Its display evidencing the depth of public interest in urban renewal, the architect's sweeping proposal left hardly a trace of the city untouched. It included the fusion of the islands of the river into one; the construction of twelve bridges; the creation of quais, new public promenades, and new streets; and the building of a new Place Louis XVI. As if to

Fig. 54. Charles De Wailly (French, 1729–98)
Projet d'utilité et d'embelissement pour la ville de Paris (Project for the utility and embellishment of the city of Paris), 1789, etching with additions by hand in ink and body color, 62 × 83.3 cm (24⅜ × 32¾ in.)
Paris, Bibliothèque nationale de France

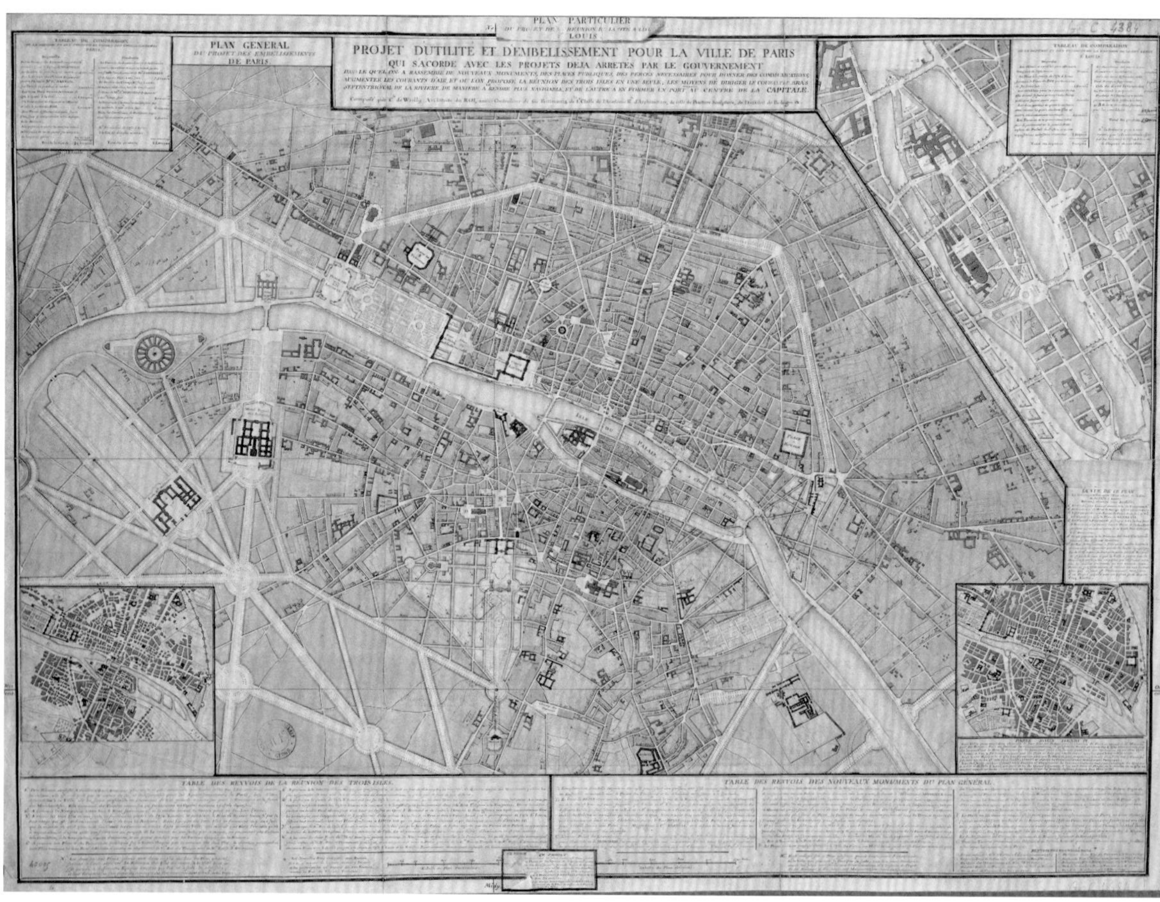

contain the shock of the new, De Wailly presented his citywide renovation agenda as the synthesis of proposals previously submitted to the government concerning "new monuments, *places publiques,* [and] passages necessary to enhance communication" as well as "the flow of air."[62]

The boldness of De Wailly's proposal well matched the mood of 1789, as expressed by a critic writing for the *Spectateur français.* The review begins dramatically: "I will not lie, this immense work frightens at first glance: but if, like Epimenides, I were to sleep for fifty years and this were to be executed by a free nation, I would congratulate myself for having slept as long as he, in order to see Mr. Wailly's intentions realized." De Wailly's "patriotic" efforts, the author continues, contrast markedly with the private interests that have long presided over urban embellishment. With the recent arrival of liberty, no longer will "ministerial despotism begin what it never finishes," nor "elevate at great cost enormous heaps of stone" in an already densely built urban center. The innumerable access routes envisioned by the architect, designed to advance the "commerce of the capital and the navigation of its citizens," heralded nothing less than the end of "slavery" and "poverty." Thus did the critic align the building industry with the evils of the old regime, and De Wailly's program of erasure with the advent of freedom. In short, the work exhibited the promise of urban reform to deliver the nation to a future radically distinct from its past.[63]

Unimpeded thoroughfares, endless communicability: as De Wailly's *Projet* illustrates, the river was superseding architecture as a source of urban identity, offering the public a reflection of the disembodied values upon which the city of the future would ideally be modeled. Robert's homage to the "Monuments of Kings" could hardly have differed more from the architect's proposal to build the people's city. The profusion in De Wailly's project of empty passages in place of "heaps of stone" marked the transference of urban resources away from the despots and private speculators and to the greater public. In internalizing the logic of the museum, however, the capriccio proved no less responsive than De Wailly's design to the changing tides of history. Arousing expectations of a marketplace "flood[ed]" with images of "our monuments," the painting appeared to be firmly aligned with the virtues of circulation.

The effect of the *Monuments of Paris,* remarkably, was to compel a vision of the market's channels sustaining the momentum of signs. As such, the painting's achievement, among other things, was to mollify an anxiety about circulation and to do so in the midst of the pre-revolutionary financial crisis. For the prospect of the ephemeral eclipsing the enduring haunted critics not only of urbanism, who deplored the loss of the monumental order, but also of an unregulated stock exchange that seemed poised to decimate the economy. Writing in 1788, when speculation on the Bourse hit a fevered pitch, Mercier powerfully captured the threat of fictitious capital's infinite expansion:

> One speaks today of a million as one spoke a hundred years ago of a thousand louis d'or.... These millions that dance are millions made of paper, an immense scaffold of credits and debts, mortgages on other credits and other debts in a perpetually lengthening chain, a wager on the future that can only temporarily support itself through its own movement, by the continual

> progression of voluminous transactions, and . . . by a rapidly increasing yield of the national economy: the accumulating returns of a prosperous economy—and additionally, the progressive depreciation of money by price inflation—will efface tomorrow the debts of today. Should the movement stop . . . the whole edifice will collapse.[64]

Mercier's damning assessment of an economy built on paper, prophetic of Theodor Adorno's reference to "the dance of the money veils," culminates in the image of a collapsing edifice. Aptly so, for such panic over the rule of arbitrary signs necessarily bereft of any "intrinsic connection with the concepts or things they represent" equally characterizes Quatremère's concern for the future of urban monuments.[65] It is this context that illuminates the ambition of Robert's *Monuments of Paris* to restore confidence in the fate of the capital. At a moment of grave instability, Robert enshrined the timeless authority of the city's monuments. In the midst of terror over the imminence of financial disaster, he invited absorption in a distant future. Exchanging liquidity for solidity, the painting injected the dynamics of circulation with the air of stability. Yet so too, with its amalgam of uprooted monuments, did it affirm the long-ago demise of a signified.

Boundless Debt

"Fictive values." The phrase abounded in the late 1780s in pamphlets accusing a financially asphyxiated state of placing the nation's fortunes at the mercy of a volatile stock market. The outsourcing of urban improvement initiatives to joint-stock companies that floated their ventures on the Bourse intensified the conviction that the city was hovering on the brink of financial collapse. As Mercier wrote, projects for the capital—once matters of "patriotism and disinterest"—were being hijacked by "brokers" and "magicians" who lured the public with offerings of "immense and chimerical capital."[66] Foremost among the perpetrators of this "audacious roguery" were the Perier brothers, founders of the Compagnie des eaux de Paris (Paris water company), which promised such services as the distribution of clean water from the Seine and the paving of streets. Foul-crying pamphleteers accused the Periers of acting not to advance the public good but to inflate their company's already exaggerated stock values—and the government, moreover, of secretly subsidizing their machinations.[67]

The controversy provoked by the Compagnie des eaux de Paris helped galvanize panicked predictions of a stock market crash and national bankruptcy. In his *Dénonciation de l'agiotage au roi et à l'Assemblée des notables* (1787), Honoré-Gabriel Riqueti, comte de Mirabeau, warned that the monarch's failure to rein in *agiotage*—the pejorative appellation for reckless speculation on the stock exchange—would result in "successive calamities."[68] Yet he also recognized that speculative enterprise—and the state's complicity in it—would flourish so long as the government remained mired in debt. Indeed, little was sacred in the face of a desperate campaign to replenish the royal treasury—least of all the Crown's obligation to keep royal institutions from being "drained by the scourge of *agiotage,*" as it was complained in 1789, when the monarch seemed intent on selling state-run enterprises to the highest bidder.[69] (Nor was the handing off of municipal services to joint-stock companies the only sign of the implosion of debt-infested public institutions: in 1769, in a bizarre episode of which Robert was doubtlessly aware, the Académie royale de peinture et de sculpture sought the Crown's permission to construct a series of boutiques on the Pont Neuf that would provide it with a source of much-needed revenue. Six years later, the Académie was publicly accused of speculating and of masking its "vile interest"—as well as its disregard for "the embellishment of the city"—behind claims of advancing "public utility.")[70]

Like Mercier, Mirabeau foresaw the mortgaging of the future to manage the exigencies of the present, wondering "for how many years will we be condemned to value the greatest resources of the Kingdom only in sad relation to an immensity of unpaid debts?" He invokes the "tides of currency" in the capital—a "place of dissipation and vertigo," "where millions... pass from one wallet to another, without creating anything." Should the king fail to contain the speculative mania, he warns, the "esprit" of the city could extend itself throughout the country. The provinces would surely be "steril[ized]" by *agiotage,* an "art" that "knows nothing of limits... it corrodes, it taints all that it touches." And Mirabeau, too, describes the endless circuitry by which "the insufficiency of... loans is announced immediately following their promulgation. Countless expedients... to attract still more money fill the interval that is necessary between these loans; if we make reimbursements, it's through contracting a debt more onerous than the one paid off."[71]

Such economic dread substantiates what scholars have described as the coincidence between the discourse of the sublime—that which "exists only by overspilling"[72]—and the unchecked expansion of debt following the Seven Years' War. For Peter de Bolla, describing Burke's England, the sublime is "marked by the emergence of a discursive excess, the production of an inflationary element within the bounds of the legislated territory." He cites "the increased flow of paper credit" (itself a phenomenon of discursive excess) alongside "the infinite transferability" of financial instruments as activations of the sublime—images to which may be added Mercier's "perpetually lengthening chain of speculation and mortgage."[73] Relatedly, Patrick Brantlinger observes that Burke, in his *Reflections on the Revolution in France* (with its worry that "nations are wading deeper and deeper into an ocean of boundless debt"), treats "the financial mysteries of state"—no less than "the ruin of monarchs and the revolutions of kingdoms"—as "sublime objects of terror."[74]

In light of this discussion, Mercier's account of the "audacious roguery" whereby urban initiatives became a launching pad for "immense and chimerical capital" further testifies to the sublime processes that engulfed the city on the eve of 1789. And it is in peculiar accordance with the unrepresentability of this interim that neither Robert's *Pont Notre-Dame* nor his *Pont-au-Change*—records, both, of the crowning feats of urbanism—was exhibited at the Salon. Yet the painter nonetheless produced several versions of each painting—evidently intending them for a private clientele. One such series was acquired by Louis-Auguste Le Tonnelier, baron de Breteuil, the royal minister who oversaw the city's public works projects.[75] Surely, writes Cayeux, Robert's paintings (like the views of the Opéra before them) would have also found a captive audience in the banker Girardot de Marigny—a key patron of the arts as well as of municipal improvement: it was his loan that financed the demolitions.[76] Further common to Breteuil and Girardot is that both were accused of capitalizing on enterprises deemed detrimental to the public. In 1786, the capital's unskilled laborers went on strike (with popular support) to protest a government-granted monopoly to a transport company—one in which Breteuil was rumored to have financial interests. As for Girardot, at least one pamphleteer accused him of engaging in a plot to destabilize the country's finances.[77] Such allegations of compromised loyalties were endemic to the prerevolutionary period's climate of suspicion, and the demolitions played no small role in fueling them. Breteuil, who was reputed to speculate in the urban improvement ventures that he oversaw, collaborated with Girardot to maximize the profitability of the operations along the Seine—not to the city, but to the lending institution that bore Girardot's name as well as to the king.[78]

From the royal government's point of view, the main benefit of the demolitions appears to have been neither functional nor aesthetic. The king agreed to the demolitions on the grounds that the loan of thirty million livres contracted from Girardot, Haller et Cie (with a 1 percent cut to the company), despite being guaranteed by the city, be placed directly into the royal treasury and distributed to Paris in installments. Thus did the Crown co-opt the financing of the renovations to ward off its own undoing.[79] Needless to say, the king did not meet his obligations, much to the despair of the city and its displaced residents. As the *bureau de ville* was forced to admit to one Antoine Mollard—an elderly hatmaker, "père de famille," and former resident of the rue de la Pelleterie, who complained in 1789 of not having received compensation for his losses and of being on the verge of "losing his liberty"—the city was not presently in a position to honor its debts.[80]

The very means by which urbanism sought to avert one calamity—by improving the quality and flow of air—thus appeared to expedite the arrival of another. Rapidly, the demolitions ignited a crisis of indebtedness, and behind the renovations' purported promise of enriching urban life lay the threat of a chain reaction of bankruptcies. Legions of displaced residents, vainly seeking reimbursement, pleaded with the city to save them from discredit. A number of them accused the city of speculating—of seizing and destroying their homes in order to rebuild at a profit. Given the capital's desperate predicament—enforced by the Crown's long-standing practice of coercing Paris into bearing the financial brunt of its own failed policies—such charges were not unfounded.[81]

The clearing of the bridges thus marked the culmination of what was at once a progressive campaign to restore the health and beauty of the city and an inglorious history of the mortgaging of urban operations in order to forestall economic collapse. As such, the demolitions served two distinct agendas for the future: the first motivated by the goal of "restoration," the other by the urgent necessity of deferral. It seems somehow fitting that the ambition behind the demolitions of furnishing citizens with a view entailed widening the scope of debt, for the prospect of its retirement appeared no more attainable than the horizon itself. Executed amidst rumors of an impending credit crisis, the great undertakings along the Seine must have been understood—and by more than the aggrieved former denizens of the bridges—not only as great public works but also as last-ditch speculative efforts to fend off catastrophe. Robert, for one, appears to have registered them as such. His paintings, indefinitely postponing the resolution of their subjects, no doubt appealed, in their depictions of mounting ruination, to a contemporary conviction that the greater the wreckage in the present, the more promising the rewards to come. Yet they also exhibited the ineluctable character of promissory notes, signifying a future that was forever deferred.

Urbanism had enticed imaginations with its Rousseauist project for a capital redeemed—a Paris brought into line with the intrinsic principles of nature, a city taken back from an outmoded order. With the demolitions, urbanism pursued its vision of the city as a tabula rasa, summed up by Friedrich Nietzsche's axiom "No happiness . . . no hope . . . no *present,* without forgetfulness." Nietzsche, appropriately, identified forgetfulness not only as the key to liberation from the crushing burden of remembrance but also as a state that would remain unavailable so long as man was doomed to an existence of perpetual oscillation between the fulfillment of obligations and the exacting of recompense.[82] Such a conjunction of emancipation and entrapment—the one furthering the effects of the other—encapsulates the modernity of the prerevolutionary city as Robert captured it: at once poised on the cusp of release from the confines of the past and bearing the burden of anticipation. It was precisely from such landscapes—ones that the imagination could not, dared not, finish—that the *Pont Neuf,* with its dreamy pliancy, and the *Monuments of Paris,* with its projection of a future anterior, promised refuge.

Chain of Associations

The Seine, though absent from the *Monuments of Paris,* made an appearance in another painting that Robert exhibited at the Salon of 1789: a view (now missing) of the river covered in ice, captured during the snowstorms that had besieged the city the previous winter, and even during the summer, when a "disastrous hailstorm," recalled Bernardin de Saint-Pierre, "swept through the whole country on 13 July." For the author, the horrific episode was inextricably tied to the other emergency of the day: the menace of "public bankruptcy . . . hovered over our fortunes, at the same time that the horrible cloud of the hailstorm traversed our countryside: the exhaustion of our finances . . . brought down several branches of our commerce, as the terrible winter did many of our fruit trees." Drawing attention to Bernardin de Saint-Pierre's recollections, Jean Starobinski notes that "the freeze" and "the deficit," punishing the country simultaneously, were perceived as two sides of the "same obscure malevolence."[83]

Robert's view of the ice-capped Seine featured the city's main commercial artery in a state of paralysis at the very moment when the "scourge of *agiotage*" had helped sterilize the nation's wealth. The work would thus have stood in contrast not only to De Wailly's *Projet,* with its image of a free-flowing river befitting an emancipated population, but also to the view captured in the pendant to Robert's painting: *The Bastille in the First Days of Its Demolition* (fig. 55). These two urban landscapes—both identified as sketches in the Salon *livret*—were clearly meant to relate to each other as antithetical opposites: presumably, the frozen imagery of the first view had its counterpoint in the cauldronesque heat emanating from the doomed fortress.[84] If the first work showed the city subjugated by natural disaster, the second one treated the theater of revolutionary upheaval as the site of humankind's vindication: in Robert's hands, the volcano-like Bastille—radiating an infernal glow and occupying a fiery chasm—poses the menace of a meteorological monster. The heroic attempt of the minuscule masses to dismantle the prison—a colossus rising uncannily from the earth

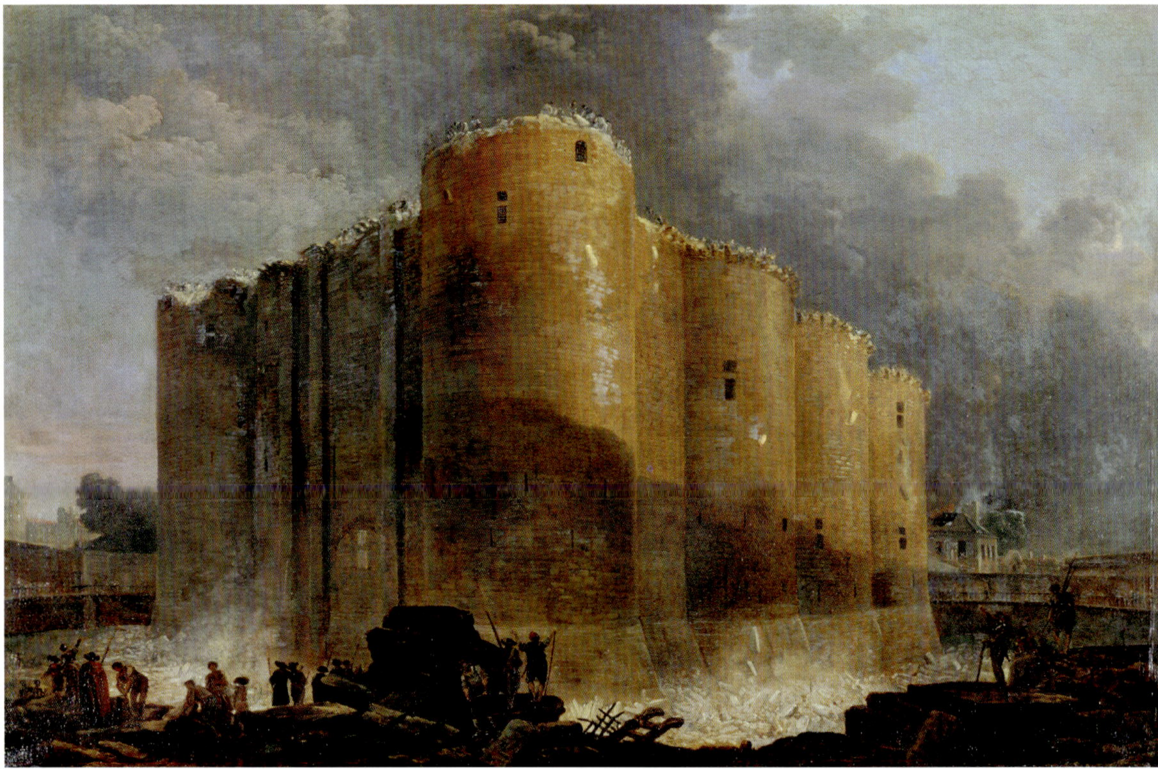

Fig. 55. Hubert Robert (French, 1733–1808)
The Bastille in the First Days of Its Demolition, 1789,
oil on canvas, 77 × 114 cm
(30⅜ × 44⅞ in.)
Paris, Musée Carnavalet

with the fury of a thousand leveled monuments—thus finds its symbolic equivalent in the wresting of power from the gods.

Even in the absence of its pendant view, the *Bastille* may be recognized as affording catharsis in a drama whose climax was long overdue. Robert relished the subject for this very reason, treating it as the grand finale in a trilogy of demolition events that began with the clearing of the Pont Notre-Dame and the Pont-au-Change. His view of the prison reverses the effect of the inverted *repoussoir* in the *Pont-au-Change:* the giant, frontal wedge of the Bastille, jutting into the space of the viewer, serves as a corrective to the soaring vacancy of the earlier work. And in place of the fragmented temporality and spatial inconsistencies of the *Pont Notre-Dame,* with its atomized and disparate focal points, the Bastille—its monolithic presence filling the canvas—offers a resoundingly unified subject. With the *Bastille,* the vague sense of malaise aroused by the previous works gives way to gleeful expectancy: if the *Pont-au-Change* portrayed the city made alien, the *Bastille* portends the forging of a communion between a newly freed people and a freshly liberated terrain. Importantly, the capital's reclamation by its residents, the molding of the city in the image of a self-determining populace, remains an event in the making, an ambition on the verge of fulfillment. Robert has taken pains to heighten the improbability of the prison's expiration: its delicately crumbling edges only underscore its mammoth inviolability. The effect of the unfinished sketch was clearly to catalyze anticipation, and with it, the desire to accelerate the process of ruination, to hurry the pace of time.

Robert's *Bastille* qualifies all the more as a successor to the previous demolition views given that a common logic united the clearing of the bridges and the dismantling of the dungeon: well before 14 July, projects were introduced to raze the

Bastille, its obstruction of circulation and access to the Seine deemed as intolerable as the despotic injustices it symbolized.[85] And like the clearing of the houses, the destruction of the fortress posed a welcome opportunity to consolidate the identity of the capital as a space of flow. With the Bastille's demolition, an architecture of confinement literally gave way to an instrument of circulation: stones from the prison were used to complete the Pont Louis XVI, in the spirit of Mercier's observation in 1771 that "republicans construct aqueducts, canals, highways."[86]

The downfall of the tyrannical institution, not unlike the removal of Guillain's monument from the Pont-au-Change, advanced urbanism's policy of magnifying the economic promise of the capital's terrain to the detriment of its symbolic uses. Immediately perceptive to the financial possibilities unleashed on 14 July was Pierre-François Palloy, overseer of the four-month demolition, who milked the "Bastille Business" for all it was worth. In 1792, he presented to the Assemblée législative a plan to convert the site into an expansive commercial and residential neighborhood, replete with thirty new streets, a bridge, and an aqueduct.[87] His vision was dwarfed by the scale of subsequent initiatives. By 1794, proponents of integrating the city more fully with the Seine called for connecting the terrain to a national network of canals: in this way, declared Jacques Auvraÿ, Paris would become "the principal depot of commerce in Europe." Five years later, the engineer Jean-Pierre Brullée envisioned a series of factories and commercial zones from which goods would be distributed to "almost all points of the Republic."[88] Thus did plans for the demolition zone proceed from considerations of urban embellishment to agendas for a nationwide marketplace.

That the Bastille's demolition so manifestly served the economic interests of the city makes Bernardin de Saint-Pierre's remembrances all the more relevant to Robert's sketch of 1789. The attack on the prison and the image of the freeze were antipodes to each other; more pointedly, it was the miseries unleashed by the latter—inseparable, as the author wrote, from the despair of commercial paralysis—that helped precipitate the events of 14 July. Viewed through the lens of Paris urbanism, the demolition of the Bastille—prefigured in the dismantling of so much ancien régime architecture before it—marked the confluence of the political revolution with an economic one.

"The urban wall has long been breached by an infinitude of openings and ruptured enclosures," writes Paul Virilio of the postmodern city. He adds, "While less apparent than those of antiquity, these are equally effective, constraining and segregating." Virilio relates such spatial alchemy—in which "radical erasure" resembles "abrupt confinement"—to an age of speed, observing that the "modern crisis of grand narratives betrays the effect of new technologies, with the accent, from here on, placed on means more than ends."[89] The statement recalls Simmel's comment that "monetary life means that life is caught up . . . in its means."[90] Robert's attention to the "means" rather than the "ends" of embellishment itself evidenced the spatialization, so to speak, of monetary life. But so too did it denote an inability to determine whether the removal of the city's meaningful forms, the dematerialization of the histories they had formerly embodied, marked the disintegration or the birth of "grand narratives." Postponing the fall of the prison—maximizing the monument's power as a symbolic structure—served to sustain the joy of anticipation, while keeping the resolution of the question at bay.

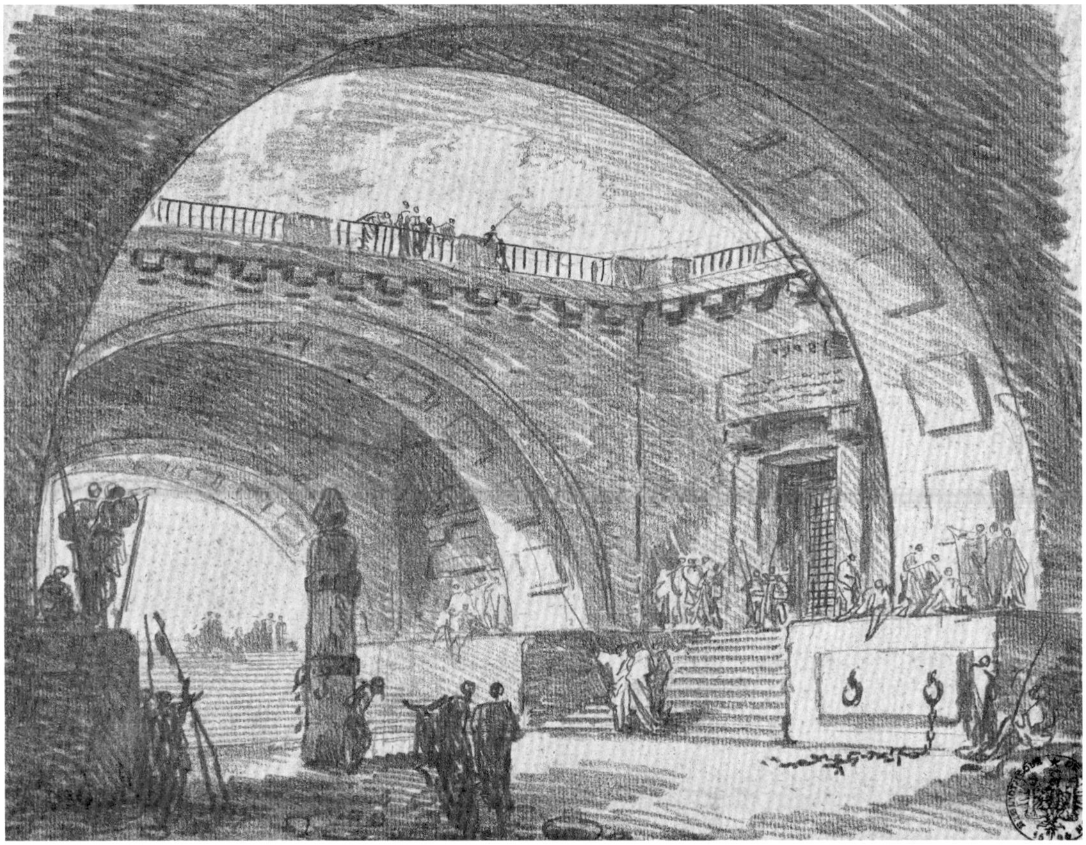

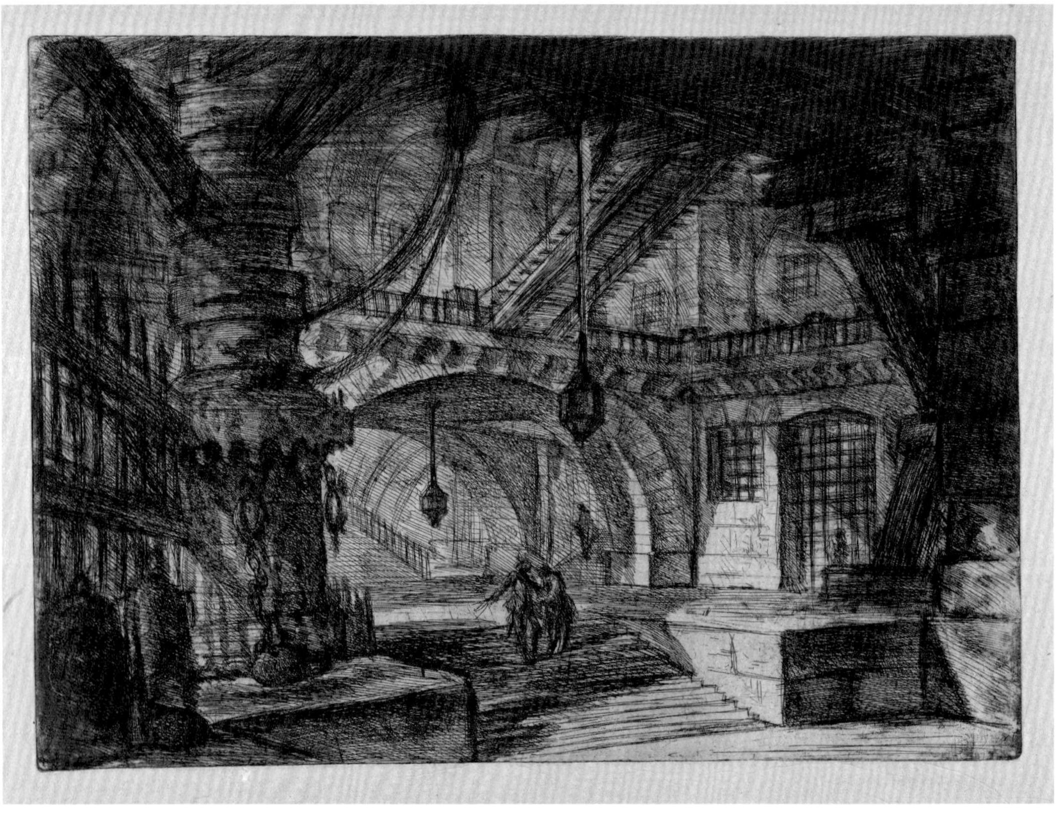

Fig. 56. Hubert Robert (French, 1733–1808)
Bridges with Prison, ca. 1760, counterproof with red chalk, 22.1 × 27.7 cm (8¾ × 10⅞ in.)
Besançon, Bibliothèque municipale

Fig. 57. Giovanni Battista Piranesi (Italian, 1720–78)
The Pier with Chains (first state), in the *Invenzioni capric di carceri*... series, 1749/1750, etching, 40.5 × 55 cm (16 × 21⅝ in.)
Los Angeles, Getty Research Institute

Fig. 58. Hubert Robert (French, 1733–1808)
Triumphal Bridge with Staircase, ca. 1760, counterproof with red chalk, 22.1 × 27.7 cm (8¾ × 10⅞ in.)
Besançon, Bibliothèque municipale

The frozen Seine, the crumbling Bastille: Robert's pendants of 1789 together and separately conflate the subjects of movement and stasis, access and confinement. Such is equally the case of Robert's earliest images of circulatory structures—works that are remarkable for their debt not so much to Piranesi's bridges and ports as to the etcher's prisons. Consider, for instance, a drawing Robert produced in about 1760, entitled *Bridges with Prison* (fig. 56). The page quotes specific features of Piranesi's *Pier with Chains* from the *Carceri:* the barred door at right has been retained, along with the two figures at center (fig. 57). But the vaulted archways in the etching have been replaced by two massive bridges, and Piranesi's tense weave of scrawlings has been resolved into chilling details: a chain at right, a prisoner at center, and a crowd that has gathered, presumably, to witness his torture. Similarly, a counterproof by Robert of a study for his painting *The Old Bridge* (also dating from about 1760) borrows motifs from the *Carceri's Grand Piazza*—including the stairway and the hanging lanterns (figs. 58, 59).[91] Once again, the arch of the etching has been modified in the drawing into a triumphal bridge. In *The Old Bridge,* the lantern—dangling in the foreground in Piranesi's print—has been set in the background, and the dense airlessness of the etching has given way to the expansive pathways proper to a "grand piazza" (fig. 60). Yet the position of the arch parallel to the picture plane renders it less an open channel than an impenetrable screen. And the stairway, accessible only by way of a sliver of space, offers no visible exit to those climbing it. The painting's account of passage depends upon the precedent of Piranesi's print, for in both, it is not the people who possess the means of circulation but the circulatory structures that appear to take possession of the people. The tiny figures stationed behind the balustrade on Robert's bridge are transplants from Piranesi's penitentiary. Even the atmospherics of the painting

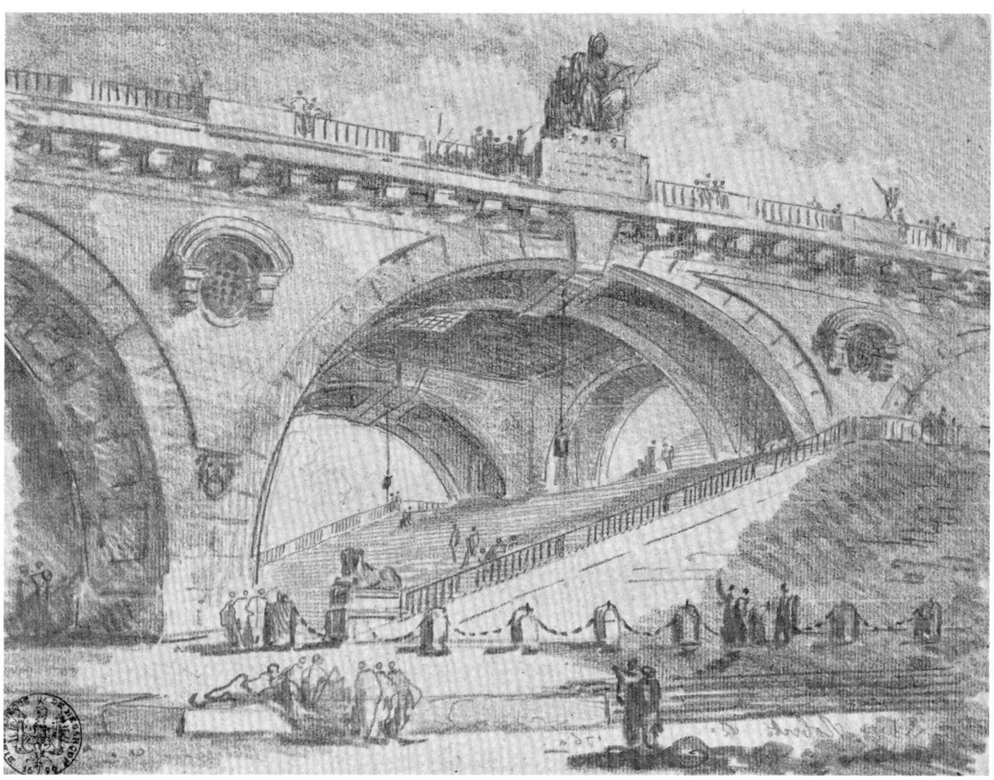

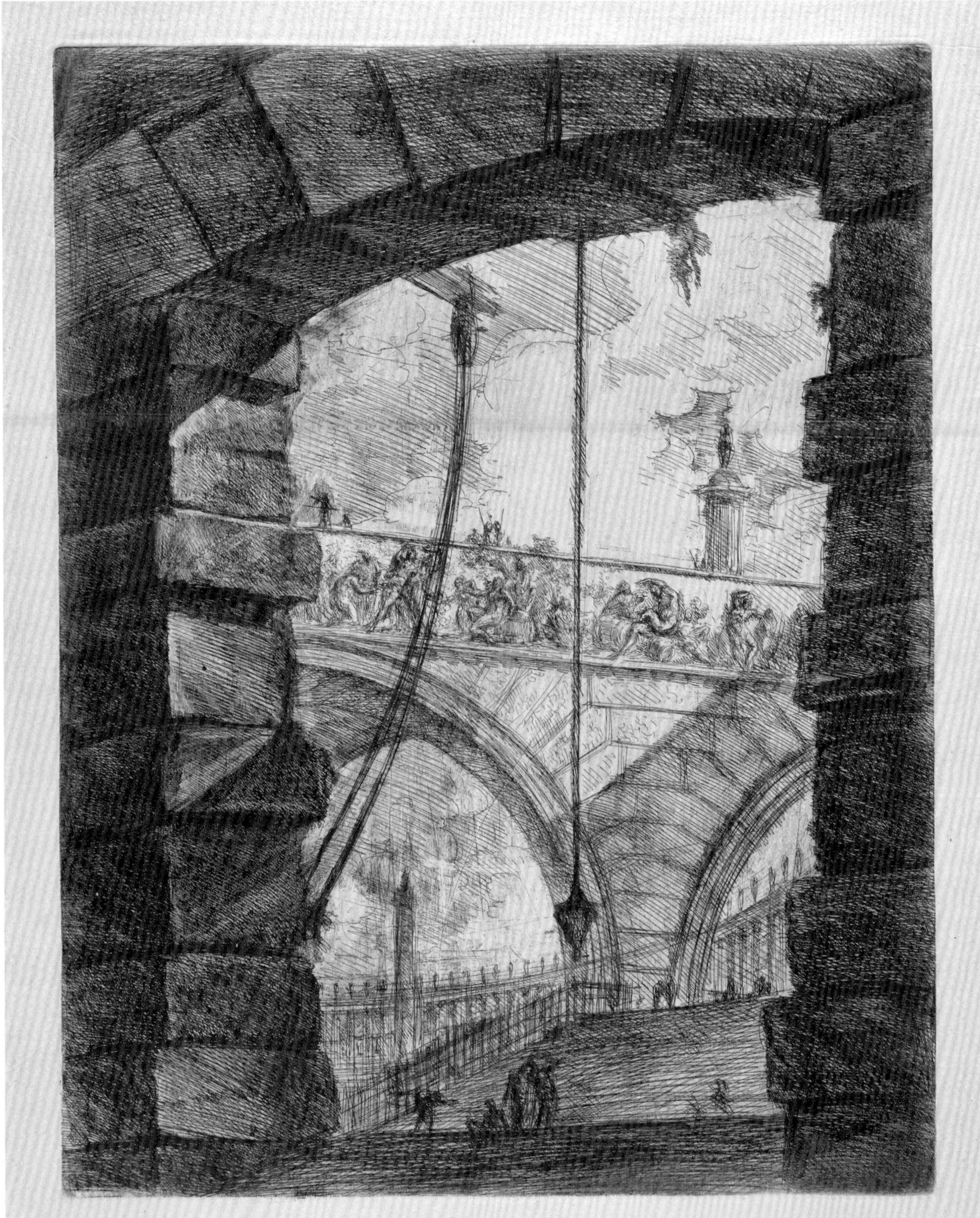

Fig. 59. Giovanni Battista Piranesi (Italian, 1720–78)
The Grand Piazza (first state), in the *Invenzioni capric di carceri...* series, 1749/1750, etching, 55 × 41 cm (21⅝ × 16⅛ in.)
Los Angeles, Getty Research Institute

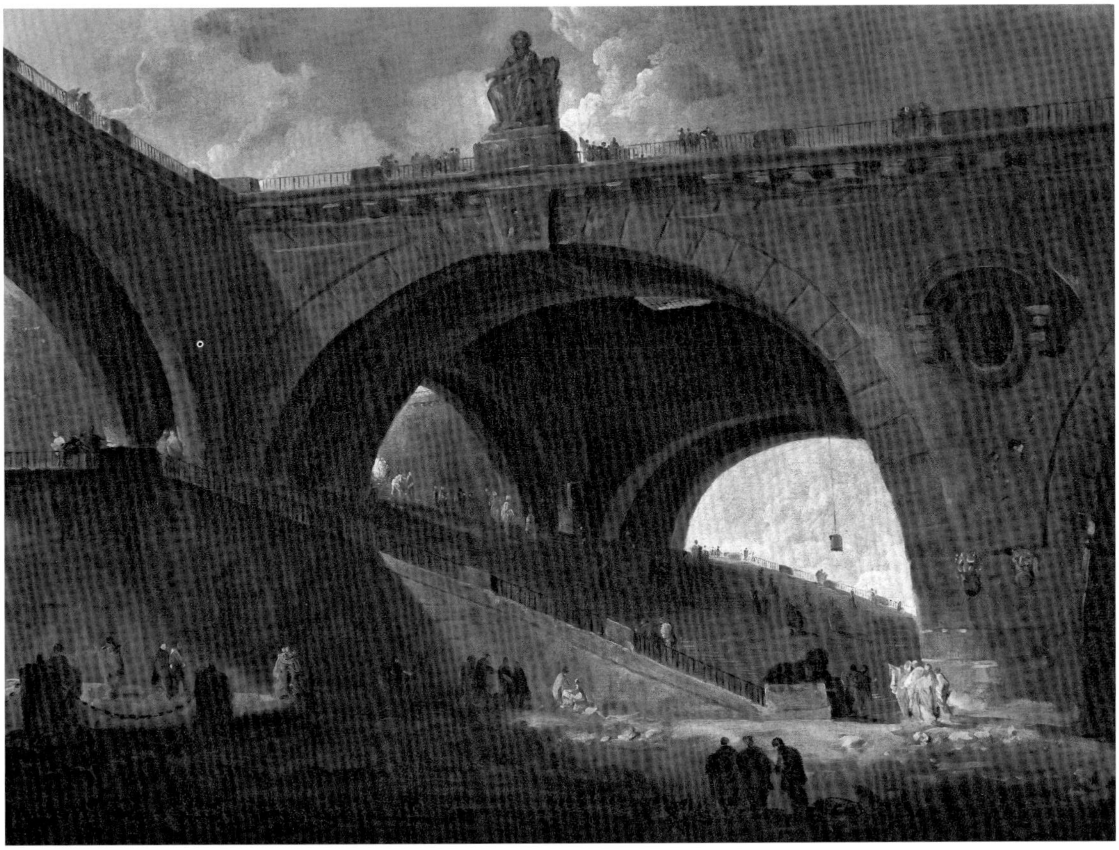

Fig. 60. Hubert Robert (French, 1733–1808)
The Old Bridge, ca. 1760–61, oil on canvas, 76.2 × 100.3 cm (30 × 39½ in.)
New Haven, Yale University Art Gallery

are mobilized to claustrophobic effect: storm clouds hover in the narrow margin of sky, and beneath the bridge, the semicircular wall of fog asserts the opacity of the picture plane. The gaping arc is echoed in the sweep of a chain hanging in the left foreground, contrasting but also conjoining communicability and confinement.

It is worth noting that the iconic status of Piranesi's most influential of bridge views—his *Magnificent Bridge*—reflected the work's remoteness from the irrational terrain of the *Carceri* (fig. 61). The etching presents a harmonious view of the magnificent bridge, an ideal of elemental clarity.[92] And yet, when Robert adopted the *Magnificent Bridge* as the basis for an enigmatic port scene he executed in about 1760—*Harbor with Architecture*—he also availed himself of a carceral imagery. The exoticized characters who populate the imaginary harbor include the two men at center transporting a barrel, their ankles in chains (fig. 62). The port's association with access and flow is undermined not only by the shallowness of the space—in contrast to the *Magnificent Bridge,* the body of water is abruptly cropped—but also by a peculiar sense of time suspended. Most of the figures are shown idling; the group at right, absorbed in some obscure activity, may even be engaged in a game of chance. Far from echoing the vibrant commercial energy of Vernet's renowned *Ports of France* series (exhibited between 1753 and 1765), Robert's port appears to have fallen into desuetude.[93]

The *Harbor,* torn between the vaguely menacing and the playfully indolent, reveals a labored—and ultimately aborted—attempt to ingest and reinterpret Piranesi's macabre pictorial vocabulary. The brawny stevedores would soon be excised from

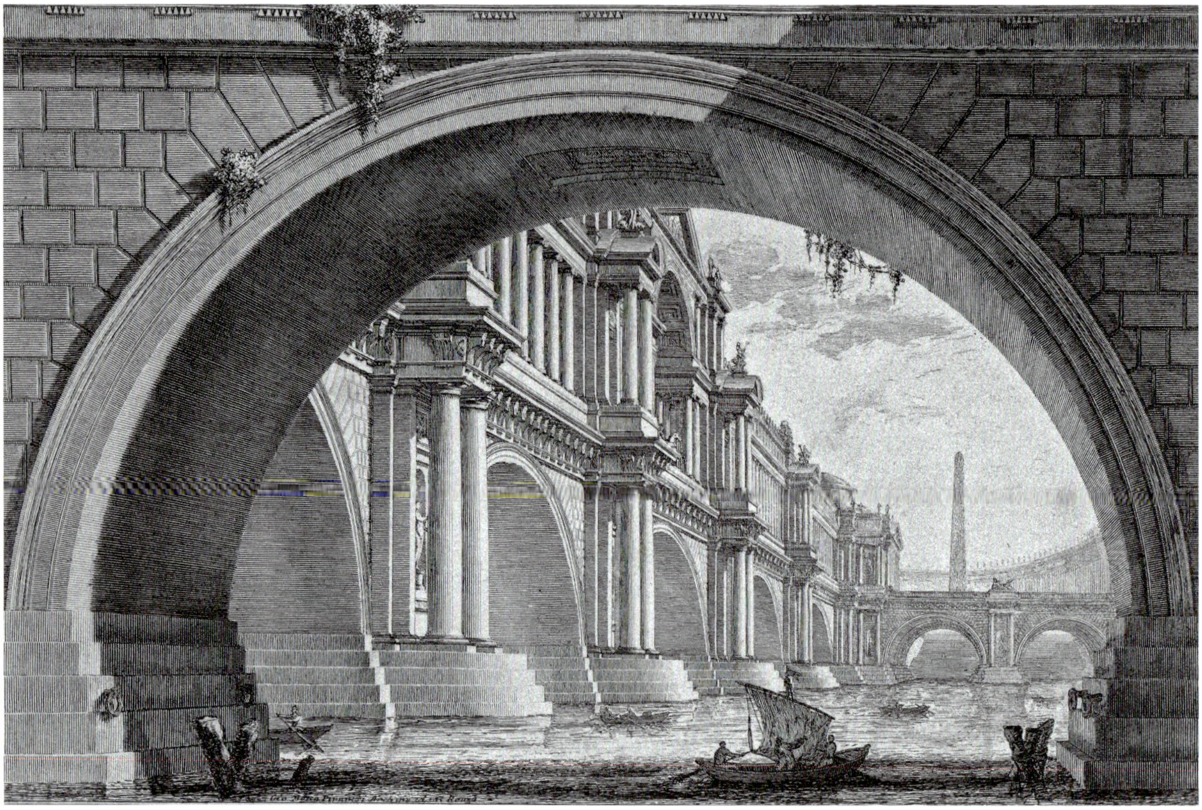

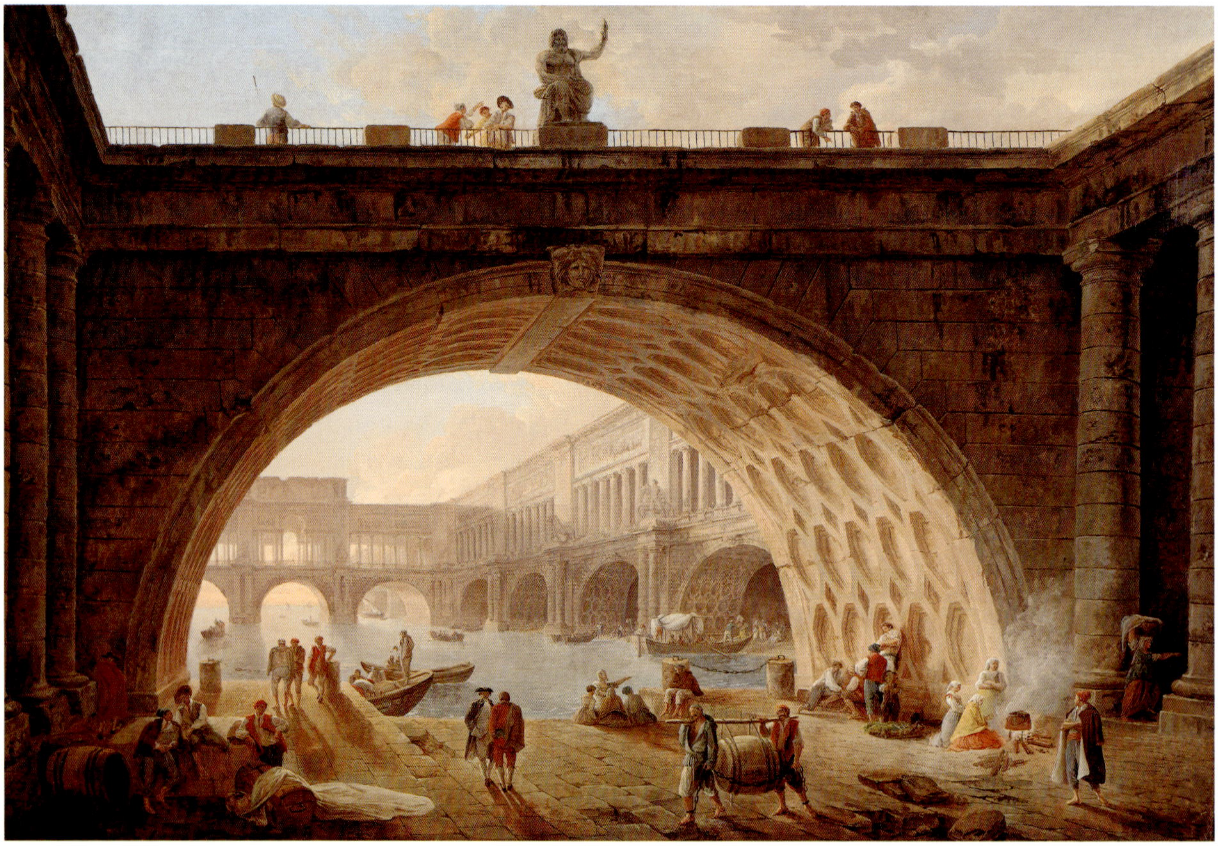

Fig. 61. Giovanni Battista Piranesi (Italian, 1720–78)
Magnificent Bridge
From Giovanni Battista Piranesi, *Prima parte di architetture e prospettive,* pl. 8, from the third edition of *Opere varie di architettura prospettive grotteschi antichità sul gusto degli antichi romani* (Rome, 1750)

Fig. 62. Hubert Robert (French, 1733–1808)
Harbor with Architecture, ca. 1760, oil on canvas, 105 × 145 cm (41⅜ × 57⅛ in.)
Dunkirk, Musée des beaux-arts

Fig. 63. Hubert Robert (French, 1733–1808)
The Demolition of Houses on the Pont Notre-Dame in 1786, 1786, oil on canvas, 86.5 × 159.5 cm (34 × 62¾ in.)
Paris, Musée Carnavalet

Robert's cast of primarily pastoral characters. Similarly, one detects in *The Old Bridge* a youthful effort to manufacture sublime effects in the absence of technical proficiency. Yet the paintings nonetheless present themselves as prototypes. In their remembrance of the *Carceri,* they suggest that within Robert's views of monumental passageways lived the theme of imprisonment.

The pairing of bridge and prison, extension and enclosure, was hardly unique to Robert. From Piranesi's carceral fantasies to Legeay's impenetrable capricci, eighteenth-century aesthetics revealed a perception of confinement as the underlying condition of the unbound imagination. An "[invitation] to a voyage" with no return is Tafuri's verdict on the capriccio—a genre that unleashed in the mind's eye an endless "chain of associations."[94] The prison, as much as it catalyzed a longing for escape, stood as a reminder of the dangers of unfettered flow. In the context of Paris urbanism, however, with its ideal of limitlessness, the lingering image of confinement functioned not only as an outmoded object of repugnance but also as a bulwark against the very future that was so ardently desired. It is perhaps for this reason that when Robert painted his views of the demolitions on the Seine's bridges, he felt compelled to draw on his *Harbor* of two and a half decades earlier. The dramatic archways of the earlier work resurface in his *Pont Notre-Dame,* as do certain of the figures: in the Carnavalet version of the painting, the woman perched on a toppled column at right, seated amidst the remnants of a dismantled order, assumes the position of the dreamers in the harbor scene who rest against the barrels (fig. 63). Traversing the riverbank at the center of the landscape, a pair of laborers commemorates the enchained figures of the *Harbor*—and with them, that which could not circulate.

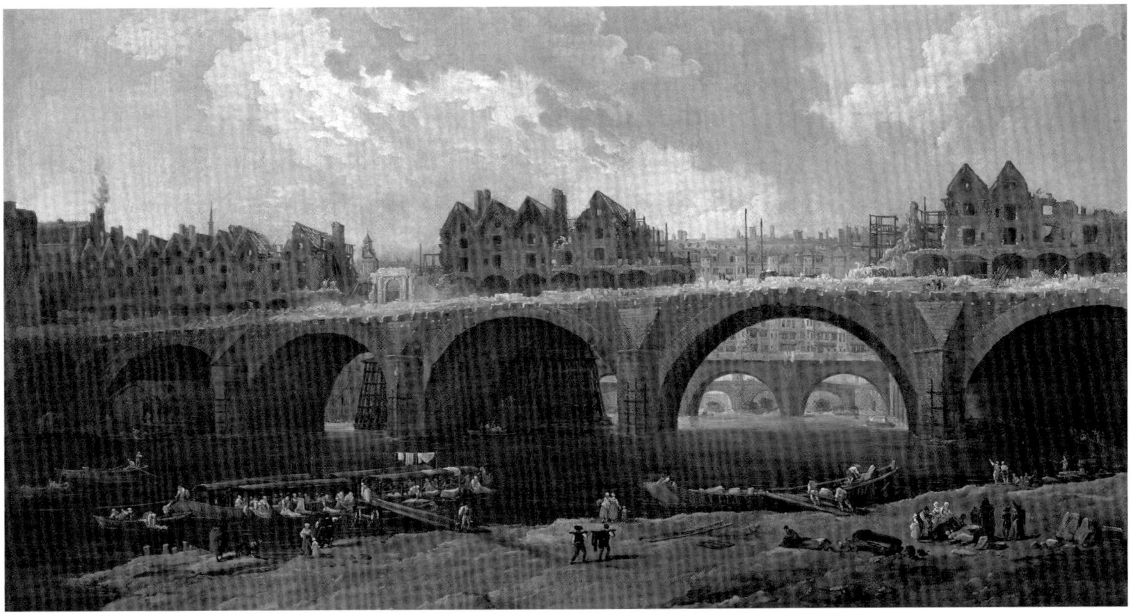

NOTES

1 Giovanni Battista Piranesi, "Opinions on Architecture: A Dialogue," in idem, *Observations on the Letter of Monsieur Mariette . . . ,* trans. Caroline Beamish and David Britt (Los Angeles: Getty Research Institute, 2002), 110–11.

2 Voltaire, "Des embellissements de la ville de Cachemire," in idem, *Oeuvres complètes de Voltaire,* ed. Adrien-Jean-Quentin Beuchot (Paris: Garnier Frères, 1879), 23:474.

3 Guillaume Poncet de La Grave, *Projet des embellissemens de la ville et fauxbourgs de Paris,* 3 vols. (Paris: Duchesne, 1756); Jean-Baptise-Jacques Élie de Beaumont, "Lettre sur l'embellissement et l'amélioration de Paris, sur les moyens de procurer en même temps sa salubrité sans qu'il en coûte rien" (11 November 1785), in Julien Hayem, ed., *Mémoires et documents pour servir à l'histoire du commerce et de l'industrie en France* (Paris: Hachette, 1921), 6:1–52; Pierre Patte, "Des embellissemens de Paris," in idem, *Monumens érigés en France à la gloire de Louis XV . . .* (Paris: Chez l'auteur, Desaint [&] Saillant, 1765), 212–29; Jean-Baptiste-Michel Renou de Chevigné dit Jaillot, *Lettres sur les embellissements de Paris* (Paris: A. M. Lottin, 1778). Isabelle Backouche provides an overview of the significance of these texts in her "Ponts et urbanisme (1760–1810): Du lieu de vie à la voie de communication," in Guy Lambert, ed., *Les ponts de Paris* (Paris: Action artistique de la ville de Paris, 1999), 57–63.

4 Jean-Baptiste Pujoulx, *Paris à la fin du XVIIIe siècle; ou, Esquisse historique et morale des monumens et des ruines de cette capitale . . .* (Paris: B. Mathé, an IX [1801]), 107; cited in Isabelle Backouche, *La trace du fleuve: La Seine et Paris, 1750–1850* (Paris: Éditions de l'École des hautes études en sciences sociales, 2000), 242. Archival sources relating to the demolitions are reproduced, and the operations detailed, in L. Taxil, "Une opération de voirie au XVIIIe siècle: Démolition des maisons construites sur les ponts de Paris et établissement de quais en bordure de la Seine," *Commission du vieux Paris, annexe au procès verbaux de la séance du 10 novembre 1909* (Paris, 1909).

5 Manfredo Tafuri, *The Sphere and the Labyrinth: Avant-Gardes and Architecture from Piranesi to the 1970s,* trans. Pellegrino d'Acierno and Robert Connolly (Cambridge: MIT Press, 1987), 25–54. See also Manfredo Tafuri, *Architecture and Utopia: Design and Capitalist Development,* trans. Barbara Luigia La Penta (Cambridge: MIT Press, 1976), chap. 1.

6 Tafuri, *Sphere,* 26, 35–36.

7 Lewis Mumford, *The City in History: Its Origins, Its Transformations, and Its Prospects* (San Diego: Harcourt, Brace, 1989), 413, 415.

8 In Piranesi's *Campo Marzio,* "the Tiber, with its sinuosity," writes Tafuri, "contributes to the dissolution of every residue of order." *Sphere,* 36.

9 Tafuri, *Sphere,* 31.

10 Patte, "Des embellissemens," 212, 222.

11 Moreau's unpublished *Plan générale du cours de la rivière de Seine et de se abords dans Paris avec les différents projets d'embellissements dont cette partie de la ville est susceptible* (1769) is conserved in the Bibliothèque nationale de France, Cabinet des estampes, Ve 36.

12 The words are Louis XV's, in the *lettres d'anoblissement* he issued on the architect's behalf in May 1771; an excerpt has been published in L. de Grandmaison, *Réunion des Sociétés des beaux-arts des départements* (1903), 378–80; cited in Sophie Descat, "Pierre-Louis Moreau et la Seine," in Michel Le Moël and Sophie Descat, eds., *L'urbanisme parisien au siècle des lumières,* exh. cat. (Paris: Action artistique de la ville de Paris, 1997), 82.

13 Louis Chevalier de Jaucourt, "Ville," in Denis Diderot and Jean Le Rond d'Alembert, *Encyclopédie; ou, Dictionnaire raisonné des sciences, des arts et des métiers* (Paris: Briasson [et al.], 1754–72), 17:277–80; cited and discussed in Nicholas Papayanis, *Planning Paris before Haussmann* (Baltimore: Johns Hopkins Univ. Press, 2004), 16.

14 Poncet de La Grave, *Projet des embellissemens,* 1:119, 2:197. Discussed in Backouche, *Trace du fleuve,* 185–86.

15 Papayanis, *Planning Paris,* 45. Nicolas Delamare, *Traité de la police où l'on trouvera l'histoire de son etablissement . . . ,* 2nd ed. (Paris: M. Brunet, J. F. Hérissant, 1719–38), 4:168; translated in Papayanis, *Planning Paris,* 36.

16 See the discussion in Backouche, "Ponts et urbanisme," 57; the quotation is from Archives nationales, H 2167; cited in Backouche, "Ponts et urbanisme," 58.

17 Backouche, "Ponts et urbanisme," 61.

18 The dyers were among the rare groups who successfully petitioned for a greater indemnity. See "Mémoire des teinturies de la rue de la Pelleterie à M. de Calonne, septembre 1786," Archives nationales, H 2167; cited in Backouche, *Trace du fleuve,* 233–34.

19 The phrase comes from a project submitted by the architect Pierre Giraud to construct a bridge between the faubourgs Saint-Antoine and Saint-Marcel; see Pierre Giraud, *Projet de bateaux mouvans et suspendus en l'air... inventé l'An 5,* s. 1. n. d., Bibliothèque nationale de France, VP 641; cited in Backouche, *Trace du fleuve,* 266.

20 On these relics—sculptures of the White Virgin and Saint Denis—see Jutta Held, *Monument und Volk: Vorrevolutionäre Wahrnehmung in Bildern des ausgehenden Ancien Régime* (Cologne: Böhlau, 1990), 293.

21 Dietmar Lüdke draws attention to the Seine's connotations of the eternal in the *Pont Notre-Dame* in his *Hubert Robert, 1733–1808, und die Brücken von Paris,* exh. cat. (Karlsruhe: Staatliche Kunsthalle Karlsruhe, 1991), 15.

22 Edmund Burke, *A Philosophical Enquiry into the Origin of Our Ideas of the Sublime and Beautiful,* ed. Adam Phillips (Oxford: Oxford Univ. Press, 1990), 59, 66–69.

23 Robert's affinity for this subject is analyzed in André Corboz, *Peinture militante et architecture révolutionnaire: À propos du thème du tunnel chez Hubert Robert* (Basel: Birkhäuser, 1978). Burke describes the sublimity of the colonnade in his *Philosophical Enquiry,* 128–29.

24 It was on such grounds that the *prévôt des marchands* rejected Passemant's proposal; see Backouche, *Trace du fleuve,* 192. Passemant's "Extrait du memoir presenté au roi le 2 octobre 1765... pour rendre Paris port de mer" is conserved at the Bibliothèque historique de la ville de Paris, MS N.A. 147, fol. 376.

25 In the realm of planning, nature, it should be noted, was conceived of as a force to be subdued—rather like the town itself, along with its residents. See Antoine Picon, *French Architects and Engineers in the Age of Enlightenment,* trans. Martin Thom (Cambridge: Cambridge Univ. Press, 1992), esp. 192–227; and Anthony Vidler, "The Scenes of the Street: Transformations in Ideal and Reality, 1750–1871," in Stanford Anderson, ed., *On Streets* (Cambridge: MIT Press, 1978), esp. 32–38.

26 Louis-Sébastien Mercier, *Tableau de Paris,* new ed. (Amsterdam, 1782–88), vol. 4, chap. 336, p. 198. Physiocracy, writes John Shovlin, "legitimated commerce by giving [it] a firmer ontological grounding" and diluting its associations with the uncertain terrain of "fancy, imagination, and the passions"; see his *The Political Economy of Virtue: Luxury, Patriotism, and the Origins of the French Revolution* (Ithaca: Cornell Univ. Press, 2006), 110–11. On the capitalist logic of the rhetoric of nature in the city, see Manfredo Tafuri, "Toward a Critique of Architectural Ideology," in K. Michael Hays, ed., *Architecture Theory since 1968* (Cambridge: MIT Press, 1997), 2–35.

27 Cited in Taxil, "Opération de voirie," 10.

28 Louis-Sébastien Mercier, *L'an deux mille quatre cent quarante: Rêve s'il en fût jamais;* translated by W. Hooper as *Memoirs of the Year 2500* (Boston: Gregg Press, 1977), 26, 28–29. Oettermann emphasizes the political component of this desire for a panoramic view—noting that the first successful hot air balloon flight, in 1783, seemed a symbol of freedom—as well as its disillusionment in the nineteenth century. The panorama, he writes, was intimately tied to the panopticon; see Stephan Oettermann, *The Panorama: History of a Mass Medium,* trans. Deborah Lucas Schneider (New York: Zone, 1997), 14–15 and introduction.

29 Richard Wittman, *Architecture, Print Culture, and the Public Sphere in Eighteenth-Century France* (New York: Routledge, 2007), 208–9.

30 Oettermann, *Panorama,* 25.

31 Mercier, *Tableau de Paris,* vol. 4, chap. 336, p. 198; Charles-Louis de Secondat, baron de Montesquieu, *Essai sur le goût* (1757), translated in Alexander Gerard, *An Essay on Taste* (London: Printed for A. Miller, A. Kincaid & J. Bell, 1759), 269–70.

32 Pierre Patte, *Mémoires sur les objets les plus importans de l'architecture* (Paris: Rozet, 1769), 5.

33 Jean Barbault, *Les plus beaux monuments de la Rome ancienne; ou, Recueil des plus beaux morceaux de l'antiquité romaine qui existent encore* (Rome: Bouchard & Gravier, 1761); and idem, *Les plus beaux édifices de Rome moderne; ou, Recueil des plus belles vües des principales églises, places, palais, fontaines, etc. qui sont dans Rome, avec la description historique de chaque édifice* (Rome: Bouchard & Gravier, 1763). Robert's inventory of prints included "Monuments antiques, la plupart dessinés par Barbault"; see Claude Gabillot, *Hubert Robert et son temps* (Paris: Librairie de l'art, 1895), 270, no. 371. On Barbault, see Nathalie Volle and Pierre Rosenberg, *Jean Barbault (1718–1762): Catalogue,* exh. cat. (Beauvais: Musée départmental de l'Oise 1974); see also Pierre Rosenberg, "Quelques nouveautés sur Barbault," in Georges Brunel, ed., *Piranèse et les Français: Colloque tenu à la Villa Médicis, 12–14 mai 1976* (Rome: Edizioni dell'Elefante, 1978), 499–508. On the theme of urban embellishment in Barbault's *Les plus beaux édifices de Rome moderne,* see Nina L. Dubin, "Anti-Edifice: Jean Barbault's *Rome Moderne,*" in Rebecca Zorach, ed., *The Virtual Tourist in Renaissance Rome: Printing and Collecting the "Speculum Romanae Magnificentiae,"* exh. cat. (Chicago: Univ. of Chicago Press, 2008), 85–93.

34 Quoted in Maurice Andrieux, *La vie quotidienne dans la Rome pontificale au XVIIIe siècle* (Paris: Hachette, 1962), 165.

35 Papayanis, *Planning Paris,* 38. See pages 35–39 for Papayanis's discussion of volume 4 of Delamare's *Traité de la police.*

36 As Lewis Mumford writes, "In France the stage-coach . . . killed more people annually than the railroad that followed it. This increase in the tempo of life, this rapid motion, these superficial excitements and dangers, were the psychological sweetening of the bitter pill of autocratic political discipline"; see his *City in History,* 370. Malcolm Campbell notes Barbault's tendency to crop the foreground margins of his prints in "Piranesi and Innovation in Eighteenth-Century Roman Printmaking," in Edgar Peters Bowron and Joseph J. Rishel, eds., *Art in Rome in the Eighteenth Century,* exh. cat. (Philadelphia: Philadelphia Musem of Art, 2000), 566.

37 Barbault, *Plus beaux édifices de Rome moderne,* n.p.

38 *Journal de Paris,* no. 28 (28 January 1787): 121.

39 *Journal de Paris,* no. 46 (15 February 1787): 197.

40 The monument's history is recounted in Geneviève Bresc-Bautier, "Le monument royal du Pont-au-Change," in Béatrice de Andia, Michel Le Moël, and Joëlle Jezierski, eds., *Du Châtelet à Beaubourg: 15 siècles d'histoire* (Paris: Action artistique de la ville de Paris, 1997), 108–17.

41 Writes Peter Burke of Louis XIV, "The cult of the king . . . represented—indeed, incarnated—the power of the centre"; see his *The Fabrication of Louis XIV* (New Haven: Yale Univ. Press, 2003), 153.

42 See Jean-Marc Dudot et al., *Le devoir d'embellir: Essai sur la politique d'embellissement à la fin de l'ancien régime* (Nancy: CEMPA, 1978), esp. 27–55. Diderot's remark appears in *Correspondance littéraire, philosophique et critique,* ed. Maurice Tourneux (Paris: Garnier Frères, 1878), 4:249, and is discussed in Thomas Cassirer, "Awareness of the City in the *Encyclopédie,*" *Journal of the History of Ideas* 24, no. 3 (1963): 388.

43 On the festive role of the sculpture, see Bresc-Bautier, "Monument royal du Pont-au-Change," 111. On assaults on monuments, see Jeffrey Merrick, "Politics on Pedestals: Royal Monuments in Eighteenth-Century France," *French History* 5, no. 2 (1991): 234–64; as well as Dudot et al., *Devoir d'embellir,* esp. 21. The argument that monuments posed health hazards was used against the tax barriers erected around Paris by the hated *fermiers généraux;* see, for instance, the unsigned pamphlet *Réclamation d'un citoyen contre la nouvelle enceinte de Paris, élevée par les fermiers généraux* (Paris, 1787).

44 Christopher Mead, "Urban Contingency and the Problem of Representation in Second Empire Paris," *Journal of the Society of Architectural Historians* 54, no. 2 (1995): 156–57. Moreau, in his embellishment plan of 1769, criticizes the houses as "so incompatible with the decoration of the city and the ease of navigation, it is astounding that they were allowed to be built there"; cited in Dudot et al., *Devoir d'embellir,* 39.

45 Christopher Prendergast, *Paris and the Nineteenth Century* (Oxford: Blackwell, 1995), 14. The quotations are from Anne Querrien, "The Metropolis and the Capital," in Michel Feher and Sanford Kwinter, eds., *The Contemporary City,* special issue, *Zone,* nos. 1–2 (1986): 219–21.

46 Louis-Sébastien Mercier, *Le nouveau Paris,* ed. Jean-Claude Bonnet (Paris: Mercure de France, 1994), chap. 105. On the empty center as a leitmotif in Mercier's writings on the city, see Martial Poirson, "Entre ville imaginaire et imaginaires de la ville: Géographie symbolique et représentations économiques de Paris chez L.-S. Mercier," in Nathalie Ferrand, ed., *Locus in Fabula: La topique de l'espace dans les fictions françaises d'ancien régime* (Louvain: Peeters, 2004), 498–518.

47 Mercier, *Tableau de Paris,* 9:121, 123; vol. 6, chap. 475, pp. 72–73. The final quotation is from Louis-Sébastien Mercier, *L'an deux mille quatre cent quarante: Rêve s'il en fut jamais,* ed. Raymond Trousson (Bordeaux: Ducros, 1971), 90; all cited in Poirson, "Entre ville imaginaire," 504–8. On the king's own role in the "de-deification" of Paris prior to the Revolution, see chapter 1 in Erika Naginski, *Sculpture and Enlightenment* (Los Angeles: Getty Research Institute, 2009).

48 Jean-Louis Viel de Saint-Maux, "Septième lettre sur l'architecture des anciens," in idem, *Lettres sur l'architecture des anciens et celle des modernes* (Paris, 1787; reprint, Geneva: Minkoff Reprint, 1974), 23, 36.

49 On the area's urban renewal, see André Chastel et al., "L'aménagement du marché central de Paris, de la 'Réformation des Halles' du XVIe siècle à celle du XIXe," *Bulletin monumental* 127 (1969): 7–26, 70–106; as well as Hélène Couzy's "discussion," in Françoise Boudon et al., *Système de l'architecture urbaine: Le quartier des Halles à Paris* (Paris: Éditions du Centre national de la recherche scientifique, 1977), 1:296–97; and Mark K. Deming, "L'embellissement des Halles," in Michel Le Moël and Sophie Descat, eds., *L'urbanisme parisien au siècle des lumières* (Paris: Action artistique de la ville de Paris, 1997), 103–12.

50 Édouard Pommier, "Une intervention de Quatremère de Quincy," in Michel Fleury and Guy-Michel Leproux, eds., *Les Saints-Innocents: Ouvrage collectif* (Paris: Délégation à l'action artistique de la ville de Paris, 1990), 153.

51 *Journal de Paris,* no. 42 (11 February 1787): 181–83.

52 On the rescue of the monument by Louis Petit de Bachaumont, see A. de Barthélemy, "La colonne de Catherine de Médicis à la Halle au Blé," *Mémoires de la Société de l'histoire de Paris et de l'Île-de-France* 6 (1879): 180–99.

53 The *Pont Neuf* was not the only one of Robert's paintings to engage with the theme of *embellissement;* see Marianne Roland Michel, "A Taste for Classical Antiquity in Town-Planning Projects: Two Aspects of the Art of Hubert Robert," *Burlington Magazine* 114, no. 836 (1972): i–vi.

54 Richard T. Gray, "Buying into Signs: Money and Semiosis in Eighteenth-Century German Language Theory," in Martha Woodmansee and Mark Osteen, eds., *The New Economic Criticism: Studies at the Intersection of Literature and Economics* (London: Routledge, 1999), 96, 98–99.

55 Élie de Beaumont recommended, for example, not only that numerous structures—including churches—be relocated but that they be partially demolished to make way for the building of new streets to improve access to remote quarters; see his "Lettre sur l'embellissement," 17. More broadly, the period's boom in real estate speculation entailed the instrumentalization of monuments as opportunities to raise land values. Building projects such as the Halle au Blé and the Comédie Française were funded through risky *lotissement* operations, that is, the development of properties whose sale was counted on to finance construction and generate profit. In both cases, the building of a major monument was exploited as a catalyst for a building spree. For an overview, see Pierre Pinon, *Paris, biographie d'une capitale* (Paris: Hazan, 1999), 119–36.

56 The quotations are from Gottfried Wilhelm, Freiherr von Leibniz, "Unvorgreifliche Gedanken, betreggend die Ausübung und Verbesserung der teutschen Sprache," in idem, *Hauptschriften zur Grundlegung der Philosophie,* ed. Ernst Cassirer, trans. Artur Buchenau, 3rd ed. (Hamburg: Verlag von Felix Meiner, 1966), 2:520; and John Locke, "Of the Imperfection of Words," in

idem, *An Essay Concerning Human Understanding,* abridged and ed. Maurice Cranston (New York: Collier, 1965), 274; both cited in Gray, "Buying into Signs," 101–2, 98.

57 The statements are taken, respectively, from John Locke, "Of the Association of Ideas," in idem, *An Essay Concerning Human Understanding,* ed. Peter H. Nidditch (Oxford: Clarendon, 1975), 34; and Étienne Bonnot de Condillac, *An Essay on the Origin of Human Knowledge, Being a Supplement to Mr. Locke's Essay on the Human Understanding,* trans. Thomas Nugent (London: Printed for J. Nourse, 1756), 120, 11, 121, 4. In his *Essai sur l'origine des langues,* Rousseau refutes this idea of a "source," claiming that man's first words were based on his misinterpretation of the world. Appositely, he argues that language, originally expressive of man's free subjectivity unrooted in the real, has become a mechanism of control, encroaching upon the human psyche and the domain of the passions; see Jean-Jacques Rousseau, *Essay on the Origin of Languages,* in idem, *On the Origin of Language: Jean-Jacques Rousseau, Essay on the Origin of Languages; Johann Gottfried Herder, Essay on the Origin of Language,* ed. and trans. John H. Moran and Alexander Gode (New York: F. Ungar, 1967).

58 Gray, "Buying into Signs," 98, 100.

59 Legrand and Landon claim that Sainte Geneviève had "surpassed" the architecture of the Greeks and Romans; see Jacques-Guillaume Legrand and Charles-Paul Landon, *Description de Paris, et de ses édifices*... (Paris: C. P. Landon, 1806), 1:109.

60 "Observations sur les peintures et sculptures exposées au Salon du Louvre tirées de *L'année littéraire,* no. 35," in *Collection Deloynes: Collection de pièces sur les beaux-arts imprimées et manuscrites (1673–1808)* (Paris: Bibliothèque nationale de France, 1980), vol. 16, no. 422. Robert executed a second, slightly different version of the *Monuments of Paris* that was engraved by the artist Régine Carrey in about 1805; see Bibliothèque nationale de France, Cabinet des estampes, Dc. 12a (in-fol). The painting shows the winged lion of San Marco (brought from Venice to Paris in 1798 by Napoléon's troops) in place of the royal statue. The substitution provides further evidence for my argument, advanced below, that Robert's approach to the genre of the capriccio reflected his experience as a museum administrator. (Chapter 4 of this study discusses Robert's views of the museum in the context of the planned confiscation of Italy's art.)

61 Louis Chéronnet, "L'esprit des ruines," *Beaux-arts* no. 39 (29 September 1933): 3.

62 Charles De Wailly, *Projet d'utilité et d'embellissement pour la ville de Paris,* Bibliothèque nationale de France, Cartes et plans, Ge C-4384 (Res). The project is discussed in Monique Mosser and Daniel Rabreau, *Charles de Wailly: Peintre architecte dans l'Europe des lumières,* exh. cat. (Paris: Caisse nationale des monuments historiques et des sites, 1979), 71–72; and Backouche, *Trace du fleuve,* 270–73.

63 *Le Spectateur français au Salon de 1789, et projet d'encouragement patriotique pour les arts de l'Académie de peinture* (1789), in *Collection Deloynes: Collection de pièces sur les beaux-arts imprimées et manuscrites (1673–1808)* (Paris: Bibliothèque nationale de France, 1980), vol. 16, no. 424.

64 Mercier, *Tableau de Paris,* vol. 10, chap. 824, pp. 248–49.

65 Gray, "Buying into Signs," 103. The phrase is from Theodor Adorno, *Minima Moralia: Reflections from Damaged Life,* trans. E. F. N. Jephcott (London: Verso, 1978), 155; cited in Patrick Brantlinger, *Fictions of State: Culture and Credit in Britain, 1694–1994* (Ithaca: Cornell Univ. Press, 1996), 23.

66 Mercier, *Tableau de Paris,* 9:104–5.

67 On this period of speculative frenzy, see the following works by Jean Bouchary: *Les manieurs d'argent à Paris à la fin du XVIIIe siècle,* 3 vols. (Paris: Marcel Rivière, 1939–43); *Les compagnies financières à Paris à la fin du XVIIIe siècle,* 3 vols. (Paris: Librairie des sciences politiques et sociales, 1940–42); and *L'eau à Paris à la fin du XVIIIe siècle: La Compagnie des eaux de Paris et l'entreprise de l'Yvette* (Paris: Marcel Rivière, 1946). See also Herbert Lüthy, *La banque protestante en France: De la révocation de l'Édit de Nantes à la Révolution* (Paris: SEVPEN, 1961), 2:686–727; and George V. Taylor, "The Paris Bourse on the Eve of the Revolution, 1781–1789," *American Historical Review* 67, no. 4 (1962): 951–77. An illustrative example of the denunciations of "fictive values" concerns the Académie royale de musique's charges against

the Italian violinist Giovanni Battista Viotti, who sought the Crown's permission to manage the Opéra. To finance the enterprise, Viotti formed a joint-stock company of bankers. Scandalized by the prospect of its fate being aligned with the fortunes of the stock market, the Opéra accused the *gens de finance* intent on running the institution of being *agioteurs* who had mastered the "art . . . [of] creating fictive values that cause the ruin of credulous families"; see "Mémoire de l'Académie royale de musique," 8 May 1789, Archives nationales, O^{1} 613.

68 Honoré-Gabriel Riqueti, comte de Mirabeau, *Dénonciation de l'agiotage au Roi et à l'Assemblée des notables* (n.p., 1787), 11.

69 The quotation is from *Franches et courtes réflexions sur un mémoire au roi, publié nouvellement par M. Viotti, 10 mai 1789,* Archives nationales, O^{1} 613, no. 139, 13. See note 67 on this affair.

70 Unsigned letter, 13 August 1775, Archives nationales, O^{1} 1693, no. 73. The incident, however peculiar, typified the controversies that pitted royal institutions against municipal ones (the city opposed granting the Académie royale rights to the bridge), a sign of deteriorating relations between the capital and the Crown.

71 Mirabeau, *Dénonciation de l'agiotage* 10, 27, 11, 25, 12.

72 Jacques Derrida, *The Truth in Painting,* trans. Geoff Bennington and Ian McLeod (Chicago: Univ. of Chicago Press, 1987), 122.

73 Peter de Bolla, *The Discourse of the Sublime: Readings in History, Aesthetics, and the Subject* (Oxford: Basil Blackwell, 1989), 109–11.

74 Brantlinger, *Fictions of State,* 88, 108–9. The quotation is from Edmund Burke, *Reflections on the Revolution in France,* ed. J. C. D. Clark (Stanford, Calif.: Stanford Univ. Press, 2001), 326.

75 Robert's *Pont Notre-Dame* in the Musée Carnavalet was seized during the French Revolution from Breteuil's collection; see Bernard de Montgolfier, "Hubert Robert, peintre de Paris au Musée Carnavalet," *Bulletin du Musée Carnavalet* 17, nos. 1–2 (1964): 11, 34nn18–19. The circumstances of Breteuil's acquisition of the *Pont-au-Change* are discussed in Paula Rea Radisich, "Hubert Robert's Paris: Truth, Artifice and Spectacle," *Studies on Voltaire and the Eighteenth Century* 245 (1986): 512; see also Louis Tuetey, "Procès-verbaux de la Commission des monuments," *Nouvelles archives de l'art français,* 3rd ser., 17 (1901): 342. On Breteuil and the urban planning initiatives he oversaw, see René-Marie Rampelberg, *Le ministre de la Maison du roi, 1783–1788: Baron de Breteuil* (Paris: Économica, 1975), 239–48, 291–97. In addition to the pendants conserved in the Musée Carnavalet, a second pair is divided between the Staatliche Kunsthalle Karlsruhe and the Alte Pinakothek in Munich (the *Pont Notre-Dame*—shown here in fig. 44—belongs to the former, its companion to the latter); a third version of the *Pont Notre-Dame* hangs in the Musée du Louvre.

76 Cayeux speculates that Girardot owned a set (but does not provide evidence) in Jean de Cayeux with Catherine Boulot, *Hubert Robert* (Paris: Fayard, 1989), 343. On the loan for the operation from the bank of Girardot, Haller et Cie (Girardot's associate was Rodolphe-Emmanuel Haller), see Bouchary, *Manieurs d'argent,* 3:114–15. On Girardot as a collector, see Colin B. Bailey, *Patriotic Taste: Collecting Modern Art in Pre-revolutionary Paris* (New Haven: Yale Univ. Press, 2002), chap. 5.

77 On the former, see Marcel Rouff, "Une grève de gagne-deniers en 1786 à Paris," *Revue historique* 105 (1910): 340–41. On the latter, see "Sur l'administration de M. Necker, par un citoyen françois," in *M. Turgot à M. Necker: Sur l'administration de M. Necker* (London, 1780); cited in Lüthy, *Banque protestante,* 2:462–63.

78 Bouchary, *Manieurs d'argent,* 3:114–15. Radisich notes Breteuil's speculations, as well as his coordinated attempts with Girardot, in her "Hubert Robert's Paris," 510–11.

79 On the detrimental effects of the loan to the city, see Backouche, *Trace du fleuve,* 221–23. Floating loans on the kingdom's cities was standard practice for the credit-challenged monarch; see Kathryn Norberg, "The French Fiscal Crisis of 1788 and the Financial Origins of the Revolution of 1789," in Philip T. Hoffman and Kathryn Norberg, eds., *Fiscal Crises, Liberty, and Representative Government, 1450–1789* (Stanford, Calif.: Stanford Univ. Press, 1994), 262.

80 The letters and documents pertaining to the cases of former residents (including "Mémoire d'Antoine Mollard marchand chapellier tenturier") are contained in Archives nationales, H 2167–68.

81 On this subject, see Gail Bossenga, "City and State: An Urban Perspective on the Origins of the French Revolution," in Keith Michael Baker, ed., *The French Revolution and the Creation of Modern Political Culture,* vol. 1, *The Political Culture of the Old Regime* (Oxford: Pergamon, 1987), 115–40; Sharon Kettering, "State Control and Municipal Authority in France," in James L. McClain, John M. Merriman, and Kaoru Ugawa, eds., *Edo and Paris: Urban Life and the State in the Early Modern Era* (Ithaca: Cornell Univ. Press, 1994), 86–101; and Jean-Lucien Gay, "L'administation de la capitale entre 1770 et 1789: La tutelle de la royauté et ses limites," *Paris et Île-de-France: Mémoires de la fédération des sociétés historiques et archéologiques de Paris et de l'Île-de-France* 8 (1956): 299–370; 9 (1957–58): 283–363; 10 (1959): 181–247; 11 (1960): 363–403; 12 (1961): 135–218.

82 Friedrich Nietzsche, *On the Genealogy of Morals,* trans. Walter Kaufmann and R. J. Hollingale (New York: Vintage, 1967), 58.

83 Henri Bernardin de Saint-Pierre, "Voeux d'un solitaire," in idem, *Oeuvres complètes... mises en ordre et précédées de la vie de l'auteur,* ed. Louis-Aimé Martin (Paris: Méquignon-Marvis, 1818), 11:25, 28. Discussed in Jean Starobinski, *1789, the Emblems of Reason,* trans. Barbara Bray (Charlottesville: Univ. Press of Virginia, 1982), 13–15.

84 The *livret* for the Salon of 1789 refers to "two painted sketches made from life; the one is a view taken from the river, under one of the arches of the Pont Royal, at the time of the great snow storm of last winter; the other depicts the Bastille in the initial stages of its demolition." Académie royale de peinture et de sculpture, *Collection des livrets des anciennes expositions depuis 1673 jusqu'en 1800* (Paris: Liepmannssohn et Dufour, 1869–72), 35:16, no. 36.

85 See Claude Quétel, *La Bastille: Histoire vraie d'une prison légendaire* (Paris: Éditions Robert Laffont, 1989), 334–39.

86 Mercier makes the statement in his *L'an deux mille quatre cent quarante* (London, 1771), 415; translated in Wittman, *Architecture, Print Culture,* 197.

87 Pierre-François Palloy, "Adresse et projet générale... présenté à l'Assemblée nationale et au roi des François," *Archives parlementaires de 1787 à 1860, recueil complet des débats législatifs et politiques des Chambres françaises,* 1st ser., 39 (1792): 564–66; and annex 2, 572–89. Discussed in James A. Leith, *Space and Revolution: Projects for Monuments, Squares, and Public Buildings in France, 1789–1799* (Montreal: McGill-Queen's Univ. Press, 1991), 75–77. The quotation is from Simon Schama, *Citizens: A Chronicle of the French Revolution* (New York: Vintage, 1990), 414. See also on "the Patriot" Palloy Hans-Jürgen Lüsebrink and Rolf Reichardt, *The Bastille: A History of a Symbol of Despotism and Freedom* (Durham, N.C.: Duke Univ. Press, 1997), 118–47.

88 *Navigation intérieure de la France: Entrepôt du commerce à Paris et embellissements de cette ville,* Jacques Auvraÿ, 12 fructidor an III, Archives nationales, F^{14} 188; and *Mémoire sur les moyens de former des établissemens d'utilité publique, et d'en assurer les propriétés au profit de la Nation, sans être à charge au Trésor national,* Brullée, 20 brumaire an VIII, Archives nationales, AD XIII 13; cited in Backouche, *Trace du fleuve,* 280–81.

89 Paul Virilio, "The Overexposed City," in idem, *The Lost Dimension,* trans. Daniel Moshenberg (New York: Semiotext(e), 1991); reprinted in Paul Virilio, *The Paul Virilio Reader,* ed. Steve Redhead (New York: Columbia Univ. Press, 2004), 89, 91, 96.

90 Georg Simmel, *Philosophie des Geldes,* ed. David P. Frisby and Klaus Christian Köhnke (Frankfurt am Main: Suhrkamp, 1989), 336–37; translated in Gray, "Buying into Signs," 95.

91 Marianne Roland Michel discusses these works' debts to the *Carceri* in Villa Medici, *Piranèse et les Français, 1740–1790,* exh. cat. (Rome: Edizioni dell'Elefante, 1976), 307–10, nos. 173–74.

92 On the influence of this image on generations of French Piranésiens, see Johannes Langner, "La vue par dessous le pont: Fonctions d'un motif Piranésien dans l'art français de la seconde moitié du XVIIIe siècle," in Georges Brunel, ed., *Piranèse et les Français: Colloque tenu à la Villa Médicis, 12–14 mai 1976* (Rome: Edizioni dell'Elefante, 1978), 293–302.

93 Robert's *Harbor with Architecture* was exhibited at the Salon of 1769. The work belonged to Étienne-François, duc de Choiseul, and was among the paintings engraved by Pierre-François Basan in advance of the auction of Choiseul's collection in 1772. See Villa Medici, *Piranèse et les Français,* 311–15, no. 176.

94 Tafuri, *Sphere,* 41.

CHAPTER 4
Posterity

I was acquainted with the affairs of Rome long before I knew any thing of those of my own family. I had the Capitol and its whole figure in my mind, when the Louvre was quite unknown to me, and had heard of the Tiber before the Seine. My thoughts have run more on the condition and fortunes of Lucullus, Metellus, and Scipio, than of any of my own countrymen.

—Michel de Montaigne[1]

After having wandered over the globe, man . . . likes to return and die in the land which gave him birth. How profound must be his grief if he left his country in flourishing prosperity, and finds it, on his return, deserted.

—François-René, vicomte de Chateaubriand (1815)[2]

Robert's career culminated in his role in the formation and administration of France's first public museum. Appointed keeper of the king's pictures in 1784, he served during the Directory era as a member of the Conservatoire, the body that supervised museum operations.[3] Throughout this tumultuous period, Robert executed several dozen views of the Louvre, the majority of which either chronicled the transformation of the former palace into a national museum or put forth proposals for the design of the Grande Galerie. One of these was exhibited at the Salon of 1796, two years into the closure of the gallery for renovations. The painting—*Project for the Grande Galerie of the Louvre*—presented the site according to the artist's preferred design plan: illuminated by skylights and divided into Serlian bays (fig. 64).[4] The gallery's magnificent corridor is filled with spectators and artists, among them Robert himself, seated in the right foreground and copying from Raphael's *Holy Family.* The masterpieces of Italian art lining the newly renovated walls include many that had been on view in the museum four months earlier, in a display of paintings from the Italian, Northern, and French schools—works that were destined to hang in the Grande Galerie.[5] At the time of the Salon, only the galleries housing the exhibition were open; the rest of the museum remained closed. Robert's projected view thus served as a surrogate for an institution that would remain largely inaccessible to the public for another three years. It offered assurances that the Grande Galerie's renovations would be worth the wait, that

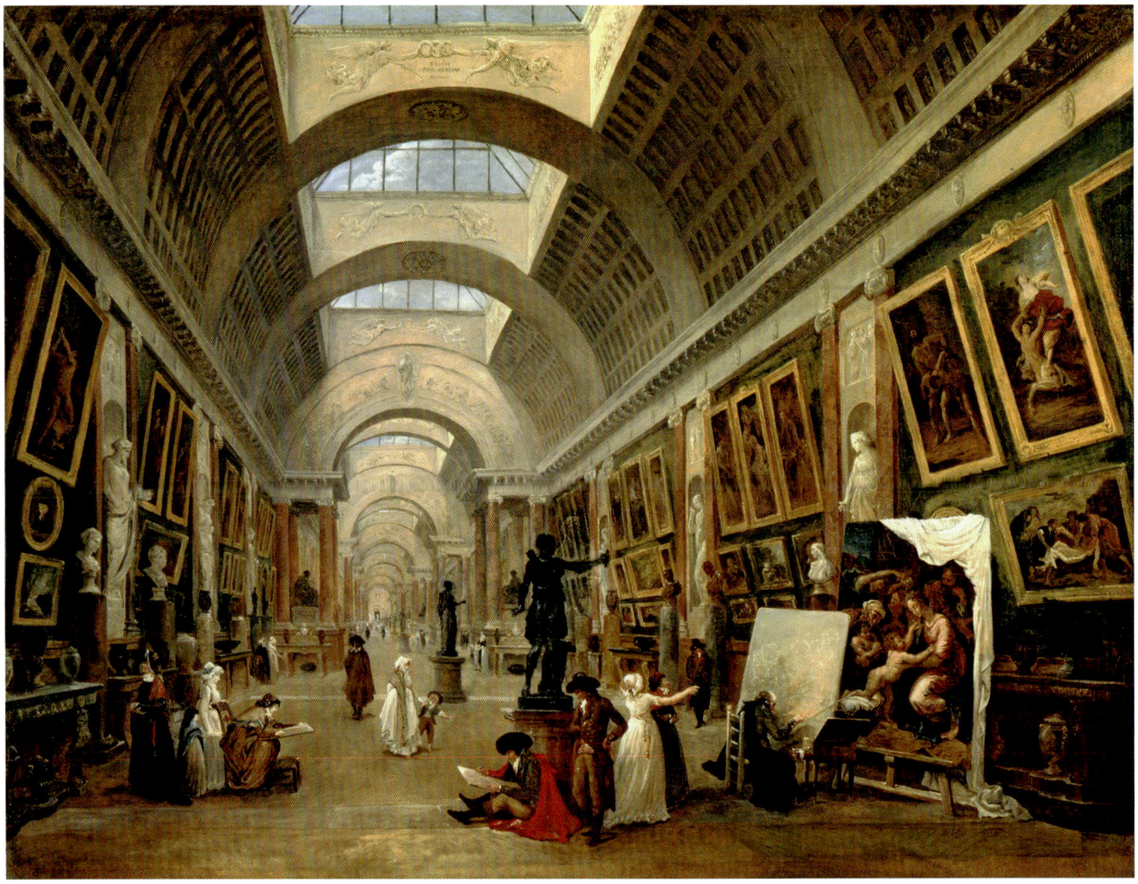

Fig. 64. Hubert Robert (French, 1733–1808)
Project for the Grande Galerie of the Louvre, 1796, oil on canvas, 115 × 145 cm (45 ¼ × 57 ⅛ in.)
Paris, Musée du Louvre

mounting expectations would be satisfied. In short, it reflected Robert's keen understanding of the responsibility of the museum to the nation—the necessity of delivering to a public that had endured the turbulent arrival of liberty the "recompense it [had] the right to demand."[6] No doubt, given the artist's position with the embattled Conservatoire—a body constrained on the one hand by exhausted finances and on the other by powerful state entities—the assurances it offered were equally self-directed.[7]

Robert's painting came with a pendant, one that similarly took the future as its subject. The scene it presented appeared, however, in the eyes of the few Salon critics who commented on it, decidedly less propitious.[8] It featured a view of the same subject in ruins—the museum as it might appear not in the near future, but in the far distant one (fig. 65). The elegant skylights have been replaced by gaping passages of sky itself, framed by crumbling coffered vaults sprouting foliage. As opposed to its pendant's display of a gallery showcasing countless pictures, the futuristic view shows the ruined museum emptied of canvases. The boundless promise of modern conservation heralded in the first view has given way to a vision of endless destruction.

Critics may have been perplexed that Robert would demonstrate his skills as an "able architect" as well as painter in the first view, only to destroy his "beautiful project" in the second.[9] Yet the *Imaginary View of the Grande Galerie of the Louvre in Ruins* presents little indication of negative intent. Despite the subject's doom-laden character, the scene is far from foreboding. The women at left, lingering by a cauldron, domesticate the decimated site with ease. For all the wreckage, the

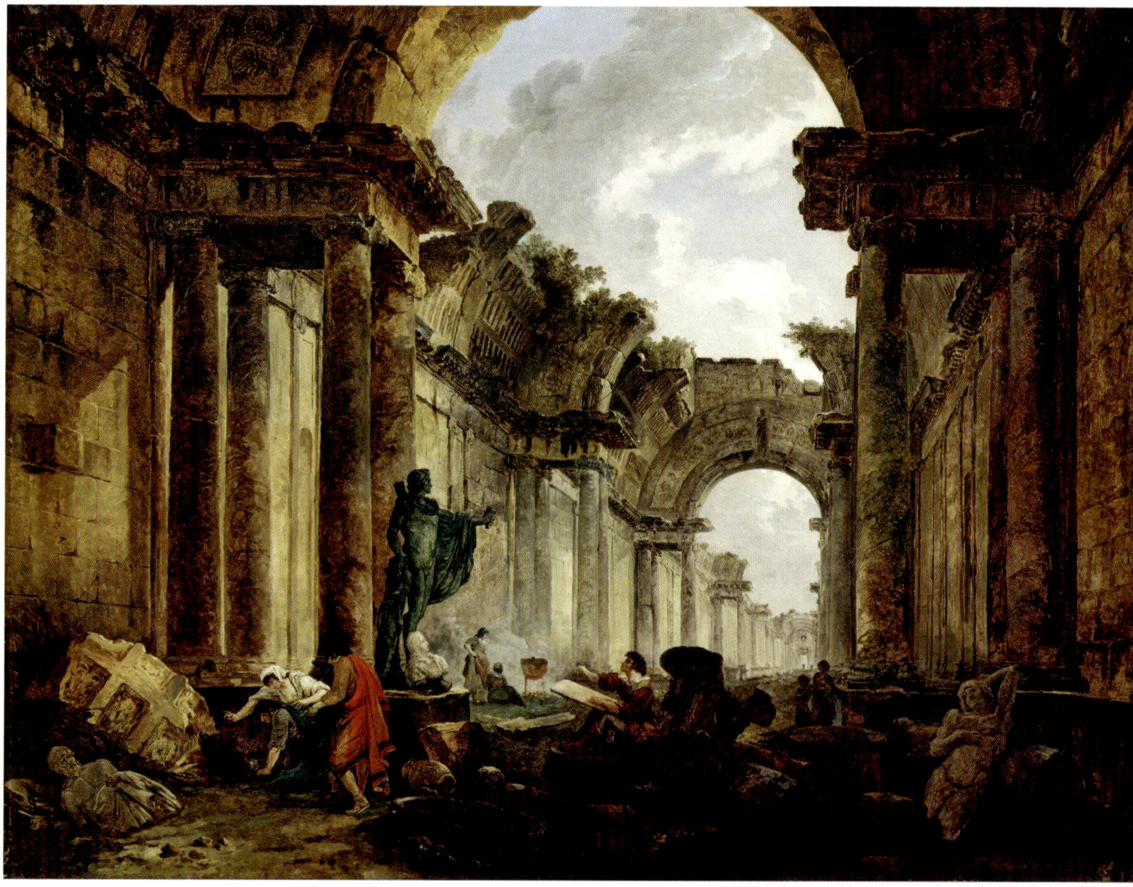

Fig. 65. Hubert Robert (French, 1733–1808)
Imaginary View of the Grande Galerie of the Louvre in Ruins, 1796, oil on canvas, 114 × 146 cm (44⅞ × 57½ in.)
Paris, Musée du Louvre

potential for cultural regeneration, embodied by the triumphant figure of the Apollo Belvedere, remains intact. The gallery's soaring perspective, directing the viewer's attention toward the depths of the ruin, is interrupted by the pregnant pause in the foreground: the suspenseful interval between the draftsman, his chalk holder poised above his sketchbook, and the iconic sculpture that arrests his gaze. It was, perhaps, with some degree of humor that Robert contrasted his own self-portrait—as an aged and wizened copyist, hunched and gray haired—with his vigorously youthful counterpart in the work's pendant.

Humor, of course, may seem an inappropriate prism through which to evaluate the second painting's relationship to the first. But if the pendants invite us to consider the draftsman before the Apollo as a version of Robert's younger self, then it may further be surmised that painting the museum in ruins marked in some way the artist's effort to privatize the prototypical institution of the public sphere: that is, to personalize the subject of the museum. The futuristic view was also a picture of Robert's past. The unfamiliar space of the first pendant, with its anonymous spectators, has been traded in for one with which the artist was intimately acquainted, and its occupants include Robert's usual repertoire of assorted ancients and moderns. An abstract and hypothetical space has given way to an architectural setting reminiscent of the painter's former haunts in Rome. With its view of a colonnade supporting a broken barrel vault, Robert's painting recovered a theme to which he had previously devoted a series of works, including his drawing *A Colonnaded Thermal Building, the*

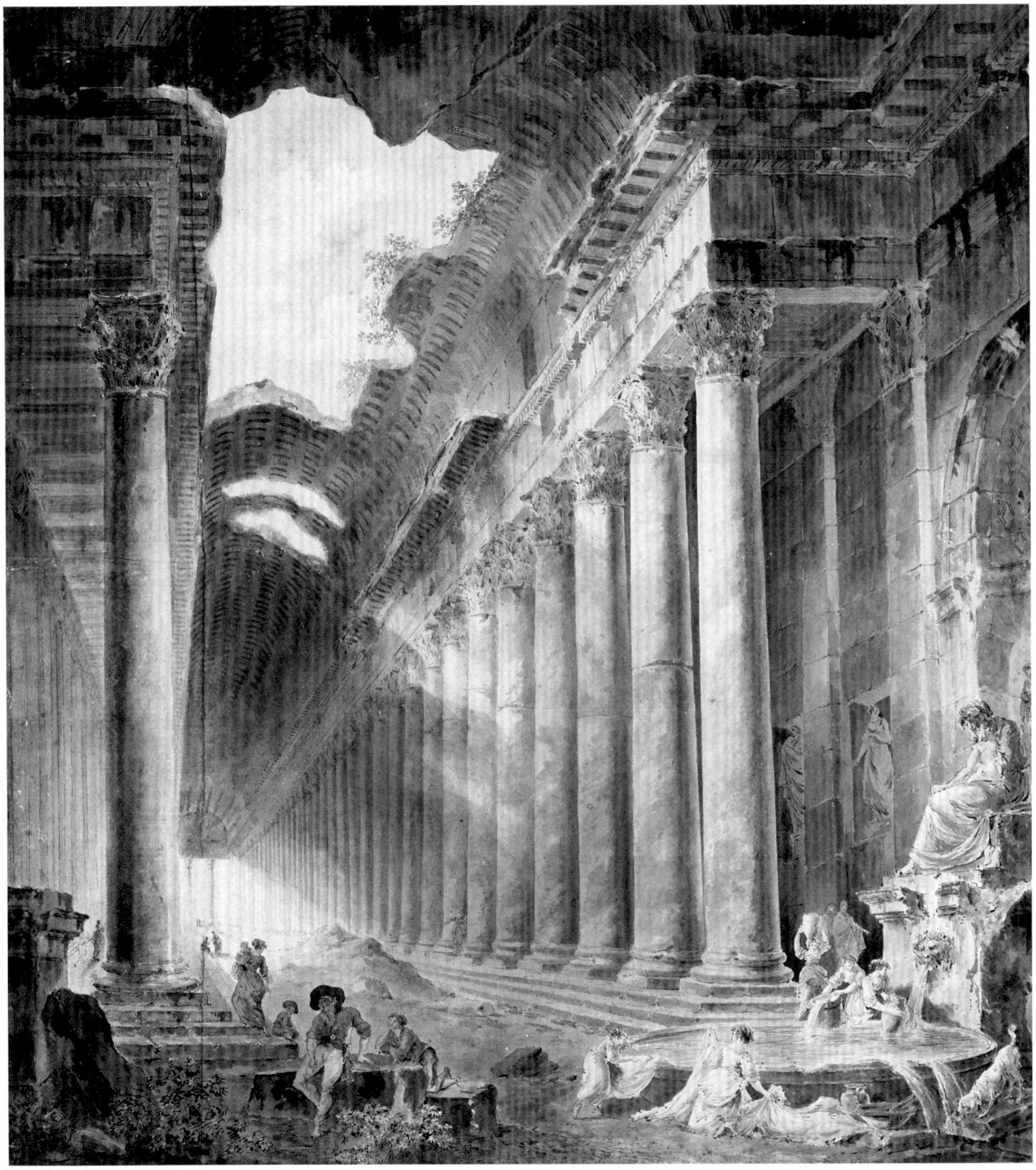

Fig. 66. Hubert Robert (French, 1733–1808)
A Colonnaded Thermal Building, the Roof Partly Open to the Sky, with Girls Washing Clothes, ca. 1780s?, watercolor, pencil, and ink, 77.5 × 68.6 cm (30½ × 27 in.)
Private collection

Roof Partly Open to the Sky, with Girls Washing Clothes (views that exerted an influence on the designs of Boullée; indeed, it was likely in recognition of his role disseminating motifs *à l'antique* to artists and architects who had not traveled to Rome that d'Angiviller placed Robert in 1778 on the committee responsible for devising a design solution for the Grande Galerie) (fig. 66).[10] In this way, Robert's view of the gallery's ruin naturalized the museum by rendering organic its relationship to his own past.

What further distinguishes the private history put forth in Robert's *Grande Galerie in Ruins* from the public one staged in its pendant is the absence of pictures. The first of Robert's gallery views, with its display of paintings shown in historical sequence, evidenced the means whereby the museum as a public institution rejected the conventions that had governed private collections. Under the influence of art theorists like de Piles, ancien régime connoisseurs had installed works by artists of different nationalities side by side so as to emphasize the distinctive traits of old masters—thus flattering the discerning gaze of the elite viewer. The museum, however, in keeping with its pedagogical mandate as well as the ideological needs of the state, organized its paintings by national school and displayed them in such a way as to instruct the public in the history of art. By hanging its works in chronological sequence, the museum sought to offer "an uninterrupted sequence of the progress of art and the degrees of perfection to which it was brought by all those peoples who have successively cultivated it."[11] Robert was immersed in this discourse on the progress of the arts. His responsibilities included managing, categorizing, and displaying the museum's (constantly expanding) collection of artworks—making recommendations about which objects should be shipped to provincial collections and which were worthy of exhibition: which, that is, merited incorporation into the historical survey that the Conservatoire endeavored to fashion.[12] In Robert's *Project for the Grande Galerie,* paintings from the Italian school (and belonging formerly to the royal collection)—by Guido Reni, Parmigianino, Francesco Mola, Titian, Caravaggio, and Correggio—are arranged according to size, with the largest ones hung closest to the ceiling following the fashion of the Salon. By displaying the Italian, Northern, and French schools in succession, as in the exhibition of 1796, museum officials (like d'Angiviller before them) were responding to the rise of historicism under the influence of Winckelmann, as well as to modern classification methods in the sciences.[13] More significantly, the chronological display subordinated individual works to a narrative of art's evolution that culminated in the French school, thus equating the native collection with modernity and the future, and the culturally exhausted foreign schools with "a receding past."[14] It is this vision of the museum as an engine of progress that Robert's *Project for the Grande Galerie* asserts. Placing the viewer at the starting point of a sprawling historical development, the painting prompts anticipation of the work of the French moderns—in effect, of a glorious future.

Such an epic conception of art's progression is ratified in Robert's first view and ravaged in the second. Yet portraying the museum in a state of decay did not necessarily represent a challenge to the positive view put forth in the pendant. In a sense, no more favorable image of the museum could exist than one that compared the institution to an ancient ruin. The *Avertissement* to Armand-Guy Kersaint's *Discours sur les monuments publics*—calling for the completion of the museum—points out that nothing remained of the Athenians but the ruins of their monuments. To the French as well, "time, perhaps, will one day bring this nothingness which menaces all that exists." Beseeching its readers to "think of posterity," the text states: "Monuments are the irreproachable witnesses of history; without their august ruins all that has been transmitted to us of the Greeks and Romans would appear as no more than a fable." In the remains of the Temple of Minerva, one discovers "the genius of a people effaced from the globe." Should not this same effect result one day from the sight of the French museum? With the completion of the Louvre renovations, "the most glorious epoch" in history would be consecrated with an edifice worthy of "a free nation," and the memory of "the liberated French" would endure in the distant future. Granted, the author recommended that "indestructible materials" be used to complete "the national palace of a people that founded its liberty on the eternal rights of man."[15] Nonetheless, his point was that the might of a nation was only as great as the capacity of its monuments to speak for it in posterity. In much the same way, the art dealer Jean-Baptiste-Pierre Lebrun, writing in 1794, envisioned a museum constructed of the most extravagant of stones—marble, granite, porphyry, etc.—arguing that "the dust of Athens is still sought after by savants and artists for the beautiful debris of its mutilated monuments... the greatest republic in the universe should obliterate and surpass all that preceded it."[16] For both Kersaint and Lebrun, the image of the museum as a resplendently finished monument was made complete by an image of ruin. When Robert exhibited his view of the completed Grande Galerie alongside a depiction of its future remains, he likely intended the works to complement rather than oppose each other.

Such inclinations are illuminated by Luhmann's observation that "around 1800 the impossibility of describing the new structures of modern society would be compensated for with projections of the future."[17] To project the monuments to come into a time yet to arrive was to endow the future with the clarity that was absent in the present. And to forecast for new institutions the longevity of ancient ones was to inspire public *confiance* in the state: as Kersaint declares, "Confidence in the stability of our new laws, which it is so necessary to inspire, will be established... by the solidity of the edifices destined to conserve and perpetuate them."[18] Comparisons of the museum with Classical monuments, moreover, legitimated an institution that itself "compensated for" the upheavals of the Revolution: like the festival of national unity that coincided with its inauguration on 10 August 1793, the museum served as an instrument of consolidation. It substituted order and civility for the chaos of bloodletting and vandalism that had tainted the recent past.[19] Indeed, Robert's treatment of the museum as a vessel to the future revealed a perspective shaped as much by his administrative position there as by his profound sense of the museum's relationship to recent events. The painter had endured the violent disruptions of the Revolution, having opted to remain in Paris (in lieu of accepting Catherine the Great's invitation to relocate to Saint Petersburg) and consequently suffering nine months of incarceration, under the charge of failing to renew his *carte de civisme.*[20] A witness to vandalism, he commemorated in paint the remaking of the city into a theater of revolution. No less than his remarkably dispassionate view of the removal of the royal tombs from Saint-Denis, Robert's paintings of the museum captured the process whereby a newly unshackled nation laid claim to the formerly sacrosanct spaces of an overthrown despotic regime (fig. 67).[21] The metamorphosis of the palace of kings into a public museum—the making available to the many that which had previously belonged to the few—crystallized the Revolution's transference of power. A monument to the revolutionary state's extraordinary novelty, the museum marked a national allegiance to conservation as opposed to destruction. Its imperative was to overcome the very history it embodied.

It was at the service of this imperative that Robert—like Kersaint and Lebrun—projected the institution into a future that auspiciously resembled the ancient past. Yet the painting alone bore the burden of translating a discourse on the museum's noble destiny into visual specifics. The abstractions cited in the texts—Lebrun's "beautiful debris"—are particularized, and brutally so, in the *Grande Galerie in Ruins:* the busts of Zeno and Minerva at left, along with the remains of Michelangelo's *Dying*

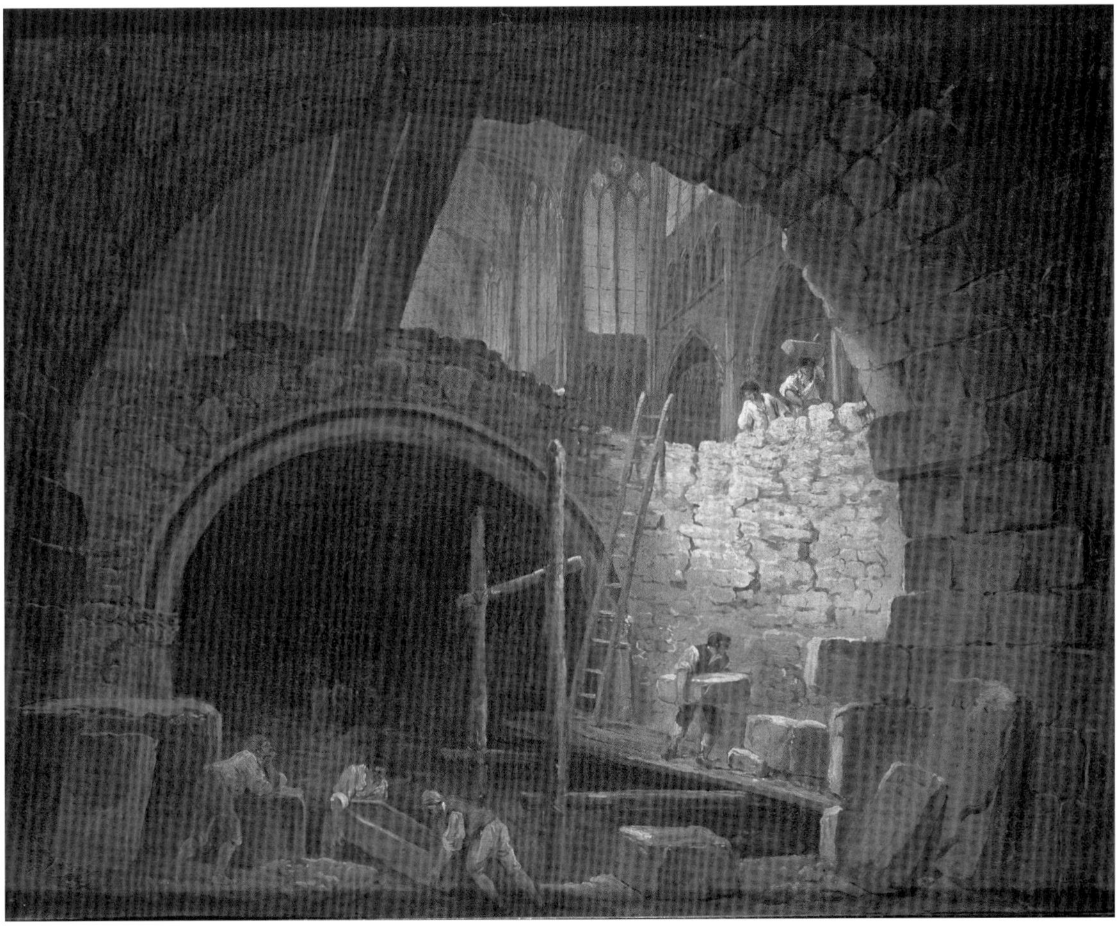

Fig. 67. Hubert Robert (French, 1733–1808)
The Removal of the Royal Tombs from the Crypt of Saint-Denis, ca. 1793, oil on canvas, 54 × 64 cm (21¼ × 25¼ in.)
Paris, Musée Carnavalet

Slave at right, appear littered on the ground like discarded objects.[22] In their ravaged condition, such details recall a recent history of vandalism. (Not for nothing did a Salon critic wonder why the painter had bothered to destroy when "so many men . . . succeed" in "destroying better.")[23] In the wake of the Terror, the goddess's severed head bears further disquieting implications. Even the undamaged Apollo Belvedere seems compromised in its personification of the stasis of Classicism. Appearing in the guise of a modern bronze replica of the ancient marble sculpture—as sign, rather than incarnation, of timeless iconicity—the sculpture promises continuity with the past, but perhaps wishfully. If Robert's projection of the future compensated for a present impenetrable to comprehension, it did not quite succeed at transcending it.

The painting, then, bespoke a revolutionary dream of recuperating the ancient past, along with its fragility. It did so, moreover, at a moment of controversy over the state's effort to manifest its destiny as "la nouvelle Athènes"—an effort that revolved around the museum: it was in the months just prior to the Salon exhibition, when Robert was likely completing the pendants, that Quatremère de Quincy fanned the flames of discord over the French army's imminent spoliation of Italy's marbles—among them, the Apollo Belvedere. For advocates of the conquest, the anticipated arrival of (what were then considered) Greek antiquities to the French museum was celebrated as a necessary impetus toward the reconstitution in revolutionary France of a golden age modeled on the achievements of the ancients. Such belief in the possibility of the ancient past's resurrection in the near future accorded with the desire of revolutionaries to read in Winckelmann's account of historical cyclicality—and of liberty as the catalyst for artistic glory—a narrative of their own regeneration.[24] For Quatremère, however, the spoliation of Rome gave the lie to the Revolution's self-identification with the virtues of the ancients. The debate polarized the artistic community. For his part, Robert—unlike his colleague on the Conservatoire, the sculptor Pajou—evidently demurred from supporting Quatremère's cause; neither does the *Grande Galerie in Ruins* reference the dismemberment of Rome in any straightforward way.[25] With the enigmatic exception of Zeno—a sculpture that did not exist in France until the arrival of the convoy from Rome in 1798—the artist based the gallery's most prominent contents on objects that were already to be found in French collections: Michelangelo's *Slave* sculptures arrived at the Louvre in 1794, following their removal by Alexandre Lenoir from the property of an émigré; bronze casts of the Apollo Belvedere decorated the palaces of Versailles and Fontainebleau.[26] And yet, given the shadow of the pending conquest, it is difficult to avoid perceiving in Robert's gallery signs of doubt about France's entitlement to the culture it believed itself to have inherited.

The *Grande Galerie in Ruins* was a product of intense temporal pressure: it was executed in the interstices between France's annihilation of its national past—the destruction of Catholic and monarchical monuments redolent of despotism—and its preparations to lay claim to another's. If Robert endeavored to naturalize the museum by prognosticating its ruin, he could do so only at the cost of suggesting that the appropriation of Italy's patrimony underscored France's lack of a culture of its own. For this reason, the painting recalls the most damning of Quatremère's arguments against the museum—his contention that the institution, far from facilitating a relationship to the past, prohibited one. Resuming his campaign—reviewed in the previous chapter—against the deracination of monuments, Quatremère argued that artworks uprooted from their rightful settings were fundamentally "denatured." The museum would "kill the instruction of the arts" by presenting as artistic models works dispossessed of their original import.[27] Consequently, the relocation of Italy's antiquities to the museum, rather than securing the status of Paris as "la nouvelle Athènes," would shake the very foundations of Classicism. Quatremère's belief in the power of artworks to function as bearers of immutable ideals could not have been further from the aesthetic interests, as we have seen, that governed the production of Robert. And yet, as if taking his cue from the museophobe, the artist hints in his painting at the prospect of Classicism being reduced to a picturesque memory, and of its beloved god available only in the form of a modern proxy.

Before exploring further Quatremère's argument against the spoliation of Rome, and examining the perspective that Robert's museum views bring to the conquest, it is worth considering his *Grande Galerie in Ruins* from the point of view of yet another author. In his review in *La décade philosophique* of the Salon of 1795, the critic Amaury Duval railed against the continued existence of degenerate artistic habits. Provoking his outrage were nine paintings by Robert—works featuring Roman ruins that the artist had produced while in prison. For Duval, the paintings (and perhaps their authorship by an artist whose loyalties to the republic had been deemed questionable) served as a reminder that "a revolution in the arts" was overdue, for "our artists produce nothing grand, sublime. All is affected, mannered." He comments sarcastically that "one must admire Robert for his memory" before taking the painter and his fellow specialists in the genre of ruins to task for basing their art in imagination rather than in the direct study of nature. Ruin painters, Duval suggests, present extreme examples of artists who produce landscapes without ever leaving Paris—a city where one can "barely apprehend a fragment of sky above the roofs of neighboring houses." In the absence of proper models, such artists end up "imitating images that others have made. . . . Vain efforts! These imitations of imitation are always cold and without truth." Thus the "tiresome uniformity" of ruin painting. The tirade formed part of a larger argument in which the author sounded the revolutionary call for direct contact with *la belle nature* and with the "truth" afforded by models as a remedy for the "false ideas" propagated under the monarchy. Nowhere were these transgressions more egregiously evidenced than in the capriccio: "What is the merit of piling up the debris of monuments that are sometimes several hundred leagues from one another?"[28]

Viewed through the lens of Duval's review, Robert's *Grande Galerie in Ruins* appears a throwback to an outmoded era—the work of a *ruiniste* whose employment at an institution dedicated to the preservation of art from the "ravages of time," to quote Diderot, was rich in perversity. And yet, if the critique incriminates the fatigued faculties of an artist unmoved by the spirit of a new order, it also illuminates Robert's canny anticipation of the contradictions that would plague the museum. Ironically, in casting aspersions on the business of unnaturally "piling up . . . monuments that are sometimes several hundred leagues from one another," Duval offers a characterization of the capriccio that pertained to the museum as well. For Robert and Quatremère alike, masterpieces relocated to the museum were no less mediated—their "originality" no less diluted—than monuments in a capriccio, or "imitations of imitation." Indeed, though a source of hope that direct access to models of unsurpassed perfection would rejuvenate art making in the present, the museum, as the recipient of plundered artworks, was also perceived as destructive of the tradition it sought to safeguard. The institution aspired to overcome the gulf between antiquity and modernity. Yet countervailing this endeavor was the museum's acceleration of the course whereby the "past and present floated free from each other," and it was this process that Robert's *Grande Galerie in Ruins* at once foresaw and forestalled.[29]

Banknotes and Curiosities

Quatremère's indictment of the museum appears to have first taken the form of a semi-clandestine series of letters, addressed to General Francisco de Miranda, that circulated in Paris in June 1796. Published thereafter under the initials *A. Q.,* his *Lettres à Miranda* fiercely opposed the French army's anticipated removal of works of art from Italy following a successful military campaign.[30] Quatremère denounced spoliation as hostile to the new body politic—"*The spirit of conquest in a republic is entirely subversive of the spirit of liberty*"—as well as to the values of "universal fraternity" and "equality" foundational to the "republic of the arts": the arts "belong to all Europe," he states, "and are no longer the exclusive property of one nation."

Quatremère elaborated on his argument that "the country is itself the museum" in a now-famous description of Rome:

> The museum of which I am speaking, is, it is true, composed of statues, of colossi, of temples, of obelisks, of triumphal columns, of baths, of circuses, of amphitheaters, of triumphal arches, of tombs, of stucco decoration, of frescoes, of bas-reliefs, of inscriptions, of ornamental fragments, of building materials, of furniture, of utensils, etc., etc., but it is also composed fully as much of places, of sites, of mountains, of quarries, of ancient roads, of the placing of ruined towns, of geographical relationships, of the inner connections of all these objects to each other, of memories, of local traditions, of still prevailing customs, of parallels and comparisons which can only be made in the country itself.[31]

Quatremère asserts that the integrity of Rome's living museum—which he contrasts with the deadening effects of the French one—is crucial to the future of the arts. The preservation of art in its rightful environment can alone guarantee a proper understanding of art's history, for a single artwork is but the sum of the infinitely varied and nuanced relationships that bind every aspect of a culture—"its discoveries, its errors, its prejudices . . . ancient customs, religious dogmas, laws, social institutions"—to the next. Only when an object of beauty is viewed in its proper context—alongside inferior objects, and through the work of "relation" and "comparison"—can its distinctive features be appreciated. Such "rapprochements" and "rapports" are the "soul of . . . instruction," states Quatremère. To "denude" and "deprive" masterpieces of "these means of demonstration" by "isolating them" in the museum would mean "no more education, no more schools, and soon no more students."[32]

For Quatremère, art remained meaningful so long as it was ensconced in what he characterizes as its natural habitat: so long, that is, as art reflected its subordination to, rather than discordance with, its surrounding institutional climate. The argument was one he resumed in a public address of 1806, which he published in 1815 under the title *Considérations morales sur la destination des ouvrages de l'art.* In the spirit of Restoration, what Quatremère valued in culture was its submissiveness to a totalizing authority. "Because it has no choice but that of belonging to what surrounds it, the Quatremèrian work of art," writes Didier Maleuvre, "yields to the tyranny of social dictates. In the end, the work of art becomes a mere instrument of cultural reproduction."[33] Quatremère's career was a testament to his conservatism. An artist turned academician who initially championed the Revolution as a vehicle for monarchical reform, he was forced into hiding in 1793 and remained fairly scarce until the Restoration. Making a name for himself thereafter as a scholar of Classicism, archaeology, and the arts, he was appointed *secrétaire perpétuel* of the Académie des beaux-arts in 1816, a position he held for the next two decades. Quatremère's creed of cultural authenticity has been interpreted as a defense of political authoritarianism; indeed, when Quatremère states that art in a museum is "unfaithful to the beliefs that watched over its making," he forecloses the possibility that culture might constitute emancipation from, as opposed to conformity with, the status quo.[34]

In 1796, however, Quatremère's antimuseum polemic reflected more than the basis for a reactionary cultural politics. Among other things, it intensified an already existing worry about whether the conquest of Italy's art amounted to triumphant republicanism or regressive barbarism. Two years earlier, the Convention nationale had legitimated the plunder of foreign collections with its adoption of the policy of "repatriation": the revolutionary doctrine of the *patrimoine de liberté* held repatriated artworks to have been victims of exile under despotism, restored by the Revolution to their rightful destiny in a free nation—their "final domicile."[35] By May of 1796, a commission of specially appointed artists and scientists was dispatched to Italy's conquered cities to earmark objects for removal (a vast range comprising manuscripts and coins, botanical and zoological specimens, in addition to paintings, prints, and sculpture) and prepare them for the journey "home."

That same month, a battle erupted in the Paris press that pitted advocates of spoliation against its detractors—and, by extension, revolutionary patriots against those who were accused of harboring antirevolutionary sentiments. For its supporters, spoliation posed an opportunity for the new republicans to embrace their destiny as reincarnations of the ancients. Thus overturning the example of France's former despots who left the monuments of conquered lands in place, preferring "to let them be destroyed by their soldiers," wrote one such proponent, spoliation enabled the French to do as the Romans had done before them but in a manner "more just... more generous, more human." Detractors, on the other hand, contended that the confiscation of Italy's patrimony undercut French interests: an act of "war on the arts" that would "wound the national honor" of Italy, spoliation would sabotage the cause of a lasting peace.[36] And just as critics of the museum worried about the harmful effects of extracting objects from their contexts ("When this Apollo, uprooted from the place where it has existed for centuries, is brought, carted to Paris, will it remain a god for our artists? Will it not be a piece of furniture?"), so did they fear that the effect of spoliation would be "to attach in the future the monuments of the arts to the chariots of victory."[37]

Indeed, what most frightened critics about spoliation was that it threatened to enslave the fate of artworks to the vicissitudes of war. The prospect hovers over Quatremère's *Lettres,* which ends with the terrifying image of Italy's collections subjugated to "the chance of war or political revolutions"—"the riches of art and science being nothing more than plunder."[38] For Quatremère, however, the possibility that Italy's antiquities would be reduced to war booty is but a more extreme version of the danger already facing art in the age of museums: that artworks would cease to exist as microcosms of an infinitely rich cultural landscape and would instead be rendered objects of mere exchange value. John Dewey echoes Quatremère's sentiments when he observes, "The contents of galleries and museums testify to the growth of economic cosmopolitanism. The mobility of trade and populations, due to the economic system, has weakened or destroyed the connection between works of art and the *genius loci* of which they were once the natural expression. As works of art have lost their indigenous status, they have acquired a new one—that of being specimens of fine art and nothing else."[39]

The menace that the museum as an outgrowth of "commercial ideas" posed to the values inscribed in artworks pervades Quatremère's *Lettres,* as when the author informs Miranda: "The shamefully mercantile profit that a city acquiring [antiquities] believes it would make would be a profit lost for the arts."[40] He goes on to note the poisonous effect that "speculators and entrepreneurs" have on the "esprit of discovery" in Roman excavation sites. Quatremère elsewhere addresses the incompatibility between art's intrinsic significance and its commercial worth. In his fourth letter, he declares the overwhelmingly "mercantile concerns" of London and Paris to be hostile to the contemplation of art, the prerequisite for which is escape (to Rome) from "the vapors that obscure... truth and beauty" in Europe's commercial centers. Artworks "lose their value" where "the distraction of business" governs the minds of spectators.[41] As he comments in the seventh letter, "What could be more contrary to the true spirit and to the enlightened love of the arts than these fiscal theories, which find in the monuments of popular instruction only objects of commerce, and who discover in masterpieces of taste and genius nothing more than indirect taxes on foreign curiosity!" What Quatremère appears to have taken to heart in this final letter was that only by showing appropriation to be commercially disadvantageous might he succeed in turning public opinion against it. Predicting that the dispersal of art objects from Rome would ultimately "impoverish" artistic production in France, he asks: "What would be the point of a monopoly over a trade without outlets and of products without consumers?" At the same time, however, Quatremère underscores the vanity of any effort to disavow the museum's relationship to the marketplace by bitterly acknowledging, "Who knows if we won't end up converting [works of art] into mortgages, and draw banknotes on antique sculpture?"[42]

From his longing for authenticity to his dread of art's commodification, Quatremère may be credited with inaugurating an abiding discourse against museums, one so central to modern thought, however, that the significance of its roots in the political economy of revolutionary France has perhaps been overshadowed. In 1796, the worry that uprooting art objects and transporting them from their proper settings would compromise their value transcended political differences: on 16 August, fifty artists—including David, Vincent, and Anne-Louis Girodet (in addition to Pajou)—signed Quatremère's petition entreating the Directory to remove nothing from Rome until a special commission "of artists and men of letters" assessed "whether it is useful to France, and if it is advantageous to the arts and to artists in general, to displace from Rome the monuments of antiquity and the masterpieces of painting and sculpture that decorate the galleries and museums of this capital of the arts." *Le moniteur universel* promptly condemned the artists for their "dishonorable demand," noting that "no modern power has so well revived the ancient Greeks; [France] has even surpassed them in their awe of liberty."[43]

Far more polemical than the petition was the counterpetition that appeared soon after in *Le moniteur,* bearing the signatures of thirty-seven artists, including Jean-Baptiste Isabey, François Gérard, and Jean-Baptiste Regnault. The signatories demanded the transport to Paris of Italy's masterpieces, pointing out that the "Romans, formerly crude, managed to civilize their Nation, by transplanting the productions of vanquished Greece. In their example, let us profit from our conquests, and bring from Italy all that which can aggrandize the imagination." Such confidence in the repeatability of ancient precedent, however, coexisted with uncertainty over the future. Nothing "guarantees," declare the petitioners, that the present circumstances of Rome's masterpieces will continue uninterrupted: "Who will assure us of the future tranquility of Italy? Who will respond to us that convulsions... will not destroy or transport elsewhere all these riches?" Already the Palazzo Farnese had been emptied of its treasures by the king of Naples, and the "Negroni collection" purchased by an Englishman.[44] The petitioners urge, "Let us hurry therefore to bring to France that which, six months from now, will no longer exist in Rome," for the "French Republic... is the only country in the world that can give inviolable asylum to these masterpieces."[45]

There was no question that spoliation served, among other things, an economic agenda; indeed, the peace treaty with Italy was drafted with the full expectation that the *patrimoine de liberté* would function as a form of indemnity. (It would thereby activate what the art dealer Lebrun had envisioned, in 1793, as the museum's potential to "rehabilitate our exhausted finances." As he put it, "Similar to the ocean to which the rivers bring the tribute of their waters, [Paris] will be the point of convergence for all the gold of Europe.")[46] Spoliation's supporters could tacitly present it as good economic policy—but not without potentially undermining their cause. Associated by its critics with the memory of revolutionary iconoclasm, spoliation stirred up recollections of monuments being removed from churches and palaces and (if not destroyed) turned into liquid assets—sold on the antiques market by the financially strapped republic.[47] To acknowledge the economic benefits of repatriation was to risk tainting the plundered objects as commodities. Still more problematically, it was to raise the specter of their ceaseless circulation: thus the necessity of presenting the French museum as the "final domicile" for the artworks in its collection. Like the petitioners who opposed the "inviolable asylum" of France to the vulnerable terrain of Rome, Joachim Lebreton of the Institut national des sciences et des arts, while professing himself to be on the side of keeping Rome's masterpieces intact, cited Austrian politics and English money as evidence of the likelihood of their removal from "the soil of Italy." Therefore, he asked, "Wouldn't the most beautiful works... of Rome be better lodged and maintained in the land where better laws and more enlightened exist, with the most forceful and industrious population, in the only nation that has a school?"[48] Advocates of repatriation appealed to the pride of a nation that identified itself with ancient republicanism; at the same time, they preyed on economic fear by warning of the imminent demise of the "indigenous status" of Italy's artworks. Suggestions that the transplanting of Rome's antiquities to Paris would make the French the equal of the liberated Greeks or of the proud Roman conquerors thus papered over the tensions between the ancient ideals subscribed to by the new republic and the modern commercial reality it inhabited.

Such tensions surface in Robert's museum views. The artist, as noted, refrained from signing either petition, yet he nonetheless produced evidence of his preoccupation with the vexed relationship between the circulation of Rome's antiquities in the museum and the institution's purported status as a "final domicile." In a painting, for instance, whose date has been disputed—*A Museum Gallery of Roman Art*—Robert imagined the Grande Galerie lined not with Renaissance masterpieces but with Roman *vedute* and housing antiquity's most celebrated marbles: these include the Laokoon, the Hermaphrodite, the Farnese Herakles, the Apollo Belvedere, the Medici Venus, the Belvedere Torso, the Callipygian Venus, the Antinous, and the Borghese Gladiator (fig. 68). The work, though its inscription indicates

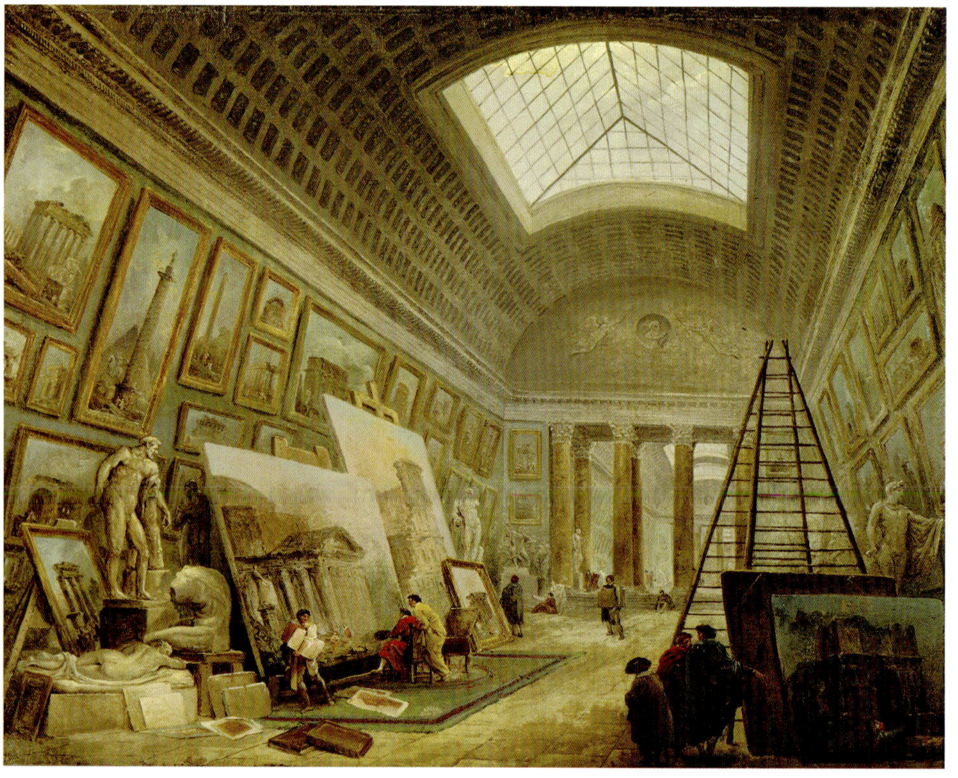

it was painted in 1789, has long been dated to the late 1790s. Evidence supporting this later execution date includes the presence of antiquities whose arrival in the museum was anticipated beginning in 1796, as well as Robert's employment of a design strategy—division of the gallery by rows of paired columns—that museum curators endorsed in 1794.[49]

The *Museum Gallery* offers a view at odds with the public address of Robert's *Project for the Grande Galerie* (see fig. 64). Whereas the earlier work, with its soaring central perspective, invites the viewer to join the ranks of the museum's enlightened community of spectators, the *Museum Gallery* places us in the position occupied by the three figures at right, who linger in the shadows and peer at the impromptu display from behind a ladder. With its casually assembled antiquities, the scene recalls the picturesque disarray of the curiosity cabinet; indeed, the pell-mell assortment of artworks, studio accoutrements, and invaluable marbles—along with crates and pedestals—suggests the in-transit condition of the objects, displayed as if in temporary storage. The labor of the seated artist, in the midst of completing an enormous view of the Pantheon that leans precariously against the canvases behind it—along with the lackadaisically stacked antiquities and drawings fallen to the floor—contributes to the scene's air of provisionality. The numerous paintings on the gallery's walls dwarf the statues below, rendering the fate of these marbles all the more ambiguous. For if, as Hegel believed, the modernity of the easel painting—that which distinguished it from sculpture—lay in its intrinsic homelessness, then the indecorous proximity of paintings and antiquities threatens to undo this distinction.[50] The *Museum Gallery* raises the possibility of ancient marbles being as mobile and transient as view paintings circulating on the art market.

Fig. 68. Hubert Robert (French, 1733–1808)
A Museum Gallery of Roman Art, 1790s (?), oil on canvas, 65 × 81 cm (25⅝ × 31⅞ in.)
Paris, Musée du Louvre

Fig. 69. Giovanni Paolo Panini (Italian, ca. 1692–1765)
Picture Gallery with Views of Ancient Rome, 1756–57, oil on canvas, 169 × 227 cm (66½ × 89⅜ in.)
Stuttgart, Staatsgalerie

Fig. 70. Giovanni Paolo Panini (Italian, ca. 1692–1765)
Picture Gallery with Views of Modern Rome, 1757, oil on canvas, 170.2 × 244.5 cm (67 × 96¼ in.)
Boston, Museum of Fine Arts

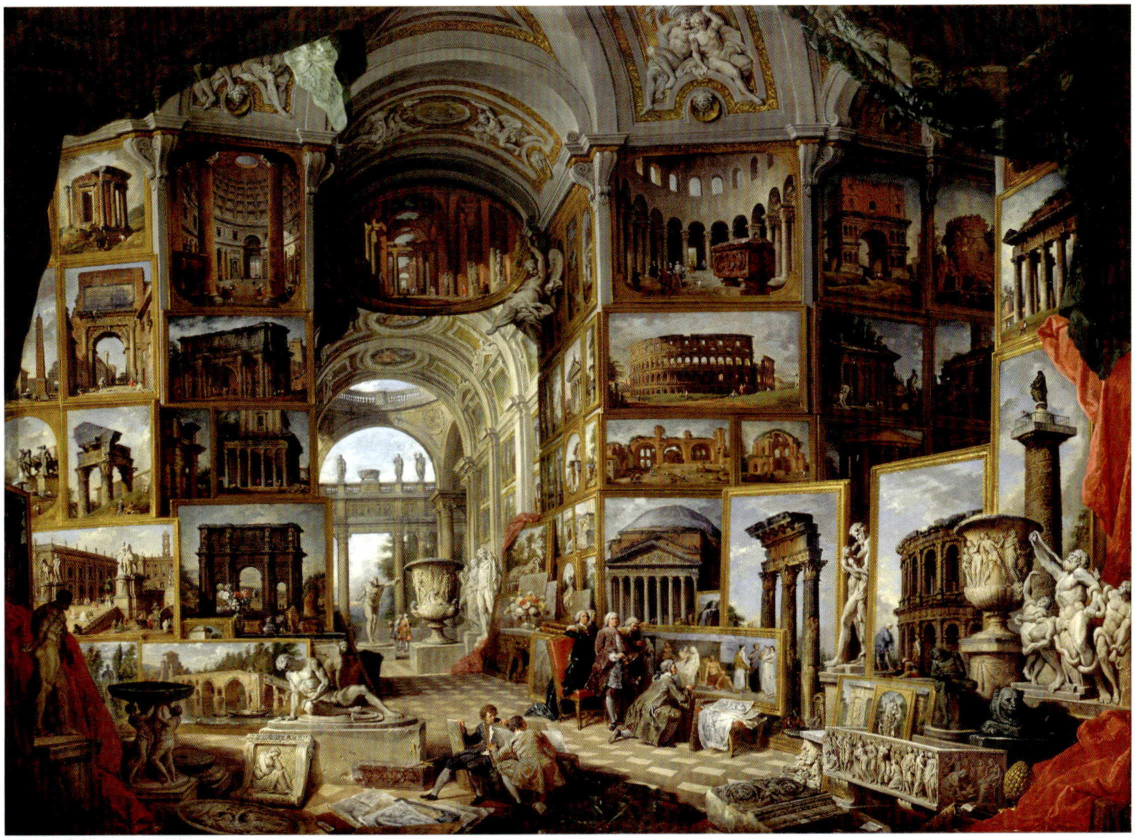

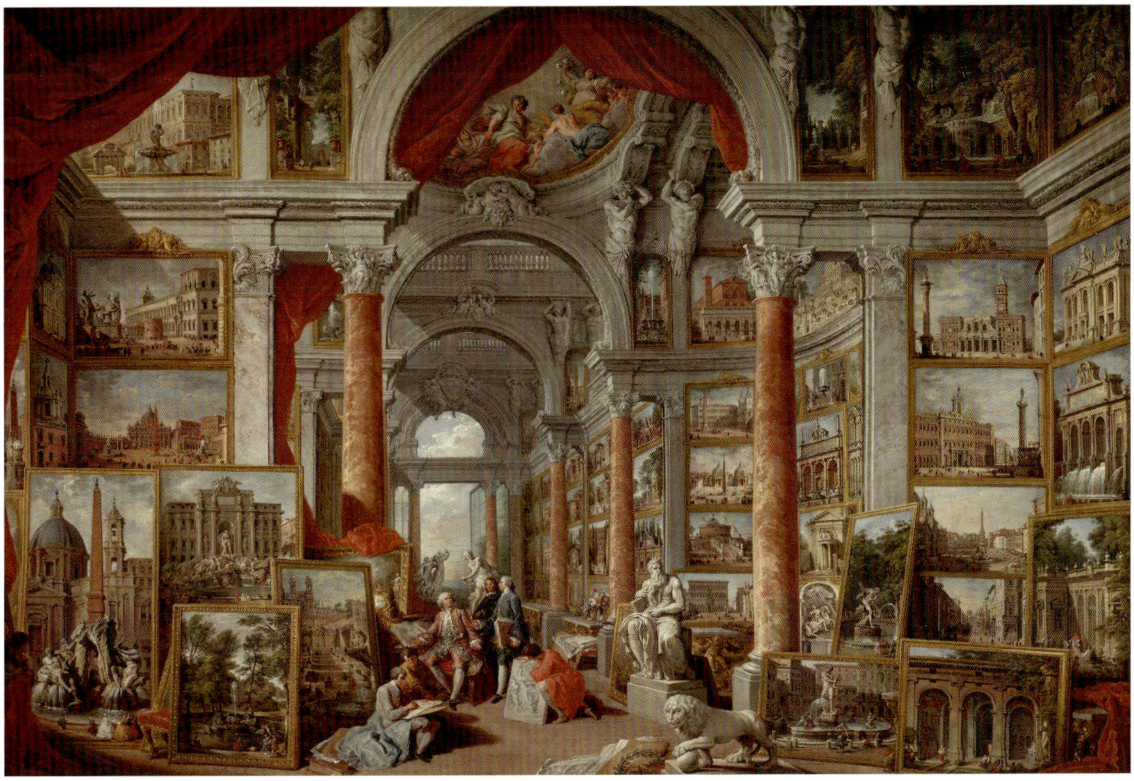

In one important respect, the *Museum Gallery* shares common ground with the pendants of 1796: all three views of the museum have their basis in Panini's pendants featuring imaginary picture galleries with views of ancient and modern Rome (figs. 69, 70). Commissioned by the duc de Choiseul to commemorate his ambassadorship to Rome, the paintings held special importance for Robert: a version of the series, signed by Panini and executed in 1757, hung in Robert's collection at the time of his death. Moreover, Robert appears to have assisted the Italian artist—his instructor at the Académie de France à Rome—in the execution of the pendants for Choiseul and may also have helped produce the 1757 replicas. Panini, in addition to portraying himself (at the center in *Ancient Rome,* holding brush and palette), included in *Modern Rome* the figure of an artist who has been identified as Robert: dressed in blue and carrying a sheaf of drawings, he appears to the right of the seated Choiseul.[51]

In his *Museum Gallery,* Robert makes pointed reference to *Ancient Rome,* featuring the same famous marbles (Herakles, the Dying Gladiator, the Laokoon, etc.) as well as *vedute* of the same monuments (including the Pantheon, the Coliseum, Trajan's Column) that appear in Panini's painting. Yet the juxtaposition of the two canvases underscores the differences between them. *Ancient Rome* evokes the leisurely yet lofty pastimes of a conversation piece: in Panini's rarefied Roman gallery, the informal display of priceless objects serves as a visual corollary to an elite, grand tour sociability. Relative to their splendid presence in this temple-like space, whose sheer sprawl evokes the abundance of Rome itself, the antiquities cluttered in the modest hall of Robert's museum appear diminished, no longer coterminous with the wealth of associations bred by the category "Roma antica." Considered alongside its antecedent, Robert's painting recalls the observations of John Scott—a tourist at the Louvre in 1814—who commented upon encountering Rome's antiquities in the alien quarters of the museum: "The finest emotions and associations of thought which these works suggested in their original seats, became dissolved and dissipated by their transportation."[52]

Yet if Robert's view offers a desublimated redux of Panini's, it does so to the extent that the latter issues an apologia for "transportation" while immunizing the gallery's contents from its debasing ramifications. In both pendants, a delight in portability is accompanied by an effort to undercut the potential standing of the works as objects fated for circulation on the art market. Along the margins of each canvas, a sweep of drapery (a flourish familiar from the curiosity cabinets dreamed up by Jan Brueghel and Peter Paul Rubens) theatrically separates the scene from a less refined world. Panini's self-presentation lends his canvases the noncommercial value of the masterpiece and the noble imprimatur of the Classical: the artist poses, palette in hand, beside the Aldobrandini Wedding (a painting that some believed to have been the work of Apelles), as if to suggest the parity of his artistic achievements with those of the ancients. The pictures on display, moreover, reiterate the compositions of the galleries, casting themselves as fixed appendages of the interiors: the *vedute* featuring the arches of Titus, Constantine, and Lucius Septimius Severus, among others, are continuous with the centrally framed view in *Ancient Rome,* while the pictures in a column at right in *Modern Rome* replicate the painting's view of an arcade seen from the right of center.[53] This blurring of the boundary between the portability of the pictures and the static space of the gallery—compounded by the effect of trompe l'oeil—places in question the commutability of the artworks. In short, in ways echoed in the capricci by Robert discussed in the previous chapter, Panini emphasizes at once mobility and, reassuringly, its regulation. Panini's galleries of movable goods, needless to say, take us far afield from Quatremère's vision of Rome, with its nostalgic conception of the city's immemorial *rapprochements* and *rapports.*

In so valorizing while containing precariousness, Panini's capricci pair the attractions of the Eternal City with the habits of perception inculcated at a time of mercantile exchange: a period when the pleasures afforded by so many collectibles were accompanied by fears that the accumulation of imports would bring about the collapse of modern nations. Rome, after all, was widely said to have been "broken by her own weight."[54] It was precisely such dread of repeating the downfall of the republic-turned-empire—one ruined by its "thirst for conquest"—that Quatremère counted on when he warned of the consequences of spoliation.[55] Among these was the mutation of the museum into a monument to imperial conquest and of its masterpieces into "denatured" commodities. In gesturing toward such a prospect, Robert's *Museum Gallery of Roman Art* dwells on the troubling implications of bringing Rome to Paris. Thus magnifying a tension already latent in Panini's pendants, Robert's painting accentuates the tremendous pressures faced by the museum—an institution premised on the mobility of art objects, yet encumbered with the necessity of presenting itself as a refuge from a world of destabilizing transactions: as the endpoint for art's movement, rather than the impetus for it.

So too, though, would Panini's precedent function for Robert as a reminder of a Rome that, by 1798, no longer existed. "Rome is no more in Rome, / It is all in Paris," went the song that greeted the convoy bearing Italy's antiquities.[56] For at least one artist whose past was rooted in "the soil of Italy," the convoy's arrival in Paris marked not the translation of Rome but its degradation. With his *Museum Gallery,* Robert corroborated the scenario envisioned by David, who scornfully predicted that the museum would fail to transcend the status of the curiosity collection. Watching the triumphal procession into Paris of Italy's art on 27 July 1798, David, ventriloquizing Quatremère, warned:

> You can be sure... that the masterpieces that have been brought here from Italy will soon be considered only curiosities. The location of a work of art and the distance one must go in order to admire it help singularly to bring out its true value... pictures, in particular... will lose a great deal of their charm and their effect when they are no longer in the spot for which they were made. The study of these masterpieces will perhaps help to form scholars—Winckelmanns—but artists, no![57]

Liquidation

A Museum Gallery of Roman Art was one of several paintings Robert devoted to the theme of antiquities in the museum. In the late 1790s, he produced a series of views, ranging from projected fantasy to accurate depiction, of the Musée des Antiques—the Louvre galleries, inaugurated in 1800, where Italy's antiquities were displayed.[58] In one such work, a sampling of ancient sculptures is arrayed against the western wall of

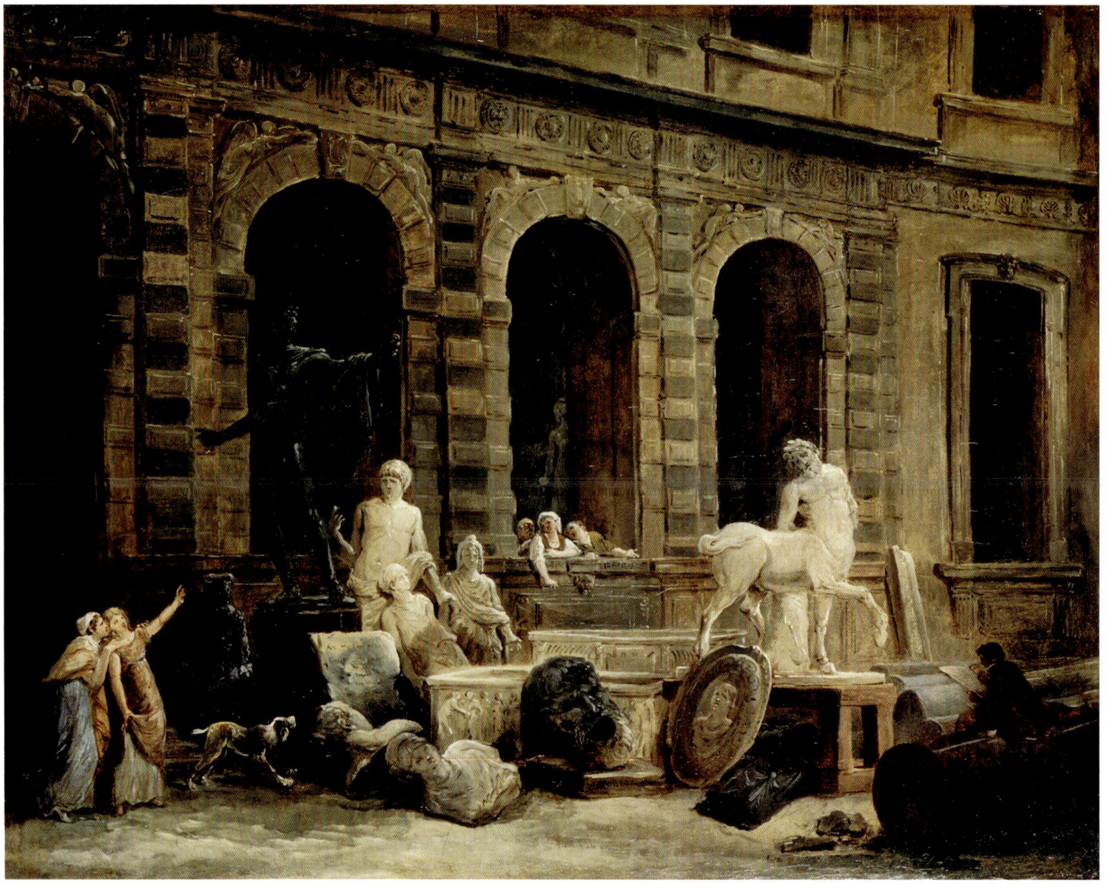

Fig. 71. **Hubert Robert (French, 1733–1808)**
Artist Drawing Antiques before the Petite Galerie, ca. 1800, oil on canvas, 46 × 47 cm (18⅛ × 18½ in.)
Paris, Musée du Louvre

the Petite Galerie (fig. 71). Included among the sarcophagi and busts are the (bronze) Apollo Belvedere; to its right, a statue of Nero with a sculpture of Isis beside it; and to the left of Apollo, a black marble bust of the Hellenistic-Egyptian god Serapis. The Centaur at right, though evidently based on a version seized from a private collection, more closely recalls the Campidoglio sculpture.[59]

Robert likely executed the painting in the later 1790s, when renovations were under way on the Musée des Antiques.[60] In typical manner, the artist capitalizes on the picturesque aspect of sculptures stored provisionally outside the Petite Galerie—as well as on the amusing dynamics of their reception: the leaning torso of the Centaur is echoed in the posture of the women behind it, and the Apollo's outstretched arm is mimicked by the visitor at left. Robert was a specialist in such playful reiterations. Here, however, they render the painting a bittersweet reflection on the accidental and haphazard *rapprochements* and *rapports* to which the sculptures, outcasts from their former contexts, were now subject. Though likely executed prior to the arrival of the convoy of artworks from Italy, the painting—in its seemingly arbitrary mix of ancient relics and modern replicas—recalls Quatremère's complaint that the artificial domicile of the museum shattered the "unity" that made works of art meaningful. As he states, "To divide is to destroy."[61] Such angst is not readily detectable in Robert's lighthearted treatment of the Petite Galerie. Nonetheless, among the implications of the painting is that the sculptures, relocated to the museum, have become empty vessels for the fantasies imposed on them by modern-day Parisians—as well as by Robert himself, whose stand-in exists in the artist at right.

If the *Petite Galerie* ruminates on the effects of decontextualization in the museum, such effects appear particularly concentrated in the Apollo, it being a bronze copy of an absent original. To suggest as much is not to overstate the existence in the eighteenth century of an anxiety about the relationship between originals and replicas per se; it is, though, to take note of a certain resonance between Robert's painting and Quatremère's implicit allegation that displacing artworks from their original settings rendered them mere copies of their former selves.[62] In the *Petite Galerie,* the condition of the Apollo as a replica finds ample reverberation: As noted, acts of mimicry abound, from the threesome at the window repeating the sculptural triad at left, to the duo of busts in the foreground, which mirror each other while also echoing the pair of women at left. The draftsman, shown copying from the collection, extends this motif of replication, in addition to being himself represented. With each instance of mediation and translation—from model to copy, from private to public collection, from one medium to the next—the erosion of the original identities of these antiquities-turned-museum-pieces is rendered ever more irreversible.[63]

As a metareflection on substitutive acts whose multiplication reinforces the irrecoverability of the thing substituted, Robert's *Petite Galerie* discloses the museum's centrality to the "shattering of tradition" that Benjamin associates with techniques of reproduction that estranged artworks from their original "use value." The painting sets in relief the parallels between the museum and the logic of reproduction: just as the museum, according to Quatremère, voids its objects of their original content, so does mechanical reproduction, as Benjamin shows, negate the "authenticity" of the object reproduced; in both cases, the artwork is detached from "its basis in ritual"; its "authority" is jeopardized, its "aura" destroyed. As Daniel Sherman writes, "The museum and reproduction... belong to the same age."[64] And the museum fascinated Robert for the same reason that reproduction did Benjamin: it marked the "liquidation" of the past.[65]

For Robert—a maker of capricci, as we have seen, that thematized deracination—the museum appears to have been as much a symptom as a cause of (art's) peripateticism; Quatremère, on the other hand, forcefully equates the institution with the latter. What Benjamin describes as the withering of the artwork's aura in an age of mechanical reproduction was anticipated by Quatremère's argument that the itinerancy of cultural capital would render its value subject to the law of diminishing returns. Indeed, Quatremère understood that persuading his readers that artworks, once uprooted from their rightful locations, would plummet in value meant undermining their belief in the institution's separateness from the marketplace. Yet more to the point, Quatremère's skepticism about the museum betrayed a lack of confidence, to put it mildly, in the fiscal health of the republic. He tacitly treated the museum as an extension of the government's disastrous economic agenda and was not unjustified in doing so. As noted, at a time when military victory proved crucial in enabling France to replenish its treasury and finance subsequent military campaigns, both pictures and payments extracted from conquered countries functioned as indemnities.[66] Thus when Quatremère, at the start of his letters to Miranda, denounced "*the spirit of conquest*" as "*subversive of the spirit of liberty,*" he condemned not only a cultural policy but an economic one as well.[67]

More specifically, the rhetoric of incommensurability Quatremère deployed—exemplified in the opposition of "conquest" and "liberty"—served at once to discredit the museum and to relate its transgressions to the problem of inflation. The arts, for Quatremère, were associated not only with the "reciprocal interest[s]" of nations that respected the international laws of patrimony but also, as we have seen, with a system of evaluation based on "comparisons, connections, analogies"—terms that ineluctably called attention to the crisis of reciprocity in financial life.[68] For the catastrophic consequences of putting into circulation objects sundered from their contexts were everywhere in evidence in 1796, when the creation of paper money in excess of its value in land caused inflation to reach its peak. The failure of the *assignat* (initially issued as an interest-bearing bond to be used as payment for nationalized properties) marked the failure of the *confiance*-boosting formula touted by proponents of the revolutionary currency: "land in a form that could circulate."[69] Its crash was followed in March of 1795 by the issuing of the *mandats territoriaux*—backed by undervalued land and fatally linked to the remaining *assignats*. The new currency collapsed while Quatremère's letters were surfacing. The state's intention to dissolve the "museum of Rome" could thus be decried as yet another attempt at liquidation whose consequences would prove no less calamitous than its failed experiment in turning land into paper.[70]

Forced loans, inflation, deflation, demonetization: the republic's persistent failure to create in currency a credible version of itself made all the more urgent the decree—issued by the minister of the interior, Jean-Marie Roland de La Platière—that the "museum must demonstrate the nation's great riches." In such a climate, the challenge of presenting the museum as a haven of unfluctuating values weighed heavily on the Conservatoire.[71] In the months prior to the arrival of Italy's antiquities, Robert and his colleagues struggled with the difficulty of readying an exhibition space worthy of the "precious plunder" while contending with the reality of their own financial penury (as if concretizing the museum's subjugation to the realities of monetary instability and the dearth of specie, its already cramped quarters were even occupied for a time by the Bourse).[72] "Soon, when the museum opens, when the fruits of our conquests abound . . . public opinion" will discover "the privation that the museum has experienced." So warned Robert in his capacity as president of the Conservatoire (a rotating position), in a letter bearing his signature. The correspondence, dated 13 February 1797, was addressed to the members of the Institut, contesting their use of space that the Conservatoire hoped to see incorporated into the Musée des Antiques. The document reveals just how acutely the Conservatoire struggled to keep the crisis of confidence from infiltrating perceptions of the museum. Pleading with the Institut to relinquish the Galerie d'Apollon and its adjoining salon, Robert called the one "the nave of the museum" and the other "the sanctuary of a temple" that "lacks only the image of the divinity to whom it was consecrated." (A century earlier, the painter Charles Le Brun had been commissioned by Louis XIV to decorate the gallery with cycles representing Apollo, the Roman sun god.) Robert dared his readers to imagine the consequences should "the Apollo Belvedere, transported to Paris, be unable to enter upon its arrival this temple that it seems destiny has prepared for it!"[73]

Left unspoken was the implication that failure to display the masterpieces properly would render criminal their removal from the "sumptuous galleries of the Vatican and the Capitol." In order to ensure that the "gods of antiquity" have their temple, André Thouin—one of the commissioners responsible for the transport of the convoy—advocated exhibiting them in a requisitioned church.[74] For the Conservatoire, such a solution was abhorrent; thus Robert's contention that the Galerie d'Apollon had already been consecrated to the deity. Symptomatic of the revolutionary will to transfer religious faith to new state institutions, the comparison of the exhibition hall to a church nave alludes to yet another anxiety: the fear that an inappropriate venue would desanctify the god. In the spirit of preserving the reciprocity between the sculpture and the ideals with which it is associated, the letter concludes by demanding that "this masterpiece of art, the object of the admiration of all ages, of all nations" be given its home in "this temple [where] everything would be analogous to it and where it would be the symbol of everything that surrounds it."

Such emphatic use of a Quatremèrian vocabulary to characterize a vision of the sculpture at one with its surroundings reflected more than a commitment to justifying the conquest of Rome's antiquities. Like his imaginary gallery views, the declaration suggests a tension between Robert's private intuitions and his public responsibilities on behalf of the institution he served. The letter expressed a knowledge already latent in his paintings: that the sacred authority of the Apollo was endangered by the museum itself, which, in its very effort to enshrine the art of the ancients, threatened to de-auraticize it.

The Terror of History

The economic turmoil of the Directory merits attention, then, not only because it formed the backdrop to Quatremère's assault on the credibility of a state institution but also because it escalated, for Robert, the challenge of solidifying the museum's image as an alternative to a world of flux. Such was the imperative facing the painter when he produced his publicly displayed pendant views of the Grande Galerie (see figs. 64, 65). Occurring within months of the collapse of the *assignat,* the exhibition of the works—particularly the first one, attesting to the future magnificence of an institution enlisted to offer the state an image of its own "stable order"—could not have been better timed.[75] Robert's canvas, with its view of artworks manifesting the evolution of painting, certified the promise of the Conservatoire to present in the gallery a "speaking history [*histoire parlante*] [of the progress], decadence and downfalls that the arts of diverse epochs have undergone."[76] Such a "speaking history"—evidencing the cycles of degeneration and renewal observable since ancient times—would assuage the uncertainty of living in a time radically discontinous from the one that preceded it.

In its application of Winckelmann's schema of the progress and decadence of ancient culture to art throughout the ages, the museum would "speak" the place of the moderns in a history that was, in effect, timeless. Summing up the infallibility of the laws of cyclicality—as well as his debts to Winckelmann—Lenoir, director of the Musée des Monuments Français, states: "The arts, like empires, experience revolutions: they pass successively from infancy to barbarity and return gradually to the point from which they started." Similarly, as Lebrun declares, "All the paintings [in the museum] should be arranged according to school and placed in such a way as to indicate the different epochs of the infancy, the progress, the perfection, and finally the decadence of the arts."[77] The adoption of Winckelmann's conception of evolutionary development (one rooted in Giorgio Vasari's biological schema of art's progress) as a natural and universal rule served the revolutionaries' agenda of identifying their "epoch" with that of the ancients. However, this compulsion to discount the sprawling temporal intervals separating one era from the next was at odds with a burgeoning historicist conception of art, one that equated the passage of centuries with an ever-widening divide between modernity and the past.[78]

Robert's pendants attest to these dueling paradigms; together, they encapsulate the process whereby the museum replaced "the contemplation of art with the retrospective contemplation of art history."[79] The first of Robert's paintings conjures the unfolding of this process—the metamorphosis of immortal masterpieces into products of a historical moment. And the second painting may well be interpreted as taking to an extreme the possibility, embedded in its pendant, that the progress of history ensured not the revival of precedent, but rather its irrecoverability. With this work, the belief—subscribed to by Winckelmann's revolutionary successors—in history's cyclicality has given way to an awareness of historical progression as enforcing the irretrievability of a past in ruins.

Already in the first of Robert's views, a "speaking history" illustrating the life cycles of the arts conflicts with a sense of history as proceeding in an open-ended march toward a future autonomous from the past. Indeed, the very immeasurability of the Grande Galerie seems to evoke the obscurity of the future, as well as its incalculable distance from the epochs preceding it. The skylights overhead take part in the work's hesitation between the ahistorical and the historicizing. For Salon viewers, top lighting—already on view in several of the city's fashionable venues—would have registered as a milestone of modern technology, the execution of a design feature whose benefits had been theorized by the ancients.[80] Four months earlier, the introduction to the catalog of Italian, Northern, and French paintings had promised viewers that the "hopes" of "amateurs" would soon be realized—that masterpieces of the three schools would "offer new charms" once they were illuminated from above.[81] The presence of skylights in Robert's view would have conveyed to Salon spectators that in the effort to fashion a museum worthy of the nation, no expense was being spared. Yet what is equally striking is the intrusion of sky that the overhead windows permit—passages of blue that have the effect of interrupting the flow below, serving as a kind of dazzling aside to, or distraction from, the gallery's sweeping trajectory. One is given to understand that without these coloristic incidents, the view would be rendered airless, confining. The gallery was, in fact, criticized for its narrow span, and Robert's clear motivation in his design proposal was to preserve the hall's "spectacle of immensity" while precluding the potential for monotony.[82] Thus the painter presented the work as a "projet pour éclairer la gallerie du musée par la voûte et pour la diviser sans ôter la vue de la prolongation du local" (project to illuminate the gallery of the museum from the vault and to divide it without sacrificing the view of the prolongation of the space). Like the series of arches and Ionic columns, the skylights envisioned by Robert complement by punctuating the flow of space. So too do they compensate for the constrictiveness of the gallery, by providing solace—both visual and conceptual—from the museum's display of the unrelenting course of history: that is, by countering an image of endless evolution with one of stasis. Insofar as the constancy of sky offers access to a space outside of the gallery—signaling the presence of an unchanging natural world—it confirms the logic of history as one of irreversible change.

By contrasting the brightness and expansiveness of the sky with the muted and contained space of the gallery, by welcoming (while excluding) nature, Robert prepares the viewer for the scene depicted in the work's pendant. The triumph of new building materials over the natural order has given way to an image of the museum in ruins. Yet if the painting presents the museum as the quintessential institution of an alienating modernity—unmasking its conservationist agenda as a fundamental hostility to the past—it also does the opposite. For Simmel, ruins mark the restoration of peace—of "unity"—between "nature and spirit," the "returning home" of human creation to its occluded "substructure."[83] It is in this sense that Robert's view may be appreciated as a portrait of alienation overcome, as an image of humankind's ceaseless repatriation to its origins, as a reaction, finally, against what Mircea Eliade describes as the "terror of history." According to Eliade, the belief in progress, in history's inexorable movement forward, rests upon the disenchantment of archetypal myths that sustained ancient peoples throughout centuries of emiseration. Inevitably, suggests Eliade, the modern realization that history is not governed by the law of cyclicality, that it proceeds independently of any preexisting paradigm, is the principle of both hope and terror. The doctrine of historical progression will necessarily prompt a resurgence of faith in a cyclical order.[84] Robert's painting may be considered a case in point, for it treats the museum as both medium and palliative for the "terror of history." The work featured the revolutionary monument reduced to rubble, to the consternation of critics at the Salon of 1796. Yet it nonetheless repaid belief in cyclicality, affirming the principle of eternal return.

It is worth noting that Robert's was not the only artwork of its time to take as its subject a future ruin. In 1798, the architect Joseph Michael Gandy executed a watercolor featuring the rotunda of the Bank of England imagined as a ruin only three years after the structure's construction by Soane.[85] Gandy, who took a job in Soane's firm after returning to London from Italy in 1797, was likely inspired by Robert's example, as he produced the work upon completing an interior view of the monument in pristine condition (fig. 72). In *The Bank of England, London: View of the Interior of the Rotunda,* a clock hangs beneath the central arch of the structure—an emblem, writes Brian Lukacher, of the "commercial schedule of the building." In Gandy's twilight view, *The Bank of England, London: View of the Rotunda Imagined as a Ruin,* observes Lukacher, "time itself has been torn from the building, the image allegorizing its own temporal disorder" (fig. 73).[86] For all the cavernous, mausoleum-like inviolability of the bank, time determines its fortunes.

Similar to Robert's authentication of the museum in his *Grande Galerie in Ruins,* Gandy's ruin honors the Classical status of a modern monument. The architect has borrowed Piranesi's trademark methods of inflating the grandeur of antiquity's remains. The massive skeletal structure—framed by savage foliage on the left and by piles of toppled columns and rubble in the foreground—along with the presence of figures with pickaxes, lends the subject the ennobling effect of an ancient Roman ruin. What further brings Gandy's picture into compelling relation with Robert's painting is its distinctive subject matter. The bank's rotunda housed the stock exchange, hub of the country's wealth and source of alarm over the effects of newfangled financial instruments on England's future.[87] Like Robert's view of the ruined museum, Gandy's watercolor incorporated an unprecedented institution

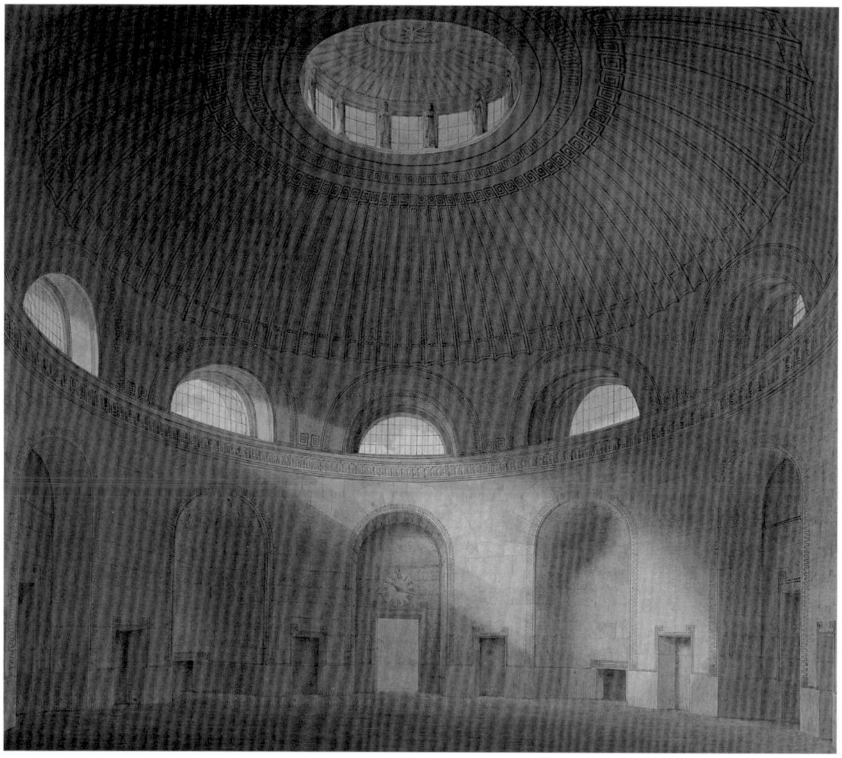

Fig. 72. Joseph Michael Gandy (English, 1771–1843)
The Bank of England, London: View of the Interior of the Rotunda, 1798, pen and watercolor, 63 × 69 cm (24¾ × 27⅛ in.)
London, Sir John Soane's Museum

Fig. 73. Joseph Michael Gandy (English, 1771–1843)
The Bank of England, London: View of the Rotunda Imagined as a Ruin, 1798, pen and watercolor, 66 × 102 cm (26 × 40⅛ in.)
London, Sir John Soane's Museum

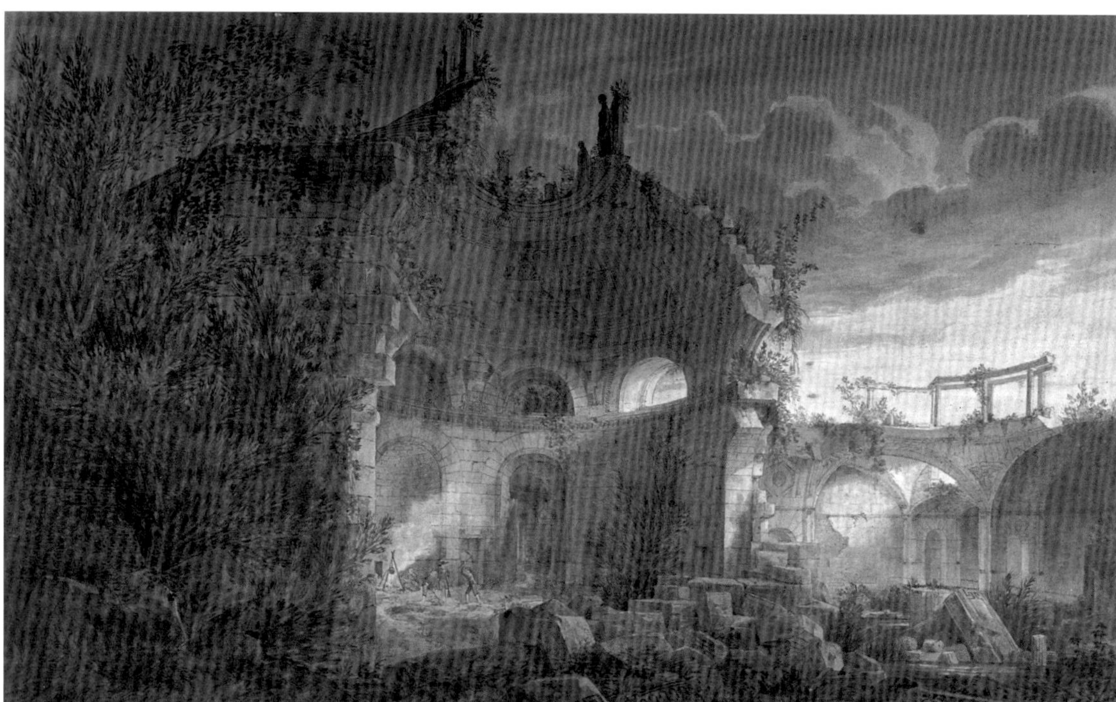

into familiar historical terrain. It turned the ultimate emblem of a frighteningly unknowable future into a vehicle for contemplating the perpetual recurrence of the past. Gandy's ruin thus functioned in a manner similar to Robert's. It prognosticated destruction, while at the same time evincing the tested capacity of the world to sustain contingency. It foretold the reunion of future and past, the better to reconcile viewers to a state of uncertainty.

Futures and Ruins

Sometime after the arrival in Paris of the convoy bearing the Apollo Belvedere and other treasures from Rome, probably in 1798 or 1799, Robert devoted a second painting, intimately sized, to the subject of the Grande Galerie in ruins (fig. 74). The picture eschews in every sense the public ambition of its predecessor: in addition to being about three times smaller than the earlier work, it bears the look of the sketch, as opposed to the finished painting. The recognizable sculptures assembled in the view of 1796 have given way to fluidly rendered forms—faceless torsos, amorphous slabs of marble—that seem on the verge of melting into indistinction. The role of narrative incident—so prominent in the first work, with its assorted peasants, mystified onlookers, and centrally placed artist—has been drastically reduced. The cast of three characters includes the ambiguously occupied woman in brown at left, a second seated woman at right, her back to the viewer, and, beside her, a watchman of sorts bearing a

Fig. 74. Hubert Robert (French, 1733–1808)
Imaginary View of the Grande Galerie in Ruins, ca. 1798–99, oil on canvas, 32 × 40 cm (12⅝ × 15¾ in.)
Paris, Musée du Louvre

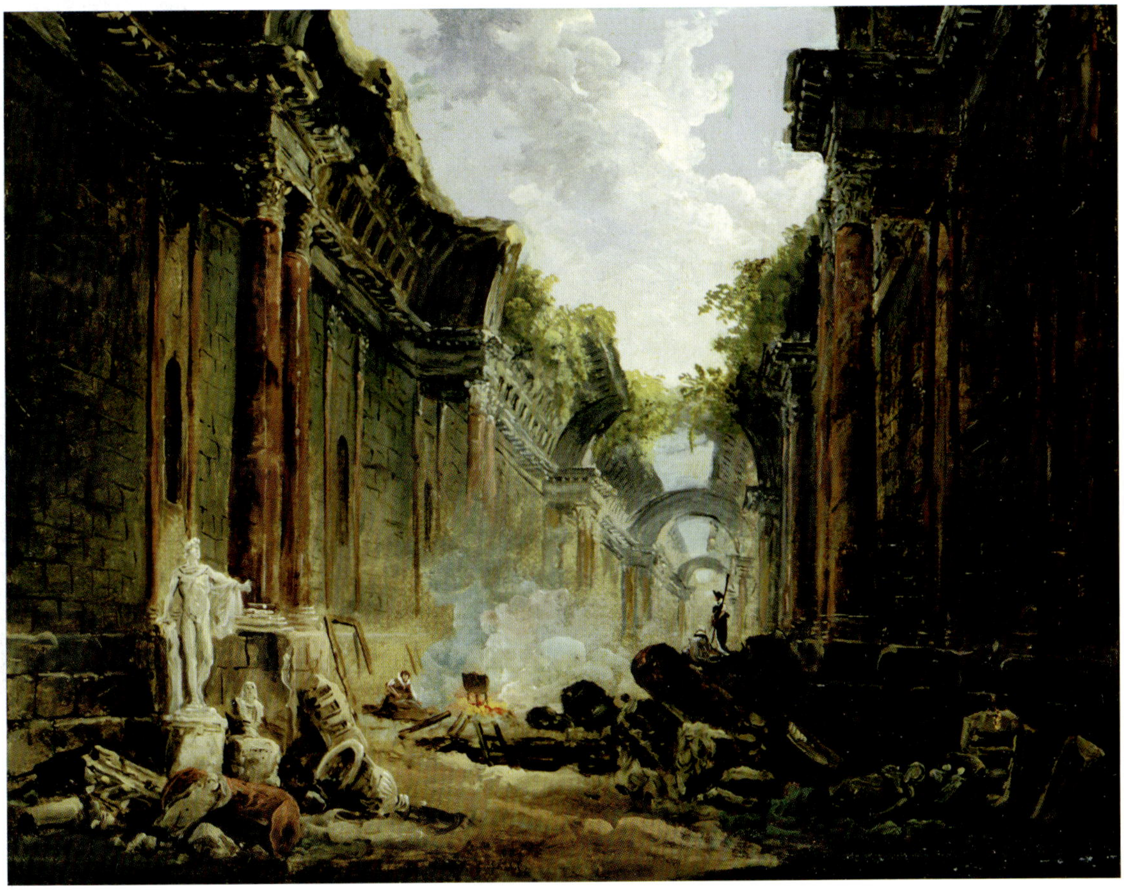

lance, his dark and minute form set in relief against the dull earth tones of the gallery's architectural backdrop. At left stands the luminous, if scrawny, figure of the Apollo, now in the form of the marble sculpture collected from Rome. Empty niches line the museum's walls, ghostly remembrances of the sculptures that formerly occupied them. As in the first version, no trace remains of the vanished paintings; also common to both views is the presence, in lieu of Raphael's picture, of Alexander Rondoni's bust of the artist, perched at the base of the Apollo.[88]

In relation to the painting of 1796, this later work captures the gallery in a state of far more advanced dereliction. The ruin is greener with foliage, its atmosphere heavier with dust and debris. The economy of means employed by Robert in his rendering of the Apollo and, by its base, an object suggestive of the Medici Vase, renders these sculptures all the more diminished, ineffectual as vessels of enduring value. The regenerative promise embodied by the artist who occupied center stage in the former work appears to have long ago expired. The nebulous figure of the watchman assumes the artist's role as absorbed beholder, though the object of his gaze remains obscure.

What is, of course, striking about this effect of pronounced decay is that it is achieved by virtue of the painting's resemblance to an unfinished sketch. And just as the picture insists on its status as a painting interrupted—as a work in the process of becoming a finished object—so too do the gallery's half-decipherable contents seem poised not only to disintegrate but also to coalesce. In characteristic fashion, Robert couples the ruin's connotation of irreversible destruction with the sketch's power to catalyze anticipation. By availing itself of the character of the sketch, the painting, more fully than the preceding work, equates ruination with possibility, decay with imminence. As such, this later view attests all the more to an uneasy historical consciousness. Disabling the eye from wandering the depths of the gallery, from uncovering traces of the museum's former magnificence, are the opaque strokes that linger on the surface—marks that stop short of being descriptive and instead serve to ensure impenetrability. The peculiarly green morass of smoke, emerging to the right of the seated woman and above the cauldron, enforces illegibility. The coloristic streaks that animate the ground plane create a sense of seismic activity; note how the woman in brown, caught in a drift of smoke, seems nearly to levitate. Such enigmatic effects invite the viewer to privilege surface over depth—the unfinished events unfolding *on* the painting, over the retreating remains of history.

This is not simply to claim that the tension in Robert's painting between depth and surface allegorizes an inability to countenance the irreversible passage of time. It is rather to suggest that the artist's insistent exaggeration of this tension—his refusal to posit progression without also interjecting suspense—functioned as a means of processing the central fact of the museum, taken by Hegel to be the basis for aesthetic experience: namely, that its very existence amounted to an admission of latecoming. Robert's *Grande Galerie in Ruins* amplifies simultaneously this state of belatedness and its antithesis in the form of the aesthetic of the unfinished object. What may be gleaned from the work is that the wish to make ruins commensurate with incompletion grew in pace with a dawning sense of occupying a belated moment in history. For following Eliade, it could be said that the anxiety of latecoming is a precondition for the wonder of unknown prospects. Such was the suppressed temporal awareness that shadowed the cult of ruins before the Revolution forced it into consciousness.

If the aesthetic of ruins functioned as an antidote to the terror of history, it did so by occasioning play in place of mourning. Robert's later view of the Grande Galerie in ruins, for all its presentiment of catastrophic loss, nonetheless places the viewer in the position of bringing the inchoate to a state of resolution. In this sense, the painting assigns to the viewer the role occupied, in the painting of 1796, by the draftsman. It is significant that the artist in this earlier view, featured in the midst of incomprehending spectators, seems alone in his capacity to salvage something coherent and recuperative from the gallery's remains. The later work extends to the viewer the challenge of making sense of the ruins or, alternatively, completing imaginatively what has been left unfinished. As such, the painting exemplifies what was most valued in the ruin: that is, its promise to turn viewers into artists. For if ruins appealed to a new consciousness of history, they did so by affirming the hallmark of the moderns—namely, their willingness to "accept the risks entailed by every creative act."[89]

I end with another view of an art collection, a drawing produced by an unknown artist sometime around 1800 (see fig. 77). The work features an elegant room lined entirely with paintings by Robert. We are presumably in the study of the figure who sits behind a desk, his wife and infant by his side. Turned to the left, they draw attention with the direction of their gaze to the presence of a clock atop the cabinet, as well as to the still life on the shelf below—sacks of money alongside perfectly stacked piles of coins. This neat arrangement is in contrast with subtle signs of potential disturbance: a document dangling over the edge of a table at left, another one cropped in the corner, overturned books in the right foreground. Not unlike the subjects featured in the paintings above—a colonnade and a bridge, a triumphal arch and a waterfall—even the stately order of a well-to-do collector's study exists in tense equilibrium with impalpable elements.

The image, as much as it testifies to Robert's lingering renown, bears traces of the artist's declining fortunes. His landscapes *à l'antique* already have an air of faded grandeur, of having been created in—and intended for—an earlier time. Displaced to a postrevolutionary context, Robert's ruins—appreciated in their heydey as unfinished objects awaiting imaginative completion—arouse remembrance. Their bygone character—the gulf between the world they once decorated and the one brought into being with the Terror—is underscored, albeit inadvertently, by one work in particular. Hanging in the first row, the second of three works, is a drawing recognizable as one that Robert executed while in prison at Sainte-Pélagie in 1793 (fig. 75). It shows the artist at right, interrupted from his reading by the arrival of a young jailer bearing provisions. The drawing is one of several works with which Robert chronicled quotidian life in prison, inscribing it with normalcy, and indeed it is the unremarkable quality of these diaristic episodes that makes them moving. The artist's precarious existence is treated with the understated sobriety of a Northern genre scene. In his cell, a composite view of Rome, hanging above his bed, takes its place among a collection of everyday objects. The drawing issues a statement of optimism and endurance against the odds, one reiterated by the Latin inscriptions along the edge of the table and above the door. They read, respectively, "As long as there is life, there is hope" and "The prison of Socrates is the house of honor."[90]

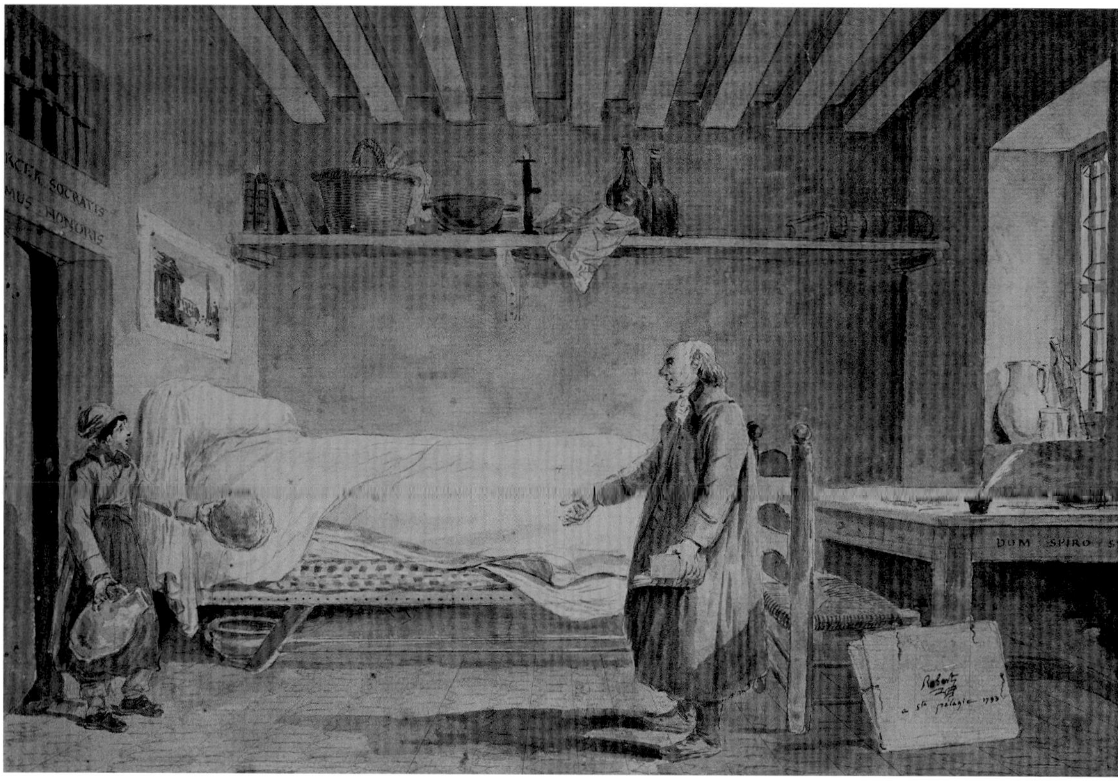

Fig. 75. Hubert Robert (French, 1733–1808)
The Artist in His Cell at Sainte-Pélagie, 1793, pen and wash with watercolor, 22.7 × 32.7 cm (9 × 12⅞ in.) Paris, Musée Carnavalet

Such maxims were nothing new in the artist's oeuvre. Yet their prominence in Robert's work of the revolutionary period suggests, perhaps, an onslaught of faith in the efficacy of ancient aphorisms—in their potential to clarify the unprecedented events of the present. While in Sainte-Pélagie, for instance, Robert produced a watercolor recycling a motif that he had treated in the past: figures amusing themselves on a seesaw—one balanced on a Corinthian capital (fig. 76).[91] A fallen antique bust rests in the foreground; in the background is a ruined triumphal arch. A slab of marble, perched beneath a watchful Farnese Herakles, bears a Latin message that reads, in the words of the Gospel according to Matthew 23:12: "Whoever exalts himself will be humbled, and whoever humbles himself will be exalted." Together, text and image assimilate unhinging incident to timeless verse, and a temporality of undivinable occurrence to one of rhythmic cyclicality.

It may be the interior of the cradle at their feet—reminder of life's renewable riches—that occupies the attention of the figures in the study interior. Yet the lateral direction of their gaze suggests they may equally be contemplating the view through the window, prefiguring the Romantic *Rückenfigur.*[92] If so, it is fitting that they turn to behold not Robert's artificial landscapes, but an absent subject whose very obscurity already signals the disenchantment of the eighteenth-century cult of ruins and its power to substitute plenitude in place of the negative.

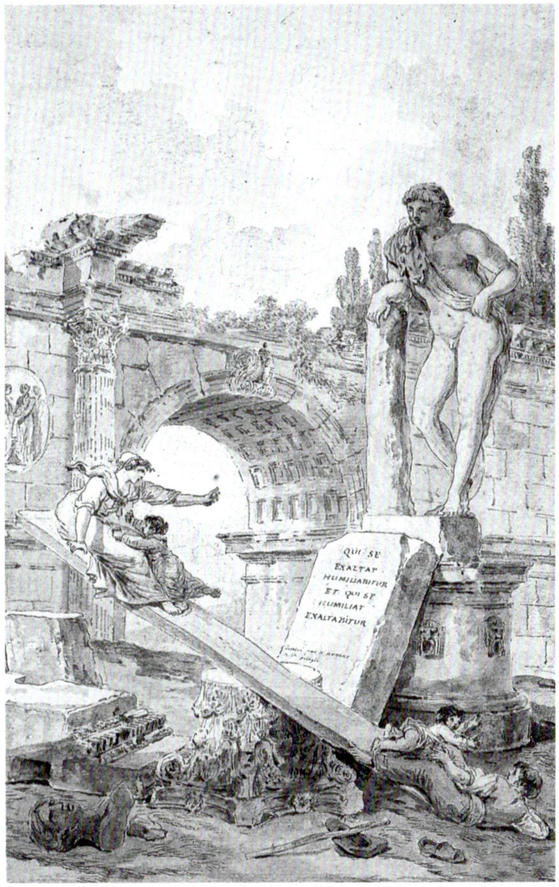

Fig. 76. Hubert Robert (French, 1733–1808)
The Seesaw, 1794?, pen, gray wash, and watercolor over black crayon, 37 × 24 cm (14⅝ × 9½ in.)
Private collection

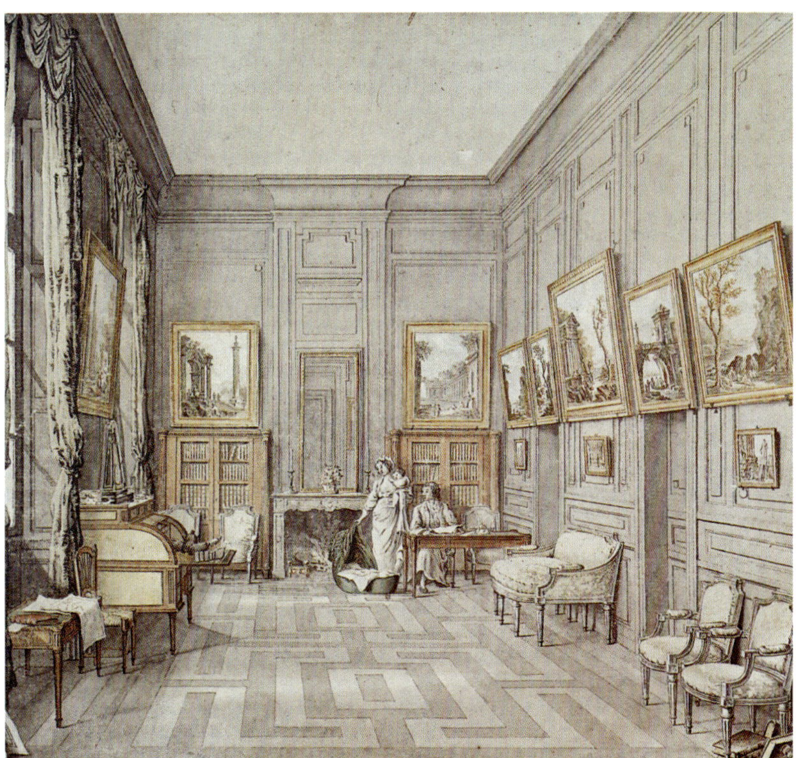

Fig. 77. *Interior of a Study*
Ca. 1800, pen, black ink, gray wash, and watercolor, 34 × 35.5 cm (13⅜ × 14 in.)
Private collection

NOTES

1 Quoted in Pierre-Jean Grosley, *New Observations on Italy and Its Inhabitants,* trans. Thomas Nugent (London: Printed for L. Davis & C. Reymers, 1769), 2:2–3.

2 François-René, vicomte de Chateaubriand, *An Historical, Political, and Moral Essay on Revolutions, Ancient and Modern* (London: Printed for J. Colburn, 1815), 32–33.

3 Robert appears to have retained this position, in which capacity he oversaw restorations and helped build the royal collection, until the fall of the monarchy. From 1795 to 1802 (when Dominique Vivant-Denon took over the museum and reconfigured its administration), Robert served as one of five members of the Conservatoire, a body charged by the Comité d'instruction publique "with recovering from all provisional depots the art objects necessary to complement the Museum and with proposing all the means of perfecting this monument." Yveline Cantarel-Besson, ed., *La naissance du Musée du Louvre: La politique muséologique sous la Révolution d'après les archives des musées nationaux* (Paris: Éditions de la Réunion des musées nationaux, 1981), 1:xix. Robert's colleagues included Fragonard, Pajou, De Wailly, and the restorer Jean-Michel Picault. See Marie-Catherine Sahut, ed., *Le Louvre d'Hubert Robert,* exh. cat. (Paris: Éditions de la Réunion des musées nationaux, 1979).

4 The challenge of how to light the gallery—whether by overhead windows or by the less costly method of flank lighting—had preoccupied museum officials since 1778, when Robert joined a committee headed by the architect Soufflot to resolve the issue. (Indecision over how best to proceed kept the museum from being inaugurated under the ancien régime.) Also subject to debate was the issue of whether and how to divide the gallery. See James L. Connelly, "The Grand Gallery of the Louvre and the Museum Project: Architectural Problems," *Journal of the Society of Architectural Historians* 31, no. 2 (1972): 120–32; Andrew McClellan, *Inventing the Louvre: Art, Politics, and the Origins of the Modern Museum in Eighteenth-Century Paris* (Cambridge: Cambridge Univ. Press, 1994), 53–60; and Georges Teyssot, "'The Simple Day and the Light of the Sun': Lights and Shadows in the Museum," translated from the Italian by Jessica Levine, *Assemblage,* no. 12 (1990): 59–83.

5 A complete list of the works included in Robert's painting appears in Sahut, *Louvre d'Hubert Robert,* 28–29, no. 58. Works that had hung in the recent exhibition and that are featured in Robert's view include, in addition to Raphael's *Holy Family,* Caravaggio's *Alof de Wignacourt with His Page,* Pier Francesco Mola's *Saint Bruno,* Guido Reni's *Daianeira Abducted by the Centaur Nessus,* Andrea del Sarto's *Charity,* and Titian's *Entombment of Christ.* See *Notice des tableaux des trois écoles choisies dans la collection du Muséum des Arts, rassemblés au Salon d'exposition, pendant les travaux de la galerie au mois de prairial an 4,* in *Collection Deloynes: Collection de pièces sur les beaux-arts imprimées et manuscrites (1673–1808)* (Paris: Bibliothèque nationale de France, 1980), vol. 18, no. 482.

6 T. B. Éméric-David, *Musée Olympique de l'École vivante des beaux-arts* (1796), republished in *Histoire de la peinture au moyen-âge...* (Paris: Charles Gosselin, 1842), 296.

7 Part of the Grande Galerie was reopened on 7 April 1799 with an exhibition featuring French and Flemish painting; the public had to wait an additional two years—until 14 July 1801, when an exhibition of Italian painting was unveiled—to see the Grande Galerie in its near entirety. For a concise history of the museum's renovations and early history, see J. J. Marquet de Vasselot, *Répertoire des vues des salles du Musée du Louvre* (Paris: A. Colin, 1946): xi–xix. The dual challenges faced by the Conservatoire—appeasing a critical public and working under the authoritarian Comité d'instruction publique—are described in Édouard Pommier, "L'administration du Musée du Louvre entre pouvoir politique et opinion publique (1795–1799)," in *Mélanges en hommage à Françoise Cachin* (Paris: Gallimard / Réunion des musées nationaux, 2002), 46–61. The hurdles facing the museum and causing the postponement of its opening are recounted in *Musée Central des Arts: Pièces relatives à l'administration de cet établissement...* (Paris: Imprimerie de la république, 1798).

8 Robert was advised by one such critic, "D'ôter ce tableau, pour détruire / Le mauvais effet qu'il produit" (Remove this painting, in order to destroy / The unpleasant effect that it produces); *Les étrivières de Juvénal; ou, Satire sur les tableaux exposés au Louvre, l'an V* (Paris:

Chez les marchands de nouveautés, 1796), n.p. Following the suspension of a jury, the Salon of 1796 featured a staggering number of (notoriously mediocre) artworks—more than one thousand—which likely accounts for the scant number of critics who took note of Robert's pendants. On this "failed" and meagerly attended Salon, see Régis Michel, "L'art des Salons," in Philippe Bordes and Régis Michel, eds., *Aux armes et aux arts! Les arts de la Révolution, 1789–1799* (Paris: Adam Biro, 1988), 66–74.

9 *Critique du Salon; ou, Les tableaux en vaudevilles* (Paris: Imprimerie des frères rapsodistes, 1796), n.p.:

> Du *Muséum,* dans un tableau,
> *Robert* en architecte habile,
> Tu fis un projet assez beau:
> Mais le pendant est inutile.
> Pourquoi détruire, dis-le moi,
> Tous les objets qui l'embellissent
> A le détruire mieux que toi,
> tant de gens si bien réussissent.

(Of the *Museum,* in a painting, / *Robert* as an able architect, / you made a rather beautiful project: / but the pendant is pointless. / Tell me, why destroy, / all the objects that embellish it / In destroying it better than you, / so many men so well succeed.)

10 The influence of such works by Robert on Boullée is discussed in André Corboz, *Peinture militante et architecture révolutionnaire: À propos du thème du tunnel chez Hubert Robert* (Basel: Birkhäuser, 1978), 6–11.

11 Quoted in Cantarel-Besson, *Naissance du Musée du Louvre,* 1:xxv. McClellan discusses the installation methods employed in private picture galleries and their replacement by the museum's chronological display in *Inventing the Louvre;* see esp. "Introduction," chaps. 1, 2. Hans Belting contrasts the ancien régime collector's "elitist" ideal of a "school of taste" with the inclusive spirit of the museum's "school of history" (27) in *The Invisible Masterpiece,* trans. Helen Atkins (Chicago: Univ. of Chicago Press, 2001), chap. 1.

12 The challenges of realizing this ambition included not only the task of inventorying the vast number of objects in the museum as well as the acquisition of artworks (through either purchase or exchange) that the Conservatoire considered necessary to its collection but the elimination of items deemed unsuitable (most commonly because they smacked of the overthrown feudal order). For a summary, see Cantarel-Besson, *Naissance du Musée du Louvre,* 1:xxv–xxix. It is also worth noting that the artist's friend, the painter Charles Fournier des Ormes, credited Robert with being the first advocate of hanging paintings according to school—an erroneous claim, but one that nonetheless signals the artist's allegiance to the historicist approach; Charles Fournier des Ormes, *Épître à Hubert Robert* (Paris: Persan, 1822), 117–18.

13 So great was the impact of Johann Joachim Winckelmann's *Geschichte der Kunst des Alterthums* that the Commission temporaire des arts decreed that copies of Hendrik Jansen's French translation (*L'histoire de l'art de l'antiquité*) of 1790–94 be "placée dans chaque musée d'art et dans les principaux bibliothèques de la République." *Procès-verbaux de la Commission temporaire des arts,* 13 February 1795, 117; cited in Dominique Poulot, "La naissance du Musée," in Michel and Bordes, *Aux armes et aux arts!* 226.

14 McClellan, *Inventing the Louvre,* 81.

15 Armand-Guy Kersaint, *Discours sur les monuments publics, prononcé au conseil du département de Paris, le 15 décembre 1791* (Paris: Imprimerie de P. Didot l'ainé, 1792), v–vii.

16 Jean-Baptise-Pierre Lebrun, *Quelques idées sur la disposition, l'arrangement et la décoration du museum national* (Paris: Imprimerie de Didot jeune, an III [1794–95]), 12.

17 Niklas Luhmann, *Observations on Modernity,* trans. William Whobrey (Stanford, Calif.: Stanford Univ. Press, 1998), 66.

18 Kersaint, *Discours sur les monuments publics,* 3.

19 See on this subject Andrew McClellan, "Nationalism and the Origins of the Museum in France," in Gwendolyn Wright, ed., *The Formation of National Collections of Art and Archaeology* (Washington, D.C.: National Gallery of Art, 1996), 29–39.

20 See Catherine Boulot, "Hubert Robert: Un peintre emprisonné sous la Terreur," in Catherine Boulot, Jean de Cayeux, and Hélène Moulin, *Hubert Robert et la Révolution,* exh. cat. (Valence: Musée de Valence, 1989), 19–27. Catherine the Great's oft-cited letter of 5 June 1791 to Friedrich Melchior, Freiherr von Grimm—"Because this painter prefers to paint ruins, and now has so many before his eyes, he has great reason not to move from the land of ruins"—is reprinted in Louis Réau, "Correspondance artistique de Grimm avec Catherine II," in Louis Réau, G. Lundberg, and R. A. Weigert, *L'art français dans les pays du nord et de l'est de l'Europe (XVIIIe–XIXe siècles)* (Paris: A. Colin, 1932), 186.

21 Less dispassionately, Robert produced artworks while in prison that reflected with remorse on the violent turn of the Revolution; one such drawing in the Albertina collection in Vienna—*The Sleep of Marat*—satirizes David's painting of the slain journalist, depicting him not as virtuous martyr but rather as drunken brute, emblematic of the madness that had led to the painter's own misfortune. For an interpretation of Robert's Revolution-era works and of their negative allusions to contemporary events, see the epilogue of Paula Rea Radisich, *Hubert Robert: Painted Spaces of the Enlightenment* (Cambridge: Cambridge Univ. Press, 1998).

22 Statues of Minerva feature in a number of works by Robert executed during the revolutionary period. On the symbolic use made by Robert of the goddess of wisdom during the Terror, see Boulot, Cayeux, and Moulin, *Hubert Robert et la Révolution,* 108, no. 32.

23 See note 9.

24 Paris was hailed as "le Nouvel Athenes" beginning in 1789. On efforts in the arts to secure the city's status as such, see in particular Édouard Pommier, *L'art de la liberté: Doctrines et débats de la Révolution française* (Paris: Gallimard, 1991). On the import of Winckelmann's *Geschichte der Kunst des Alterthums* in the Directory period, see Édouard Pommier, *Winckelmann, inventeur de l'histoire de l'art* (Paris: Gallimard, 2003), 272–78.

25 Pajou was among the artists to sign Quatremère's petition protesting the spoliation. Curiously, the newspaper *L'éclair* inaccurately listed Robert among the signers (1er fructidor an IV/18 August 1796: 4). Cited in Pommier, *Art de la liberté,* 435. The petition is printed in Antoine Quatremère de Quincy, *Lettres à Miranda sur le déplacement des monuments de l'art de l'Italie* (1796), ed. Édouard Pommier (Paris: Macula, 1989), 141–42.

26 Included in both of Robert's pendants is Alessandro Rondoni's *Bust of Raphael*—after the seventeenth-century original by Paolo Naldini then in the Pantheon in Rome—which was in the Musée du Louvre's collection as of 1793. Robert has also included in the *Grande Galerie in Ruins,* behind the artist, what appears to be the Borghese Vase—an object that entered the Louvre's collection only after Napoléon's purchase of the Borghese antiquities in 1807. On the former, see Sahut, *Louvre d'Hubert Robert,* 29, 60n138; on the latter, see Charles Saunier, *Les conquêtes artistiques de la Révolution et de l'empire; reprises et abandons des alliés en 1815; leurs conséquences sur les musées d'Europe* (Paris: H. Laurens, 1902), 42–43.

27 Quatremère de Quincy, *Lettres,* 129.

28 *La décade philosophique,* no. 56 (30 vendémiaire an IV/22 October 1795): 334–35, 337. Duval wrote under the pseudonym "Polyscope." (Regrettably, the artworks he reviewed the following year did not include Robert's pendants.)

29 Peter Fritzsche, *Stranded in the Present: Modern Time and the Melancholy of History* (Cambridge: Harvard Univ. Press, 2004), 5.

30 The original title of the work was "Lettres sur le préjudice qu'occasionneraient aux arts et à la science, le déplacement des monuments de l'art de l'Italie, le démembrement de ses écoles et la spoliation de ses collections, galeries, musées, etc." The diffusion of Quatremère's writings prior to their publication is discussed by Pommier in his introduction to Quatremère de Quincy, *Lettres.*

31 Quatremère de Quincy, *Lettres,* 87–88, 97, 115, 102; the paragraph is translated in Francis Haskell and Nicholas Penny, *Taste and the Antique: The Lure of Classical Sculpture, 1500–1900* (London: Yale Univ. Press, 1981), 110.

32 Quatremère de Quincy, *Lettres,* 97, 110–11, 128.

33 Didier Maleuvre, *Museum Memories: History, Technology, Art* (Stanford, Calif.: Stanford Univ. Press, 1999), 32.

34 See, for instance, Maleuvre's account. The quotation is from Antoine Quatremère de Quincy, *Considérations morales sur la destination des ouvrages de l'art* (1819) (Paris: Fayard, 1989), 84–85; translated in Maleuvre, *Museum Memories,* 33. Sylvia Lavin challenges this view of Quatremère as conservative academic in *Quatremère de Quincy and the Invention of a Modern Language of Architecture* (Cambridge: MIT Press, 1992). Quatremère's biography is recounted in this study as well as in René Schneider, *Quatremère de Quincy et son intervention dans les arts (1788–1850)* (Paris: Hachette, 1910).

35 The concept was introduced by Luc Barbier on 20 September 1794; cited in J. J. Guillaume, *Procès-verbaux du Comité d'instruction publique de la Convention nationale* (Paris: Imprimerie nationale, 1914), 5:75. Henri Grégoire invokes the "dernier domicile" in *Rapport sur les destructions opérées par le vandalisme et sur les moyens de le réprimer* (Paris, 31 August 1794); both quoted in Pommier, *Winckelmann, inventeur de l'histoire de l'art,* 239. On repatriation, see Pommier, *Art de la liberté,* esp. 397–403.

36 *Le rédacteur,* 25 messidor an IV/13 July 1796: 3; *Le véridique ou courier universel,* 10 messidor an IV/28 June 1796: 2; and *Le censeur des journaux,* 17 prairial an IV/5 June 1796: 2. Quoted in Pommier, *Art de la liberté,* 408, 405, 404.

37 Pierre-Louis Roederer, "Des tableaux d'Italie," *Journal de Paris,* 19 messidor an IV/7 July 1796: 1159–60; and *Journal de Paris,* 27 messidor an IV/15 July 1796: 1292. Quoted in Pommier, *Art de la liberté,* 407, 410.

38 Quatremère de Quincy, *Lettres,* 138.

39 John Dewey, *Art as Experience* (New York: Capricorn Books, 1959), 8–9; cited in James H. Bunn, "The Aesthetics of British Mercantilism," *New Literary History* 11, no. 2 (1980): 319.

40 On Quatremère's critique of the museum as a site of commercial transaction, see Daniel J. Sherman, "Quatremère/Benjamin/Marx: Art Museums, Aura, and Commodity Fetishism," in Daniel J. Sherman and Irit Rogoff, eds., *Museum Culture: Histories, Discourses, Spectacles* (Minneapolis: Univ. of Minnesota Press, 2000), 123–43. Quatremère de Quincy, *Lettres,* 139; the second quotation, on 96, is translated in Sherman, "Quatremère/Benjamin/Marx," 130.

41 Quatremère de Quincy, *Lettres,* 96, 116.

42 Quatremère de Quincy, *Lettres,* 133–34, 136–37; translated in Sherman, "Quatremère/Benjamin/Marx," 130–31.

43 *Le moniteur universel,* no. 335 (5 fructidor an IV/22 August 1796): 1; cited in Pommier, *Art de la liberté,* 436.

44 In 1777, the remains of an ancient house located on the grounds of the Villa Negroni (between Santa Maria Maggiore and Santa Maria degli Angeli) were discovered and promptly excavated. The residence's perfectly preserved wall paintings were purchased by the painter and dealer Henry Tresham, who, in turn, sold them to Frederick Hervey, bishop of Derry (later earl of Bristol). See Hetty Joyce, "The Ancient Frescoes from the Villa Negroni and Their Influence in the Eighteenth and Nineteenth Centuries," *Art Bulletin* 65, no. 3 (1983): 423–40.

45 The counterpetition is printed in Quatremère de Quincy, *Lettres,* 143–46.

46 Jean-Baptise-Pierre Lebrun, *Réflexions sur le muséum national* (Paris: Réunion des musées nationaux, 1992), 8. Lebrun interestingly proposes that museums might function as a substitute for the commercial port, recommending the establishment of provincial museums in the nation's interior as sources of supplementary income. See Lebrun, *Quelques idées,* 26–27. Little wonder that the minister of the interior, Jean-Marie Roland de La Platière, anxious to ensure that no suggestion of commercial interest taint the museum, campaigned to keep Lebrun from joining the institution's administration. See on this subject Pommier, "Postface," in Lebrun, *Réflexions sur le muséum.*

47 Christopher M. Greene, "Alexandre Lenoir and the Musée des Monuments Français during the French Revolution," *French Historical Studies* 12, no. 2 (1981): 202. On the equation of spoliation with vandalism, see Pommier, *Art de la liberté,* 405–6.

48 Joachim Lebreton, *La décade philosophique,* no. 81 (30 messidor an IV/18 July 1796): 183. Translated in Jane Van Nimmen, "Responses to Raphael's Paintings at the Louvre, 1798–1848" (Ph.D. diss., University of Maryland, 1986), 44.

49 The painting's inscription—"H. Robert/1789"—appears on the box of pigments in the middle ground at left. See in support of this date Boulot, Cayeux, and Moulin, *Hubert Robert et la Révolution,* 146, no. 47. My description employs details provided in Sahut, *Louvre d'Hubert Robert,* 42, no. 109, in which she proposes an execution date of circa 1800—based in part on the ornamental pattern of the rug at left. She has since suggested an execution date of 1789, in Bernadette Caille and Edit Kiss, eds., *Ombres et lumières: Quatre siècles de peinture française,* exh. cat. (Budapest: Musée des Beaux-Arts, 2005), 178, no. 52. (The later date is maintained in such recent Louvre catalogs as Michael Kiene, *Pannini* [Paris: Réunion des musées nationaux, 1992], 162, no. 54.) Further evidence in favor of the later date exists in a sketch the artist appears to have produced after 1794 that similarly features antiquities in the Grande Galerie. In the sketch—*Project for the Museum of Antiques, at the Louvre*—one finds the same two rows of columns that appear in the painting. The sketch may document a project envisioned by Robert to display the museum's sculptures in the west end of the Grande Galerie. Marianne Roland Michel, "From the 'Museum' to the Musée du Louvre: Schemes and Transformations in Connexion with Two Paintings by Hubert Robert," *Burlington Magazine* 105, no. 720 (1963): i–iv. Robert's painting, if indeed it was executed in the late 1790s, would not be the only one of his museum views to bear a misleading inscription; a painting discussed below—*Artist Drawing Antiques before the Petite Galerie*—bears an inscription date of 1781 but is believed to have been executed in the late 1790s.

50 Georg Wilhelm Friedrich Hegel, *Aesthetics: Lectures on Fine Art,* trans. T. M. Knox (Oxford: Clarendon Press, 1975), 2:797–811.

51 Ferdinando Arisi, *Gian Paolo Panini* (Piacenza: Cassa di Risparmio, 1961), 215–16, nos. 249–50.

52 John Scott, *A Visit to Paris in 1814; Being a Review of the Moral, Political, Intellectual, and Social Condition of the French Capital,* 4th ed. (London: Printed for Longman, Hurst, Rees, Orme & Brown, 1816), 248. My thanks to Andrew McClellan for alerting me to this source and for sharing with me his unpublished research on reactions against the museum.

53 My discussion draws on accounts of the pendants offered in Henry A. Millon, ed., *The Triumph of the Baroque: Architecture in Europe, 1600–1750,* exh. cat. (New York: Rizzoli, 1999), 426–27, nos. 1–2; and Edgar Peter Bowron and Joseph J. Rishel, eds., *Art in Rome in the Eighteenth Century,* exh. cat. (Philadelphia: Philadelphia Museum of Art, 2000), 425–27, nos. 275–76.

54 The quotation—cited in Bunn, "Aesthetics of British Mercantilism," 315—is from James Harrington, *Oceana,* ed. Sten Bodvar Liljegren (Heidelberg: C. Winter, 1924), 185. The fall of Rome was widely attributed, as Bunn notes, to the effects of its plunder. On the French context for this discourse, see John Shovlin, *The Political Economy of Virtue: Luxury, Patriotism, and the Origins of the French Revolution* (Ithaca, N.Y.: Cornell Univ. Press, 2006); J. G. A. Pocock, *Barbarism and Religion* (Cambridge: Cambridge Univ. Press, 2003), 3:325–71; and Andrew Jainchill, *Reimagining Politics after the Terror: The Republican Origins of French Liberalism* (Ithaca, N.Y.: Cornell Univ. Press, 2008), chap. 4.

55 A.-C. Thibaudeau, *Mémoires sur la Convention, et le Directoire* (Paris: Baudouin frères, 1824), 1:181; translated in Jainchill, *Reimagining Politics after the Terror,* 149.

56 Printed in *La décade philosophique,* 10 thermidor an VI/28 July 1798: 230–32; cited in McClellan, *Inventing the Louvre,* 123.

57 Daniel Wildenstein, *Documents complémentaires au catalogue de l'oeuvre de Louis David* (Paris: Fondation Wildenstein, 1973), 171, no. 1474; translated in Robert Goldwater and Marco Treves, *Artists on Art, from the XIV to the XX Century* (New York: Pantheon Books, 1947), 206.

58 For an overview, see Sahut, *Louvre d'Hubert Robert,* 45–50; as well as Christiane Aulanier, *La Petite Galerie: Appartement d'Anne d'Autriche, Salles Romaines* (Paris: Éditions des musées nationaux, 1955), 62–77.

59 My thanks to Hérica Valladares for helping me with these identifications. A Centaur taken from the collection of the comte d'Orsay and a bronze Apollo were placed in the museum circa 1795–97. See Sahut, *Louvre d'Hubert Robert,* 61–62n183.

60 Robert was likely inspired by the storage of sculptures being moved in and out of the Jardin de l'Infante, where antiquities were temporarily placed on display. Aulanier, *Petite Galerie,* 64–65.

61 Quatremère de Quincy, *Lettres,* 100.

62 On issues of originality and reproduction in the eighteenth century, especially as they pertain to the dissemination of copies of ancient sculpture, see in particular Haskell and Penny, *Taste and the Antique;* Viccy Coltman, *Fabricating the Antique: Neoclassicism in Britain, 1760–1800* (Chicago: Univ. of Chicago Press, 2006), chap. 5; as well as the relevant essays in Anthony Hughes and Erich Ranfft, eds., *Sculpture and Its Reproductions* (London: Reaktion, 1997); and "Art and Replication: Greece, Rome, and Beyond," special issue, *Art History* 29, no. 2 (2006).

63 Viccy Coltman details similar effects of mediation in Johann Zoffany's famous painting of Charles Townley's study, in "Representation, Replication and Collecting in Charles Townley's Late Eighteenth-Century Library," *Art History* 29, no. 2 (2006): 304–24. It is interesting to consider that a discourse against replication informed reactions against the French Revolution; a "fatal copy" is how Chateaubriand derisively characterizes the Revolution's emulation of antiquity. François-René, vicomte de Chateaubriand, *Essai historique, politique et moral sur les révolutions anciennes et modernes considérées dans leurs rapports avec la Révolution française* (1797) (Paris: Gallimard, 1978), 81; cited on p. 30—and discussed as exemplary of the critique of imitation—in François Hartog, "La Révolution française et l'antiquité: Avenir d'une illusion ou cheminement d'un quiproquo?" in Marcel Gauchet, Pierre Manent, and Pierre Rosanvallon, eds., *Situations de la démocratie* (Paris: Seuil-Gallimard, 1993), 30–61. Quatremère similarly contests the possibility of repeating the achievements of the ancients; see Alex Potts, "Political Attitudes and the Rise of Historicism in Art Theory," *Art History* 1, no. 2 (1978): 191–213.

64 Sherman, "Quatremère/Benjamin/Marx," 137. It is instructive in this respect to consider the case of the engraver Pierre Laurent, who received permission from the king in 1791 to reproduce in print the museum collection in its entirety. His efforts resulted in the publication *Musée français,* which appeared between 1803 and 1811. Alexander Tuetey and Jean Guiffrey, eds., *La commission du muséum et la création du Musée du Louvre (1792–1793), Archives de l'art français,* n.s., 3 (Paris, 1909), 84–85, 104–6.

65 Walter Benjamin, "The Work of Art in the Age of Mechanical Reproduction," in idem, *Illuminations,* ed. Hannah Arendt, trans. Harry Zohn (New York: Schocken Books, 1968), 221, 224.

66 Denis Woronoff, *The Thermidorean Regime and the Directory: 1794–1799,* trans. Julian Jackson (Cambridge: Cambridge Univ. Press, 1984), 72.

67 Quatremère de Quincy, *Lettres,* 87.

68 Quatremère de Quincy, *Lettres,* 90, 135.

69 Rebecca L. Spang, "The Ghost of Law: Speculating on Money, Memory and Mississippi in the French Constituent Assembly," *Historical Reflections / Refléxions historiques* 31, no. 1 (2005): 21.

70 Eugene Nelson White, "The French Revolution and the Politics of Government Finance, 1770–1815," *Journal of Economic History* 55, no. 2 (1995), esp. 246–47; see also Woronoff, *Thermidorean Regime,* 91–117. In this sense, Quatremère's hostility to the theft of artworks earmarked for the museum may be likened to what Manuela Albertone describes as the fierce clerical opposition to the state's claim to credibility, resting as it did on the confiscation of church property; see Manuela Albertone, "Le débat sur le crédit public en France et la naissance des assignats," *Économies et sociétés* 24 (1990): 405–29. On the ravaging effects of Directory-era economic turmoil more generally, see Judith A. Miller, "The Aftermath of the Assignat: Plaintiffs in the Age of Property, 1794–1804," in Howard G. Brown and Judith A. Miller, eds., *Taking Liberties: Problems of a New Order from the French Revolution to Napoleon* (Manchester: Palgrave, 2002), 70–91.

71 *Le moniteur universel* 14 (1792): 263; cited and translated in McClellan, *Inventing the Louvre,* 91. Christine Boyer describes this challenge, writing that at a time of "newfangled credit systems and speculative stock markets," the rise of the museum marked the pursuit of "stabilizing roots and permanent values in rare and treasured works of art . . . [whose] material value . . . was enhanced as monetary value dematerialized." Because, she suggests, the need to create a sanctuary of permanent values only underscores their imperiled status in the modern world, the museum "produces more anxiety than it absorbs." M. Christine Boyer, *The City of Collective Memory: Its Historical Imagery and Architectural Entertainments* (Cambridge: MIT Press, 1996), 131.

72 The reference to "precious plunder" is from *La décade philosophique,* 20 prairial an VI/8 June 1798: 496, in an article hailing the arrival of Italy's riches on the anniversary of the Bastille; cited in McClellan, *Inventing the Louvre,* 123. The Bourse was placed below the Galerie d'Apollon, by decree of the Comité de salut public (Committee of public safety) on 13 May 1795; it retained the quarters until 14 January 1796, much to the dismay of the Conservatoire. See Aulanier, *Petite Galerie,* 63–65.

73 The letter is reproduced in Yveline Cantarel-Besson, ed., *Musée du Louvre (janvier 1797–juin 1798): Procès-verbaux du Conseil d'administration du "Musée Central des Arts"* (Paris: Réunion des musées nationaux, 1992), 44.

74 Both quotations are from André Thouin, letter of 6 vendemiaire an VI/27 September 1797. Archives nationales, F^{17} 1275. Thouin was right to worry. The antiquities were taken to the basement of the Louvre and stored there for nearly eighteen months. Not until Napoléon came to power were they put on display in the Galerie des Antiques; see Haskell and Penny, *Taste and the Antique,* 111–12.

75 On 30 March 1795, the Comité d'instruction publique declared that it was "urgent" that the new Conservatoire "accelerate the organization of the Museum . . . and place in stable order the administration of the establishment"; see Cantarel-Besson, *Naissance du Musée du Louvre,* 1:xix.

76 Séance du 13 messidor an III (1 July 1795), no. 294; see Cantarel-Besson, *Naissance du Musée du Louvre,* 1:194.

77 Alexandre Lenoir, *Musée des Monumens Français; ou, Description historique et chronologique . . .* (Paris: L'imprimerie de Guilleminet, an IX [1800]), 1:25; Lebrun, *Réflexions sur le muséum national,* 9. Winckelmann's elaboration of the theory of cyclicality is analyzed in Alex Potts, "Winckelmann's Construction of History," *Art History* 5, no. 4 (1982): 377–407.

78 See in particular Potts's account of the tension between these two modes of understanding history, as borne out in Winckelmann's *Geschichte der Kunst des Alterthums,* in Alex Potts, *Flesh and the Ideal: Winckelmann and the Origins of Art History* (New Haven: Yale Univ. Press, 1994), esp. 11–46, as well as Wolfgang Ernst, "Frames at Work: Museological Imagination and Historical Discourse in Neoclassical Britain," *Art Bulletin* 75, no. 3 (1993): 481–98. For its role in the early history of museums, see, for instance, Belting, *Invisible Masterpiece,* chap. 1; and Anthony Vidler, *The Writing of the Walls: Architectural Theory in the Late Enlightenment* (Princeton: Princeton Architectural Press, 1987), 167–73.

79 Belting, *Invisible Masterpiece,* 39.

80 McClellan notes that the ideal of a top-lighted *pinacotheca* (picture gallery) is discussed by Vitruvius in *De architectura,* translated by Claude Perrault in 1673. See *Inventing the Louvre,* 57. Robert's client, the notary Duclos-Defresnoy, had in his *hôtel* in the faubourg Poissonnière a gallery with a windowed ceiling, as noted in Jean de Cayeux with Catherine Boulot, *Hubert Robert* (Paris: Fayard, 1989), 177. More famously, the public exhibition space opened by Lebrun on rue de Clery featured skylights; it was the favorable impression left by his gallery that persuaded the committee convened by d'Angiviller to recommend top lighting, despite the staggering costs. See Sahut, *Louvre d'Hubert Robert,* 19.

81 *Notice des tableaux des trois écoles choisies dans la collection du Muséum des Arts,* 6.

82 Kersaint notes the narrowness of the Grande Galerie in *Discours sur les monuments publics,* 46. The quoted words belong to the architect Charles-Axel Guillaumot, describing the thrill

he felt upon first visiting the space in 1778, alongside his colleagues on the design committee. Charles-Axel Guillaumot, *Mémoire sur la manière d'éclairer la galerie du Louvre* (Paris, 1797), 21–22; cited and translated in McClellan, *Inventing the Louvre,* 54.

83 Georg Simmel, "The Ruin" (1911), in Kurt H. Wolff, ed., *Essays on Sociology, Philosophy, and Aesthetics* (New York: Harper & Row, 1965), 260–63.

84 Mircea Eliade, *The Myth of the Eternal Return; or, Cosmos and History,* trans. Willard R. Trask (Princeton: Princeton Univ. Press, 1971), chap. 4.

85 On the genre of anticipatory ruins, see Philippe Junod, "Ruines anticipées ou l'histoire au futur antérieur," in *L'homme face à son histoire* (Lausanne: Payot, 1983), 23–47; Philippe Junod, "Future in the Past," *Oppositions* 26 (1984): 46–63; and Günter Metken, "Les ruines anticipées," in Anne Poirier and Patrick Poirier, eds., *Domus Aurea: Fascination des ruines* (Paris: Centre Georges Pompidou, 1978), 19–24.

86 Brian Lukacher, *Joseph Gandy: An Architectural Visionary in Georgian England* (London: Thames & Hudson, 2006), 165.

87 See Daniel M. Abramson, *Building the Bank of England: Money, Architecture, Society, 1694–1942* (New Haven: Yale Univ. Press, 2005), esp. chap. 5. Werner Oechslin suggests that Gandy's views of the Bank of England in ruins not only legitimized Soane's building by likening it to an ancient monument but also brought transparency to an otherwise mysterious institution. See his "Die Bank of England—und ihre Darstellung als Ruine," *Archithese* 11, no. 2 (1981): 19–25.

88 See the entry on this painting in *L'empire du temps: Mythes et créations,* exh. cat. (Paris: Réunion des musées nationaux, 2000), 174, no. 169.

89 Eliade, *Myth of the Eternal Return,* 156.

90 See on both drawings—the *Interior of a Study* as well as Robert's drawing of his cell—Boulot, Cayeux, and Moulin, *Hubert Robert et la Révolution,* 160, no. 52; 80, no. 20.

91 On this drawing and related works, see Boulot, Cayeux, and Moulin, *Hubert Robert et la Révolution,* 118, no. 37. A drawing in the Fogg Art Museum, circa 1780–85, features the same theme. See Victor I. Carlson, *Hubert Robert: Drawings and Watercolors,* exh. cat. (Washington, D.C.: National Gallery of Art, 1978), 138, no. 56.

92 I have in mind such works by Caspar David Friedrich as his *Woman at the Window* (1822). On the *Rückenfigur*—the figure within the painting who turns away from the viewer—as Romantic trope, see Joseph Leo Koerner, *Caspar David Friedrich and the Subject of Landscape* (New Haven: Yale Univ. Press, 1995), esp. 159–66.

Illustration Credits

Fig. 2 © Collection Rijksmuseum, Amsterdam
Fig. 3 Fitzwilliam Museum / The Bridgeman Art Library
Fig. 4 The Pierpont Morgan Library, New York. Purchased as the Gift of The Fellows with the Special Assistance of an Anonymous Contribution from a Foundation. 1958.5
Fig. 5 Getty Research Institute, acc. no. 88-B19555. © J. Paul Getty Trust
Fig. 6 Courtesy Musée Valence
Fig. 7 © Musées de la Ville de Rouen. Bequest of Jules Hédou, 1907. Photo: Catherine Lancien / Carole Loisel
Fig. 8 Property of the Conseil général de l'Oise, Ermenonville, France. Photo: © Denis Mariolle
Fig. 9 Courtesy Didier Aaron
Fig. 10 Getty Research Institute, 95-FO. © J. Paul Getty Trust
Fig. 11 Getty Research Institute, 92-F51. © J. Paul Getty Trust
Fig. 12 Bibliothèque nationale de France
Fig. 14 Image courtesy of the Board of Trustees, National Gallery of Art, Washington, D.C. Gift of Ivan E. Phillips and Jacqueline Getty
Fig. 15 Bibliothèque nationale de France
Fig. 16 Getty Research Institute, 90-B18412. © J. Paul Getty Trust
Fig. 17 Getty Research Institute, 90-B18427 © J. Paul Getty Trust
Fig. 18 © The Metropolitan Museum of Art / Art Resource, New York. Edward Pearce Casey Fund, 1979 (1979.572)
Fig. 19 Getty Research Institute, 94-F121. © J. Paul Getty Trust
Fig. 20 Reproduction by permission of the Syndics of the Fitzwilliam Museum, Cambridge
Fig. 21 © Erich Lessing / Art Resource, New York
Fig. 22 © Réunion des musées nationaux / Art Resource, New York
Fig. 23 Bibliothèque nationale de France
Fig. 24 © Erich Lessing / Art Resource, New York
Fig. 25 Restricted gift of Alan Rutenberg, Margaret Day Blake and Harold Joachim Endowments, 1990.140, The Art Institute of Chicago. Photo © The Art Institute of Chicago
Fig. 26 Bibliothèque nationale de France
Fig. 27 Getty Research Institute, 2001.PR.3**. © J. Paul Getty Trust
Fig. 28 Getty Research Institute, 88-B19555. © J. Paul Getty Trust
Fig. 29 Getty Research Institute, 88-B19555. © J. Paul Getty Trust
Fig. 30 Purchased in 1983 with donations from Sophia Giesecke and Sara and Johan Emil Graumanns (NM 6765)
Fig. 31 Photo: © Städel Museum–ARTOTHEK
Fig. 32 The Art Institute of Chicago, Gift of Clarence Buckingham, 1900.383. Photo © The Art Institute of Chicago
Fig. 33 Bibliothèque nationale de France
Fig. 34 Musée des beaux-arts, Pau
Fig. 35 Museum-Estate Arkhangelskoye, Moscow region
Fig. 36 Pushkin Museum of Fine Arts, Moscow
Figs. 37, 38 © Musée Carnavalet / Roger-Viollet
Fig. 39 The Pierpont Morgan Library, New York. Gift of Mrs. Allerton Cushman in honor of Mr. Janos Scholz. 1973.51
Figs. 40, 41 Bibliothèque nationale de France
Fig. 42 Getty Research Institute, 1376-798. © J. Paul Getty Trust
Fig. 43 © Musée Carnavalet / Roger-Viollet
Fig. 44 © Staatliche Kunsthalle Karlsruhe 2009. Photo: W. Pankoke
Fig. 45 Photo: Scala/White Images / Art Resource, New York
Fig. 46 Getty Research Institute, 90-B18428 © J. Paul Getty Trust
Fig. 47 Getty Research Institute, 90-B18416 © J. Paul Getty Trust
Fig. 48 Getty Research Institute, 84-B30675. © J. Paul Getty Trust
Figs. 49, 50 Bibliothèque nationale de France
Fig. 51 © Musée départemental d'art ancien et contemporain, Epinal. Photo: Bernard Prud'homme, 2006
Fig. 52 © Musée départemental d'art ancien et contemporain, Epinal. Photo: Bernard Prud'homme, 2006
Fig. 53 The Power Corporation of Canada Art Collection
Fig. 54 Bibliothèque nationale de France
Fig. 55 © Bridgeman-Giraudon / Art Resource, New York
Fig. 56 © Bibliothèque municipale de Besançon
Fig. 57 Getty Research Institute, 2007.PR.103** © J. Paul Getty Trust
Fig. 58 © Bibliothèque municipale de Besançon
Fig. 59 Getty Research Institute, 2007.PR.103** © J. Paul Getty Trust
Fig. 60 © Yale University Art Gallery / Art Resource, New York. Gift of Mr. and Mrs. James W. Fosburgh, B.A. 1933, M.A. 1935. 1957.34.1
Fig. 61 Getty Research Institute, 90-B18412 © J. Paul Getty Trust
Fig. 62 Musée des beaux-arts, Dunkirk, France / Giraudon / The Bridgeman Art Library
Fig. 63 Réunion des musées nationaux / Art Resource, New York. Photo: Agence Bulloz
Fig. 64 © Réunion des musées nationaux / Art Resource, New York. Photo: G. Blot / J. Schor
Fig. 65 © Réunion des musées nationaux / Art Resource, New York. Photo: G. Blot / J. Shormans
Fig. 66 © Christie's Images / The Bridgeman Art Library
Fig. 67 © Réunion des musées nationaux / Art Resource, New York. Photo: Agence Bulloz
Fig. 68 © Erich Lessing / Art Resource, New York
Fig. 69 © Staatsgalerie Stuttgart. Photo: Staatsgalerie Stuttgart
Fig. 70 Charles Potter Kling Fund 1975.805. Photo: © 2010 Museum of Fine Arts, Boston
Fig. 71 © Réunion des musées nationaux / Art Resource, New York. Photo: C. Jean
Figs. 72, 73 By courtesy of the Trustees of Sir John Soane's Museum
Fig. 74 © Réunion des musées nationaux / Art Resource, New York. Photo: J.G. Berizzi
Fig. 75 © Réunion des musées nationaux / Art Resource, New York

Index

Page references to illustrations are in italic.

Académie de France à Rome, 16–17, 18, 28, 30, 38, 166
Académie des beaux-arts, 160
Académie royale de musique, 148n67
Académie royale de peinture et de sculpture, 8n13, 18, 65, 105n81, 107n98, 132–33
académies, 17
actresses, and inheritance of property, 90
Adorno, Theodor, 132
aesthetic experience: gambling as, 12; imagination and, 5, 11–13; unquantifiable events and, 1
aesthetic of play, ruins and, 16, 177
aesthetic of the picturesque, development of, 15
aesthetics, danger of, 3, 27
aesthetics of disaster, cult of ruins and, 61
aesthetics of incompleteness: in aesthetic theory of 18th century, 5, 12–13; credit and, 50; and emotion as aesthetic criterion, 27; gambling and, 12, 13, 14–15; and imagination, excitement of, 11–13, 27; picturesque and, 23–27; Robert's early predilection for, 17–18; in Robert's *A Game of Dice*, 11–12, 14; in Robert's *Grande Galerie in Ruins*, 176; Robert's Opéra fire paintings and, 79–81; in Robert's works, 96–97; ruins and, 12–13; secularization of chance and, 14–15, 44. *See also* unfinished buildings
aesthetics of precariousness: picturesque gardens and, 21–27; in Robert's *A Game of Dice*, 11, 43
aesthetic style, real estate speculation and, 94–95
aesthetic theory, 18th century: on aesthetic value of dematerialization, 5–6; destabilizing enterprise of, 27–28; emphasis on vagaries of time and space, 54n57; iconoclastic character of, 1–2; and interdisciplinarity, 28–29; and introduction of paper money, 5–6; paradigm shift toward artwork's effect on viewer, 12; and ruins, meaning of, 15
aesthetic theory, emphasis on subjective experience, 2–3
aesthetic theory, pre-18th century: meaning of ruins in, 13, 15
agiotage, 132–33
Albertone, Manuela, 185n70
Aldobrandini Wedding, 166
Alquier (newspaper commentator), 121
American War of Independence, financial markets following, 78
The Ancient Monuments of France (Robert), 76, 129
Androuet du Cerceau, Jacques, 36
Angoulême affair, 47
L'année littéraire, 129
annuities, and 18th-century culture of risk, 45
Le antichità romane (Piranesi), 36, *38*
anticipation, ruins as instrument of, 13
anticomanie, 18; and attractiveness of urban disaster, 68–69; emphasis on exotic and singular, 41; print technology and, 33–36, 41; undermining of Classicism by, 68
L'antiquité dévoilée par ses usages (Boulanger), 72–76, 98–99
Les antiquités d'Herculanum (Maréchal), 70
Antiquitez de Rome (du Bellay), 13
antiquity, disasters in: echoes of in disaster paintings of Robert, 65–66, 75–76; 18th-century fascination with, 69–70; perceived replay of, in 18th-century disasters, 65–66, 70–76; pleasure derived from contemplation of, 64. *See also* Herculaneum; Pompeii
antiquity, irrecoverability of: and imaginative pleasure of ruins, 2, 12; and museum's shattering of tradition, 169; progress of history and, 172; in Saint-Non, 19
anxiety of latecoming, 176–77
Apollo Belvedere: display of, in Louvre, 167–68, 169, 170–71; in Robert's *Imaginary View of the Grande Galerie of the Louvre in Ruins* (1796), 153, 157, 158; in Robert's *Imaginary View of the Grande Galerie of the Louvre in Ruins* (1798-99), 176
Arcadian Shepherds (Poussin), 42–43, *43*, 57n91
archéofiction, 29–43. *See also* capriccio
Architectural Fantasy (Challe), 39, *39*
Architectural Fantasy (Legeay), 39–40, *41*
architecture: decline of, in building mania, 95; painterly, Robert and, 18; rules of, Piranésiens and, 36–39, 41–42
architecture, modern: lack of content, 78; loss of form, 110; and market economy, 78, 110; Viel de Saint-Maux on, 77–78
art: corruption of, 79; historical progression of, 155; market economy and, 8n13, 83–84; modern, prominent figures in development of, 3–4; and precariousness, 167; real estate speculation and, 91; significance of, commercialization and, 162
art, commercialization of: Académie resistance to, 8n13; and contentlessness of decontextualized artworks, 6, 120–24, 129–30, 147n55, 157–63, 167, 168–71; and diminishment of cultural capital, 169–70; museum collections and, 161–63, 166–67, 169–70; and precariousness, 167; and revolutionary iconoclasm, 163; Robert and, 79; Viel de Saint-Maux on, 78–79
art and antiquities trade, Piranésiens and, 41, 57n85
Art et argent en France au temps des premiers modernes (Poirson, ed.), 8n13
Artist Drawing Antiques before the Petite Galerie (Robert), 167–69, *168*
The Artist in His Cell at Sainte-Pélagie (Robert), 177–78, *178*
Artist Sketching a Statue in a Ruin (Dumont), 30, *32*
Artois, comte de, 91–92, 94, 105n80
assignat, failure of, 170, 171
astonishment, in Robert's disaster and demolition paintings, 97
Auvraÿ, Jacques, 137

Bachofen, Johann Jakob, 98
Bagatelle, comte d'Artois' *folie* at, 91
Bamboccianti, 13–14
The Bank of England, London: View of the Interior of the Rotunda (Gandy), 173–75, *174*
The Bank of England, London: View of the Rotunda Imagined as a Ruin (Gandy), 173–75, *174*

bankruptcy, public, fears of, 46, 91, 132, 134, 135. *See also* financial collapse, fears of
Banque générale, 46
Barbault, Jean, 118–20, *119*
Baridon, Michel, 22
Barré, Jean-Benoît-Vincent, 21
Barry, James, 57n85
Basilica of Constantine (Rome), 2
Bastille: demolition of, as confluence of political and economic revolution, 137; as obstruction to circulation, 136–37; proposed uses of site, 137
The Bastille in the First Days of Its Demolition (Robert), 135–39, *136*
Baudet, Étienne, *68*
Baumgarten, Alexander Gottlieb, 2
Beaumarchais, Pierre-Augustin Caron de, 103n53
Bélanger, François-Joseph, 21
Belisarius (David), 65
Bellicard, Jérôme-Charles, 28
Benjamin, Walter, 50, 169
Benveniste, Émile, 42
Bernardin de Saint-Pierre, Henri: recollections of 1789, 135; on ruins, 11, 13; on taste for destruction, 61, 64, 68, 78
Bernini, Gian Lorenzo, 89
Berthélemy, Jean-Simon, 65
Blondel, Jacques-François, 55n61, 91
Bolla, Peter de, 133
Bouchard, Edmé, 125
Bouchard and Gravier, publishers, 118
Boucher, François, 79, 103n52
Boulanger, Nicolas-Antoine, 72–76, 98–99
Boullée, Etienne-Louis, 28, 154
Bourse: *agiotage,* failure to rein in, 132–33, 135; crash, predictions of, 132–33; and excesses of speculation, 131–32; and gambling mania, 36–37; and insurance speculation, 44–45
Boyer, M. Christine, 186n71
Brantlinger, Patrick, 133
Breteuil, Louis-Auguste Le Tonnelier, baron de, 133–34
Brice, Germain, 83, 91
Bridges with Prison (Robert), *138,* 139
Brongniart, Alexandre-Théodore, 93
Brosses, Charles de, 2, 3
Brueghel, Jan, 166
Brullée, Jean-Pierre, 137
Buffon, George-Louis Leclerc de, 72
building industry: magic of, 90, 93–94, 132; and old regime, 131
building mania, 91–92; expansion of credit markets and, 78, 91, 102n47; and fear of collapse, 83, 91, 93; impermanence of, 90–91; paper money introduction and, 83; and poor construction, 95; Robert's awareness of risk in, 91–92
Bullant, Jean, 125, 128
Burke, Edmund: on aesthetic experience of unquantifiable events, 1; on national debt, 133; obsession with catastrophe, 1; *Philosophical Enquiry into the Origin of Our Ideas of the Sublime and Beautiful,* 69; on pleasure of incompleteness, 12; *Reflections on the Revolution in France,* 133; on the sublime, 69, 116; on unexpected, effect of, 61
The Burning of Rome (Robert, Salon of 1785), 76
The Burning of Rome (Robert, 1773), *75,* 76, 88
The Burning of the Opéra at the Palais-Royal (Robert), *vi,* 4, 79–81, *81,* 103n54
Bust of Raphael (Rondoni), 182n26

Caillois, Roger, 42, 98
Caisse d'escompte, 45, 46, 64
Calonne, Charles Alexandre de, 114–15
Canaletto, 116
capital, fictitious: credit as, 47–50; and loss of form in architecture, 110; Mercier on, 131–32; and overheating of economy, 132–35; paper money as, 47–50; transformation of urban fabric into, 83. *See also* paper money
capitalism: and delirium, 47; triumph over social hierarchy, 45–46. *See also* market economy; speculation
capriccio, 56n75; as barometer of 18th-century modes of perception, 4, 167; and bridging of substantialist and functionalist views of value, 127–28; Duval on, 159; and 18th-century attitudes toward circulation, 127; Tafuri on, 143
capricci of Panini, 127, *165,* 166–67
capricci of Piranésiens, 30, 34–43
capricci of Robert: as effort to assimilate modernization process, 124–32, 135; *Monuments of Paris, 128,* 128–32, 135, 148n60; *A Museum Gallery of Roman Art,* 163–67, *164; The Pont Neuf, 124,* 124–28, *128,* 130, 135; and portability of artworks, 166–67
Caravaggio, 155
Carceri d'invenzione (Piranesi), 38, 40, *138,* 139, 141, *142,* 143
Carmontelle, Louis Carrogis de, 22
Carrey, Régine, 148n60
Cassirer, Ernst, 3, 27
catastrophe. *See* disaster
Catherine de Medici, Queen, 125
Catherine the Great, 182n20
Cayeux, Jean de, 21–22, 88, 133
Caylus, Anne-Claude-Philippe, comte de, 12
ceremonial aspects of Paris, eclipsing of by priorities of circulation, 113–14, 121–22
Cesi Juno (Musei Capitolini), Robert's sketch of, *17,* 17–18
Chalgrin, Jean-François-Thérèse, 92, 93
Challe, Charles Michel-Ange, 28, 39, *39*
Challe, Simon, 28
Chambers, William, 21, 69
chance: age of, and cult of ruins, 16; and credit as analogue of ruins, 48; picturesque and, 23; role in history, 19; ruins and, 11, 16, 24, 48; secularization of, and aesthetic of the unfinished, 14–15, 44; world ruled by, Robert's Opéra fire paintings and, 81–83. *See also* Fortuna; fortune, vagaries of; gambling
Chanteloup, garden at, 21
Chardin, Jean-Baptiste-Siméon, 4
Chateaubriand, François-René, vicomte de, 151
Chaussée d'Antin, 90, *90,* 91–92, 93–94, *94,* 97
Chaussinand-Nogaret, Guy, 45–46
Chinea, Festa della: history of, 55n60; Piranésiens' contributions to, 28, *29,* 29–30
Choiseul, Étienne-François, duc de, 17, 21, 45, 92, 93, 166
Choiseul-Gouffier, Marie-Gabriel-Florent-Auguste de, 92
Christ's crucifixion, gaming at, 13–14
church demolitions: *Demolition of a Church* (Robert), *x,* 85, *86; Demolition of the Église Saint-Jean-en-Grève in 1800* (Robert), 85, *87.* *See also* demolition paintings of Robert
circulation: Bastille as obstacle to, 136–37; 18th-century attitudes toward, 127; as goal of demolition of houses on bridges of Seine, 109, 110–15, 117; of imagination, and aesthetic pleasure, 5, 11–13; museums as conduits of, 129–30; paper money and, 47–48; Paris's reconfiguration as city of, 4; prioritizing of, and doctrine of laissez-faire, 117; Robert's image of Seine covered in ice and, 135; Robert's images of confinement as resistance to, 137–43; urban reform and, 126–27. *See also* monuments, decontextualization of
circulation of currency: and circulation in urban reform, 126–27, 134; Law's theories on, 5–6; and magic of credit, 94; and risk of collapse, 126–27, 131–32, 170. *See also* paper money
city, modern concept of, as unbounded, 113, 117
Classicism, crumbling of: *anticomanie* and, 68; and time of contingency, 2, 44; and triumph of subjectivism, 24–43
The Clearing of the Colonnade of the Louvre (Demachy), 96, *96*
clergy, invisibility of, in Paris, 122
Clérisseau, Charles-Louis, 30–33, *33*
Cobham, Richard Lord Viscount, 54n49
Colbert, Jean-Baptiste, 46
Coleridge, Samuel Taylor, 42
Colisée, 93
collapse, financial, fears of. *See* financial collapse, fears of
Collège de Navarre, 16
colonization of the future, 3, 95
A Colonnaded Thermal Building, the Roof Partly Open to the Sky, with Girls Washing Clothes (Robert), 153–54, *154*
color mezzotint, 70
color prints, 33–34
Comédie Française, 92–93
comet strike, impending, rumors of (1784), 73
commercial developers: criticisms of, 93; rise of, 78. *See also* building mania
commercialization of art: Académie resistance to, 8n13; and contentlessness of decontextualized artworks, 6, 120–24, 129–30, 147n55, 157–63, 167, 168–71; and diminishment of cultural capital, 169–70; museum collections and, 161–63, 166–67, 169–70; and precariousness, 167; and revolutionary iconoclasm, 163; Robert and, 79; Viel de Saint-Maux on, 78–79
Compagnie des eaux de Paris, 132
Compagnie des Indes, 46
Condillac, Étienne Bonnot de, 126–27
Confessions of an English Opium-Eater (De Quincey), 42
confinement: in art of Legeay, 39–40; in art of Piranesi, 38; in 18th-century aesthetics, 143; Robert's images of, 137–43
Conservatoire du Muséum des Arts, 151, 152, 155, 158, 170, 171

Considérations morales sur la destination des ouvrages de l'art (Quatremère de Quincy), 160
The Construction of the École de Chirurgie (Robert), *88*, 88–90, 91
content, cult of ruins' abjuring of, 42–43
contentlessness: of belief systems, 73, 77; emptiness as emancipatory, 122; of modern architecture, 78; of modern world, as Robert's subject matter, 1, 6; of out-of-context art works, 6, 120–24, 129–30, 147n55, 157–63, 167, 168–71; of Paris, urban reform and, 122; past as void, 19; and the picturesque, 88–89; Robert's appreciation of negative space, 18; Robert's evacuation of tradition, 4, 65, 68, 70, 84; in ruin aesthetic, 42
context of artwork, importance of, 6, 120–24, 129–30, 147n55, 157–63, 167, 168–71
contingency, consciousness of, and cult of ruins, 44–50
contingency, time of, 44; credit and, 50; crumbling of Classicism and, 2, 44; ruins genre as adjustment to, 2–3
continuity with the past: and Paris as la nouvelle Athènes, 157–59, 161, 162–63, 172; and Robert's *Imaginary View of the Grande Galerie of the Louvre in Ruins*, 156–59. *See also* Classicism, crumbling of; Rome, French army's spoliation of
Convention nationale, and spoliation of Rome, 161
Cook, James, monument to, in garden at Méréville, 22
Correggio, 155
Correspondance secrète, 64
creative destruction, Paris demolitions as, 5
creativity, risks of, 177
credit: as analogue of ruin, 48–50; aesthetic appeal of, 46; as circulation of fiction, 47–50; critics of, 48–50; Defoe on, 47–48, 50; dematerialization and, 48; double nature of, 91; fire as metaphor for, 91; imaginative appeal of, 46, 47–48; and impression *vs.* reality of wealth, 46; indebtedness of Parisians, 102n47; of Louis XVI, 45, 46; magic of, 94, 97, 99; obscurity of future and, 91; and Paris building mania, 78, 91, 102n47; and pleasure of the incomplete, 50; replacement of money with, 46–47; and time of contingency, 50. *See also* national debt
Croquis faits à Rome par Hubert Robert en 1760 (Robert), *17*, 17–18
cult of ruins: abjuring of content by, 42–43; aesthetics of catastrophe and, 61; and age of chance, 16; consciousness of contingency and, 44–50; Diderot on, 13; as embrace of uncertainty, 2, 48; and obsession with impermanence, 95; secularization and, 15, 44; and triumph of time, 178; Viel de Saint-Maux on, 77, 78
cultural reproduction, art and, 160, 169
culture of risk: annuities and, 45; consolidation of, 64; development of, 84; Law's Système and, 46; and modern sense of time, 16
currency. *See assignat*, failure of; *mandats territoriaux*, failure of; paper money
cyclicality, historical: fears of, 73–76. *See also* antiquity, disasters in; continuity with the past; disaster (catastrophe); Rome, as precedent for Paris; Vyverberg, Henry; Winckelmann, Johann Joachim

d'Angerville, Mouffle, 65
d'Angiviller, Charles Claude Flahaut de La Billarderie, comte, 154, 155
Daston, Lorraine, 98
David, Jacques-Louis, 3–4, 65, 162, 167
death: awareness of, sublimated in ruin aesthetic, 24–25, 43; and play, 98
debt: City of Paris defaults, 134; crisis magnified by demolition of houses on bridges of Seine, 134; unchecked expansion of, as sublime, 133
debt, national: and bankruptcy fears, 46, 91, 132, 134, 135; and institutionalization of risk, 16, 45–46; and speculative enterprises, necessity of, 132–33
La décade philosophique, 158
Defoe, Daniel, on credit, 47–48, 50
Delamare, Nicolas, 76, 113, 119
De la passion du jeu depuis les temps anciens jusqu'à nos jours (Dusaulx), 84–85
Della magnificenza ed architettura de' romani (Piranesi), 36
Delle magnificenze di Roma antica e moderna (Vasi), 119
Demachy, Pierre-Antoine, 33, 96, *96*, 107n98
dematerialization: and credit, 48; of money, and inherent confusion of signs, 126–27, 132; in Robert's renditions of unfinished buildings, 89; of Rome, in *archéofiction*, 29, 36; and value, 5–6
demolition(s), as creative destruction, 5
Demolition of a Church (Robert), *x*, 85, *86*
demolition of churches: *Demolition of a Church* (Robert), *x*, 85, *86*; *Demolition of the Église Saint-Jean-en-Grève in 1800* (Robert), 85, *87*. *See also* demolition paintings of Robert
demolition of houses on bridges of Seine, 109; and bronze sculpture of Louis XIV and family, relocation of, *120*, 120–22; circulation as goal of, 109, 110–15, 117; Crown's co-opting of financing for, 134; as cultural turning point, 122, 134; debt crisis magnified by, 134; displaced persons, indemnity for, 114–15, 134; ignoring of human costs in, 117; profiteers and, 133–34; public opinion on, 120–21; Robert's understanding of, 134–35; sublimity of, 110, 116–17; and triumph of future over local and particular, 117–18; unimpeded prospects as objective of, 117–18, 134. *See also The Demolition of Houses on the Pont-au-Change, Paris* (Robert); *The Demolition of Houses on the Pont Notre-Dame in 1786* (Robert; Musée Carnavalet); *The Demolition of Houses on the Pont Notre-Dame in 1786* (Robert; Staatliche Kunsthalle Karlshrue)
The Demolition of Houses on the Pont-au-Change, Paris (Robert), *108*, 109–13, 115–16, 125, 133, 134–35, 136; courting and compromise of uninterrupted progression in, 118; ignoring of human costs in, 117; sources for, 118–20, *119*
The Demolition of Houses on the Pont Notre-Dame in 1786 (Robert; Musée Carnavalet), 114, 143, *143*, 149n75
The Demolition of Houses on the Pont Notre-Dame in 1786 (Robert; Staatliche Kunsthalle Karlshrue), *108*, 109–13, 125, 133, 134–35, 136; courting and compromise of uninterrupted progression in, 118; ignoring of human costs in, 117; juxtaposition of rapid transformation with immemorial behavior in, 113–15; sources of, 143; versions of, 149n75
Demolition of the Église Saint-Jean-en-Grève in 1800 (Robert), 85, *87*
demolition paintings of Robert, 135–39, *136*; and nightmare of market economy, 83–84; as site of suspense, 85; theatricality of, 97. *See also The Bastille in the First Days of Its Demolition*; *Demolition of a Church*; *The Demolition of Houses on the Pont-au-Change, Paris*; *The Demolition of Houses on the Pont Notre-Dame in 1786* (Musée Carnavalet); *The Demolition of Houses on the Pont Notre-Dame in 1786* (Staatliche Kunsthalle Karlshrue); *Demolition of the Église Saint-Jean-en-Grève in 1800*
Dénonciation de l'agiotage au roi et à l'Assemblée des notables (Mirabeau), 132
de Piles, Roger, 154–55
De Quincey, Thomas, 42
Descourtis, Charles-Melchior, 33–34
Description de la ville de Paris (Brice), 83
Desgodets, Antoine, 30
Desprez, Louis-Jean, 19, 70, 72, *72*, 75
dessinateur des jardins du roi, Robert as, 19
destruction: creative, Paris demolitions as, 5; modernity's capacity to envision its own, 1; pleasure of, 64; senselessness of, in Robert's Opéra fire paintings, 68. *See also* disaster; time of continuity, ending of
Détail des nouveaux jardins à la mode (Le Rouge), 28
Devil's Bridge, in garden at Méréville, 22
De Wailly, Charles, 92–93, *130*, 130–31, 135
Dewey, John, 161
Diderot, Denis: on bad monuments, 121–22; connecting of modern catastrophe and cult of ruins, 61; on decimation of Paris, 68; on Demachy, 96, 107n98; on Laborde, 93–94; obsession with catastrophe, 1; on poetics of ruins, 13; on power of incompleteness, 12–13, 24; on reconciliation of truth and falsehood, 11; on Robert's debut exhibition, 12–13, 43, 44, 48, 61, 95–96, 97; *Salon de 1771*, 95; *Salon de 1767*, 43, 48, 68, 95
disaster (catastrophe): aesthetics of, cult of ruins and, 61; *anticomanie* as craving for, 68–69; commodification of, Robert's Opéra fire paintings and, 70; 18th-century anticipation of, 64, 68, 69, 73, 155–56; 18th-century attraction to, 1–2, 6, 44, 61, 69; exploitation of, in art and financial life, 96; hints of, in *Monuments of Paris*, 129; impending, Robert's fascination with, 97; as investment opportunity, 95; obsession with, secularization and, 1–2, 6; public utility of, 77; as source of religion, 72–74, 98–99; sublimity of, 1–2, 69, 97–99. *See also* financial collapse, fears of; *entries under* fire
disaster paintings of Robert, 61; associations with speculative economy, 64; echoes of ancient disasters in, 65–66, 75–76; fears of Paris's

impending doom and, 64; and future, failure of confidence in, 91; inciting and dispelling of terror in, 75–76; and nightmare of market economy, 83–84; and pleasure of destruction, 64; sublime in, 97–99; theatricality of, 64, 69, 75, 79–81, 97; and thrill of gambling, 84–85; undermining of tradition in, 65, 68, 70, 84; unexpected and, 84–85
disasters in antiquity: echoes of in disaster paintings of Robert, 65–66, 75–76; 18th-century fascination with, 69–70; perceived replay of, in 18th-century disasters, 65–66, 70–76; pleasure derived from contemplation of, 64. *See also* Herculaneum; Pompeii
Discours sur les monuments publics (Kersaint), 155–56
Discours sur les sciences et les arts (Rousseau), 83
Dissertation on Oriental Gardening (Chambers), 69
The Drawbridge (Piranesi), 110, *112*
du Bellay, Joachim, 13
Dubos, Jean-Baptiste, 12, 54n57
Duclos-Dufresnoy, Charles-Nicolas, 92, 186n80
Dulaure, Jacques-Antoine, 28
Dumont, Gabriel Pierre Martin, 30, *31*, *32*
Dupaty, Charles-Marguerite-Jean-Baptiste Mercier, 68–69
Dusaulx, Jean, 84–85
Duval, Amaury, 158–59
Dying Slave (Michelangelo), 156–57, 158

École de Chirurgie (Robert), *88*, 88–90, 91
economic policies of France, and commercialization of art, 169–70
economy of anticipation, ending of time of continuity and, 3
Édifices antiques de Rome (Desgodets), 30
Église des Saints-Innocents, 61, *123*, 123–24
Église Sainte-Geneviève, 128
Eidophusikon, 69
Eliade, Mircea, 173, 176
Élie de Beaumont, Jean-Baptiste-Jacques, 109, 147n55
embellissement, 77, 102n42. *See also* urban reform
Des embellissements de Paris (Voltaire), 110–13
enchantment: picturesque as agent of, 19; sublime's transformation of terror into, 99
Encyclopédie (Diderot and d'Alembert), 46, 91, 113
Entwurff einer historischen Architectur (Fischer von Erlach), 30
Ermenonville, 24–27, *25*, *26*
Essai sur l'architecture (Laugier), 38
Essai sur les jardins (Watelet), 18, 22–23
Essai sur l'origine des langues (Rousseau), 148n57
Étude de la nature (Bernardin de Saint-Pierre), 11

fabriques: appeal of, 24, 27; commodification of, 33, 55n58; cost of, 27–28; for garden at Méréville, 21, 22; as naturalizations of obsolescence, 95; in Parc de Monceau, 22, 48; terror-inducing, 18th-century delight in, 69
Farnese Herakles, 178
Ferme générale, 45
Festivities at the Pont de Neuilly (Robert), 100n8
fictitious capital: credit as, 47–50; and loss of form in architecture, 110; Mercier on, 131–32; and overheating of economy, 132–35; paper money as, 47–50; transformation of urban fabric into, 83. *See also* paper money
fictive values, 132. *See also* fictitious capital
Figures in a Vaulted Portico (Clérisseau), 30, *33*
financial collapse, fears of: building mania and, 83, 91, 93; circulation of currency and, 126–27, 131–35, 170; and Musée du Louvre as haven of unfluctuating values, 170–71; Rome as precedent for, 5, 84; in 1789, 135; urban reform and, 126–27. *See also* bankruptcy, public, fears of
financier class, public opinion on, 79
fire, 76, 88; as instrument of urban reform, 76–77; as metaphor for credit, 91; as metaphor for gambling, 84; valences in 18th-century imaginations, 76. *See also The Burning of Rome* (Robert, Salon of 1785); *The Burning of Rome* (Robert, 1773); *The Burning of the Opéra at the Palais-Royal* (Robert); *Fire Amidst the Principal Edifices of Rome* (Robert); Hôtel-Dieu fire; Opéra fire; Opéra fire, Robert's paintings of; *Ruins of the Opéra after the Fire of 1781* (Robert); volcanoes, 18th-century fascination with
Fire Amidst the Principal Edifices of Rome (Robert), 92
The Fire at the Hôtel-Dieu in Paris, 1772 (Robert), 4–5, *74*, 75–77, 88, 97
Fire at the Opéra of the Palais-Royal, Viewed from a Crossing in the Louvre (Robert), *62*, 64–70; inciting and dispelling of terror in, 75–76; taming of threat in, 85
fire insurance, perception of, as speculation, 84
fireworks, Enlightenment critics of, 84
Fischer von Erlach, Johann Bernhard, 30
Fontaine des Innocents, *123*, 123–24, 128, 129
Fontaine des Quatre Saisons, 125, 128
Forbonnais, François Véron Duverger de, 46
Fortuna, 15, 97
fortune, vagaries of: and credit as analogue of ruins, 48; ruins as monuments to, 11. *See also* chance
found objects, Piranésiens' valuation of, 30
The Fountain of the Église des Saints-Innocents in 1787 (Sobre), *123*
Fragonard, Jean-Honoré, 18, 19, 34, 79
freedom: flowing water as invocation of, 23–24; modern system of values and, 127; urban reform and, 117–18, 131
French Revolution: and circulation as goal of urban reform, 137; continuity with the past following, 156–59; financial possibilities of, 137; and iconoclasm, 121, 156–57, 163; Musée du Louvre as compensation for, 156; premonitions of, in *Monuments of Paris*, 129; Robert and, 156–57, 177–78, 182n21; and transfer of religious faith to new institutions, 171; and urban reform, 117, 121–22, 133–34
future: colonization of, 3, 95; 18th-century anxiety about, 73; 18th-century fixation on, 2, 4; secular, creation of, 16, 44; and shape of history, debate over, 171–75; triumph of over local and particular, in demolition of houses on bridges of Seine, 117–18. *See also* collapse, financial, fears of; precariousness; Rome, as precedent for Paris
future, obscurity of: credit and, 91; and inability to distinguish promise from menace, 85

gambling: as aesthetic pastime, 12; and aesthetics of the unfinished, 14–15; as culture-wide obsession, 84; fire as metaphor for, 84; history of works on, 13–14; insurance speculation in 18th century, 44–45, 84; and pleasure of incompleteness, 12, 13, 14–15; as surrender to uncertainty, 98; state-sponsored lotteries, introduction of, 45, 84; thrill of, Robert's disaster paintings and, 84–85. *See also* play; real estate speculation
A Game of Dice amidst Roman Ruins (Robert), *10*, 11–16; abandonment to the unexpected in, 11; and cult of ruins' abjuring of content, 42–43; gaming and aesthetics of the unfinished in, 14; pleasure of incompleteness in, 11–12, 14; secularization of chance and, 15; source for, 42–43, *43*
Gandy, Joseph Michael, 173–75, *174*
garden at Chanteloup, 21
garden at Ermenonville, 24–27, *25*, *26*
garden at Méréville: Robert's designs for, 19, 21–22; Robert's paintings of, 23, *23*
garden design: and imagination, excitement of, 22; and primacy of painting, 4; Robert and, 19, 21; Robert's designs for garden at Méréville, 19, 21–22; theatricality in, 22, 69
gardens, picturesque: and the aesthetics of precariousness, 21–27; as avant-garde, 22–23; commodity culture and, 27–28, 33, 55n58; development of, 18; imagination and, 22; Robert's design of, 19, 21–22. *See also* garden at Ermenonville; garden at Méréville; Moulin Joli; Parc de Monceau
gardens, "terrible," 69
genre painting, Northern tradition of, 13
Gérard, François, 162
Gersaint, Edme-François, 114
Giambologna, 125
Giddens, Anthony, 3
Girardin, René-Louis, marquis de, 24
Girardot, Haller et Cie, 134
Girardot de Marigny, Jean, 45, 64, 77, 133–34
Girodet, Anne-Louis, 162
Gondoin, Jacques, 88, 89
Goujon, Jean, 124
Goulet, Nicolas, 102n42
Grande Galerie of the Louvre: lighting in, 151, 172, 180n4, 186n80; planning committee for, 121; scientific classification methods, and arrangement of paintings in; 155. *See also Imaginary View of the Grande Galerie of the Louvre in Ruins* (Robert, 1796); *Imaginary View of the Grande Galerie of the Louvre in Ruins* (Robert, 1798–99)
The Grand Piazza (Piranesi), 139–41, *140*
Gray, Richard T., 126, 127
Greuze, Jean-Baptiste, 3–4
Grimm, Friedrich Melchior, Freiherr von, 12, 97
Grimod de La Reynière, Alexandre-Balthazar-Laurent, 33
Groethuysen, Bernard, 75
Grotta di Pausilippo, 19, *20*
guidebooks: on Paris, 78, 83; on picturesque gardens, 27–28

Le guide de ceux qui veulent bâtir (Le Camus de Mézières), 104n74
Guillain, Simon, 120–22
Guimard, Marie-Madeleine, 90

Hadrian (Museo dei Conservatori), Robert's sketch of, *17*, 17–18
Halle au Blé, 92, *92*
Halle au Blé and rue de Viarmes (Maréchal), 92, *92*
Harbor with Architecture (Robert), 141, *142*, 143
Hardy, Siméon-Prosper, 76
Haussmann, Georges-Eugène, 122
Hegel, Georg Wilhelm Friedrich, 176
hell: 18th-century conjurations of, 69; gambling dens as metaphor for, 84; as last remnant of religious faith, 75. *See also* fire; volcanoes, 18th-century fascination with
Henri IV (king of France), equestrian statue of, 125
Herculaneum: discovery of, 19, 61; evocation of modern destruction by, 70; response of Académie *pensionnaires* to, 28, 29; visitors' disappointment with, 19
Hervey, Frederick, bishop of Derry, 184n44
historicism, and terror of history, 172
history: debate on direction of, 171–75; role of chance in, 19; terror of, and aesthetics of ruins, 171–77
history painting, and moral instruction, 79
Holbach, Paul Henri Dietrich, baron d', 72, 73
Holy Family (Raphael), 151
Hôtel-Dieu, efforts to relocate, 77
Hôtel-Dieu fire: *The Fire at the Hôtel-Dieu in Paris, 1772* (Robert), 4–5, *74*, 75–77, 88, 97; welcoming of, by urban reformers, 76–77
Hôtel Thélusson, 93–94, *94*
House of Mademoiselle Guimard, rue de la Chaussée-d'Antin, Ledoux (Maréchal), 90, *90*
Hume, David, 72, 73
Huquier, Gabriel, *80*
Hutcheson, Archibald, 47

Ichnographiam Campi Martii (Piranesi), 110, *111*
iconoclasm: of aesthetic thought, 18th century, 1–2; and commercialization of art, 163; French Revolution and, 121, 156–57, 163; Robert's ruins and, 157
Île des Peupliers, at Ermenonville, 24–27, *26*
Imaginary Tombs on the Via Appia (Piranesi), *38*, 41
Imaginary View of the Grande Galerie of the Louvre in Ruins (Robert, 1796), *i*, 1, 2, 4, 152–59, *153*; and continuity with the past, following French Revolution, 156–59; described, 152–53; and museum's destruction of tradition, 159; and replacement of art with art history, 172; reviews of, 152, 180n8, 181n9; revolutionary critique of, 159; and terror of history, 171–75
Imaginary View of the Grande Galerie of the Louvre in Ruins (Robert, 1798–99), *175*, 175–77
imagination: and aesthetic pleasure, 5, 11–13; and credit, 46, 47–48; financial markets and, 47; garden design and, 22; irretrievability of past and, 2, 12; and pleasure of incompleteness, 11–13, 27; power of sublime over, 69; Robert's predilection for the fantastical, 17–18; suspension of judgment and, 22; unbounded, confinement as underlying condition of, 143
Imperial Mausoleum (Piranesi), 36, *37*
impermanence: of luxury, 90–91, 93; obsession with, cult of ruins and, 95; ruins as allegory of, 13; *vs.* solidity, distrust of distinction between, 91. *See also* circulation; precariousness
incompleteness, aesthetics of: in aesthetic theory of 18th century, 5, 12–13; credit and, 50; and emotion as aesthetic criterion, 27; gambling and, 12, 13, 14–15; and imagination, excitement of, 11–13, 27; picturesque and, 23–27; Robert's early predilection for, 17–18; in Robert's *A Game of Dice*, 11–12, 14; in Robert's *Grande Galerie in Ruins*, 176; Robert's Opéra fire paintings and, 79–81; in Robert's works, 79, 95–97; ruins and, 12–13; secularization of chance and, 14–15, 44. *See also* unfinished buildings
infinity, conjurations of in Robert, 117
Institut national des sciences et des arts, 163, 170
insurance speculation in 18th century, 44–45, 84
The Interior of a Study (anon., ca. 1800), 177–78, *179*
Interior of the Opéra of the Palais-Royal after the Fire (Robert), 65, *67*
Interior of the Opéra of the Palais-Royal the Day after the Fire (Robert), *63*, 64–70, 75, 79, 97–98
irrecoverability of past: and imaginative pleasure of ruins, 2, 12; and museum's shattering of tradition, 169; progress of history and, 172; in Saint-Non, 19
Isabey, Jean-Baptiste, 162

Jaillot, 109
Jameson, Fredric, 94
Janinet, Jean-François, 33–34, *34*, *35*, 48, *49*
Jardin, Nicolas-Henri, 28
jardins à l'anglaise, Viel de Saint-Maux on, 94–95
Journal de Paris, 78, 120–21, 123–24

Kavanagh, Thomas M., 46, 98
Kent, William, 54n49
Kersaint, Armand-Guy, 155–56
Kew, Chambers's pagoda at, 21
Koselleck, Reinhart, 15

Laborde, Alexandre, comte de, 22
Laborde, Jean-Joseph, marquis de: background, 45; and Chaussée d'Antin, 93–94; and French national debt, 45–46, 58n99; and garden at Méréville, 19, 21, 22, 103n53; and Hôtel-Dieu, efforts to relocate, 77; real estate speculation, 91
La Font de Saint-Yenne, Étienne, 79, 83, 93
laissez-faire doctrine, prioritizing of circulation and, 117
Lajoue, Jacques de, 79
Lallemand, Jean-Baptiste, 96
landscape painting(s): *anticomanie* and, 18; of Robert, triumph of nature in, 24; Robert's interest in, 18
Landscape with the Funeral of Phocion (Poussin), 65, *68*
Langeac, Charlotte-Christine-Antoinette de Lenoncourt, marquise de, 92
The Large Limekiln (van Laer), 13, *14*
latecoming: anxiety of, 176–77; in Robert's *A Game of Dice*, 43
Laugier, Marc-Antoine, 38
Lavedan, Pierre, 93
Law, John, 5–6, 46–47, 79, 84
Lebreton, Joachim, 163
Le Brun, Charles, 170
Lebrun, Jean-Baptiste-Pierre, 156, 163, 171, 184n46
Le Camus, Louis-Denis, 21, 93
Le Camus de Mézières, Nicolas, 92, 104n74
Le Comte, Marguerite, 18
Ledoux, Claude-Nicolas, 28, 61, 90, 93–94, *94*, 105n78
Legeay, Jean-Laurent, 39–41, *40*, *41*, 143
Legrand, Jacques-Guillaume, 94
Leibniz, Gottfried Wilhelm, Freiherr von, 126
Le Lorrain, Louis-Joseph, 28, 29, *29*
Lenoir, Alexandre, 158, 171
Le Nôtre, André, 22
Leonardo Dying in the Arms of Francis I (Ménageot), 65
Lequeu, Jean-Jacques, 28
Le Rouge, Georges-Louis, 28
Lettres à Miranda (Quatremère de Quincy), 159–60, 161–62, 169
Les lettres persanes (Montesquieu), 48–50
Lettres sur l'architecture des anciens et celle des modernes (Viel de Saint-Maux), 77–79
Lévi-Strauss, Claude, 42
linguistic signs, and potential for confusion, 126–27
Lisbon earthquake, 61
Livron, Charles-François Lubersac de, 48
Locke, John, 72, 126
London: destruction of, Burke on, 69; fire of 1666, 76
Lorraine, duc de, 16
lottery, state-sponsored, introduction of, 45, 84
Louis XIV (king of France), 125, 128, 170
Louis XV (king of France), 125
Louis XVI (king of France), 4, 45, 46
Loutherbourg, Philippe de, 69
Louvre. *See* Musée du Louvre
Luhmann, Niklas, 15–16, 156
luxury: 18th-century concerns about, 83; impermanence of, 90–91, 93

Macchina for the Chinea festival with the Temple of Venus Genetrix (Le Lorrain), 29, *29*
macchine, Piranésiens' designs for, 28, *29*, 29–30
magic: of credit, 94, 97, 99; of neoclassical architecture, 90, 93–94
Magnificent Bridge (Piranesi), 141, *142*
Maleuvre, Didier, 160
mandats territoriaux, failure of, 170
Maréchal, Jean-Baptiste: *Halle au Blé and rue de Viarmes*, *92*; *House of Mademoiselle Guimard, rue de la Chaussée-d'Antin, Ledoux*, 90, *90*
Maréchal, Sylvain, 70
Mariette, Pierre-Jean, 16

Marigny, Abel-François Poisson, marquis de, 17, 52n28

market economy: art and, 8n13, 83–84; building mania and, 83; disaster and demolition paintings of Robert and, 83–84; and loss of form in architecture, 110; and modern architecture, 78; picturesque gardens and, 27–28, 33, 55n58; and religion, 99; unpredictability of, 83–84. *See also* capitalism; commercialization of art

Martin, Pernette-Elisabeth, 45

McClung, William Alexander, 57n81

McGowan, Margaret M., 36

mechanical reproduction: and fate of antiquity, 33–36, 41; and relation to museum, 169

Mémoires secrets, 65

Mémoire sur les prêts d'argent (Turgot), 47

Ménageot, François-Guillaume, 65

Mercier, Louis-Sébastien: on building industry, 90, 93, 95; on clearing of Seine's bridges, 117, 118; on fictitious capital, 131–32; on fire, 76; on imminence of disaster, 73; *Le nouveau Paris*, 122; obsession with catastrophe, 1; on precariousness of prosperity, 90–91, 93, 95; on Republican architecture, 137; on speculators, 94, 132; on spiritual emptiness of Paris, 122; on the sublime, 69; *Tableau de Paris*, 73, 90–91, 122

Mercure de France, 64–65, 70

Méréville, garden at: Robert's designs for, 19, 21–22; Robert's paintings of, 23, *23*

Métra, François, 64, 79, 96

metropolis, transformation of Paris into, 122

Michelangelo, 156–57, 158

Mirabeau, Honoré-Gabriel Riqueti, comte de, 132, 133

Miranda, Francisco de, 159

modernity: aesthetic strategies enabling acclimation to, 2; and capacity to envision own destruction, 1; contentlessness of, as Robert's subject matter, 1, 6; experience of risk and, 5, 177; liquidation of values in, 78; and sense of time, 15–16, 44, 171–75

modernization: Robert's effort to assimilate and make palatable, 124–32, 135; Robert's works as commentary on, 5

Mola, Francesco, 155

Mollard, Antoine, 134

monarchy: decline of, and urban reform, 121–23; invisibility of, in Paris, 122

moneyed class, as threat to public morality, 79

Le moniteur universel, 162

Montaigne, Michel de, 151

Montesquieu, Charles-Louis de Secondat, baron de: on decline and fall, 5, 61; on gambling, 85; *Les lettres persanes*, 48–50; on limitlessness, 118

Monumental Tomb with Tree Branches (Legeay), 39, *40*

monuments: and confidence in political institutions, 156; decontextualization of, 6, 120–24, 129–30, 147n55, 157–63, 167, 168–71; Musée du Louvre as post-catastrophe monument of French culture, 155–56; Robert's capricci and, 124–32

Monuments of Paris (Robert), *128*, 128–32, 135, 148n60

Moreau, Pierre-Louis, 113, 114

Morel, Jean-Marie, 53n47

Mouffle d'Angerville, 65

Moulin Joli, 18

Mumford, Lewis, 110, 146n36

municipal services, contracted to joint-stock companies, 132

Musée du Louvre: arrangement of paintings in, 154–55; and commercialization of art, 161–62; as compensation for French Revolution, 156; as engine of progress, 155; as haven of unfluctuating values, 170–71, 176, 186n71; Musée des Antiques, 167–68; and museum's destruction of tradition, 159; and post-Revolution Paris's continuity with the past, 157–59; Quatremère de Quincy's critique of, 158, 159–62; Robert as curator-administrator at, 121, 129, 148n60, 151–52, 155, 156, 170, 171, 180n3, 181n12; in Robert's capricci, 125, 128, Robert's views of, *151*, 167; and shape of history, 171–72. *See also Artist Drawing Antiques before the Petite Galerie* (Robert); Conservatoire du Muséum des Arts; Grande Galerie of the Louvre; *Imaginary View of the Grande Galerie of the Louvre in Ruins* (Robert, 1796); *Imaginary View of the Grande Galerie of the Louvre in Ruins* (Robert, 1798–99); museum(s); *A Museum Gallery of Roman Art* (Robert)

museum(s): and commercialization of art, 161–63, 166–67, 169–70; as conduit of circulation, 129–30; decontextualization of art in, 6, 129–30, 168–71; and economic crisis, 170; as monument to conquest, 167; museological paradigm in Robert's *Monuments of Paris*, 129. *See also* Conservatoire du Muséum des Arts; Musée du Louvre; Rome, French army's spoliation of

A Museum Gallery of Roman Art (Robert), 163–67, *164*

mystification, the picturesque and, 22–24

national debt: and institutionalization of risk, 16, 45–46; and speculative enterprises, necessity of, 132–33

Natoire, Charles-Joseph, 17, 18

nature: as corrective model, revolutionary call for, 159; creation of ruins by, 11, 13; Rousseau on Paris and, 117

nature, triumph of: in landscapes of Robert, 24; picturesque as imitation of, 22; in Saint-Non, 19

negative space, Robert's appreciation of, 18

Negroni collection, 163

Neoclassicism: associations with decadence, 91; associations with simplicity, 79, 103n53; associations with speculation, 91–92, 93–94; Paris's aspiration toward splendor of, 90; Piranésiens and, 28; Robert as transitional figure in, 91

Nietzsche, Friedrich, 135

nominalism: cult of ruins and, 5–6; Robert and, 6

Le nouveau Paris (Mercier), 122

la nouvelle Athènes, post-Revolution Paris as, 157–59, 161, 162–63, 172

Nouvelle description des environs de Paris (Dulaure), 28

novels, and paper money as fiction, 47

The Obelisk **(Robert)**, *80*

Oechslin, Werner, 187n87

Oettermann, Stephan, 117

The Old Bridge (Robert), 139–43, *141*

ontological values, destabilization of, 3, 5–6

Opéra fire(s): history of, 76; as investment opportunity, 95; perceived echoes of ancient disaster in, 65–66, 70–72, 75

Opéra fire, Robert's paintings of: and aesthetics of incompleteness, 79–81; and chance, world ruled by, 81–83; Christian symbolism in, 97–98; and commodification of disaster, 70; critical reactions to, 64–65, 70; and 18th-century fascination with the sublime, 69–70; *Fire at the Opéra of the Palais-Royal, Viewed from a Crossing in the Louvre*, *62*, 64–70, 75–76, 85; historical echoes in, 65–66; *Interior of the Opéra of the Palais-Royal*, 65, *67*; *Interior of the Opéra of the Palais-Royal the Day after the Fire*, *63*, 64–70, 75, 79, 97–98; *Ruins of the Opéra after the Fire of 1781*, 65, *66*; sale of, 64; at Salon of 1781, 61, 64, 65; subversiveness of, 65, 68, 70

Oppenord, Gilles-Marie, 79, *80*

Orléans, Louis Philippe, duc d', 48

painterly architecture, Robert and, 18

painting: Robert's views on, 4; as site of communion between past and present, 4

Pajou, Augustin, 21, 120–21, 129, 158

Palais du Luxembourg exhibition of the king's pictures (1750), 27

Palais Mancini, 28, 30, 52n23. *See also* Académie de France à Rome

Palazzo Farnese, 163

Palloy, Pierre-François, 137

Panini, Giovanni Paolo, 4, 33, *165*, 166–67

paper money: and building mania, 83; and circulation in urban reform, 126–27, 134; as circulation of fiction, 47–50; destabilizing impact on social hierarchy, 45; and 18th-century aesthetic theory, 5–6; introduction of, 46; Law (John) and, 5–6, 46–47, 79, 84; and risk of collapse, 126–27, 131–35, 170. *See also* fictitious capital

Parc de Monceau, 22, 48

Parere su l'architettura (Piranesi), 38

Paris: debt defaults, 134; demolitions and remodeling, 64; as disaster-prone city, 64, 76; and ending of time of continuity, 4; municipal services, contracted to joint-stock companies, 132; Robert's fascination with metamorphosis of, 4; Robert's works on, 4–5; as theater of Revolution, 156; transformation from capital to metropolis, 122. *See also* building mania; ceremonial aspects of Paris, eclipsing of by priorities of circulation; urban reform; *entries under* demolition *and* real estate speculation

Paris, destruction of: building mania and, 83; 18th-century anticipations of, 64, 68, 69, 155–56; urban reformers' interest in, 76–77

The Park at Ermenonville (Robert), 24–27, *26*

Parmigianino, 155
Passemant, Claude-Siméon, 117
past, continuity with: and Paris as la nouvelle Athènes, 157–59, 161, 162–63, 172; and Robert's *Imaginary View of the Grande Galerie of the Louvre in Ruins*, 156–59. *See also* Classicism, crumbling of; Rome, French army's spoliation of; tradition, erosion of
past, irrecoverability of: and imaginative pleasure of ruins, 2, 12; and museum's shattering of tradition, 169; progress of history and, 172; in Saint-Non, 19
Patte, Pierre, 76, 77, 78, 109, 113, 118
Perier brothers, 132
Pernet, Jean-Henri-Alexandre, 34
Perrault, Claude, 125
Petit de Bachaumont, Louis, 93
Petitot, Edmond-Alexandre, 28, 29
Petit-Radel, Louis François, 85
Peyre, Marie-Joseph, 52n28, 92–93
Philip Augustus (king of France), 123
Philosophical Enquiry into the Origin of Our Ideas of the Sublime and Beautiful (Burke), 69
Philosophie des Geldes (Simmel), 5
Physiocrats, 117
pictorial, the: abandonment of, by late-20th-century artists, 1
Picture Gallery with Views of Ancient Rome (Panini), *165*, 166–67
Picture Gallery with Views of Modern Rome (Panini), *165*, 166–67
picturesque, the: aesthetic of, development of, 15; and chance, 23; emphasis on sensory pleasure over fact, 19; as imitation of work of nature and time, 22; irretrievability of past and, 19; and pleasures of incompleteness, 23–27; Robert's exposure to, 18, 19; and ruins, 11, 15, 16, 48; as source of mystification, 22–24; and tradition, erosion of, 4, 28; triumph of subjectivism in, 24–27; and unpredictability, 23, 43; Viel de Saint-Maux on, 94–95. *See also* *Voyage pittoresque*
picturesque gardens: and the aesthetics of precariousness, 21–27; as avant-garde, 22–23; commodity culture and, 27–28, 33, 55n58; development of, 18; imagination and, 22; Robert's design of, 19, 21–22. *See also* garden at Ermenonville; garden at Méréville; Moulin Joli; Parc de Monceau
The Pier with Chains (Piranesi), *138*, 139
Piganiol de La Force, Jean-Aymar, 83
Piles, Roger de, 5
Pinto, Isaac de, 94
Piranesi, Giovanni Battista: *Le antichità romane*, 36, *38*; and art and antiquities trade, 41, 57n85; *Carceri d'invenzione*, 38, 40, *138*, 139, 141, *142*, 143; defiance of Classicism, 42; *Della magnificenza ed architettura de' romani*, 36; and development of modern art, 3–4; *The Drawbridge*, 110, *112*; French, call for, 129; *Ichnographiam Campi Martii*, 110, *111*; *Imaginary Tombs on the Via Appia*, *38*, 41; *Imperial Mausoleum*, 36, *37*; influence of, 4, 29, 93, 110, 118, 139–43, 173; *Magnificent Bridge*, 141, *142*; on monotony in architecture, 109; painterly inclinations of, 18; *Parere su l'architettura*, 38; *Prima parte di architetture e prospettive*, 36; relations with French artists, 28–29, 96; Tafuri on, 38, 110; and triumph of subjectivism, 28–30, 34, 36–43
Piranésiens: and art and antiquities trade, 41, 57n85; grandiose aspirations of, 55n61; interdisciplinarity of, 28–29; inventiveness of, and foreclosing of possibilities, 40–41; triumph of subjectivism in, 28–43; valuation of singular and unpredictable, 30
"Plaisir de la ruine" (Bernardin de Saint-Pierre), 11, 61, 78
play: abjuring of content in, 42–43; aesthetic of, ruins and, 16, 177; dark side of, 38; and death, 98; disabling of fear through, 98; imperviousness to decay, 14. *See also* gambling
Les plus beaux édifices de Rome moderne (Barbault), 118, *119*
Les plus beaux monuments de la Rome ancienne (Barbault), 118
Pocock, J. G. A.: on credit economy, 93; on 18th-century institutionalization of risk, 16; on times of continuity and contingency, 2, 44
Poirson, Martial, 8n13, 122
Pommier, Édouard, 27, 123
Pompeii: discovery of, 61; evocation of modern destruction by, 70; pleasure derived from contemplation of, 64; response of Académie *pensionnaires* to, 28, 29; Temple of Isis, Desprez recreation of, 70, 72, *72*
Poncet de La Grave, Guillaume, 109, 113
Pont-au-Change: and sculpture of Louis XIV and family, *120*, 120–22. *See also* demolition of houses on bridges of Seine; *The Demolition of Houses on the Pont-au-Change, Paris*
Pont Louis XVI, 137
Pont Neuf, Académie boutiques on, 132
The Pont Neuf (Robert), *124*, 124–28, *128*, 130, 135
Pont Notre-Dame, 125. *See also* demolition of houses on bridges of Seine; *The Demolition of Houses on the Pont Notre-Dame in 1786* (Robert; Musée Carnavalet); *The Demolition of Houses on the Pont Notre-Dame in 1786* (Robert; Staatliche Kunsthalle Karlshrue)
Porte Saint-Denis, 125, 128
Ports of France series (Vernet), 141
Poussin, Nicolas, 4; *Arcadian Shepherds*, 42–43, *43*, 57n91; *Landscape with the Funeral of Phocion*, 65, *68*
Poyet, Bernard, 77, 93
precariousness: commercialization of art and, 167; in Panini's capricci, 167; picturesque gardens and, 21–27; of prosperity, 90–91, 93, 95; in Robert's *A Game of Dice*, 11, 43; ruins and, 2, 11, 41–43, 116. *See also* impermanence; uncertainty; unpredictability
Prima parte di architetture e prospettive (Piranesi), 36
print technology, *anticomanie* and, 33–36, 41
progress, 18th-century doubts about, 73
Project for the Grande Galerie of the Louvre (Robert), 151–52, *152*, 154–155, 164; and replacement of art with art history, 172; and terror of history, 171–75
Projet d'utilité et d'embelissement pour la ville de Paris (De Wailly), *130*, 130–31, 135
prosperity, impermanence of, 90–91, 93
Pujoulx, Jean-Baptiste, 109, 110, 117

Quatremère de Quincy, Antoine-Chrysostôme: *Considérations morales sur la destination des ouvrages de l'art*, 160; on decontextualizing of monuments, 123–24, 125, 126, 132, 160, 168, 169, 171, 185n70; on Fontaine des Innocents, 123–24, 129; on French economic policies, 169–70; *Lettres à Miranda*, 159–60, 161–62, 169; on museums, 159–62, 167, 169–70; on spoliation of Italy, 157, 159–62, 167

Radix de Sainte-Foix, Maximilien, 94
Raphael, 151
real estate market, volatility of, and Robert's disaster paintings, 84–85
real estate speculation: aesthetic style and, 94–95; building mania and, 78; and corruption of art, 91; cult of ruins and, 95; and impermanence, 93; and inevitability of market collapse, 83, 91, 93; Parisian anxiety about, 83; Paris urban reform and, 78
Reflections on the Revolution in France (Burke), 133
Réflexions critiques sur la poésie et sur la peinture (Dubos), 12, 54n57
Réflexions sur les richesses (Turgot), 47
Réflexions sur quelques causes de l'état présent de la peinture en France (La Font de Saint-Yenne), 79
Regnault, Jean-Baptiste, 162
Reith, Gerda, 14–15
religion, disaster as source of, 72–74, 98–99
Remains of the Palace of Pope Julius (Robert), 48, *49*
The Removal of the Royal Tombs from the Crypt of Saint-Denis (Robert), 156, *157*
Reni, Guido, 155
Renou, Antoine, 64
Réstif de La Bretonne, 70–72
risk: of building mania, Robert's awareness of, 91–92; creativity and, 177; culture-wide acceptance of, 84; ending of time of continuity and, 3; experience of, and perceptions of modernity, 5; infatuation with, in 18th century, 16, 44–45; Neoclassicism and, 91–92, 93–94; picturesque gardens and, 27–28; problem of, in financial markets, 47; stylistic manifestations of, 92–93. *See also* gambling
risk culture: annuities and, 45; consolidation of, 64; development of, 84; Law's Système and, 46; and modern sense of time, 16
Robert, Hubert: accusations of monetary motivations, 79, 95–96; and aesthetics of incompleteness, 79, 95–97; annuity investments by, 45; background, 16; and committee on the Grande Galerie of the Louvre, 121; connections to financial world, 45; debut exhibition of 1767, 12–13, 43, 44, 48, 61, 95–96, 97; Diderot on, 12–13, 43, 44, 48, 61, 95–96, 97; Duval on, 158–59; entrepreneurial instincts of, 64; fascination with Rome, 13; French Revolution and, 156–57, 177–78, 182n21; Grande Galerie design of, 172–73; in history of painting,

4; influences on, 4–5, 139–43; as Louvre curator-administrator, 121, 129, 148n60, 151–52, 155, 156, 170, 171, 180n3, 181n12; and print technology, 33, 34; role on museum Conservatoire, 151, 152, 155, 170; scholarship on, 2; shortcomings as artist, 3; and spoliation of Rome, 158; and tradition, erosion of, 4
Robert, Hubert—works: *The Ancient Monuments of France*, 76, 129; *Artist Drawing Antiques before the Petite Galerie*, 167–69, *168*; *The Artist in His Cell at Sainte-Pélagie*, 177–78, *178*; *The Bastille in the First Days of Its Demolition*, 135–39, *136*; *Bridges with Prison*, *138*, 139; *The Burning of Rome* (1773), *75*, 76, 88; *The Burning of Rome* (Salon of 1785), 76; *The Burning of the Opéra at the Palais-Royal*, *vi*, 4, 79–81, *81*, 103n54; *A Colonnaded Thermal Building, the Roof Partly Open to the Sky with Girls Washing Clothes*, 153–54, *154*, *The Construction of the École de Chirurgie*, *88*, 88–90, 91; *Croquis faits à Rome par Hubert Robert en 1760*, *17*, 17–18; *Demolition of a Church*, *x*, 85, *86*; *The Demolition of Houses on the Pont-au-Change, Paris*, *108*, 109–13, 115–20, 125, 133–36; *The Demolition of Houses on the Pont Notre-Dame in 1786* (Musée Carnavalet), 114, 143, *143*, 149n75; *The Demolition of Houses on the Pont Notre-Dame in 1786* (Staatliche Kunsthalle Karlsruhe), *108*, 109–13, 113–17, 125, 133, 134–36, 143, 149n75; *Demolition of the Église Saint-Jean-en-Grève in 1800*, 85, *87*; *Festivities at the Pont de Neuilly*, 76; *Fire Amidst the Principal Edifices of Rome*, 92; *The Fire at the Hôtel-Dieu in Paris, 1772*, 4–5, *74*, 75–77, 88, 97; *Fire at the Opéra of the Palais-Royal, Viewed from a Crossing in the Louvre*, *62*, 64–70, 75–76, 85; *A Game of Dice amidst Roman Ruins*, *10*, 11–16, 42–43, *43*; *Harbor with Architecture*, 141, *142*, 143; *Imaginary View of the Grande Galerie of the Louvre in Ruins* (1796), *i*, 1, 2, 4, 152–59, *153*, 171-75, 180n8, 181n9; *Imaginary View of the Grande Galerie of the Louvre in Ruins* (1798–99), *175*, 175–77; *Interior of the Opéra of the Palais-Royal*, 65, *67*; *Interior of the Opéra of the Palais-Royal the Day after the Fire*, *63*, 64–70, 75, 79, 97–98; *Monuments of Paris*, *128*, 128–32, 135, 148n60; *A Museum Gallery of Roman Art*, 163–67, *164*; *The Obelisk*, *80*; *The Old Bridge*, 139–43, *141*; *The Park at Ermenonville*, 24–27, *26*; *The Pont Neuf*, *124*, 124–28, *128*, 130, 135; *Project for the Grande Galerie of the Louvre*, 151–52, *152*, 154–55, 164, 171–75; *Remains of the Palace of Pope Julius*, 48, *49*; *The Removal of the Royal Tombs from the Crypt of Saint-Denis*, 156, *157*; *Ruins by the Water*, *82*; *Ruins of the Opéra after the Fire of 1781*, 65, *66*; *The Seesaw*, 178, *179*; Seine covered in ice (lost work), 135; *The Sleep of Marat*, 182n21; *Soirées de Rome*, 18; *The South Façade of the Palazzo Poli with the Trevi Fountain under Construction*, 88–89, *89*; *Tempietto di San Pietro in Montorio*, 21, *21*; *Temple de la Piété Filiale, Seen from a Rustic Bridge*, 23, *23*; *Triumphal Bridge with Staircase*, *139*; View of the entrance to the Grotta di Pausilippo, 19, *20*
Robert's oeuvre: and centrality of ruins in 18th-century aesthetics, 2; impact of time on, 177–78, *179*
Rococo: La Font de Saint-Yenne on, 79; Robert and, 79–83, 91
Rohan-Chabot, Louis-Antoine-Auguste, 19
Roland de La Platière, Jean-Marie, 170, 184n46
Roman Ruins (Pernet), 34
Rome: appropriation and redeployment of ruins in, 21; dematerialization of, in *archéofiction*, 29, 36; as ideal of durability, 5; modernization, costs of, 120; as museum, 159–60; Nero's burning of, 61, 68, 76; Robert's etchings of, 18; Robert's residence in, 17–19
Rome, as precedent for Paris, 5, 83, 84, 88-97, 153–54; as convergence of fear and hope, 5, and French "repatriation" of Roman art, 157–63; Robert's *Imaginary View of the Grande Galerie in Ruins* (1796) and, 153–54
Rome, French army's spoliation of, 167; debate over, 157–63; exhibition space for, 170–71; Robert on, 163–67
Rondoni, Alexander, 176, 182n26
Rosa, Salvatore, 39
Rothschild, Emma, 47
Rousseau, Jean-Jacques: *Discours sur les sciences et les arts*, 83; *Essai sur l'origine des langues*, 148n57; on French culture, 83; on Paris and nature, 117; tomb of, at Ermenonville, 24–27, *26*
Rubens, Peter Paul, 166
Rückenfigur, 178
ruin painters, Duval on, 158–59
ruins: and aesthetic of play, 16, 177; aesthetics of, and terror of history, 171–77; and aesthetics of disaster, 61; in aesthetic theory before 1700, 13, 15; in aesthetic theory of 18th century, 15; associations with speculation and commerce, 95; and awareness of future, 6, 13, 48; and chance, 11, 16, 24, 48; credit as analogue of, 48–50; fake (*fabriques*), as naturalizations of obsolescence, 95; as figure of reversal, 48; future, purpose of imagining, 156; gambling and, 12, 13, 14–15; and obsolescence, 95; and the picturesque, 11, 15, 16, 48; Piranésiens' interest in, 28–43; and pleasure of incompleteness, 2, 12–13, 64; and precariousness, 2, 11, 41–43, 116; and secularization, 14–15, 44; as sites of accident, 11; as sites of divestment from the past, 16; and sublimation, 2–3, 48, 98, 166; traditional meaning of, 13, 15; and transition to time of contingency, 2–3; and triumph of subjectivism, 2–3, 28; and *vanitas*, 14. *See also* cult of ruins; *entries under* incompleteness
Ruins by the Water (Robert), *82*
Ruins of the Opéra after the Fire of 1781 (Robert), 65, *66*
rustic bridges, in garden at Méréville, 23, *23*
Rykwert, Joseph, 30

Saint-Non, Jean-Claude Richard de, 18, 19, 70
Salon de 1767 (Diderot), 43, 48, 68, 95
Salon de 1771 (Diderot), 95
Salon of 1767, 12–13, 43, 44, 48, 61, 95–96, 97
Salon of 1781, 61, 65, 96
Salon of 1785, 76
Salon of 1789, 128, 130–31, 135
Salon of 1795, 158–59
Salon of 1796, 151, 181n8
Salon of 1800, 85
Santa Trinità dei Monti convent, ruin room at, 30–33
Scherzi di fantasia series (Tiepolo), 39
Scott, John, 166
Scott, Katie, 79
sculptures, interactions between living figures and, in Robert, 115
secularization: of chance, and aesthetic of the unfinished, 14–15, 44; and cult of ruins, 15; and demolition of churches, 99; and ending of time of continuity, 4, 44; and modern sense of time, 15–16, 44; and obsession with catastrophe, 1–2, 6; and the sublime, 97, 99, 118
The Seesaw (Robert), 178, *179*
Seine: as key to circulation within Paris, 117, 125; as site of immemorial routine, 113–14; and urban reform, 130–31
Seine covered in ice (lost Robert work), 135, 137–39
XVIe vue de la Grece (Pernet), 34, *35*
Seven Years' War: financial markets following, 78; and French national debt, 45, 133
Shell, Marc, 46
Sherman, Daniel J., 169
Sherman, Sandra, 47
Simmel, Georg, 5, 81–83, 137, 173
singularity, Piranésiens' valuation of, 30
The Sleep of Marat (Robert), 182n21
Slodtz, Paul-Ambroise, 16
Slodtz, René-Michel (Michel-Ange), 16
Slodtz, Sébastien-Antoine, 16
Soane, John, 42, 173
Sobre, Jean-Nicolas, *123*
social hierarchy, destabilizing impact of money on, 45
Soirées de Rome (Robert), 18
solidity, *vs.* transience, distrust of distinction between, 91
Sonenscher, Michael, 5, 91
The South Façade of the Palazzo Poli with the Trevi Fountain under Construction (Robert), 88–89, *89*
Spectateur Français, 131
speculation: associations with Neoclassicism, 91–92, 93–94; on Bourse, Crown's failure to rein in, 132–33, 135; on Bourse, excesses of, 131–32; and ending of time of continuity, 3; and inevitability of catastrophe, 131–32; in insurance products, in 18th century, 44–45, 84; triumph of subjectivism in, 47
speculation in real estate: aesthetic style and, 94–95; building mania and, 78; and corruption of art, 91; cult of ruins and, 95; and impermanence, 93; and inevitability of market collapse, 83, 91, 93; by Robert's patrons, 91-92
spoliation. *See* Rome, French army's spoliation of
Stainville, François Joseph de Choiseul, marquis de, 16

Starobinski, Jean, 135
stock market. *See* Bourse
subjectivism: aesthetic theory's emphasis on, 2–3; and the art of the Piranésiens, 28–43; cult of ruins as triumph of, 5–6; dangers of, 28; and dissolution of coherence, 27; expression of, in picturesque, 24–27; triumph of, in financial markets, 47; and value of art, 27
sublime, the: Burke on, 69, 116; demolition of houses on bridges of Seine and, 110, 116–17; disaster and, 1–2, 69, 97–99; in disaster paintings of Robert, 97–99; and distance from danger, 85; as exemplified in *Imaginary View of the Grande Galerie of the Louvre in Ruins*, 1; fascination with, late 18th-century sense of doom and, 69; and pleasure of destruction, 64; power over imagination, 69; secularization and, 97, 99, 118; sublime city as recompense for lost past, 120; and terror, 69, 99; triumph over human specificity, 118; unchecked debt expansion as, 133
Suite de ruines d'architecture (Dumont), 30, *31*, *32*
suspense, Robert's demolition paintings as sites of, 85
Suvée, Joseph-Benoît, 65
Swanevelt, Herman van, 14, *15*

Tableau de Paris (Mercier), 73, 90–91, 122
Tafuri, Manfredo, 38, 57n85, 110, 143
Tempietto di San Pietro in Montorio (Robert), 21, *21*
Temple de la Philosophie at Ermenonville, 24–27, *25*, *26*, 54n49
Temple de la Piété Filiale, in garden at Méréville, 22, *23*
Temple de la Piété Filiale, Seen from a Rustic Bridge (Robert), 23, *23*
Temple of Ancient Virtue at Stowe, 54n49
Temple of Isis in Pompeii as It Would Have Appeared in the Year A.D. 79 at the Time That It Was Destroyed by the Eruption of Vesuvius (Desprez), 70, 72, *72*
Temple of Modern Virtue at Stowe, 54n49
terror: *fabriques* inducing, 18th-century delight in, 69; of history, and ruin aesthetic, 171–77; inciting and dispelling of, in disaster paintings of Robert, 75–76; as source of religion, 72–74, 98–99; and the sublime, 69, 99
theatricality: in garden design, 22, 69; of Robert's disaster paintings, 64, 69, 75, 79–81, 97
Théorie des jardins (Morel), 53n47
Thiry, Leonard, 36
Thouin, André, 170–71
three-dimensional media, Robert's gravitation toward, 16
Tiepolo, Giovanni Battista, 39
time: and cult of ruins, 178; picturesque as imitating workings of, 22; pre-18th-century sense of, 13, 14; and Robert's oeuvre, 177–78, *179*; and *vanitas* theme, in 17th-century painting, 14
time, emergence of modern sense of, 15–16, 44
time of contingency, 44; credit and, 50; crumbling of Classicism and, 2, 44; ruins genre as adjustment to, 2–3
time of continuity, ending of, 44; cultural awareness of, 4; and fascination with ruins, 2–3; Robert's painting as commentary on, 5; secularization and, 4, 44
Titian, 155
tradition, erosion of: Classicism, crumbling of, 2, 24–43, 44, 68; Robert's art and, 4, 65, 68, 70, 84
transience. *See* impermanence
Tresham, Henry, 184n44
Triumphal Bridge with Staircase (Robert), *139*
Turgot, Anne-Robert-Jacques, 47

uncertainty: age of, and fear of collapse, 91; cult of ruins as acceptance of, 2, 48; gambling as embrace of, 98; picturesque and, 22; and terror of history, 171–77. *See also* precariousness
unfinished, the. *See* incompleteness, aesthetics of
unfinished buildings: relation of, to ruins, 88, 95; Robert's works on, *88*, 88–90; threat to dissolve into ruin, 90
unpredictability: Burke on effect of, 61; market economy and, 83–84; picturesque and, 23, 43; Piranésiens' valuation of, 30; Robert's disaster paintings and, 84–85; in Robert's *A Game of Dice*, 11. *See also* precariousness
unquantifiable events, and aesthetic experience, 1
Urban VIII (pope), 89
urban reform: and anti-monumentality, 120–24, 129–30, 147n55, 157–63, 158, 159–60, 161, 167, 168–71; as avenue to political change, 131; circulation as objective of, 110–13, 119, 122, *130*, 130–31, 137; and circulation of currency, 126–27; city without limits as goal of, 113, 117; commercial developers and, 78; and decoration, demotion of, 122; De Wailly's plan for, *130*, 130–31; economic potential of, 117; *embellissement* and, 77, 102n42; financial exploitation of, 133–34; fire as instrument of, 76–77; and freedom, 117–18, 131; French Revolution and, 117, 121–22, 133–34; homogenization of behavior as consequence of, 114; and laissez-faire, 117; and monarchy, decline of, 121–23; and museum mentality, 129–31; and nature, 117, 135; need for, 76, 77; outsourcing of, 132–33; and risk of collapse, 126–27; Robert's engagement with, 4, 64, 124–132; Seine and, 130–31; and surveillance, 119; and transfer from substantialist to functionalist theory of value, 126–27; unimpeded prospects as ambition of, 117–18, 122–23, 134. *See also* demolition of houses on bridges of Seine

value, theory of, shift from substantialist to functionalist, 126–27
vanitas, as theme in 17th-century painting, 14
van Laer, Pieter, 13, 14, *14*
Vasari, Giorgio, 172
Vasi, Giuseppe, 18, 29, 119
Veduta del Palazzo Sacchetti (Barbault), 118–20, *119*
Venus (Musei Capitolini), Robert sketch of, *17*, 17–18
Vernet, Joseph, 19, 70, 116, 141
Vesuvius: 18th-century fascination with, 69; Robert's view of, 70, *71*
Vidler, Anthony, 93
Viel de Saint-Maux, Jean-Louis: on age of *incertitude*, 91; on commercialization of art, 78–79; on cult of ruins, 77, 78, 83–84, 94–96; on expendability of monuments, 122–23, 126; on innovators, ephemerality of, 105n78; on *jardins à l'anglaise*, 94–95; *Lettres sur l'architecture des anciens et celle des modernes*, 77–79; on modern architecture, 77–78; on corruption in Paris, 94–96, 97; on urban expansion, 83
viewer, artwork's effect on, paradigm shift toward, in 18th-century aesthetic theory, 12. *See also* subjectivism
View of the Campo Vaccino in Rome (Swanevelt), 14, *15*
View of the entrance to the Grotta di Pausilippo (Robert), 19, *20*
Views of Greece (Pernet), 34, *35*
Views of the Environs of Rome (Descourtis), 33–34
Vigée-Lebrun, Elisabeth-Louis, 58n98, 79
Villa Negroni, 184n44
Vincent, François-André, 65, 162
Viotti, Giovanni Battista, 148n67
Virilio, Paul, 137
Visscher, Cornelis de, *14*
void, as emancipatory space, 122
Volaire, Pierre-Jacques, 70
volcanoes, 18th-century fascination with, 69. *See also* Herculaneum; Pompeii; Vesuvius
Volney, Constantin-François, comte de, 1
Voltaire: on credit, 50; *Des embellissements de Paris* and role in urban reform, 113; on Law's Système, 47; on London fire of 1666, 76; on the sublime, 69
voyage pittoresque, garden at Méréville as, 19
Voyage pittoresque; ou, Description des royaumes de Naples et de Sicile (Saint-Non), 18, 19, *20*, 70, *71*
Vyverberg, Henry, 54n57

Watelet, Claude-Henri, 18–19, 24, 27, 54n57
water cascading over rocks, and picturesque, *23*, 23–24
Watteau, Antoine, 3–4, 13, 79, 114
Weiskel, Thomas, 97
Winckelmann, Johann Joachim, 167; and historicism, 155; influence of, 181n13; on Roman *vs.* Greek art, 36; and theory of historical cyclicality, 158, 171–72
Wittman, Richard, 117
wonder, experience of, in picturesque gardens, 23

Also published by the Getty Research Institute

The Aztec Calendar Stone
Edited by Khristaan D. Villela and Mary Ellen Miller
ISBN 978-1-60606-004-9 (hardcover)

Visual Planning and the Picturesque
Nikolaus Pevsner
Edited by Mathew Aitchison
ISBN 978-1-60606-001-8 (hardcover)

Printing the Grand Manner: Charles Le Brun and Monumental Prints in the Age of Louis XIV
Louis Marchesano and Christian Michel
ISBN 978-0-89236-980-5 (hardcover)

Bernard Picart and the First Global Vision of Religion
Edited by Lynn Hunt, Margaret Jacob, and Wijnand Mijnhardt
ISBN 978-0-89236-968-3 (paper)

Harry Smith: The Avant-Garde in the American Vernacular
Edited by Andrew Perchuk and Rani Singh
ISBN 978-0-89236-735-1 (paper)

Sculpture and Enlightenment
Erika Naginski
ISBN 978-0-89236-959-1 (hardcover)

The Walls of Algiers: Narratives of the City through Text and Image
Edited by Zeynep Çelik, Julia Clancy-Smith, and Frances Terpak
ISBN 978-0-295-98868-9 (paper)

The Fragment: An Incomplete History
Edited by William Tronzo
ISBN 978-0-89236-926-3 (paper)

Laurence Bertrand Dorléac, *Art of the Defeat, France 1940–1944* (1993)
Translation by Jane Marie Todd
ISBN 978-0-89236-891-4 (hardcover)

Meyer Schapiro Abroad: Letters to Lillian and Travel Notebooks (1926–1927)
Edited by Daniel Esterman
ISBN 978-0-89236-893-8 (hardcover)

Jacqueline Lichtenstein, *The Blind Spot: An Essay on the Relations between Painting and Sculpture in the Modern Age* (2003)
Translation by Chris Miller
ISBN 978-0-89236-892-1 (paper)

Dilettanti: The Antic and the Antique in Eighteenth-Century England
Bruce Redford
ISBN 978-0-89236-924-9 (hardcover)

The Getty Murúa: Essays on the Making of the "Historia general del Piru," J. Paul Getty Museum Ms. Ludwig XIII 16
Edited by Thomas B. F. Cummins and Barbara Anderson
ISBN 978-0-89236-894-5 (hardcover)

Historia general del Piru: Facsimile of J. Paul Getty Museum Ms. Ludwig XIII 16
Martín de Murúa
ISBN 978-0-89236-895-2 (hardcover)

California Video: Artists and Histories
Edited by Glenn Phillips
ISBN 978-0-89236-922-5 (hardcover)

Ephemeral Bodies: Wax Sculpture and the Human Figure
Edited by Roberta Panzanelli
ISBN 978-0-89236-877-8 (hardcover)

Allan Kaprow—Art as Life
Edited by Eva Meyer-Hermann, Andrew Perchuk, and Stephanie Rosenthal
ISBN 978-0-89236-890-7 (hardcover)

Le Corbusier, *Toward an Architecture* (1924)
Introduction by Jean-Louis Cohen
Translation by John Goodman
ISBN 978-0-89236-899-0 (hardcover)
ISBN 978-0-89236-822-8 (paper)

China on Paper: European and Chinese Works from the Late Sixteenth to the Early Nineteenth Century
Edited by Marcia Reed and Paola Demattè
ISBN 978-0-89236-869-3 (hardcover)

Titian Remade: Repetition and the Transformation of Early Modern Italian Art
Maria H. Loh
ISBN 978-0-89236-873-0 (hardcover)

The Life and the Work: Art and Biography
Edited by Charles G. Salas
ISBN 978-0-89236-823-5 (hardcover)

Art, Anti-Art, Non-Art: Experimentations in the Public Sphere in Postwar Japan, 1950–1970
Edited by Charles Merewether with Rika Iezumi Hiro
ISBN 978-0-89236-866-2 (hardcover)

Rethinking Boucher
Edited by Melissa Hyde and Mark Ledbury
ISBN 978-0-89236-825-9 (paper)

Late Thoughts: Reflections on Artists and Composers at Work
Edited by Karen Painter and Thomas Crow
ISBN 978-0-89236-813-6 (paper)

Making Up the Rococo: François Boucher and His Critics
Melissa Hyde
ISBN 978-0-89236-743-6 (paper)